White Summer Dress

White Summer Dress

The story of a shoeshine boy

Thomas R. Sawyer

TANDOR PRESS, Santa Rosa

Second American TANDOR PAPERBACK edition published 2006.
Some names of persons have been changed.

Second edition published by Tandor Press, Santa Rosa, California.
(707)546-7262 Printed in the United States of America by Malloy
Incorporated, Ann Arbor, MI.

Edited by Anila Manning and Pauline Goslovich
Cover art in watercolor by John Hodapp

Second Edition
Tandor Press

White Summer Dress
ISBN 0-9770875-8-1
www.whitesummerdress.com

```
Publisher's Cataloging-In-Publication Data
(Prepared by The Donohue Group, Inc.)


Sawyer, Thomas R.
   White summer dress : the story of a shoeshine boy / Thomas R.
Sawyer. -- 2nd ed.
     p. ;  cm.
   ISBN: 0-9770875-8-1

1. Quihuis-Sawyer, Mari. 2. Sawyer, Thomas R.  3. Spouses--United
States--Biography. 4. Spiritual biography--United States.
5. Breast--Cancer--Patients--Biography. 6. Love. I. Title.

CT275.S29 A3 2006
920                                            2006900556
```

To
MARIJANA

Forward

First off, let me make the disclaimer that I knew the woman in the white summer dress, and it was wonderful to spend time with her and her true love in these pages. However, no one should miss this story. IT is so unusual, so brave, so raw and revealing, and so full of aliveness and courage. Plus, one heck of a good adventure story...and it's all TRUE. Trust me, you won't be able to put it down. And you will look at life in a new way after reading it.

Mari, the woman of the title, is someone her husband is sharing with the world, and she enriches each of us with her presence...almost an archetype of a Woman with Heart. You will learn. You will grow. You will love her and be grateful to Tom for sharing their story. They are two people who color outside the lines and love beyond measure.

It is the magical story of how a man and a woman meet, fall in love, take joyous gypsy road trips, and alas - well, I won't tell you. There is tragedy and loss, for this is real life...but the spiritual redemption they garner from their approach will move and inspire you.

–Naima Shea, Taos, NM

Author's Preface

Mates, those who have touched upon Divine love through their humanness, have a tendency to reach across the veil with such force as to lose sight of typical reality, living in multiple dimensions simultaneously inseparable, even in death. *White Summer Dress* was written in the way of Vipassana: from the point of view of the observer. If you read mindfully, you will find out who "I" is at the end of the book.

A piece of paper blew across the road on its way to the other side, how was I to know ...

-TRS

Contents

Acknowledgements

Pauline Goslovich for her courage and understanding in editing the initial draft and Anila Manning for spending months lovingly poring over the details of the final edit and John Hodapp for capturing, in watercolor, the essence of the woman in the white summer dress.

Dr. Rosemary Ward, Linda Sundhiem, Deirdre Robson, Theresa Sawyer, Debbie Drake, Diana Bowland, Seela Lewis, Azza, Dr. Fancessca Manfredi, Kamila Al-Najjar, Babette Dailey, Dennis Darrow, June Jamerson, Betty Finch, Komala Lyra, George Shepard, Cathryn Sawyer, and Roger House for proof reading the drafts and giving openhearted criticism.

Angela Goslovich and Cathy Snipper for lighting the fuse, and Robert Quihuis for his life's wisdom, and my children, Larry, Tiffany, Adam and Jacob for their memories of unending connection. Tom and Kathleen, June Jamerson and Georgette Goslovich for their encouragement and loving support.

Didger, who patiently waited by the keyboard.

And to all those who provided inspiration —
O *esprit.*

White Summer Dress
The story of a shoeshine boy

MARI 1987 *(photo by T. Sawyer)*

1

"Ja'vat'ma -The heart lotus
is like unto the steady tapering
flame of a lamp in a windless place."
Sir John Woodroffe

Falling

Through a set of unusual circumstances I watched Buck White and Tom Sawyer reunited in a restaurant on January 21, 2001 at a place called Strawberry Hill, a fashionable resort nestled 3,000 feet straight up in the Blue Mountains of Jamaica, 25 miles northeast of Kingston Town. Strawberry was built there years ago by music industry mogul Chris Blackwell and was famous for its restaurants and spas.

Buck was in the restaurant bar sipping on a Jack Daniels when he heard a helicopter fly in and hover over the grassy lawn area normally used for weddings and special gatherings. Buck watched it slowly land and wind down its blades. A tattooed man in grubby clothes stepped out carrying a backpack. Jenny Wood, manager of the resort, greeted the man and pointed to the restaurant. He walked in, sat down at a table and ordered a drink. The waiter whispered something in his ear. He looked towards the bar. It was in that instant that Buck realized it was Tom. They had met years before in the West Indies, when Tom was working as an engineering consultant and living in Parham, a small fishing village on the north coast of Antigua.

Tom bought Buck a drink and began telling him as best he could what was in his heart—a story that Buck never heard the like. It began like all good stories, with loss.

It was the spring of '87, a low point in Tom's life. He was still reeling from his divorce of a year ago, and had just lost most everything he owned in a venture capital start-up in Oregon. He packed up a few items and climbed on an Amtrak train bound for a small forty-niner gold-mining town called Grass Valley in northern California. He and his brother had decided to build a house there for their parents.

Several weeks later he boarded an airplane for the buffalo ranch in Oregon where his stuff was stored and came back with a U-haul truck containing books, a filing cabinet, a box of clothes, some tools and "Ol' Gal," as he respectfully calls his Harley-Davidson motorcycle.

His mother had designed a 2700-square-foot dream home in the pines above Grass Valley. His brother Ray was a building contractor and well equipped to take on such an adventure. The project was to be a resting place before life moved him downstream to his next rite of passage. He was being brought back into the circle of his family.

During work breaks he would lie down at the jobsite and daydream. He dreamed of a beautiful barefoot woman with wild dark brown hair, wearing a long white summer dress and an ankle bracelet. Her image first appeared to him in the trees when the sun was just right.

As weeks passed the dreams became exceedingly vivid; he was now capable of seeing her with his eyes wide open. He could even summon the glow of her smile, the sparkle in her eyes and smell her.

It became such an obsession with him that every spare moment was spent thinking of her. On an old napkin from Mama Sue's he scribbled down a poetic description:

> She walks naked in the forest on a full moon night. She's a white witch with dark hair, deeply spiritual, yet wild. Her purpose is the surcease of suffering. She's Aphrodite in body, mind, and spirit. She says, push into me slowly, and I into you, let us become one spirit in two bodies. She's a no-bullshit lady, grounded in truth. The wilderness is her sanctuary, the city a playground for her practice.

However, he had no idea of who *she* was. He started going to town hoping he would find her. His favorite hangout was Mama Sue's, a little hole-in-the-wall breakfast/lunch place on the edge of Nevada City where all the local color hung out. Hill people and hippies would gather there. He asked Tatyana, the barefoot belly-dancing waitress, where he might find the white witch dream girl of his visions. Tatyana was young with blond dreadlocks and wild blue eyes. You got the sense that there was something ancient about her. She told him about Laluna Pool, a secret swimming hole 15 miles west near North San Juan on the north fork of the Yuba River, "Go, witness your thoughts, you may find her there," she whispered as Tom was leaving Mama Sue's one morning.

Encouraged by Tatyana's words he started skinny-dipping at Laluna after work. He walked every day two miles upstream to an enchanted waterfall surrounded by garnet boulders and cave ledges. Local pundits gathered there to bask naked in the sun and dive into the freshwater pools that adorned the supernatural setting. Often he was the only one there.

One especially hot day, while the cool blue water was passing over his body, he dreamed he was on the Ganges River in India. From the edge of the rocky stone bank appeared a dark wild-haired Hindu woman miraged in a white dress, presenting *pranamah* (Hands pointed, held together in front of the heart, silently saying, *I bow to the Divinity within you*). A soft breeze blew her hair outward as he returned the *pranamah*, summoning her. She entered the water and swam to him. She held him close—he was transported to another place in time.

After this golden moment he realized he was dreaming, but the vision remained real in his mind. Now most every quiet moment was spent with the dream girl. He started to fall in love with *her*. Even though he knew *she* was a dream, he started to take on all the signs of a person in love. Singing, smiling for no apparent reason, you know—with that glow in his eyes. This went on for weeks. His brother thought perhaps he'd slipped a gear.

In July, he received a phone message from his sister Theresa, "Come to a Wirikuta Meeting in Santa Rosa tomorrow afternoon." He wasn't sure what that was, but it sounded like a good idea. He arrived at Linda Wren's house for the meeting, and after the usual introductions, Tom and Theresa sat down on the couch. He didn't know anyone and was nervous. Staring at the pictures on the wall, he started rocking back and forth hoping for relief.

Theresa got up and went into the kitchen. He continued gazing at the pictures, rocking autistically, occasionally looking down at the dust on his boots. With out warning a woman appeared in the doorway. She was beautiful; beautiful like an angel, like nothing he had ever seen before in real life. She was barefoot, wearing a long white summer dress. He could see the sun shining through her wild dark hair. Light behind her dress accented the silhouette of her long slender legs. His eyes dropped to the hardwood floor where she was standing. For a second his mind tumbled, then it hit him—just above her left foot she wore a beaded ankle bracelet!

His heart stopped for a moment, then started racing. She looked over at him, making "three second" eye contact. Suddenly she began to walk toward the couch. Chills ran up and down his spine. He whispered to himself, "Is she going to sit down beside me?" He couldn't breathe. As her body sank into the cushion, she lifted her legs; tucking her bare feet underneath his right thigh, smiling, "Hello, my name is Mari. Who are you?" He tried to tell her, "My name is Tom Sawyer," but the words stumbled out. He was frozen. Every bell and whistle that could possibly go off inside of a person was going off in him. With a red face and whispered voice, he finally got out the words, "T-o-m—Theresa's brother."

Saying no more, he got up and went into the kitchen and continued out the back door. In the backyard he looked at the dog chained to the garage, and mentally surveyed what he might look like to someone else. He used to ride with an outlaw motorcycle gang, but never spoke much of that and at this point in his life he was looking quite ragged; long dirty hair and straggly beard, Levis he never changed, and work boots that he almost never took off.

He kept saying to himself, *Who is she and why is she being so nice to me...could she be the woman of my dreams?* Coming back in the house he spotted dishes piled in the kitchen sink. "Thank God for dishes," he muttered to himself. After washing all the plates, pots and pans, and wiping down the counter, he walked back to the hallway and watched her from a distance.

Just as he was beginning to feel safe, an announcement rang out, "It's time to go to the coast. Jaichima is waiting." Mari walked out the front door and disappeared. Tom followed the crowd, and was squashed into the back of a Ford van with a bunch of people and two small boys. They were all on their way to the Sonoma coast to find suitable ceremonial grounds for Jaichima and Vicente Rutury, Huichol Indian medicine people. Tom was hoping to God that Mari was in one of the other cars in the caravan. After traveling for a while in tight quarters, the two small boys jumped up on his lap and sat there for the remainder of the trip—one on each knee. They seemed to like him, pinching and squirming around and pulling at his mustache.

After miles of winding back roads, they finally arrived at Siminow Lodge north of Goat Rock. There was a building there with a creek and a small archway bridge. Theresa and Tom sat on a wooden deck that bordered the creek. The sound of birds and talking people filled the air.

He looked over at the bridge and saw Mari standing there by herself overlooking the water. He watched her for a while with the thought of approaching her. Noticing he had no control over the pounding of his heart, he argued with his doubting mind, *How can I begin to say anything to her if I can't breathe properly?* To be sure, he sorted through all his one-liners, hoping for something brilliant; nothing sounded good. He settled on, "Isn't it a wonderful day." That wasn't too long—he could remember that. Like a blind man walking across traffic, with all the courage he could muster, he started toward the bridge. He was halfway there when he lost his one-liner and by the time he arrived at the bridge he was speechless. He started rambling on about his log cabin in Oregon…anything that might impress her. She listened for a few minutes and then walked away without a word, strolling down the bridge toward the crowd that had gathered near a large tree. He felt as though someone had just knocked the wind out of him.

As she sauntered away he watched her every nuance, the way her heels shifted with each placement of her bare feet, her long elegant neck, the way her elbows brushed her hips as she moved, the sway in her walk—everything about her was a wonder to behold. In an obvious effort to become part of her world he followed her, saying nothing. After 50 feet, and a thousand years later, she stopped and turned towards him. With her hands on her hips, looking him dead in the eye, she flipped her hair to one side, "I'm the kind of woman that takes the kids, the dishes, and the clothes and puts them in the shower and does them all at the same time." That did it—he was hopelessly in Love.

The ice had broken. They walked and talked for a little while. Tom was beginning to lighten up. He could smell the sea breeze, and pine, the moss growing along the banks, and her musk as he inadvertently brushed up against her. Everything was heightened. As they ambled along their hands occasionally made contact. Both pretended not to notice the obvious silver-gold energy sparking off each tender accidental touch.

An announcement blasted out from the group leader with the sound of a noon whistle, "It's time to go." Everyone was getting ready to leave for Goat Rock for some kind of ceremony. He turned to Mari and asked if she was going, "I have to take my boys home." That's when it hit him; the two boys that sat on his lap in the van were her ten-year-old twins, Adam and Jacob. He prayed to all the Gods he knew hoping he would see her again.

That night he stayed at his sister's house, a colorfully quaint place near Petaluma. He had brought a box of fireworks acquired from an Indian reservation and he and his sister celebrated the Fourth of July, but that wasn't all he was celebrating.

His sister woke him early the next morning; "Mari will be at the Smoke Ceremony at the Catholic high school in the afternoon, do you want to go?" That's all it took, he was up and bright-eyed—another thread leading to the new purpose in his life. Deep things were going on inside; he wanted to know *Who was this gorgeous creature?* He asked Theresa if she knew anything about her. She only knew Mari was not married, that she was thirty-six years old, had twin boys, was of Croatian descent and was very close to Jaichima. Oh, and she was a Sannyasin (disciple), a follower of Bhagwan Shree Rajneesh, and had traveled around the world for several years with a Thai monk named Dhiravamsa.

Theresa had car troubles and they arrived late at the high school. The smoke ceremony was almost finished. More than 500 people were gathered in the field listening to the drums and wisdom of the Huichol medicine people as Jaichima gave blessings with smoke from bundles of burning sage. Tom and Theresa walked through the crowd and spotted Mari. His heart skipped a beat. As the ceremony was ending, he noticed everyone was hugging. This was his big chance; he worked his way through the crowd to Mari.

He looked at her with puppy dog eyes and tenderly put his arms around her. He could feel her guarded at first, then her hands pressed into his back and they melted. It was like nothing he had ever experienced. He didn't want to let go—ever. They were spiraling in a violet-gold-silver-blue tunnel that went upward to Ever. As they held each other everyone else disappeared, all voices ceased; they had transformed into their own special dimension. After 15 minutes, they slowly let go. He whispered, "That has never happened to me before." Mari looked back at him with a *He's trying to net me* look on her face and said, "Well, it's happened to me before." He didn't know what to say, so entranced by the moment yet blown away—like a child blowing a bubble into the wind to watch it glimmer in the sun and pop.

He said goodbye and went back to his sister's car. Still spinning from Mari's embrace, he got in, rolled down the window, cocked the seat back and stared out into the distance. He felt blue from his perceived rejection and waited for his sister's return.

Not more than five minutes passed when Theresa showed

up. "You know, I have to go pay the nuns over there for renting the school grounds." She went on, "I see Mari sitting on the steps. Why don't you walk with me and we'll stop and talk with her." Tom sighed, "OK." As they walked toward the steps where Mari was sitting, he started to get a sense of knowing, an overlay of the woman in his daydreams with Mari's no-nonsense persona. He knew her by instinct. They were both wanderers looking for signposts just over the edge.

Theresa started a conversation with Mari and the other girls. After a few minutes Mari turned toward Tom and said, "I like your tattoos." He replied, "Thank you." Theresa exclaimed, "Well, you ought to see his back." Mari motioned with her hand and said, "Yeah—take off your shirt, I want to see your back." He alluringly replied, "No—we will have to make a date to go swimming if you want to see my back." Mari retorted, "I don't go out on dates." He stumbled for a second then the words came, "Then let's just go swimming." She looked at him with a gleam in her eyes, "OK, meet me at my house tomorrow around 1:00, we'll go to Lake Ilsanjo." She told him where she lived and gave him her phone number. He was in dog heaven; he heard bells and saw rainbows in his head. Happy and struggling to be cool, he articulated as best he could, "See you tomorrow." She smiled back as he walked away.

The next morning he got up early and started working on his brother-in-law's car. Steve's brakes had gone out the day before and Tom had promised to help. By the time they finished the brakes it was almost 1:00. He had to hurry over to Mari's house, un-showered, greasy and grubby. He finally found the house and knocked on the door. In the driveway sat a new Cadillac. The home was in a wealthy neighborhood. He wasn't sure if he had the right place. It didn't compute: she was a new age barefoot goddess and this was an upper-class home.

When Mari opened the door, he melted. She looked at him with reserve and invited him in. The hallway was covered with family pictures. Out of the kitchen came a stunning older lady dressed in casual attire from the '50s. She was as beautiful as Mari but from a different era. With a sweet, almost reverent tone in her voice Mari introduced Tom, "This is Noni, my mother." Feeling a little self-conscious he looked over at Noni. He could see the serenity in her eyes, the kind that comes from hard times and strong faith. Her presence was "from the old country." He reached out his hand, "It's a pleasure to meet you."

Noni welcomed him without reservation, like family. The look on Mari's face was one of shock; she couldn't figure out why her mother was so accepting of this bearded, longhaired, near-homeless-looking man. Noni excused herself and went back into the kitchen. She was cooking Croatian lamb. The smell was taking him off to foreign lands when Mari looked over, "Let's take my car."

He gathered his backpack and got into Mari's little Honda. They drove to a residential area in the hills near Bennett Valley. She pulled over and stopped the car. Tom said, "Where's the lake?" She pointed and replied, "Up that trail about two miles."

They walked part way up the trail and stopped at a bronze plaque framed in cement alongside the path. She read out loud, "Dedicated to the Men and Women Who Served in Vietnam." They continued along the trail into a canyon and crossed a creek on the other side to a wash. Following a steep incline to the top of the hill, they finally ended up at the lake. Tom tried to breathe easy so as not to let her know that he was out of breath. Mari looked back and said nothing—she knew he was faking it.

They sat beside each other near the dam staring out into the water. He wanted to reach over and touch her hand, but he dared not. He went on and on about how he was looking for a partner and how wonderful it would be to wake up in the morning with a woman by his side. It was starting to get a little pathetic. He was proposing with every word without actually saying it—anyone who could read between the lines could get his meaning.

Mari picked up her pack and started walking around the edge of the lake. He followed her steps, watching her every movement. He noticed how elegantly she moved with her head held high, the way her slinder arms moved with the rhythm of her body.

She arrived at her self-designated swimming spot and laid out a blanket. From her pack came a little picnic basket with food and drink and a flowered towel. Tom took his brown-stained blue towel from his backpack and laid it next to hers. Then he removed what looked like a book and placed it on the towel next to her. As she glanced at the book, she caught him observing her, and quickly turned away.

Tom was used to swimming nude in the Yuba River. He carelessly took off his clothes and dove into the water. She watched for a minute and then started removing her dress exposing a bathing suit underneath. Leisurely she moved in to her waist. They began swimming and splashing at one another. She was splattering large quantities of water with one hand while protecting her eyes with the other. All of a sudden she dropped her hand from her face and said, "Stop. Turn around." She might as well have said, "Have him washed and brought to my tent." Peering at the skin illustrations on his back she became fascinated. He was covered with themes from the *Bhagavad Gita* (Hindu Bible). In the center of his back was tattooed a cobra encircling the god *Shiva* (the force of change in nature), transforming into the form of a lion. Moving her gaze away to the horizon in a blank stare, she caught him looking back and quickly changed to an unimpressed expression. She grinned as she skimmed her hand across the lake, splashing water in his eyes.

After playing for some time, they got out and sat on the blanket. It was a hot day. Tom looked over at her. He noticed the tiny white hairs on her legs, and how the cold water had erected and tightened every cell. He loved everything about her; the way she talked, the way she smiled, the way she walked—everything. He adored her.

She became curious about the book he'd brought. Trying to impress her, he explained that it contained the business plan for a corporation he was involved in a few years back and that he had lost almost everything he owned in the deal, except for his property on the Hill and Ol' Gal. "What's the Hill?" she asked.

He gave her a long description. The Hill is an 80-acre parcel of sacred ground 30 miles southeast of Hood River. Deer, elk, bear, coyote and bobcat roam there, and life is free, save the wrath of Mother Nature herself. It borders the Mount Hood National Wilderness Area. There are places there where no man's foot has touched the ground. It's the place where Tom built a log cabin and lived with his wife and their two small children for three years. He began to ramble. Mari stopped him and said, "Tell me, where is Hood River?" Tom replied, "It's a town situated along the Columbia River Gorge, 90 miles east of Portland on Highway 84, headin' towards Idaho." He told her he would take her there someday.

She seemed interested, perhaps even impressed by the Hill story and then glanced back over at the book. "What's this book?" He told her that when he was working as a consultant to Intel Corporation, he had met Bob Davis, one of the founders and former CEO of Tektronix, which employed 20,000 people in Oregon. Bob owned an island called Long Island off the coast of Antigua in the Caribbean. He gave the island to his developer son Homer who put $20,000,000 into restoration and new development, making it a world-class resort later known as Jumby Bay. Bob had sent Tom to the island to help re-establish portions of the infrastructure back in the '80s. Back then Bob lived on the island and practiced his hobby of traveling around the world buying up old merry-go-rounds, carousels and steam calliopes, restoring and donating them to parks all over the United States. Bob was mainly interested in circus logistics, circus history and old-timers that used to work the sideshows. Bob had become Tom's third mentor.

In 1985, after Tom returned from the island, he and Bob and several other partners started a company called Paratechnology. Tom had designed a search engine architecture that performed 1 billion string searches per second called ASAP (Associative Search Array Processor). He was made Chief Engineer and the company filed a patent; a corporation was formed using venture capital. Before the company could get their second round of funding, their primary customer got into financial troubles and was forced to cancel the $22,000,000 contract. Losses were big and dominoes fell, but Tom continued to meet with venture capital groups in the Bay Area hoping for a second round.

Mari was very impressed and she was not easy to impress. She told him that she wanted her dad to look at the business plan someday. Tom didn't know who her dad was, but if it meant more time around Mari, that was good.

She suggested they go back to the house. On the way to the car she raised her hands to stop him from talking. "You're falling in love with me, aren't you?" He swallowed, "How do you know that?" "Because you're giving me a headache." She then gave him her why-relationships-don't-work speech and he gave her his why-relationships-do-work speech.

They drove back to her house and she invited him in for lemonade in the backyard. They chatted for a while then she abruptly said, "It's time for you to go." He didn't dare ask her for another date. She had already told him adamantly that she didn't go out on dates.

The next day he drove back to Grass Valley and started working with his brother on the house. Ray would look over at him with an *Is that all you can think about?* look. All Tom could do was think about her. He couldn't eat or sleep. An enchanting Mari song befell him. He kept singing it over and over while he worked. How was he going to see her again? Weeks went by. Finally, he asked his sister, Theresa, if she could somehow let Mari know that he was interested.

Two weeks later Tom's mother handed him a note she'd taken by phone from Theresa. It said, "Come to Armstrong Woods campground on Saturday, Mari will be camping there, come if you like." Tom thought to himself, *IF YOU LIKE?* He was singing and dancing like a kid before Christmas. He couldn't sleep, but that was just fine—he couldn't wait for morning.

At the crack of dawn he had all his gear ready. Leaving a note for his brother, he slipped out the door. Two-and-a-half-hours later he drove into Santa Rosa, making it in record time.

He arrived at Armstrong Woods State Park around 9:00 AM; however, there were several campgrounds in the area and he had to go through each one to find the goddess. He didn't find her till around noon. He spotted her lying on a sleeping bag reading a book. They greeted each other and talked for a while. She wanted to walk around. As they passed each campsite, she psychically exposed the inner life of each occupant. Tom asked her how she could know such things, and she answered, "By the way they set up camp."

Time flew by and night was coming on. She asked if he would build a campfire. She was watching him very closely. He put on his best mountain man persona, wishing he'd brought his flint and steel to impress her with a fire made by primitive means. He gathered wood, made kindling and settled for a box of matches. They sat around the fire and warmed their hands, conversing into the late evening. He got up, put more wood on the fire, then placed his sleeping bag down gently next to hers; pulling the zipper back, he got in. She began explaining all the constellations and how the stars seemed to rule our lives. She talked of the zodiac and what the different signs meant. His heart was full. He was surprised that his thoughts didn't go to a sexual realm. For now, their connection was immersed in a sweet delicate place. They did not kiss or make love that night even though nature had provided the perfect setting.

The next morning they woke and broke camp. Mari said cheerfully, "I'm going to Salt Point campground, you can come along if you like." They got into her car and drove along the coast for what seemed like an hour, winding along Highway 1. When they arrived at the Salt Point registration office Mari did all the talking, "We would like to have a campsite away from other people." The ranger replied, "Camp number 11, you're a couple of lucky kids, it just became available!"

They got their campsite tag and drove over to the parking area. Mari said she needed to call her friends Asha and Bodhi to let them know her whereabouts. She and Tom started walking towards the phone booth. When they arrived someone was already using it. Mari turned and said, "I also need to call my mom and let her know that I won't be back tonight, she's watching the boys." Tom repeated with a grin, "We won't be back tonight!"

What happened next will be recorded in his DNA forever. They sat down on a rough piece of wood, a parking-place stop. She sat south. He sat north. Back to back they waited for the person on the phone to finish. This was the moment, a moment he would remember for the rest of his life. It was the feeling of home—he was HOME. It was the most powerful, peaceful, blissful moment that he had ever known—just sitting there, back to back, not saying a word. It overpowered the memory of the time he spent at Rudy's, the old hermit who taught him how to play the accordion—the time the rain was falling on Rudy's tin roof and the cuckoo clocks were ticking and he was covered with a blanket, drifting off into his first lucid flying dream. This moment with Mari was even more than that.

When the person in the phone booth finished, Mari got up and made her calls. They walked back to the car and drove to campsite number 11. They pulled out their camping stuff; two sleeping bags and two small backpacks, and looked at each other with a smile. She asked if he'd go collect firewood. Off he went to do his manly job of providing for the home fire. Trying to impress her with how much he could carry, he gathered a large bundle of wood and headed back to camp like a Boy Scout about to receive a merit badge.

When he returned, Mari was lying there nude, face down on her sleeping bag, basking in the sun. He could hardly believe his eyes; he could see her Tampax string trailing down one side of her leg. He was somewhat shocked, yet honored she would feel so comfortable with him. She just lay there reading her book without saying a word. She was so beautiful. He watched her breathe; she was calm and composed. Without any sign of self-consciousness she lifted her left leg up, bending it at the knee, and scratched her ankle. The move sent waves through every molecule in his body.

Turning away from the hormonal whirlpool, he started

stacking firewood. He kept looking at her. She rolled onto her side holding the book in her right hand, "Tom, will you read to me from this book?" He felt liberated hearing her speak his name and knelt down next to her. Looking up at him caringly, she handed him the book. It was titled *White Buffalo Woman.*

He became frightened; he was dyslexic and couldn't read out loud very well. Figuring she would think he was stupid and all would be lost in the next moment, he hesitated. Then strength came to him; he thought *if she can lie there with her Tampax string hanging out, then the least I can do is show her my weakness.* He began to read. The words stumbled off his lips like a fourth grader, not a grown man. Her eyes sprang open wide like an animal's. She looked up and said, "I love the way you read."

He was overwhelmed; embarrassment and joy hit him at the same time. He told her that he could read OK to himself, since he was able to make mental adjustments for the changing characters on the page, but to read out loud was difficult. She turned to him, lifting herself up on one arm. Reaching out to touch his elbow she said, "You should read out loud more often." In that moment he felt a profound healing envelop his condemned childhood memories; an acceptance of himself from someone he respected so much poured into his being.

That night they sat around the campfire and told stories about themselves, details they wouldn't have told just anyone; concepts of life, the soul, God, and their innermost secrets. When they woke the next morning Mari said she wanted to go for a walk by the ocean. As they walked along the waters edge, barefoot in the sand, not only could they hear the crashing of the waves, they heard the blending of their souls. Mari stopped and sat on a nearby rock. "Tell me a joke and if you can make me laugh, I will sing you a song." "Umm…let's see," he said out loud.

He told her his Kodachrome joke from the '60s—she laughed a free, open, unrestricted belly laugh. He was pleased. Laughing with her, he looked over with waiting eyes. She was about to sing him a song. Suddenly she got quiet and looked away. He waited while she stared out at the sea gripping his hand. He held on hopefully, then verbalized with excitement, "OK, your turn, you sing me a song."

She got up and walked away saying nothing. He protested, "You said you'd sing me a song if I made you laugh." She remained quiet and kept walking. Running to catch up, he jogged up in front of her. Facing her as though it meant everything in the world he said, "Aren't you going to sing me a song?" She stopped walking and looked into his eyes, "I can't," she replied. He whispered tenderly, "Why?" She looked deeper into his eyes, "Because I'm falling in love with you." They kissed for the first time, an ever-so-sweet kiss felt from the tips of their toes to the tops of their heads. They embraced without words; all else seemed to disappear save the essence of self. Us had been born. They had just given birth to We, completely, hopelessly in Love.

Like seedpods floating gently in the breeze they walked arm-in-arm down the beach, intoxicated with ecstasy. They walked for miles until they could see no sign of where they had come from. They watched foam form around rocks jetting out onto the beach. The perpetual thunder of the surf, the sound of seagulls flying, the smell of the salt air and the moisture on their faces transformed their vermilion light into a field of paradise; time had ceased to exist. All meaningful communication took place without words. Mari leaned her head on his shoulder and whispered, "We should probably go back."

They walked back to the campsite in a trance and packed up the Honda. As they drove past the ranger station they waved goodbye to the attendant with clasped hands. She was driving with her left hand on the steering wheel, working the clutch with her left foot. He worked the gearshift with his right hand so neither would have to let go of the other.

It was a long, winding trip back to Armstrong Woods. On the way he asked to touch her hair. He loved the way her hair was, all wild and frizzy. She said, "It's OK." He was more fascinated by her hair than a cat is with a string. All the way back he played with her hair while she drove, twisting and rolling it back and forth in his fingers while shifting gears with his other hand.

After an hour they rolled into Armstrong Woods and parked next to Tom's borrowed Subaru truck. They sat there looking at each other. Mari put her head on his shoulder. He lifted her hair and placed it over his face. Tiny sunbeam prisms sparkling through from the sunlight danced in his eyes.

Unexpectedly she sighed, "Why are you being so nice to me?" He replied, "Because you're letting me." She smiled softly. Lifting her chin slightly, she pressed her lips together as if to say, *How sweet.* They kissed tenderly one more time. He opened the door and got out. She got out and stood by her door. They reached across the top of the car, touched hands and stood gazing at one another.

Slowly he released her fingers and reached into the back seat, grabbing his backpack. He dropped it onto the front seat of his truck and looked over again. Neither one wanted to leave. He walked around the Honda and put his arms around her. Again they kissed goodbye.

He walked back to his truck and started the motor, never losing her eyes. He sat there for a few minutes, then shut the motor off and got out. He walked to her window and squatted down at face level, "When will I see you again?" She replied, "Soon, I hope." He told her he needed to go back to Grass Valley to help Ray with the house and when he got to a good spot he'd come see her again.

She left first. He stood there, watching, as she drove away. He got back in the truck and sat staring out at the trees. If he looked just right, he could see her there, dancing in the breeze.

2

"Avoiding danger is no safer in the long run than outright exposure. The fearful are caught as often as the bold."

Helen Keller

Exposure

The sun is setting over the Malakoff Diggings. Streaks of violet-red bands peek through the sandstone crevasses of the once gold-rich hydraulic mining region. Tom turns his head back to watch the road. He's got 150 pounds of nails in the back of his truck. He slows for the next turn and looks back at the sunset. Up ahead a deer scurries across the road and crashes through the woods on the other side. Everything beautiful reminds him of Mari. He has just picked up building supplies at the Old Nail Factory north of Malakoff and has 11 miles to go. He's hoping to make it to Grass Valley by suppertime. Ray is waiting there at the construction site of their Mom's new house. They hope to start framing by first light.

The next morning the sound of hammers echoed down the canyon. The brothers were up early. Tom was eager. If all went well they should have the frame up in three weeks.

Tom made phone calls to Mari now and then, but it was hard having his sweetheart so far away. Several weeks went by. Finally, the two brothers reached a good stopping point and Tom set out for Sonoma County the next day.

Coming across the windy Mayacamas Mountains, he headed for Santa Rosa in his borrowed Subaru truck. He was supposed to be there by 6:30 PM. Noni was cooking dinner for the entire family and he was invited. All the way he sang his "O Mari" song or "I'm going to be home in time for dinner."

He arrived on time. As he approached the house, Mari

appeared in the doorway wearing a violet cotton dress that shifted with the breeze. Her skin sparkled with the look of love. She put both arms around his neck and softly whispered, "I missed you," then led him by the hand into the house where a tall man was standing. "Tom, I would like you to meet my father, Carl." Tom said, "Good to meet you sir."

Carl was a well-built Telly-Savalas-looking Croatian man wearing a polo shirt, yellow slacks and white shoes. His face was distinguished, strong and intelligent. With authority, he replied, "Just call me Gus." Noni and Mari's sister, Pauline ambled in from the kitchen beaming *Mari's in love* smiles, then scurried back.

Adam and Jacob were in the back playing "chase your brother." Mari escorted Tom to the backyard, the boys ran to him, each grabbing a leg, tugging profusely at his tattered Levis. With a studied gaze he questioned, "Tell me again, how old are you boys?" "Ten," they both chimed. Squeezing Tom's tattooed arms, she dug her fingernails into his bicep and said, "I'm so happy the boys like you." The twins scampered off to the family room and turned on the TV. A few minutes later they began yelling for "Mom and Tom" to come watch the program. They all cuddled on the couch, curled up in a moment of union. Suddenly the doorbell rang, marching through all 8 bells. It was Cheeze, the next-door neighbor boy. Mari yelled, "The boys can't play right now, they have to eat dinner." Three-quarters of the way through "I Love Lucy," Pauline came in from the kitchen and announced, "Dinner will be ready in a few minutes. Better wash up."

They all chaotically wandered to the bathroom and stood in front of the sink slopping water onto the floor, emulating the affectionate family they might become. Noni announced dinner. The four rustled around the corner to the dining room and sat along a large mahogany table covered with a white embroidered tablecloth. Gus sat at the head and Noni at the opposite end. The boys seated themselves across from Mari and Tom, next to Pauline. The table was attractively set with porcelain bowls of Croatian lamb, potatoes, salad, wine, bread and other delicacies. Mouthwatering smells of a home-cooked sit-down dinner filled the air. Noni straightened her utensils and began to pray. After grace, everyone smiled and turned toward the head of the family. Slipping his chair forward, Gus motioned graciously and said, "Tom, please help yourself." Tom politely began serving himself, noticing that the boys had already taken the lion's share.

During dinner all kinds of subtle questions came forth seeking the intentions of the newcomer. Afterwards Tom and Mari picked up everyone's dishes and put them in the kitchen, then disappeared to her bedroom, hanging out like adult teenagers.

Mari asked him about his family. He took her on a diverse journey, spelling out a shorthand version.

"My mother June is beautiful, part beloved Romanian gypsy, part savvy business woman. My stepfather Bob is a good-hearted redneck with a talent for restoring cars. My biological father is named Robert. He's a LA County toe-the-line plumbing inspector, tough guy. Sister Theresa is a world traveler, psychic, housewife to her musician husband. Sister Cathryn is a long-legged beauty who owns an interior design company in Bend, Oregon. Brother Ray is a work-hard, play-hard, stay-hard building contractor and Fire Chief for the Grass Valley Fire Department.

"I'm not sure how to describe myself—perhaps one foot in the responsible, the other in the wandering gypsy—the one who looks for signposts along the edge of life. A searcher. My major in college was electronic engineering. I worked for Raytheon, The Bell System, AT&T, trained with Bell Labs and was a consultant to Intel Corporation. I was involved with Paratechnology, and several high-tech startups, and was a construction-engineering manager for Arawak Corporation in the Caribbean.

"I've lived in communes, lived out of a cardboard box, been lost in the fog, tried farming, was a fireman, a shoeshine boy, a musician, a pilot, ran a halfway house for parolees out of prison, lived like an 1850s wilderness family, owned a tattoo shop, traveled the West Indies, experimented with sex, drugs, and rock & roll and lived in a village where I was the only white man in four hundred people.

"Yet there's been a spiritual awareness through it all. I've attended every kind of church, listened to endless speakers of truth and found that there's no one who can do it for you, save yourself, with the Divine. My spiritual teachers are Jesus Christ, Paramahansa Yogananda, Shri Yukteswar, Mahatma Gandhi, Nimkaroli Baba, and Ananda Moyi Ma. You could call me a Hindu-Christian, a seeker of Love through Bhakti Yoga (devotion), although, I'm not so sure how good I've been at it all."

Tom asked Mari about her family.

"My father, 'Mr. G', Gus, or Didi (Croatian for grandfather) is the CEO of one of the largest privately-owned food distribution companies in the United States. My mother, Georgette, or Noni (Croatian for grandmother) takes care of the family and is devoted to her husband and church. Sister Pauline is one of the few woman 747-jet pilots in the world. My brother Carl is a manager for a division of my dad's company. Although we don't speak of it, I deeply love my brother.

"To my family I am the mother of the twins, the light in their future vision and for that I am honored. I love my boys dearly. They are the most important things in my life. I am a disappointment in the eyes of my family, yet they will always love me. I am the 4.0-educated rebel.

"I existed. I was born. If I told you where and when this took place, this would be no more than an income tax return. If I told you why this took place, it would be no more than an echo of some philosopher's words. So I will merely continue.

"My first years were full of impressions, lights, colors, sounds, thoughts, confusions (they still are)—but it was different then. I could look at a cloud and not think of rain. I could admire a flower and not know it was a weed. But those days are gone and I am much wiser now (?). I see people spending hours talking about war, God, and Love without listening to what is being said. I have seen others who have hardened themselves against their 'enemy's' reproach, not realizing that he is actually a friend trying to show concern and love. I have seen those who say they have learned to face 'reality.'

I've noticed that some think food to be more important than fasting, and conversation more important than contemplation. I have been told that success means cars, houses, clothes and influential friends. I have been told that Love is only a superficial word that no one believes in. My life has been a series of lessons and since the beginning, I have been trying to sift through the superficial lining and discover a truth. I have found that there is much good in the world and that I have much to learn. My life thus far could be summed up in one word—search.

"I went to private Catholic girls' schools most of my childhood and attended Santa Barbara and Sonoma State Universities, traveled to Yugoslavia, Europe, South America, Mexico and India. I work as a massage therapist at a spa in Calistoga and live with my parents. My father has been both father and grandfather to my boys since they were very young.

"Even as a child I searched for the truth beyond the day-to-day beneficial exchange, beyond survival, beyond the pursuit of greatness and control. Looking for it in flowers, in the *darshan* (seeing with awareness) of a sunset, the play of children and in the silence of myself.

"My main practice is *Vipassana*, silently creating the observer. My teachers have been Bhagwan Shree Rajneesh, Krishnamurthi, Jesus Christ, Ananda Moyi Ma, Tara, Tantra, Tibetan Buddhism and motherhood. My battle has been to gain independence from the little self, the one that judges, compares and competes through endless head-trips. Watching myself without judging expands that part of me that just watches. It increases my awareness of THAT which I am a part of. Think of it, someday everyone you have ever loved will die, including yourself. In the end, all you have are moments of NOW, separated by self-imposed filler. To live more in the NOW, seeking the flow and truth in life has been my goal."

It was nearing nightfall. Mari explained that her parents would not approve of him sleeping at the house. He remembered seeing a park one block from the house that would be an excellent place to lay his head. He left his truck at Mari's and the lovers walked to the park arm-in-arm. He found a little clearing atop a knoll with bushes all around. They laid out his sleeping bag and talked and kissed into the night. With her face beard-burned and her lips noticeably swollen, she squeezed his hand and said softly, "It's getting late. You can go to school with me tomorrow. See you in the morning." Without looking back she walked away.

Getting into his sleeping bag he propped up his junkyard jacket for a pillow and looked at the night sky. Gazing up at the stars, he thought *This is not so bad.* He remembered once having slept in a downtown L.A. flophouse. This was surely better than that. Anyways, love was just a block away.

The sun woke him at the crack of dawn, too early to set out for the house. Mari had said to be there around 8:00 AM for breakfast. The morning air was invigorating and the smell of cooking bacon from the neighborhood proclaimed civilization nearby. He wandered through the trees and stopped to pick up a snail scooting along the leaf of a bayberry bush. "Hello Mr. Snail, how are you this morning?" The snail pulled in its translucent antennae and sucked into its shell. "Probably better before I came along." He placed the curious creature back on its leaf and wondered on.

Birds had gathered by a nearby dumpster appreciating an apple that hadn't quite made it in. He walked to the edge of the clearing and entered the wet tall grass. The dew soaked his scuffed boots. The sun was poking up through spaces between the houses at the rear of the park. Dogs were barking off in the distance. He stood there with his brown-stained T-shirt hanging out over his pants, when he spotted a baseball field. Climbing the fence, he made for the bleachers and sat staring out at second base, the Little League position he had played when he was a kid.

Suddenly the crackle of tires on pavement accented the sound of a police radio. A black-and-white pulled into the parking lot, shocking him into present time. A policeman stepped out, situating his nightstick as he walked briskly toward left field. The officer had received a call from a neighbor stating there was a "homeless man" sitting in the bleachers. The officer yelled from a distance, "What are you doing?" Not knowing what to say, Tom mumbled, "I'm waiting for my girlfriend." Now, Tom looked more like a homeless person who had just slept in the park, than someone waiting for his girlfriend. The cop stepped forward, "I think you better be moving along." Tom glanced at his watch; it was 7:30 AM. Without saying anything he walked across the field and headed for Mari's. It was too early to knock on the door, so he waited across the street, watching Noni prepare food behind the kitchen window. Noni looked up and saw him standing there. She looked away for moment, then Mari appeared at the window, signaling Tom to come over.

He walked up the driveway to the side door and knocked. From inside came the clink-clink sound of a wooden spoon hitting the sides of a mixing bowl. A few minutes later she came to the door with bowl in hand and invited him in, "Do you like waffles?" "Oh, yes," he replied. Tom helped with the preparations and again the boys ate the lion's share. Noni had eaten early and Gus had his banquet in bed. Mari said she was going to Sonoma State University for a biofeedback assignment—she was finishing her degree in clinical psychology and needed more lab time.

Climbing into the car, he noticed she was sporting a really tight pair of pants. He said, "What kind of pants are those?" She crooked her head around to look at the tag on the back, "They're called Rose's." Tom said bashfully, "You can see the lips." "What do you mean?" He replied with a schoolboy grin, "You know, the lips, in front." She smiled erotically, "Maybe I'd better go change?" Apologetically he exclaimed, "No, no, please don't, they look wonderful on you." From that day on he called those pants his Santa Rosa Roses. If she wasn't wearing them, he'd go, "Where's your Santa Rosa Roses" and she'd always smile and look away.

At Sonoma State University they walked across campus past the library. It reminded him of the three months he'd spent at Oberlin College installing a library management system that he and Dr. Ralph Shoffner had designed. Tom had spent a year writing the operating system that would became the first bar-coded library in the country. Hoping to impress her, he told her the story. She looked at him with a save-your-breath expression and continued walking to a room marked BIOFEEDBACK LAB. She told him she was going to hook him up to different monitors and ask questions. He thought, *This could be fun!* Like a mad scientist, she connected him to temperature sensors, EKG, EEG and blood pressure monitors and ran him through a battery of tests. He was hanging out in Beta/Delta most of the time, which didn't make much sense to her. A man his age should be mostly in Alpha. She was puzzled for a while, then it hit her—he must be IN LOVE. She tried other tests like sitting on his lap—his heart rate and blood pressure went through the roof and his hand and face temperature rose exponentially. During her school years, she would "hook him up" every time she got the chance!

Afterwards she said she knew a great restaurant not too far from campus in the accordion-festival town of Cotati. Of course he couldn't help but tell her that he played the accordion. They drove to Rafa's, a little mama-papa Mexican restaurant—the real thing. After eating huevos rancheros she wanted to lie down in the park near the center of town. She got a blanket and laid it on the lawn placing her head on his chest, moments later confessing she liked to hear his heart beat FASTER.

With a shaky voice he whispered, "Will you go steady with me?" Silence ensued while she addressed her inner self. Then she explained she would have to tell her estranged juggler/street-performer boyfriend, Sudan, in San Francisco, that she had met someone new.

She began laying out the ground rules. "If you ever hit me, I will leave you." He assured her that he would never hit her and paused, coming out with his own little rule, "If you ever lie to me, I will leave you." She said she would try not to. And with that, they became girlfriend/boyfriend. It was a serious moment, a sign of commitment. They lay there oblivious to anyone else, not saying a word, not even "I love you"—it was inferred through their bodies.

It was getting to be afternoon. Mari wanted to see an Indian saint named Ammachi staying near Mill Valley. Tom replied, "Let's go." Off they went, Tom playing with Mari's hair most of the way. An hour later they arrived in a residential area west of town and circled the block twice before Mari spotted the open front door where people were wandering in and out.

Someone from the flower-covered front porch yelled, "Come, come, Ammachi is in the back." The lovers parked and walked through the house into the backyard. On a chair covered by a blanket, surrounded by several East Indian men, sat Ammachi in a bright purple sari with flowered leis around her neck. Her long black hair glistened in the sunlight as did her eyes. Three men stood to the left and two to the right. Tom and Mari stared in awe. Ammachi motioned them to come over. Holding hands, they walked forward and knelt in front of the saint. The fragrant Mother reached out, gently placing their heads in her lap. One of the men uttered words in *Malayalam,* a dialect of Kerala, India. Something began to manipulate the energy around them. A sensation moved through their spines like a string being pulled through their bodies. Their ears filled with a sound like dripping water, while rays of swirling colors danced in their heads. A moment later they were immersed in calm, like a child being held by its mother.

One of the East Indian men started speaking. He was reading the Sanskrit writing tattooed on Tom's right arm, "Tomas, Karma, Jana." Ammachi asked, "What's on the other arm?" Another man on the left chimed in, "Bhakti Man." Ammachi lifted their heads from her lap and smiled into their eyes. Raising her hands in *pranamah*, she said, "Om shanti, Om shanti, peace, peace, peace, amen."

Feeling blessed, they left the saint and went into the house to help with the cleanup. Once back in the car, Tom said, "Where to now?" "Let's go to Stinson Beach," Mari shouted excitedly. Stinson Beach is where she had hung out in the early days, when she was a teenage rebel.

After driving an hour on winding roads, they stood holding hands on a windswept beach. Once past the rocks, he took his boots off and tied the laces together, throwing them over his shoulder. The feel of the sand reminded him of where he was and where he had once been. Mari motioned him to follow.

She ran between two jagged cliff rocks and disappeared on the other side. He followed. There through the rocks was a secret beach; people were basking in the sun, nude. She turned and smiled like a little girl and exclaimed, "Isn't this cool." Most of the women were walking around with no tops. It reminded him of La Luna on the Yuba River. She told him someday she'd take him to Harbin Hot Springs, a place that would be sure to expand his mind. He didn't know what that was, but felt excited about the prospect of going anywhere with her.

It was getting late; she had to get back to her boys. Two hours later, rolling into Santa Rosa, Mari asked, "Where are you going to sleep tonight?" She knew a place near her house, by a creek with a field of oak trees. That sounded good to him; he loved the enchantment of oak trees. They were part of his growing-up years in Thousand Oaks and made him feel comfortable.

That night he slept under the oaks in a field a mile from Mari's house. The smell of the creek mixed with the odor of moss took him back. As a boy he remembered exploring Saltos Creek Canyon with his dog Chico and wondering about the ancient spirits that he believed lived there.

The next morning Mari came and woke him. They walked to a nearby creek where she used to play as a little girl. She talked about her strict Croatian Catholic upbringing and how the creek was a place where she went when she got angry with her parents, or to watch the water and write poetry.

Tom said, "You like to write?" She said she loved to write. She told him about attending the University of Santa Barbara; lodging with health-food hippies in the mountains above Santa Barbara and living in a wooden shack that had an outdoor bathtub with a view of the sea—she had loved that place. She was the editor of the university newspaper. She'd sit out on the wooden steps of her little handmade house and write articles on medicinal herbs and organize the campus news.

Tom asked, "What did you do after that?"

"Later I moved to New York and worked at a Park Avenue Greek belly-dancing joint to make ends meet. On breaks I would write sonnets about the bizarre characters I saw there. Then I traveled to France in '73 where I met a lady in a coffee shop who asked me to write her memoirs. I stayed in France for six months, and then moved to Berkeley, California where I met the African American novelist Cecil Brown. We fell in love and moved in together. Later I became the editor for one of the novels he was writing at the time.

"My girlfriend Janet, Cecil and I made the Beverly Hills scene, hanging out with Richard Pryor, attending wild parties and hobnobbing with the rich and famous. After breaking up with Cecil in '74, Janet and I left for Mexico, traveling for six months by train, bus and any other way we could get around.

"When I finished my Mexican adventures, I moved to San Diego and rented a renovated chicken coop from the wife of a karate instructor who taught me how to dive for abalone. I met the father of my twin boys, Beto, at a gas station in Chula Vista. We were married in January of '76 and the twins were born that February. We moved to Arizona where I met Jaichima, Beto's mother, a Huichol Indian Shaman. Beto and I lived together for about a year, and then I moved in with my parents in Santa Rosa. We divorced in 1981."

"That's probably more than you need to know."

Mari went on, "And how about you, do you write?" He told her that when he was ten years old he wrote a cowboy story about a blacksmith. She laughed. He went on hoping to impress her, "While working at the Portland Plant Training Center for Pacific Northwest Bell, I had a chance to do some technical writing for a new course curriculum on Centrex Analysis. It's where I met my second mentor, Al Toler—the hermit Rudy was my first. Al taught me how to pack my own chute and fly an airplane."

Then he started telling her about the farm he bought in Oregon in 1969, living in a barn before moving in. Wrapping up his long-winded story, he told her he'd worked the farm by day and the telephone company by night. He sold the farm in '74, bought an 80-acre parcel in the mountains, built a log cabin and lived there until '77.

Mari exclaimed, "Oh shit, I have to pick up the boys and you've got to go back to Grass Valley." They started walking back up the trail from the creek toward the car. She spotted dandelions, bent over and picked one. Making eye contact, she reached out and handed Tom her gift. She smiled, picking another and headed back to the creek. He followed. When they arrived she lifted her flower into the air, pushing it toward the sky three times. Tom followed her lead. They threw their yellow blossoms into the water and watched them flow downstream, as if to say, "We are moving downstream together."

That afternoon Tom drove back to Grass Valley.

He and Ray worked on the house two more weeks. They got all the trusses up and were beginning to put the plywood sheathing on the roof. Tom loved to put up sheathing; it was his favorite. Pulling eight-penny nails from his pouch and pounding them in with two whacks, two stories up in the air, was his idea of a good time. He stopped for a moment, leaning back on the heels of his boots, and stretched out his back. As he did this he heard a car coming up the driveway. It was Mari in her little Honda! He quickly went back to work pretending he didn't see her. He wanted her to see him in action, working high on the roof. She drove around in front of the house where she had a clear view. He stopped working and knelt on one knee and waved to her with hammer in hand. He thought, *Oh, there's my sweetie, how wonderful she would drive all this way to see me.* He stood up and yelled down, "What a great surprise. I'll be right down. I was just thinking about you." Of course he was, he was always thinking about her. They were so glad to see each other tears formed in their eyes.

Mari was hungry, and Tom suggested Mama Sue's in Nevada City. When they arrived Tatyana greeted Tom with a big hug. Mari wanted to know who she was. He explained to Mari how Tatyana had told him about the Yuba River and how he had

had the vision of Mari there before ever meeting her.

Old Max, the local, tattered, dredge miner, yelled out something to Tatyana from across the room. Max was missing all his teeth and you could hardly understand what he was saying. "Who's that pretty gal with Tom?" "She's from Santa Rosa." Max murmured, "You tell her to come over and sit at my table." Tom knew Max was a sweet old man so he brought Mari over and introduced them. Max, spitting while he talked, garbled out the words in a gruff voice that the whole place could hear, "Hot damn Tom, she's a good looker. How in da hell you get so lucky?" Tom told him, he'd wondered that himself. Max was right, she was a gorgeous creature; every guy in the place had his eyes on her. They ordered Mama Sue's famous chiliburger and spent the afternoon visiting with all the local characters.

After saying goodbye to everyone in the café, Tom decided to take Mari up to North San Juan and show her the swimming hole. Mari loved it. She was free of the home front; all her responsibilities for schoolwork, and her parents' expectations had disappeared. She took off her clothes and jumped into the water. He followed, fulfilling the dream he had there a few months back. This time she was there in flesh and blood. The sun was shining and nothing else mattered. They held each other, merging off into some distant land. They basked in the hot sun on the rocks above the falls looking down at the swimming-hole below. The crash of the waterfall making its way through the smooth rock basin beneath them set the background for several hours until the cool mountain air began sweeping over their naked bodies around dusk. It was time to head back.

She was hungry for Chinese food and wanted to stop somewhere interesting. He took her to a quaint Chinese place in downtown Grass Valley; they held hands through most of the meal. He knew she would have to go back that night and was already getting the blues. After dinner they drove back to the house and kissed goodbye. He waved until she was out of sight.

The next day Tom began thinking about the meeting that he had set up with a venture capital group at Sand Hill in Menlo Park. He was hoping to raise additional capital for the barely-alive company he had so intensely worked to save. He was going to have to get a haircut and shave before having an audience with these folks and it was scaring the hell out of him. His fear wasn't about meeting with the venture capitalists, but that Mari might not like his looks after seeing him all cleaned up. It bothered him for days.

He called her on the phone and told her about his proposed metamorphosis. She assured him that it would be OK. He found a barbershop in old downtown Grass Valley and proceeded with the feat. Afterwards he was so shook up over his new looks, he asked the barber for a lollipop hoping the childhood gesture would make him feel better. He kept looking in the mirror and saying, "I don't know, she's not going to like this." .

Now that he was all clean-cut, his brother Ray, who was Fire Chief at the time, suggested that he join the Grass Valley fire department. Tom had had some training as a volunteer fireman in Cornelius, Oregon when he had the farm years ago and remembered feeling a sense of belonging. He figured it would help with the loneliness of missing Mari. The next day he showed up at the Grass Valley firehouse for First Arrival training and became the department's newest member.

Ten days later, a major wildfire broke out near Grass Valley. Large sections in the mountains above Nevada City were on fire. The press called it the "Forty-Niner Fire." The California Dept. of Forestry had command control and thousands of firemen were brought in from all over the state. Tom was assigned to an engine company protecting an industrial area in the northern mountains near the Grass Valley Group's high-tech manufacturing facility. There were several large industrial buildings on the property. The real danger was the two 2,000-gallon propane tanks next to the tree line.

Tom's engine company drove several miles with 20-foot flames on either side of the road, coming out into a clear area near the manufacturing facility. The battalion chief gave instructions to protect the buildings at all costs. In other words, if the tanks went, no one was coming out alive; they had to stop the fire at the crest. Wind-driven 150-foot flames were roaring up the canyon in front. The explosions of burning pine trees below sounded like a locomotive coming up the canyon.

Three engines held the frontline. If the flames came up over the hill and got into the propane tanks, everything within an eighth of a mile would be toast. They stood their ground with hoses ready, waiting for the wall of flame to change direction, praying for the wind to shift. They looked at each other, *This is it.* The thought raced through Tom's mind, *I really never got a chance to know her.*

Just when the flames crested over the hill, a 100 feet from the engines, coming directly at them, a borate bomber flew low over the treetops dropping red fire retardant. It covered the engines, propane tanks, trees and the firemen working the line. Thank God for borate bomber pilots!

That night they all ate steak at CDF command headquarters and slept on top of their fire trucks, ready for the next morning's run. The wildfire burned 33,000 acres of watershed lands and destroyed over 150 homes. Tom's crew fought the fire for four days.

Exhausted, Tom headed for Santa Rosa. He had just had his close call and was ready to see the love of his life. The story of the fire had been in the news and he received a hero's welcome from Mari and her family. He had almost forgotten about his new clean-shaven look when Mari said, "You look handsome." That's what he needed to hear; she still loved him. That night he went to Theresa's house to sleep and Mari went with him. They slept together just cuddling. They still hadn't made love.

The next morning Tom woke and told her he was constipated from all those days out on the fire line. She said he probably needed to take an enema. He asked her if she would help. Theresa's husband Steve was quite shocked at the idea. He went on and on about what in the heck they were doing in there. To Tom and Mari it seemed so natural; they were just helping each other, regardless of what anyone else thought.

That morning he left for a meeting in Menlo Park that Bob Davis had arranged with some venture capitalists. They wanted Tom to disclose the algorithms for the ASAP (Associated Search Array Processor) technology. After much discussion about the terms of their nondisclosure agreements he bid them goodbye. They told him that they would have their attorneys prepare the necessary changes and he could meet with one of their high-tech companies, Wetek Corporation, in the coming weeks in San Jose.

Tom arrived at Mari's house in the evening and discussed Paratechnology's business plan with Gus. He told Tom he should prepare a letter to the president of Wetek confirming the meeting and outline his goals. Tom spent the rest of the evening with Mari preparing the letter and then showed it to Gus. Gus began reading the letter out loud, stridently verbalizing his response as he read, "SO WHAT." He read on some more, "WHO CARES." Flipping the page, "BIG DEAL." He told Tom to remove all references to any personal feelings and get to the point. Tom and Mari rewrote the letter, shortening it to one page. Gus was somewhat happy.

Mari told him that her parents were going away for three days to a Frank Sinatra concert in Las Vegas. The two teenage adults started scheming about what they might do while the parents were away. Tom slept at Theresa's house that night.

Tom arrived at Mari's house next morning; the parents and Pauline had already left. Tom made pancakes for Mari and the boys. No one was really saying it, but they were all pretending to be a family. They took the boys to Scandia, an amusement park south of Santa Rosa and played together all day. Tom liked the batting boxes and the little motorized racecars and the boys loved all the high-energy stuff.

When they got back to Mari's house that afternoon the boys went off with the neighbor kids and Tom and Mari were alone. They started making out on the couch. Tom slowly, very slowly moved his hand under her blouse and touched her breast. It was incredibly exciting, kind of like "While the parents are away the teenagers will play." He stopped there, she whispered with a smile, "You're not supposed to do that." They both giggled.

That evening, Mari asked Tom if he would spend the night. He told her that he would, but Gus had given him the 'ground rules', "No sleeping over." Mari said, "What if you call my dad and ask his permission? Just tell him you're going to sleep on the couch." Tom called their Las Vegas hotel room; Gus answered. Tom blurted out, "Hello Gus, this is Tom." Gus replied, "Is everything all right?" Tom choked up a little, "Yes, I was hoping to get your permission to sleep on the couch tonight?" Gus responded in a deep business voice, "Absolutely NOT." Tom replied, mirroring his corporate persona, "Very good. We'll see you when you arrive home," and that was that. Tom slept in the park again that night and Mari was mad at both of them.

The next morning all was well. They made plans to help at a benefit cookout in Petaluma for the Wirikuta organization. They arrived at the park around 10:00 AM. The parking lot was full of people with painted faces, dressed in bright colors, feathers and such, ready to help with the cooking. Jaichima and Vicente were just arriving and stopped to say hello to Mari. They all went into the rec hall. Mari helped the performers and Tom prepared food in the kitchen with Randy and Ulu. After the performance and eats, Jaichima and Vicente Rutury gave a Huichol Indian blessing to the crowd. The lovers were the last ones to leave the hall and as they did Mari turned to Tom, "Everyone's going to the beach for the harmonic convergence, will you come with me?"

Off they went to the beach for the Mayan Quetzalcoatl celebration. When they arrived people were drumming and dancing in the sand. Jaichima and Vicente Rutury were leading an ancient ceremony for the 25th year of the Mayan cycle of 13 moons. According to the Mayan calendar this was the time when the veil thinned between earth and other dimensions. It was a time when prayer and intention affected the fabric of reality the most. They all prayed for peace on earth.

While dancing with Mari on the sand he moved her hair back. Placing his mouth near her ear he began to whisper a song, "Many a tear has to fall, but it's all in the game. The wonderful game of love... "

That evening Tom left again for Grass Valley to start house wiring with Ray. A week later he set out for Santa Rosa, this time on Ol' Gal. He laid her down in the corners, pushing her 100 miles per hour on the straights, and made it to Santa Rosa 45 minutes ahead of schedule.

He had arranged with Theresa to stay at her house, but went directly to Mari's. He was home in time for dinner! Mari told him that she wanted him to meet her friends who lived in Guerneville. They wound around into the hills above the Russian River, onto a narrow one-lane road. Mari set the brake in her little Honda and climbed out, "Come on Tom, I want you to meet Asha and Bodhi." It was beautiful. The house looked out over the valley and down onto the river. Mari and Asha immediately went into the other room for Tom-talk. Bodhi, a carpenter by trade, started talking to Tom about the house he and Ray were building.

An hour later Tom noticed Mari walk out onto the deck. She stood at the railing overlooking the river, gazing out at the horizon. He excused himself and joined her. Coming up behind her he pressed his body against hers. They ogled each other in silence, occasionally looking at the valley below; their heads stuck together, their bodies entangled. Mari got that look on her face—a good idea was about to manifest. With a cat like smile she said, "Let's go to the Armstrong Woods parking lot." He knew what she meant. They said their goodbyes and drove five miles up a narrow winding road to their real destination.

She spun the wheel around pointing the car downhill. Setting the brake with one hand she seized his neck with the other and pulled him towards her. They kissed for hours. They kissed until Mari's lips were red and swollen. He wanted to explore other places with her, but refrained with whatever will power he had left. He felt she was saying, *Stop it some more*. He didn't want to cross the line.

Driving back to Santa Rosa he played with her hair, watching her beaded earrings sway with each corner. The silhouette of her nose, the elegance of her neck, were all being stored in indelible memory.

The next day he assisted Theresa around the house and played ping-pong with Steve. The phone rang. It was Mari. She wanted to know if Tom would go to a Rajneesh party with her. Of course he would, he would have gone to a tailgate party at the North Pole. Mari said she would pick him up at 7:00 PM.

She pulled up in her little Honda dressed to kill, wearing a flesh-colored short skirt with black nylons and a white see-through top. The kind of top that when the wind blew her controls magically rose up, saluting like a cherry on top of a chocolate sundae. Tom was wearing his usual grubby Levis and work boots; at least he was clean-shaven.

They arrived at the party spiritually in style. Hand in hand they walked in the open front door of the fancy Montecito Heights home. There were 50 people there. People were coming from everywhere to say hello to Mari—they knew her by her Rajneesh name, *Santosh*. Santosh means, "responsibly reserved and dignified" in Hindi.

Mari seemed proud to introduce her newfound lover to all her Bhagwan friends even though he looked like a dog. She acquainted him with Anila and Anunado, old friends from Rajneeshpuram, the ranch where Mari and her boys had lived and worked together. Mari and Tom walked around hugging, playing, singing little short tunes, and laughing with everyone. Tom really liked that everyone was fond of everyone else, regardless of his or her appearance or station in life. Certainly they liked him—he was with the goddess. He made friends with Ken and Ritma, the dentist and the schoolteacher. Ritma loved Mari and was particularly sweet with Tom. Mari's friends seemed like one big happy family. He met a host of other folks that would soon become friends. They left the party late that night and tried to find a motel in downtown Santa Rosa. Every place was full up. So Tom slept in the park on Fourth Street under a tree near a bag lady who snored all night.

Mari came and woke him early. She wanted him to go to breakfast with her at the Rusty Nail in Forestville. An old boyfriend/lover named Prabhat, who had spent six months with her at the Pune ashram in India in the '70s, was in town and wanted to meet her for breakfast. She told Prabhat she would come, if she could bring her new boyfriend Tom along. Tom was a little jealous; however, he knew that she was being straight-up honest and it would be a big mistake to turn into an idiot now. She introduced the tall, handsome contractor-type to Tom. Tom pulled Mari's chair back so she could sit down like a lady. It was also a secret signal to Prabhat, *This is my girl.* She was so sweet to both of them, as if to say, *I love you both, but I'm with Tom.*

Prabhat wanted to have one last look at her before he left the country on some far-off journey. They all walked out to the parking lot and stood by Prabhat's truck. Tom could tell that they needed time alone and walked back to the car. Mari soon returned and told Tom she appreciated the goodbye time—good *q'uecha* (inner energy) all around.

After Prabhat drove out of sight Mari turned to Tom and said, "Let's make a picnic. I know a beautiful park outside of Petaluma and it's not too far from Theresa's." They stopped off at a roadside fruit stand near Forestville and got all the fixin's. Mari took the back roads to Petaluma and then headed west toward the ocean. About six miles out of town, she turned off onto Park Road and stopped alongside an oak tree. They bagged up food and blankets and walked through steep rolling green hills to the top of an oak-crested ridge. There they had a 360-degree view of the east and west valleys of Sonoma County. They were so in love. It would have been sickening for anyone to see them, unless they too were in love.

Mari sat on an old downed oak log. Pushing aside the cheese and apricots, she slipped off her sandals and lifted her long skirt up onto her knees. Tom moved the green grass back from around her feet and sat facing her. He kissed each foot tenderly and laid his head on her lap. She scooted down to the ground with her back against the log. Her hair fell forward across her bare shoulders. They began exploring each other's bodies. It was the first time they had touched with so much passion. After going as far as they dared without crossing the point of no return, they lay in each other's arms staring up at the sky. Suddenly, they broke into laughter and ran down the hill holding hands, giggling like naughty little children all the way to the car.

He left that night riding an iron horse chasing a white line with the wind in his face and tears in his eyes, screaming down the blacktop for Grass Valley.

3

"You cannot have sex without having sex with me.
You cannot kill without killing me.
You cannot walk barefoot in the grass without touching me.
Everywhere you are I AM. Everywhere I AM you are."

Jaiamata

Cross Roads

Tom's mom is in the kitchen of the old house near the new construction site. She's been cooking all day, mixing up a secret sauce for one of her special Gypsy dishes. Bob just got back from Humpty Dumpty's, the local hamburger joint. He's up at his shop above the old house banging and scraping on a body, performing his transformational magic on a '68 Volkswagen. Tom and Ray are pounding. The thud, bang, echo sounds of hammers boom across the valley.

Suddenly Tom's mom yells out, "TOMMY!" She always calls him Tommy. He keeps working, pretending not to hear her. "Tommy, you and Ray take a break. There's lemonade on the counter."

The sun blazed yellow. Tom wiped the salty sweat from his eyes and hollered back, "Yes Mom." Soon construction clatter died behind the sound of a barking dog. They walked over to the old house and sat down at the counter. The glasses were dripping with condensation. Tom ran his finger down the side of the glass and took a drink. Mom continued, "I got a call from Mari." Tom became all ears, "She said not to interrupt your work. She's arranged some kind of camping trip. You better call her."

While walking towards the phone Tom ate the lime from the edge of the glass and gulped down the lemonade, making a sound like a cat with a hairball. Picking up the receiver, he dialed Mari's number in Santa Rosa and waited while it rang. He heard the line pick up and grinned. Noni answered, "Hi Tom, Mari's not here, she just went to Safeway." Tom cleared his throat, "Nice to hear *your* voice, will you please tell Mari I'll try calling back in a half hour."

With leather tool belts still strapped to their waists, Tom and Ray strolled out on to the front lawn and sat cross-legged in the dry grass. They looked across at their work smiling at each other. Ray said, "N-O-W what are you guys up to?" Tom knew that Ray was getting a little frustrated with all those Santa Rosa trips. Tom replied, "I don't know, maybe a camping trip!" Ray nodded slowly. Both their heads turned at the crackling sound of tires coming up the gravel driveway. It was Guy, Bob's gold-panning cousin, barreling up in his '53 Ford pickup. He went past the house waving as he headed for Bob's backyard body shop.

Tom heard the phone ring, sending shockwaves up his spine, "Tommy, its Mari on the phone." Tom made a beeline for the front door, tripping on the last step. He gently took the phone from his mother's hand and spoke into the mouthpiece, "Hi sweetie." A no-nonsense loving voice echoed, "Hi sweetie, I made arrangements with my parents and work for a one-week camping trip at Frog Pond. What do you think?" He told her to hold just a minute and went outside. Ray was sitting there nervously counting nails in a leather pouch, anticipating Tom's next absence. Tom asked. Ray reflected, gazing at the sky; with a reluctant partial grin he cocked an eye over at Tom and said, "Go for it." Although Ray supported Tom in his new love, he thought he was a bit off his rocker.

Tom packed his camping gear in the Subaru and left the next morning for Santa Rosa. This time he took the back road through Marysville, on to Williams, over the hills at Calistoga and on in to Santa Rosa. He even knew the back roads to Mari's house.

When he arrived at the house, Gus was waiting by the door. Gus took him off to the side. Tom began to get nervous; sweat formed on the palms of his hands. Gus said, "Sorry to be so damned mysterious. Seriously, why do you drive all that way?" Tom looked at Gus with a perplexed look, and then smiled,

"Because it's worth it!" At first Gus had a kind of dirty-old-man expression. Then he shifted to Oh-I-see, an almost proud look, as if to say, *Yes, she's my daughter.*

Mari's twins were running around all excited about the trip. They kept asking, "What are we going to do?" Mari said, "We're going camping, we'll have a campfire and marshmallows, we'll go hiking, see the animals, look at the stars, and eat." They liked that idea, but Tom could tell that wasn't going to keep them busy. Finally the car was packed and ready to go. Pulling out of the driveway, Noni and Pauline stood at the door and waved them off.

As they drove down Highway 116 towards Guerneville the boys were pushing and shoving, playing license plate games in the back seat. They passed Davy's Tree Farm, Mom's Apple Pie, wound around the Forestville Cemetery, and onward to the Canyon Rock Mine, passing Shanti's geodesic dome glass shop on the left.

At the town of Guerneville, there was J's old amusement park and penny arcade on the right. They stopped at the only signal and went straight. Mari said, "Tom, pull over here, I want to get something to drink." The Twice Told Book Store Laundromat was also a tie-dye dress shop and soda fountain place, all rolled into one. Mari ordered a cherry Italian soda. The boys wanted 7-up and Tom tried a boysenberry Italian. He wanted to be like Mari.

Two gay men holding hands came around the corner and moved slowly down the pavement. Strange characters sat at tables lining the sidewalk in front of the building. A couple caught Tom by surprise; two girls kissing, one wearing excessive red lipstick, the other with short orange-colored hair and green mascara. They goggled and giggled in the fog-spray under the steel pipes near the misting machine. Between the mist and the sloppy kisses, mascara ran down the face of the orange-haired woman wedging its self in the wrinkles of her smile. Being an Oregon boy, Tom had never seen anything like it. A tad blown away at first he took a double take, then refocused on Mari and the boys. Mari observed his momentary flash and smiled, "It's all part of your education."

They finished their drinks and were back on the road again. Up Armstrong Woods Road they passed the River of Life Pentecostal Church with its white picket fence, and Ring Canyon Camp Grounds where Mari had asked Tom to go camping the first time IF HE LIKED. They pulled into the guard station at the entrance to the redwood grove and stopped. The lady ranger greeted them, "Welcome to Armstrong Redwoods State Reserve, are you staying long?" She was talking to Tom. He didn't know what to say. Mari covered for him, "We're going to Frog Pond camp ground for a few days." The ranger explained that they could pay the patrol ranger each afternoon.

They started into the park, speed limit 5 MPH. The redwood trees stood 200 feet tall, blocking out the sun even in the afternoon. Strobe light sunbeams blasted through the trees as the car moved along. Mari was pointing out the flora and fauna near the road when something caught her eye, "Stop here, T-o-m, pull over." She told the boys "Wait in the car, I'll be right back, I want to show Thomas something." They both started whining, "We want to come." Mari said, "OK, but you have to be quiet because we're going to meditate," Jacob replied, "We'll wait here."

Mari steps out of the car and walks across the road, jumping over the wooden divider intended to keep people out. She lifts her dress in midair, first one leg then the other. Tom follows. Light catches her body like a thousand floodlights going off as she scampers through the trees. Tom runs to catch up. Mari stops, "Look, see this tree, it's been struck by lightning, we can go inside." Just by the way she says it, he can tell she's been here many times before. The base of the tree is hollowed out on one side where lightning had struck. Inside is a black charcoal wall, a literal tree cave, yet the tree is still alive, rising up almost 150 feet. Mari removes her leather sandals and goes inside, "Come Tom, come meditate with me." Tom squats next to her. She reaches over and holds his hand, "Let's be quiet for a moment, it's so wonderful here." With eyes closed they drift off to some remote aspect in time.

Her face emitted a translucent glow. Tom stilled his thoughts. He could feel her merging within. After a few minutes they came out from the tree. He looked over at Mari. Looking down at her charcoal-blackened bare feet against the green grass, he was immediately transported to a long-ago scene.

She was tending sheep in a field of wildflowers. Her dark sinuous hair flowing down the back of her hand-made dress glistened in the sun. She carried the staff of a Highland Welsh herder. Tom stood transfixed on a muddy wagon-rutted road gazing toward her. He felt the sun hitting his back through holes in his shirt. She stopped and turned. Her eyes flickered with the joy of life. Their eyes met—it was a moment so strong, the feelings could still be recaptured 400 years later.

Tom, coming back from his collision with the past, uttered, "Did anything happen to you?" Mari replied, "Yes, we went to a past life." Tom felt affirmed, complete, and at home with the rebirth that was bubbling to the surface of his consciousness.

Mari grabbed his hand and ran back to the car. The boys had been fighting and were getting restless. She started telling them a story about magic bullfrogs, "When we make our camp, if you boys go to the pond you might find one." Adam said, "Why are they magic?" She replied, "If you find one you can make a wish." The boys forgot about their fighting and were white-eyed with the prospects of seeing a magic bullfrog!

On they went, passing through a cathedral of redwood trees, ancient giants with thousands of moss-covered stories to tell. After driving two miles Mari pointed to a little side road that wound up the hill. Tom read the sign, "Bull Frog Pond, 3 miles, Winding One Lane Road." After hearing that, in the minds of the boys it was confirmed; there were going to be magic frogs.

Zigzagging through hairpin turns, Tom spotted a ranger's patrol car coming down the hill. He stopped and backed down the hill to a pull-off point. As the ranger passed he rolled down his window and waved "Thank you." They continued up the road, passing what looked like an old homestead surrounded by withering apple trees. Mari told Tom about a guy that had run a pottery studio at the old cottage years ago. Coming around a blind corner, they veered to the right to let an old man on a bicycle pass. The look on the old man's face was serene and peaceful. As they approached the 1,000-foot level, oak and madrone trees begin to appear. To the left was a small meadow truncated by a steep drop-off descending into a canyon below. At the last turn, they looked back; a clear view, reaching 25 miles back to Santa Rosa. At 1,250 feet, the coastal range silhouetted the skyline. Its grandeur was breathtaking; not a single manmade object as far as the eye could see.

Along the road, a half mile from the campground area, someone had stacked rocks on a forked oak branch forming a "Y," the question that can never be answered. Mari instructed Tom to pull into campsite number 14, then commented, "Not many people camp at Frog Pond, it's kind of a secret place; you almost need to be a local to know that it's even up here." Two campsites away, along a turn in the road, was a phone box mounted on a redwood stump. Mari told Tom she had promised to call Noni when they arrived. While Mari made the call, Tom unloaded the car and started setting up the tent. Adam and Jacob scoured the area for firewood, stacking small pieces in one pile and larger ones in another. The scent of pine and oak balls filled the air. Mari nonchalantly mentioned so the boys could hear, "Wild pigs, raccoons and sometimes bears raid the camp at night—it's best to leave the food in the car." It was getting to be dusk. Nocturnal creatures were striking up their ancient musical ragas and their little gypsy camp was all set for the night.

The boys kept asking about "magic bullfrogs." As Mari was cutting fruit and getting things ready for dinner, she said, "Tom, will you take the boys to the pond to see the M-A-G-I-C bullfrogs?" Each boy scurried to Tom, grabbing either hand, dragging him in the general direction of the pond, "Thomas, where do we go, how far is it?" Adam and Jacob were quite confident they would find magic frogs. Adam pulled out a small black and white stuffed killer whale from his pocket. Jacob sounded out, "Ask Orca, he will know if there's any magic frogs." Because the boys are identical twins, each one knows what the other is going to do before they do it. They consulted Orca. In a language known only to the boys, "Orca says yes!"

By the time they reached the pond it was almost dark. The bullfrogs were vibrating the air with double-bass notes. The boys became very excited. They approached the water's edge. Jacob spotted a large green-gold frog in shallow water next to a water-paddy, something only the eyes of a child could spot. They both screamed out with glee—the whole pond went dead quiet. Adam shouted, "What happened? Let's make a wish and don't tell."

Without disclosing their secret, they turned and headed back to camp. Climbing the hill towards their encampment, they could see their mom's Coleman lamp lighting up dinner, casting shadows into the night. Mari was surrounded by a ball of luminous light—a magical fairy painted against the black of night.

She asked the boys, "Did you find a magic frog?" They both yelled, "We made a wish!" Mari questioned, "And what did you wish for?" With somewhat serious looks they uttered simultaneously, "It's secret." Mari replied, "Oh yes, that's the most powerful kind."

Tom built a roaring campfire and they all prepared for dinner. The boys were being picky so Mari made something special for them and then dished out a lovers banquet with fruit, cheese and bread. During dinner the boys went on and on about roasting marshmallows, prompting Tom to carve roasting sticks, turning them loose to send white overcooked balls of sweet-smelling flame into the fire. The lovers did K.P. and settled down for the evening. The boys slept in the tent that night while Tom and Mari slept out under the stars.

Several days and nights went by. The lovers could only take the boys on so many nature walks. They were running out of things to keep the scamps occupied and Tom's made-up yarns about "Circus Boy" were becoming unacceptable. Of course if all else failed, they would get Tom to read "The Grinch." They loved that. When he read, it sounded like a second-grader. They would laugh and laugh, occasionally chanting, "Dummo

Thomas, dummo Thomas." Tom would laugh too. He knew how ridiculous it sounded coming from an adult. Anyways, Mari said it would be good for him, "The more you read out loud, the better you'll get."

Mari said, "I've got an idea." Without elaborating she ran to the phone. She came back skipping with a smile on her face. Tom said, "W_h_a_t?" Mari disclosed the news, "I called my friend Linda Wren, she said she'd set up camp next to ours and watch the boys. She's also going to take them to town and maybe to the movies!" Well, Tom liked that idea; he knew he'd get some one-on-one with Mari. The boys liked it too. They needed more STIMULUS!

Linda showed up the next morning in an old Chevy pickup truck and organized herself at campsite number 13, right next to Tom and Mari. Linda is a spiritually powerful lady with short white hair and a great loving soul who loves children. She could see the love in Tom and Mari's eyes and chuckled throughout the day, "I'm in a love field." She had brought a big green army tent, enough for six people. The boys moved into her camp and Tom and Mari kept the little blue one-man tent at their site. After situating the kids and announcing their departure, the lovers were off on their *own* nature walk.

They would just wander, his arm around her waist, hers around his. They moved like a flock of birds—if one went left the other followed, and vice versa. One could never tell who was leading. It looked like time-lapse photography. They roamed the park, occasionally saying something but mostly remaining silent. They forgot to eat, wandering all day and into the afternoon.

That night around dusk they were all at the table eating dinner when the camp became acutely aware of a distant sound. Something quite large was crashing through the undergrowth...and there was more than one. The screams and grunts got closer and closer. A troop of seven 300-pound wild boars waltzed into camp as bold as you like. They rooted around the campfire ring for several minutes snorting for food then moved toward the table. The boys jumped up on the picnic table and watched. Tom instinctively went for his walking stick. The boars came toward the table brave as yellowjackets. Squeals and grunts rang out as Tom swung his stick through the air, shooing them off. The boars ran into the bushes and scoured near the edge of camp. Tom went back to telling stories as everyone listened to the wild pigs move away in the distance.

That night around the campfire, after the kids and Linda were fast asleep, Mari asked Tom if he had ever had an experience that could verify the existence of another dimension.

He began telling her about what happened at the phone company in 1966.

"I was working at Downey Toll. The building was divided into two sections, one for switching equipment, the other for office space. It was my turn for Saturday watch. It was morning and no one else was in the building. I had made all my rounds leaving the door to the switch-room open. I sat down on the office couch and started to relax. I could hear complex clicking sounds coming from the switch-room, giving me a sense of how the equipment was operating. My job for the rest of the day was to listen and be aware of alarms. As I listened I drifted off into a dream.

"With my eyes closed, before me was a beautiful angelic woman, a Goddess. I watched her for a while. She became incredibly vivid, unbelievably beautiful. The dream became lucid. I was still listening to the equipment while having a full-on Technicolor dream. Consciously I was interacting with this being without words, yet I knew I was in the office, sitting on the couch, listening to the equipment.

"All of a sudden I could sense someone at the doorway. As soon as that happened I started to lose the dream, so I quickly moved my focus back to the angelic being. I thought that my boss had caught me sleeping on the job. I didn't care. He would have to wake me up, I wasn't going to leave the dream. After a while, hoping not to lose the dream, I changed partial focus towards what was standing in the doorway. I was hoping to get some sense of breathing or movement, anything that might give a clue as to whether it was my boss or not. As I did, whatever was in the doorway floated into the room and moved in front of me, blocking out the Goddess. It was black. I saw only black. I opened my eyes. It was as if I were blind—I could see only black. Then it turned navy-blue, then blue, then light blue, then white. The white got brighter and brighter—brighter than looking into the sun. Then an explosion occurred. I heard a roaring sound like a waterfall and could hear things rattling around in the room. For a moment I felt transported, as though I had been hit by lightning. I felt light like a feather, then heavier and heavier, feeling myself sink back into the couch.

"I would have thought this entire incident a dream if it weren't for what I saw next. Now fully awake I looked around the room. The desks had been moved at odd angles, papers and documents were scattered about the office. Heavy test equipment had shifted from their stanchion bays. It looked like a bomb had gone off in the room. I spent 2 hours cleaning up the office and putting test apparatuses back to their original locations. I was a young man and from that day on, I didn't think that there were other dimensions, I knew there were."

Mari told Tom about her experience in India.

"I had just had a fight with my lover at the ashram in Pune. Dressed in my orange sari and mala, I left the ashram to wander the peasant district at night. I kept thinking of God. As I walked through a literal field of suffering, it all started to become surreal. Blind beggars, limbless children, women covered in sores, men so thin you wondered how they could be alive—I just kept thinking about God. I sat down on the curb among the filth and squalor and looked up at the stars thinking, *Here I sit in this dimension, yet the universe is infinite.* Then I asked myself, *How many dimensions are possible in an infinite universe?* At that moment a fly landed on my lip. Somehow the tickle of the fly's feet created a stimulus that triggered an internal explosion that started at the bottom of my spine and moved up to the top of my head ending in a flash of light. I gathered myself and stood up. I was in *samadhi*, complete bliss.

"I continued to wander the district in an altered state until morning. People came up to me, looking at me as if I were otherworldly. No matter who they were, I saw them as beautiful. They approached me in prayerfulness, saying, '*namaste ma, namaskar ma,*' saluting the Goddess within me. They could see the transformation that took place in me that night, that momentary gift given to me by grace. It was like being Cinderella. It went away the next day, but I have never forgotten it."

They were both silenced by each other's stories. After a few minutes Tom got up and put another log on the fire. Mari said, "Let's go to bed." With a slight breeze in the air, the night had become cold. They made one large sleeping bag out of two and crawled in. Cuddling facing each other, they fell a sleep.

The next morning Linda announced that she was taking the boys to town for a movie and they would all be spending the night at her house. Tom and Mari decided to walk the Austin Creek trail. They walked along in their usual way, pausing occasionally under an oak tree. They found one especially nice oak with thick leaves covering the ground. Making a little spot to sit among the leaves, they sat cross-legged facing each other and began to play like children, clapping their hands together, "Patty cake, patty cake, baker's man ..."

It was in the meadow just up from where they were playing that she stopped and said, "Tom, pick an oak tree, look around, find one that suits you. I will read the leaves that lie under her branches." He moved out into the meadow and scouted for a tree that most represented his feelings. After evaluating many, he settled on a large grand oak near the edge of the meadow overlooking the valley. Its branches, turned and twisted from the wind, reminded him of his childhood. He spoke, "O tree of my childhood. Where do you bring me, the one lone cow drinking by the well? It is you, old silence, that I carried next to my trusty dog, long forgotten in moments under my bed, the moon shining on me for a thousand nights, where we sat to watch dreamers dream," and with that he hugged the tree. Not knowing why he had said such words, he gazed over at Mari standing in the distance and turned and kissed the bark.

He looked back at his love standing in the meadow, how royal and lovely she looked. It was as though he were in a trance as she walked towards him. Walking under the canopy of the great oak's branches she fell to one knee and began lifting the fallen leaves from the damp ground under her, throwing them to the wind. Her hair fell forward, ushered by a strange breeze that suddenly appeared. Through the sun's reflection and cast shadows, she read Tom's life. She saw into the very depths of his soul. Such confirmation produced a faith in faith, that another could know another that way. Her feet were dirty, her dress covered in leaves, her brown eyes took on a golden manifestation—she had traveled to some far off place beyond where he could go. Standing, they put their arms around each other's waists, and went to wander some more.

A half hour into their trek to somewhere, Mari stopped and pointed, "This is the Cross Roads. We've been on the Austin Creek trail, the one crossing it is the Gilman Creek trail." A large burly root protruded from the ground near where they stood. Purple thistles flowered on either side of the trail. The morning air soughing through the surrounding oaks produced an eerie mystical dissonance.

Together they stood at the Cross Roads looking out over the western valley. Neither had bathed for a week; their clothes were covered with earth and campfire smell. Their hair was animal-like. They clasped hands, looking deep into the eyes of the other. She wore a white earth-stained skirt accenting a colorful blouse. A purple cloth belt tied to one side celebrated her waist. Black tights moved from under her skirt, passing under purple leggings to her bare feet on the ground. Her eyebrows arched deeply across her forehead accenting her large brown eyes. Her ears were adorned with Huichol beaded earrings that played with her hair in the wind. With her mouth slightly open, highlighting her full red lips, she whispered, "I love it here." Her posture was that of royalty and strength, dignified, elegant. She was alive here, here in the Now and he the same. Her face literally glowed, energized by the moment. There was nothing contrived about this meeting. No hidden agenda—just destiny fulfilling itself.

Tom ran his fingers through her tangled hair, touching her ear. He moved his hand ever so slowly to the back of her neck. While making contact with her skin he began an unspoken communication with the cells that formed it. Then came the molecules, the atoms, the atomic particles, the sub-atomics, and on to the very energy that manifested upward making up her physical creation. He was in love with every cell in her body. She spoke again, "The dream is forward with many possible probabilities. We have arrived in *this* moment." Tom knew what she meant. In fact, he heard the words before she spoke them. Her head slowly moved to his shoulder. She looked down like a shy schoolgirl and took a deep breath.

Breaking the silence she said, "I want to show you something—this way." They scrambled through the manzanita up to the top of the hill then headed east to the cliff's edge, climbing the last few feet on all fours. There it was again, a wall of mountains plunging west to the Pacific, a marriage of rock and green slicing through the canyon below. Ancient redwoods, some older than Christianity, sipped moisture from the surrounding low valley fog. Not a manmade object as far as the eye could see.

They wandered the rest of the day and into the dark. Tree frogs began winding up their nightly orchestra; the gypsies were almost back to camp. They paused to get their bearings and noticed what was left of the sunset. The last light tinted the air with myriads of violet and vermilion clouds scattered against the navy-blue sky. The mountaintops were edged with the black gold of night.

They had taken a slightly different trail coming back. It came out by an old homestead fence with hog wire on the bottom; a single strand of barbwire drooped over the top. Mari leaned against the fence facing her mate. Her eyes glimmered in the moon. Tom moved closer, drawn by an invisible silver string. His arms instinctively rose locking themselves around her waist. Holding the back of his head she escorted his lips to hers. They began kissing. The earth moved body to body. Unseen wood nymphs celebrated the inner fire. A warm feeling moved over their bodies heralding a symbiotic flashback to the past.

It took them to an ancient Anasazi tribal setting 1,000 years before Christ. Their river village was in the midst of being overthrown by a rival tribe. A warrior dressed in elk hide stood between Tom and his love. The warrior's black braid edged the red paint on his face. They battled. Mortally wounded, Tom wrapped his arms around his young bride. She was pried from his arms. Moments later he died.

They stood in present time leaning against the fence, crying, holding each other, thinking, *No one can separate us this time.* After wiping each other's tears, Mari said, "That was so real." Tom ran his hands up behind her neck and told her, "I love you sweet lady." They began to kiss. They kissed openly and without reservation as though they were the only two left on earth.

Mari lifted her skirt and pushed her left hand down into her underwear. Pulling her hand back, she showed Tom her fingers in the moonlight, "See how it strands back and forth like a rubber band, that means I'm ovulating. We will have to wait." Tom stood there in the moonlight looking into the eyes of a pagan Goddess. Together they heard the barely-audible sounds of rattles and chanting coming from spaces in between the material world. A lavender odor filled the air around them.

She grabbed his hand and led him back towards camp. They stopped to say hello to a raccoon and her babies and then continued on. Passing the phone box they made the last turn into camp. It was beginning to get cold and Tom made a fire to warm their hands. That night they slept as though they were floating in the clouds without a care in the world.

The next morning Linda arrived with the boys and three other people, including Theresa, all friends of Mari's. The boys were glad to see Momus and Thomas. They had started calling Mari "Momus" because it rhymed with Thomas. After lunch they decided to walk into the western valley and chant. Zeke and Carla had brought drums. They congregated under a large oak tree bonsai-ed by the wind and sang songs, chanting incantations into the afternoon.

The boys wanted to go to the pond. At the water's edge, inquisitive Adam asked, "What are those things sticking up?" Tom told him that they were cattails, "In a pinch the tops and roots can be cooked and eaten." They saw ducks, woodpeckers and redneck finches. Jacob spotted a chicken hawk in flight.

After dinner Mari said goodbye to her friends, and Theresa and Linda got the boys ready for bed. The hum of mosquitoes and bats in hot pursuit modulated the sounds of the night. They both went to Linda's tent and kissed the boys goodnight. Thanking Linda and Theresa for all their kindness, they walked back to their camp.

Tom had spotted a clearing overlooking the west valley on one of their earlier walks. He suggested to Mari, "Let's go sleep out on the ridge?" He described the spot, elaborating on how wonderful it would be to sleep out under the stars in the wild. She liked the idea and informed Linda of the adventure.

They got their sleeping bags and headed up Austin Creek trail. The moon was out; it made good light for walking. Fifty feet before the Cross Roads, Mari stopped and put her bag down. Tom did the like. She told him to stay there. She walked on, turning right at the Cross Roads onto the Gilman Creek trail and continued for about 50 feet. She turned around and said, "Now walk slowly toward the Cross Roads. As you walk, think of me, and as I walk, I will think of you. When we meet at the center of the Cross Roads we will think of us." They walked in matrimonial procession, in highest respect for one another. The ritual was extremely powerful, setting into motion two becoming one. What took place *within,* during this walk, is beyond the scope of this text.

At the center they touched hands. She said, "We have gone through much to arrive at this moment, here. I walked one path and you another—our paths crossed in time for us to meet. It is Grace that brought us together and Grace will take us apart. We are both the gift and the giver."

They held each other in the moonlight. The sound of a hoot owl echoed from the canyon below. Every trace of the modern world fell away. They kissed, falling to their knees.

Mari stopped for a moment. She squatted, again testing for ovulation, and whispered, "It's OK, do you have protection?" She spoke very softly, "I've been with many men, I'm afraid I might have AIDS." Tom said, "Whatever you have, I will have." She repeated, "Do you have protection?" "Yes." He reached for his wallet. She lifted her skirt and slowly moved to the ground. When they reached the terminal at the Taj Mahal no control existed, all ceased to be in a moment of breaking thunder. Their aspects were pushed upward through their spines into deep space by some invisible force. Little pieces that they called *themselves* returned to orbit the earth like intermingling stardust. The dispersement and scintillation was beyond description. Slowly fragments of their former selves combined, leaving portions immersed in the other as they re-entered their bodies. They had made love in the moonlight at the Cross Roads—a moment that combined their souls forever. In ways known only to them they were married that evening without witness, save the moon, the spirits in the forest, and the eyes of God.

Afterwards they sat holding each other like two children just starting out in life. For a half hour they didn't move or say anything—only feelings passed between them. Then Tom began picking twigs and grassy objects from her hair. She said, "I love you, Tom." With that she kissed his forehead and said, "We better find a place to sleep."

They made their way to the cliff's edge overlooking the western valley. It was a place they'd been before in ancient times, a dejá vu. Tom found a level spot in the manzanita facing the valley. He scraped the ground like an animal, clearing the rocks and large twigs away to make a soft space for their bed. Zipping the two sleeping bags together, they cuddled up for the night. He looked at her hands. Her fingers were long and supple. The dirt under her fingernails from living in the woods made him even more in love with her. She wrapped her arms around his neck. Digging his nose in under her armpit, he nuzzled his head back and forth like a gentle dog. She placed her bare feet over the tops of his and started talking about the stars.

When they woke in the early morning, the sun had just risen. Everything was wet from dew and smelled of pine and dried grass. They sat up and began to pick things from one another's hair—grooming each other like primates. Fog had formed in the valley below. Mountain peaks poked through the surreal landscape. They felt divinely isolated—it was 10,000 years ago.

4

*"When atoms form crystals
the full potential of their information
is realized."*

Jean Rostand

Crystal Cream

Punctually at 6:30 AM Tom showed up on the job. The sun had just risen, blasting a yellow glow over the tops of the mountains in the east. Sawdust smells filled the crisp Grass Valley air, setting the mood for another day's work. Ray called over at Mom's and left a message, "I'm going to be late, be in town picking up supplies."

Tom's mother walked over to the jobsite and relayed the message. She was off on her morning walk. Tom stopped her, "Mom, can I walk with you?" Laughingly she replied, "Of course you can." He went on, "I'd like to talk to you about Mari."

He told her that after the last camping trip at Frog Pond with Mari and the boys, things were beginning to move to a new level. There was no doubt in his mind; Mari was coming closer. He discussed the possibility that Mari could have AIDS, but no matter what, he loved her. He told his mother he wanted to marry Mari and asked what she thought about it. "Oh Tommy, that's wonderful. I think Mari's a brilliant girl and a good mother, but you two should get your AIDS tests." Tom replied, "Mari said the same thing. We had our blood drawn before I left Santa Rosa." She continued, "I am happy for you and Mari, but please, let me know when you get the results back." Tom interjected, "I'm going to marry her even if she has AIDS." His mother put her arm around him and they walked on to the top of the rise near the Litton plant.

They continued talking about marriage. He asked her why she had broken up with his dad. She told him, "He was a good, honest, hard-working man; he just didn't know how to have fun or express his feelings. He'd come home tired from work, read the paper, eat dinner and go to bed, then get up early the next morning and do it all over again, day after day for years. He hardly ever talked with friends or did much outside the house. I know he taught you a lot about responsibility and the construction trade but he really didn't do much else with you kids. He was a good provider for the family, but became sarcastic as the years went on. He hardly talked to me. I needed someone to express my feelings with."

Tom dug in deeper, "You know when I was a kid dad used to beat me with a razor strap. He told me if I cried I'd "get it" worse. It would leave black and blue marks on my legs that scabbed up over on the edges." His mother replied, "Your dad had a hard childhood and was brought up in a strict family, everything was about work and survival—he did that to make a man out of you at a very young age." Tom continued, "You know, I felt that you taught us kids how to openly love and dad taught us how to be strong. I'm thankful to both of you for what you taught me. I hope I've found that balance between love and strength." Tom and his mom went on walking and talking for several hours. They hadn't had a communication like that in a long time.

That afternoon Tom went back to work thinking about his father, Robert F. Sawyer. "No job is so urgent that it is not worth doing right." "Do it in a workman-like manner." "If you do it wrong, take it apart and do it right." "That's a lazy man's load." "This is the trade, stand back and look at your work, it's who you are." "If you bend a nail, pull it out and put in another." "Let's get this show on the road." "When you get tired, do some more." "Home again, home again, jiggetty jog." His father's words streamed through his mind, inspecting each task Tom performed. Words he would always be grateful for—old school. "Dammit kid, I said three-quarter-inch pipe."

Tom had been sleeping in a small outbuilding on his mother's property for the last several months. Ray came to him one day with an idea, "Why don't you move into our extra room, the kids would love it too, and if we get called out on a fire, we can ride together." Tom liked the idea. They set up a bed for Tom in the office/spare bedroom and Ray's wife Jayne made a sit-down dinner every evening.

He and Ray worked on their mother's house for a couple more weeks, then Tom got a phone call from Mari. She told him about a Huichol Indian gathering out by the coast in the little town of Bodega. He didn't need much of a reason, just a way to get there. Bob wanted to use the Subaru for a few days so Tom set out to fix the ignition on his motorcycle.

Out in Ray's garage he looked over at Ol' Gal and said, "You're a good old gal, let's see if we can get you running." He surveyed her 640-pound steel frame and ran his hands over her V-twin 1350cc shovelhead engine. When he got her new in 1980, he replaced the stock carburetor with a S&S Super, modified the heads to run four plugs with dual ignition, put in nickel-chrome-molly steel oversized valves, added tuned twin twice-pipes, converted to kick-start and put in a three-quarter racing cam. Thinking about all the trips they had been on together, he ran his fingers down her root-beer-brown gas tank, "You need a bath, too."

He found a broken lead on one of the coils, repaired it and gave her a bath. He threw his right leg over the saddle. Situating the kicker, he pulled out the choke. Throwing all his weight forward, he came down hard on the kicker. The motor coughed and popped, throwing black smoke from her exhaust. Again he positioned himself with all 155 pounds on the kicker and hit it again. That's all she needed. The engine erupted, projecting a loud rumble off the garage door. He strapped a backpack on the sissy bar of his iron horse and headed for Santa Rosa.

This time he took the Yuba City/Marysville route up over the mountains winding down into Calistoga. Pulling Ol' Gal off the road at the last grade, he looked out over the Santa

Rosa valley and thought, *Somewhere down there in this sprawling city is my sweetheart.*

Making the last corner, he pulled onto Mari's block and swung the bike around. He backed into the curb and shoved the kickstand out with his left foot. Hoping Mari would hear the deep-throated sound of the Harley, he let Ol' Gal idle for a bit. It worked. She came skipping out the side door like a teenager on the run. Her eyes were all big and excited, "Hi sweetie, I'm ready to go." She ran back into the house, appearing seconds later with stuff. Tom loaded the backpack and they were off.

A loud blast of thunder filled the neighborhood as he went through the gears at Steele Lane and Mendocino. It was a hot day. The wind was warm and blew across their faces. She wore a little red belly top and a white skirt bunched up between her legs, with her hair flying in the wind.

They were on the road about 20 minutes when she yelled, "Slow down, there's a signal up ahead." She started pointing out places, shouting at the top of her lungs, hoping he could hear her over the rumble of the engine. She hollered, "This is Sebastopol. We're on Bodega Highway, great restaurant here." They made *the* only green light through town, passing Luther Burbank gardens, the old cemetery and pulled the hill at Marty's Top of the Hill dance hall and tavern.

Six miles out they passed Linda's Spring Hill Tavern on the right, Mari shouted, "T-o-m... local nightspot. There used to be a brothel in back." Laying the bike to the left they screamed by Roses & Thorns, past Bill's Farm Basket at Sexton Rd. and tore up a windy rise overlooking Freestone. Mari yelled, "Pull over down there." Tom downshifted and stopped near the turnoff to Bohemian Highway. She went on, "Over there is the town of Freestone; my dad had a chance to buy this town a few years back, but decided not to. I wish he had. It's such a quaint little place. Down the road is the post office and general store. Oh and there's the local favorite, Rocco's beer and hamburger joint, a real hole in the wall. We'll bear left here, and a-couple miles up, right after the turnoff to Valley Ford Station, there's a little barn on the left—pull in there. I want to show you something." Off they went again, passing rolling green hills and dairy farms.

Up ahead, Tom noticed a clump of trees lining the road in front of an old barn. He pulled in the gravel driveway and stepped off. A flock of birds flew from the berry bushes and circled the barn as he shut the engine down. Mari got off on the left side; she knew better than to get off on the right – on their last trip she got pipe burns down her right leg. Taking a few seconds to adjust her skirt, she walked toward the wooden building, "This is the Crystal Barn." The place was made from moss-covered rough-cut boards, cracked in places, giving it an almost haunted look.

They walked through a large, open, sliding door. Tom looked up; daylight poked through the decomposing wood-shingled roof. Straw was scattered about the dirt floor in an attempt to cover the damp smell. Soft flute music played in the background. Tom turned just in time to catch the glance of a longhaired wizard-looking guy walking across the driveway from the house across the way. The wizard stepped forward with a strange look. Placing his finger on his nose, he said, "Can I help you?" His face altered. "Oh, Santosh. Haven't seen you for a while. How are you?" Mari introduced Tom to the wizard and they began talking about crystals and such.

Glass display cases formed the right side of the main room. Each contained various types of crystals, some for healing, others for casting spells. All kinds of witchcraft paraphernalia hung on the walls. Up above was a loft with lots of other secret stuff. To the side were more cases containing large, beautiful crystals, most too expensive for Tom's pocketbook. They walked around looking in each case, as the wizard explained each item's power. Mari spotted a section containing small hand-woven African baskets, "We must come back in the car and get this basket." Then she turned toward the wizard, making eye contact with some sort of obvious mental communication. Just about the time Tom's curiosity was about to get the best of him, she turned and kissed Tom on the lips, announcing it was time to go. Tom felt nonetheless a mysterious initiation as she whispered, "We'll come back again soon."

Wandering back to the bike, Mari leaned against the seat. He sat squatted in the dirt next to her feet. Looking up, squinting into the sun, he began talking about his meeting with Marcel Vogel and Ron Mann.

"...Dr. Marcel Vogel is an IBM research scientist who not only developed the phosphorus colors for color television, he also invented the magnetic medium used in cassette tapes to computer disc drives. While working on experimental crystal memory devices for IBM he noticed some peculiar attributes, and through a series of experiments with living plants he was able to measure electroencephalographic changes in the electrical properties of a plant's circulatory system. This led to other experiments that demonstrated how water ions were modified merely by presenting a mental intention for change while holding a tuned crystal in the palm of one's hand. Some of his early work with plants was published in abbreviated form in a book called *The Secret Life of Plants*. He and Dr. Ron Mann, a research psychologist, worked on several research projects involving the modification of human consciousness using quartz crystals. I attended a class by Dr. Vogel at Portland University on the use of crystals to effect change. Soon after taking classes on hemispherical synchronization of the brain from Robert Monroe I met Dr. Mann at a seminar in Nevada City and studied with him and a man named Mitchell. Through all this I became convinced that our intent modifies the fabric of reality and that our perception of reality modifies our intent. Some of the new age woo-woo regarding crystals has some basis in scientific fact."

Mari wanted to know more. He told her someday he'd demonstrate the crystal Dr. Vogel had made for him. And with that, they climbed on the bike and headed west for Bodega. Passing several more dairy farms and miles of rolling green hills, signs of a town showed up ahead.

"Slow 25 MPH." Off to the left was the old Potter School established in 1873, a spooky two-story white building with wooden steps leading to its "inner sanctum." Alfred Hitchcock filmed "The Birds" there in 1962. They passed St. Teresa of Avila church, the Casino Tavern, and a string of quaint antique shops. Tom down shifted to second gear and turned right on Salmon Creek Road. Mari leaned forward pressing her lips to his ear, "The Old Creamery is just up ahead, about a mile."

They pulled up to a large old wooden building complex and parked. Mari reached into the backpack and pulled out a multicolored hand-woven bag with birdlike geometric designs in the weave. Tom said, "What's that?" She replied, "This is my medicine bag." She quickly changed the subject and went on with historical facts, "This is the Bodega Creamery, built in the 1880s. It continued operating until 1950, and was later converted into art studios. In one of the studios, Janet Alder, who has a Ph.D. from Harvard University in Shamanism, started a dance group called Authentic Movement. She's arranged for Jaichima and Vicente to come and put on a Huichol Shaman ceremony here."

Cars were parked everywhere; people were gathered around in front searching for the door. Mari nonchalantly took a beaded ankle bracelet from her medicine bag and clasped it to her left leg. She grabbed Tom's hand, leading him inside to a place she'd been many times before. Hundreds of people were dressed in bright colors. Feathers, drums, rattles, handmade gifts, food and sage were being moved to their designated locations across a glossy hardwood floor. In the front, Jaichima and her brother Vicente Rutury stood addressing the crowd. They were clothed in traditional ceremonial garments with bright-colored weavings, beaded designs, and large feathers adorning their bodies.

Mari went on, "...they are Wirarikas, Huichol Indian Mara'akame medicine people from the Sierra Madre Mountains of Mexico. Jaichima was taught in both traditional tribal and ancient ways. Her father, Haka'ula, guided her in the forms of physical healing. Vicente Rutury was trained from birth as a Mara'akame, protector of the ancient ways. He is from the village of San Sebastian Teponahuastian Mesquitic."

Tom thought it was interesting and refocused his attention to Mari's hair. The ceremony was set in motion with drumming while Jaichima gave thanks to Mother Earth and Grandfather Spirit. The drums became louder and the ceremonial dance amplified into a frenzy. Mari pulled Tom into the mass of swirling bodies. Spinning, she reached into her medicine bag and pulled out a rattle, shaking it into the air. The dance continued for hours then abruptly stopped. Howchi, one of the ceremonial heads of Wirikuta put forth a prayer, speaking in the ways of the warrior. Jaichima asked several Wirikutas to come forward and speak. Tom's sister Theresa was called up. She appeared frightened at first, then something shifted; she began to speak out openly and clearly without reservation, encouraging people to thank the earth.

Jaichima lit sage and waved it in the air, spreading good fortune to all peoples. Tom and Mari stood back in reverence with their arms around each other. Then Jaichima spoke; all became quiet. She talked about the earth and future trials, events that might befall the planet if humans did not give respect to the Mother who sustains all living things. She spoke with simple wisdom. All appeared to understand the urgency of the message.

After the ceremony Mari introduced Tom to everyone. There was food and drink spread across tables from wall to wall. People came up to Tom and offered him food and opened conversation, and why not—he was with the goddess. They addressed Mari as Shetima, the Huichol name given her by Jaichima during a ceremony years ago. Tom and Mari mingled with the heads of Wirikuta and sat at the side of Jaichima and Vicente. Tom remembered, "Some of the people from my initial meeting at Linda Wren's house were so kind after learning that Mari and I were lovers." He recognized Ulu, Hamima, Howchi, and a few others. Mari was highly respected not only for her presence, power and personable-ness; Jaichima was the grandmother of Mari's children, Adam and Jacob.

After saying goodbye, she and Jaichima walked to the doorway. Tom followed behind. He noticed Jaichima place an amulet into Mari's hand. Whatever it was, it seemed private and Tom looked away. Over their shoulders he caught two boys flash by on bicycles with no hands. It's what he felt like, "with no hands." Tom and Mari leisurely walked toward the motorcycle. Tom fired up Ol' Gal. Mari nodded and swung her leg over the back. They moved away slowly, then went like the wind. Mari shouted, "Slow down, you silly, turn left on to Joy Road. It's just up ahead."

They zigzagged over a mountain heading east when Mari pointed and said, "There's Coleman Valley Road on the left. It goes all the way to the coast; we'll go there someday." Continuing until they reached the little village of Occidental, she leaned forward and spoke into his ear, "Straight ahead is the Union Hotel. They make good raviolis. Let's eat here."

They sat at an outside table feeding one another, each taking turns being the parent. Mari paid her respects to the owner and they pushed on for Santa Rosa. For those two, riding a motorcycle was Zen poetry. The future was up ahead; *they* were in the moment, and the past fell behind like clouds dispersing in the sky. Tom, Mari and the motorcycle became one thing as they moved down the road.

He dropped her off at Noni's and they began their goodbyes. You could hear the sadness in their voices as they tenderly touched lips in an undertone of words. He consciously moved his head alongside hers and whispered, "You know, if I look deep enough into your eyes, I can see God being a woman." At first she chuckled, then looked intensely. She didn't want to be on a pedestal; however she realized in the deepest sense what he was saying.

He handed her a little handmade card with two hearts on it, connected together at the top by an OM symbol. Moving down from each heart were two interconnected spiraling lines that ended at the bottom of the card with two words, "Life Together." On either side were the words: "Health, Forgiveness, Love, Kindness, Faith, Truth and Strength." Mari looked down. Lifting her head, her brown eyes were filled with tears. She said, "Oh Tom, are you sure you want to do this *again?*" Without hesitation he replied, "Yes, I wouldn't miss it for the world."

5

*"All growth is a leap in the dark,
a spontaneous, unpremeditated act
without benefit of experience."*

Henry Miller

The Red Ledge

After the deepening at Frog Pond and their visit to Bodega, Tom began to miss Mari bad. Sitting in the park east of Nevada City, watching an American flag flutter in the wind, he left the bench he was sitting on and moved farther along where inland seagulls were feeding on trash. Through a row of dumpsters he could see two small children, a girl and a boy, skateboarding a block away. He smiled at the scene reminding him of his love. Suddenly a fragmented idea drifted forward, "Mari…here."

He pulled up on his clumsy Levis and sat down next to the phone booth, waiting for a man arguing with his wife to hang up. After a few minutes the man slammed the receiver down and walked away. First, Tom called Ray, then Mari. She would come with the boys. The blackbirds sitting on the telephone wire watched him change pace from a shuffle to a perky step. He continued toward the downtown section, turning left onto Main Street. Two blocks from Mama Sue's he found a little rock shop/sidewalk stand and purchased a beautifully clear single-terminated quartz crystal.

That night at Ray's he wrapped it, along with a love note, in a little bright-colored package: "To Mari with Love," falling asleep with her picture in his hand.

Today is an ever-so-special day—Mari is coming! Stepping into the early morning air he looked down the street in anticipation; by noon his sweetheart will be there. He walked down to the intersection and looked back. Apart from the background noise of dogs barking, the street was quiet. The redneck neighbor two houses down, the suspected crank-loving, backyard appliance-repair guys on the corner and the little old lady across the way were all still asleep. In half an hour the street would come alive again. Ray and Jayne would be getting the kids up and the street would begin to take on the smell of breakfast. The little old fat lady would come out onto her porch in her nightgown and look back and forth, snapping up the newspaper and scurrying back inside. The appliance guys would be yelling and banging on things. The redneck would stumble across his chain-link front yard and put Max the pit bull on a chain for its morning dump.

At the end of the street was Ray and Jayne's, an out-of-place substantial two-story white house with a partial veranda on the second floor. Ray had converted an old ready-for-the-bulldozer building into a beautiful home.

Tom turned left at the corner and walked to the gas station. He thought about waiting there leaning against the Coke machine until Mari showed up. Then ideas started coming in. *I bet Mari and the boys would love to camp down on the Yuba River!* Running all the way back to the house, he asked Ray about using the tent and the two Honda motorcycles. They made a plan: Mari and boys could sleep at the house tonight and tomorrow they'd take what's needed down to the north branch of the Yuba River and set up a camp near Jones Bar.

After breakfast Tom went outside and looked down the driveway, hoping she might come early. No sign of Mari yet! Back inside, he kept pacing till 11:00. Gazing out the backyard window, he noticed Ray had firewood to be stacked. Slipping on his gloves, he headed for the backyard. He stacked wood till 12:15. *She's still not here.* At 12:45, stopping to stretch out his back, it hit him—*She's very near.* It was getting hot. He removed the splintered gloves, wiped his brow and walked to the driveway. Standing in the sun with a blank faraway gaze, he could feel her. *She's coming!*

The sound of a car turning the corner broke his catatonic state. There she was, coming up the driveway in her little silver Honda with Adam and Jacob in the back. Tom's heart skipped a beat. He ran down the driveway meeting her halfway and kissed her through the window. A big grin spread over Mari's face. It was an interesting smile, a smile that said *I know something you don't know.* Tom spoke out loud, "W-h-a-t?" She just kept smiling and replied, "It's a surprise. I'll tell you later. Meet you up at the house." Curiosity grabbed his hand; it was as if some beautiful creature had attached him to a moving newsstand— he couldn't quite read the print with all the motion. He ran alongside the car waving at the boys. They were in full energy, anticipating what adventures lay ahead of them. Mari stopped in front of the garage and got out. A ten-minute hug ensued while the twins ran around, communicating in "Quihuis" language.

With a loving smile, she turned and bent over, reaching into the car and pulling out a piece of cardboard with handwritten words and symbols, "THOMAS (a heart drawn in the middle) I love you, miss you—you are beautiful in every aspect, always provided for with blessings—in my thoughts, in my heart, share our Soul." There was nothing more to say— his cup ran over.

Ray, Jayne and little Ben greeted them at the porch. Jayne said, "Tom's mom called and wants everyone to meet for dinner in Rough and Ready at the Mexican Villa around 6:00." Tom interrupted, "The only restaurant in Rough and Ready." Then turned to Mari, "It's a small gold mining town west of Grass Valley. The townspeople actually seceded from the Union in 1850. Three months later they returned to being part of the United States." Mari asked, "Why?" Tom replied, "They didn't like the government taxing their mines."

Inside Ray and Jayne's house the boys were restless after the three- and-a-half-hour ride. Ray mentioned the basketball court beside the house. That did it. Adam and Jacob got busy shooting hoops while the parents swapped stories about raising kids.

"It's 5:30, we should probably go." Tom rode with Mari and the boys, and they all rendezvoused at the Mexican Villa. Mari met Tom's family: Grandma Gert, Uncle Larry, Aunt Kay, Aunt Anna Laura, Uncle Ray—about 20 in all. At dinner she kept smiling *I know something you don't know.* Again he said, "W-h-a-t?" Continuing to smile, she whispered, "I'm not going to tell you right here." He felt a moment of relief. At least she would be telling him later, in private. Grabbing his hand under the table, she said, "It's OK."

After dessert June looked over at Grandma Gert. She was getting tired; it was time to say goodbye.

Back at Ray's the boys set up sleeping bags on the living room floor in front of the TV, and the lovers put *their* big blue bag in the office that doubled as Tom's room and settled in for the night. Mari still had a grin on her face. Rolling over on one elbow, Tom looked up, "WELL, tell me?" Reaching into her backpack she pulled out a newspaper and handed it to him. He glanced down. Ignoring the print, his eyes went to a large photograph of himself and Mari dancing on the beach at the Harmonic Convergence a few weeks earlier. Ulu was playing drums and Tom was in bib overalls, Mari was barefoot dancing in the sand in a white skirt. The Press Democrat had done a full-color front page on it. He reached over and hugged her, "That's such a great picture of us." Nodding, she still had that funny smile on her face. He said, "OK, what else?" She replied, "I can stay for four days." He yelled, "YES." Moving into a half-lotus posture, she continued, "Come sit here in front of me. Put out your hands and close your eyes." Tom felt a piece of paper slowly drop into his hands, "Open your eyes and make a wish!" Tom opened his eyes and to his amazement it was the results from their AIDS tests. Both tests were negative. Neither had AIDS. They put their foreheads together. Uncontrollable tears coursed down their faces as they moved to the sleeping bag. Tom wrapped his arms around her. She laid her head on his chest and fell fast asleep.

Later there was a knock at the door. The boys wanted to have a group snuggle before going to bed. Tom and Mari lay on the bottom with Adam and Jacob stacked on top like Lincoln Logs. For several minutes all was sublime in their little huddle. Then the boys started to squirm. She chuckled, "Let's go tuck you guys in." They ran for the front room and hopped in their bags. Adam said with a grin, "We want Thomas to read us a story," Tom took the Grinch book from Jacob's hands and began to read. As he muttered over each word the boys chanted, "Dummo Thomas, Dummo Thomas." He smiled, lifting his hands, interrupting their drill-sergeant incantations. "If you keep saying that, I'm going to stop reading." With a Cheshire grin Adam vowed, "We won't, we promise." Tom started reading again. After a few minutes, "Dummo Thomas." The iterations continued until the little book was finished. They were all laughing, even Thomas. They kissed the boys goodnight and went to *their* room.

They lay on top of the sleeping bag and started talking about spiritual things. Tom interrupted the conversation by reaching for the dresser; he grabbed something wrapped in silk. Pausing to remove the cloth he returned to the floor and presented the Goddess with a double-terminated (a point on either end) four-sided quartz crystal, his secret possession. "Marcel Vogel made this for me." Mari asked, "How does it work?"

"Our bodies vibrate with a complex of frequencies. This dynamic complex represents how we are. We are constantly modulating the base frequencies of our body with our emotion and intent. If we hold an intent (i.e. emotion) that affects the body's nervous system, that in itself affects the fabric of reality. For example: if we say a prayer, 'Thank you for this food,' but have no feeling of thankfulness, then the vibrating words have none or very little effect. If we actually feel thankful when the words are spoken, our emotions are modulated by the vibrating words. You might say the vibration of speech brings the emotional state or intent closer to material reality, amplifying it. If one felt thankful and said, 'ke ke do ja ja' it would have as much effect on the fabric of reality as saying, 'Thank you for this food.' The feeling is what's important.

"Think of a crystal like an amplifier. If you have a crystal closely tuned to your body's base frequency, then it is in resonance with your common state. That means it takes very little power to affect a change in the piezoelectric properties of the crystal. Now if you modulate your nervous system with an emotion, good or bad, that energy is highly amplified by the crystal. A double-terminated crystal held in the hand with one end in the palm *chakra* (energy center) and the other end pointing at an object can effect a change in that object."

After the lengthy explanation (they could get away with this kind of stuff because they're both Virgos) Tom asked, "Would you like to have a demonstration?"

"Yes."

"Give me your hand."

He placed his hand underneath the back of her hand and pointed the crystal at her palm chakra. He began moving the crystal in a clockwise spiral motion until he felt a tingle in *his* palm. She jerked her hand away. "What was that, it felt like you were pulling a string through my hand." He replied, "My intent was to create a harmless sensation in your hand." She said, "Can I try it?" She did the same to him. They both felt the warm tingle move through their hands. Mari went on, "Is it dangerous?" He replied, "Any tool can be misused. Take a hammer; you can hit someone over the head with it or build a house."

He continued, "Lie down face up. Let me sense the energy in your chakras?" He started moving his left hand over each of her body chakras. The base chakra felt OK, indicating she was not in survival. The second chakra was elevated, signifying sexual arousal. The third chakra was strong with a healthy sense of personal power. The fourth was a little weak, signaling fear in the heart (past hurt); the fifth chakra was strong, representing her ability to speak the truth; the sixth chakra was strong and clairvoyant and her seventh chakra was highly expanded, indicating a deep spiritual connection with the Universe.

Tom went on, "Allow me to use the crystal to induce a healing energy into your heart. If something wonderful happens, it's not me; I'm only acting as a conduit." Mari said, "Go ahead." Meditating on angelic love he moved the crystal over her heart. She started crying. The sorrow lasted for just a minute, then a blissful state appeared on her face. "Oh, thank you, that was wonderful." They rested beside each other, drifting into bliss.

Tom asked her, "Is pain better than pleasure, is pain divine and pleasure evil?" She replied, "They are our teachers, they move in and out of our lives as the tide rises and falls with the sea. They are of nature, they are brother and sister, they push and pull at us. The trick is not to get caught in them lifetime after lifetime. Know them as teachers and passageways, not as the source of all being, not the un-dual infinite One from which all manifests. Through the fear of pain we create our TO DO list and through the promise of pleasure we create our TO HAVE list. From the vantage point of Oneness they are both illusions, but for now, this is Planet Earth. What most people forget in the midst of the DOs and HAVEs is the JUST BE list."

He didn't expect what happened next. She rolled over and made love to him in a most tender, loving way. Afterwards they got in the sleeping bag and cuddled up. She began to talk about lovemaking. "There are so many ways to make 'love'. It's kind of like your example of the hammer. Two people can use sex as a way to reduce their pain, using it like a drug, in lust. Or they can use it as a way to lovingly share and experience the deepest parts of their beings—to make a spiritual bond, a passage toward Oneness. Sex can be dirty and damaging or it can be beautiful and healing. It's all in the intent, in the emotion." With that they fell asleep in each other's arms, thankful for having found one another.

They woke early the next morning and loaded motorcycles, camping gear, and a tent into the truck—destination Jones Bar on the Yuba River. Taking the gravel road to within a quarter mile, they parked on a flat a quarter mile above the river. Tom took the motorcycles off the truck. One boy jumped on with

Mari and the other with Tom and they all sped off toward the river. The road was narrow, steep and winding, more of a trail than a road. Jones Bar was a rich gold-panning claim in 1849, but not many people come to this part of the river anymore. Near the shore massive boulders whipped water into rapids in front of a deep, clear swimming hole. Mari waited with the boys at the water's edge while Tom made several trips back to the truck for the gear.

By noon, camp was set up and they were swimming. Oxygenated water from rapids upstream energized the bodies of the adventurous skinny-dippers. It was very hot that day, over 100° and when not swimming they mostly hung out in the shade of the tent.

At dusk the mosquitoes came out. The boys were getting restless. They decided to go for an evening walk before dinner. Mari stayed at camp and got the food together. Tom took the boys for a boulder-hopping expedition. By the time they got back they were ready to eat and go to bed. Tom put another log on the fire and they all settled in for the night. The sky was black that night. Thousands of stars, like magic wishes, twinkled everywhere. The two lovers started their evening talk while the rest of the world slept. They talked about their previous marriages and how couples mirror each other's pasts.

They carried on about how it was and how it might be, then she asked him, "You said your first mentor was Rudy; what was he like?" Tom began telling the story:

"I must have been about eight years old. We had just moved out of central LA to a small country settlement named Newbury Park. It was a place of rolling hills and oak trees. High up on a hill over looking the Ventu valley, my grandfather Elisha had built a cabin in 1937 where he and Grandma Florence raised six children. Mom and Dad had just split up. Mom and us kids moved in with Grandma. Grandpa had already passed away when my mom was 16 years old and Grandma made a living as the Postmaster of Newbury Park.

"One Sunday afternoon I heard accordion music coming from the woods. I followed the sound into the trees and across a creek. I continued to walk north through the trees and willow brush to a fence with a wooden sign attached to a split-rail post. It read, "KEEP OUT." Being a young boy, I paid no mind to such things. Lifting up the barbwire and squeezing through, I felt a slight nervousness. The music was getting louder, blending with the sound of the rushing creek. The ground was thick with brush and trees. Wet leaves and moss along the creek created a magical aroma. I continued for about a quarter mile to the edge of a clearing and hid behind an oak tree. To my amazement there was an old man standing on the porch of a tin-roofed shack playing the accordion. He looked to be maybe 70 years old. As the breeze changed, it carried his music to other parts of the valley. I watched him for what seemed like a long time. Behind him sat a handmade rocking chair with a cane leaning against it. At his side was a small black-and-white dog. Fortunately the wind was blowing downhill and the dog wasn't able to pick up my scent. The little cabin had two small windows in front with a large rusted old-time gas station thermometer tacked above the door.

"Finally I mustered up enough courage to step forward into the clearing. The dog started barking profusely. The old man stopped playing. Setting his accordion down, he stepped off the porch and started yelling in a German accent, 'What are you doing here. You're not supposed to be here. Can't you read the signs– keep out!' I wasn't sure what to say. I replied, 'I heard the music, I have a little accordion but I can't play it very well.' Calming down a bit, he replied, 'Come over here, boy,' I studied the way he held his body and the gentle look in his eyes. Even though he was still yelling, I figured it would be OK. I stuck out my hand like a little gentleman and he did the like. I told him that my name was Tom Sawyer and that I lived in a cabin just off Ventu Park Road—he liked that. He told me that kids sometimes came and stole things off his property. I assured him it wasn't me, 'I just came to hear the music.' He asked me to sit on the porch. He went inside and came out with two glasses of what he called lemon-water; it had no sugar and was room temperature. He chuckled when my mouth puckered up. He said, 'Set a spell,' and started playing his accordion. While he played one beautiful Black Forest melody after another, I thought maybe he could be my father or even my grandfather. I had never known either of my grandfathers, so I was always on the lookout for a surrogate. That afternoon we became best friends. I was like the son he never had and he was my grandfather.

"When I got home I told my mother about Rudy. She told me that his real name was Rudolf Elston and he was a hermit. Everyone in the valley thought he was a strange old man and that I should not go over there. But I loved Rudy and would continually sneak over to his place for an afternoon of music, stories and lemon water.

"He was one of the most interesting men I have ever met. He came from Germany in 1916 via Brazil after he found his bride making love with his best friend. It broke his heart and he never remarried. When he first arrived in America he worked as a Model A Ford mechanic, and later switched his profession to watch maker. He built his small home deep in the woods and never finished the inside. The interior was bare walls and two-by-fours with all kinds of clocks and tools hanging from them. Above his handmade bed, nailed to a two-by-four, was a picture of his mother. He lived off a small pension and repaired clocks on the side. His specialty was cuckoo clocks; his little home was full of cuckoo clocks. He spoke four languages: German, Protégés, French and English. He cooked on a white gas Coleman camp stove, and carved alder walking sticks. He stained designs on them with a paste he made from oak balls and wrapped them with cut gunnysack material. Then he would cure the canes under his house for a year, finishing them with beeswax and some special brew he made from leaves. He did his own sewing and made his own clothes.

"He told me when he was a young man that he was very ill and almost died. That's when he became a vegetarian and 'beat the doctors'; he called them 'needle squeeezers.' He taught me about health food before the term ever existed, about basic electricity and magnets. We would go on walks in the woods, showing me how to identify different plants and rocks. He could out-walk most any energetic kid—up hill, down hill, it didn't matter. He showed me how to take a watch apart and put it back together again. He had a globe and showed me how the earth rotated and how with a watch you could navigate the seas; all of which I loved. But most of all, he gave me lessons on the accordion and told me stories of all his adventures. When he would let me, I would help with simple chores like hauling firewood and such.

"One rainy afternoon the wind was blowing hard from the east. With the sound of the rain on the tin roof and the cuckoo clocks, I drifted into a semi-sleep on layers of blankets that covered his handmade wooden couch. He covered me with a quilt and patted my head. After a few minutes I slipped into what I know now was a lucid flying dream, a most profound experience for an eight-year-old boy. I felt so at HOME; so peaceful, not a care in the world. That feeling has stayed with me all my life, topped only by my 'back-to-back' experience with you at Salt Point campground when we waited for the phone booth. Later in life, whenever I would despair, I'd think of being in Rudy's cabin with the rain coming down—somehow it made everything better. He taught me much—my parents never understood what great friends we had become. When I moved back to LA he gave me a silver plate, which I have to this day. What this simple poor man gave me was rich beyond any schooling I ever received. In a way you could say he was my guru—I wanted to be just like Rudy. We remained in contact until his passing in 1965 at the age of ninety-one."

Mari smiled happily. She wanted to know more, but he wanted to hear more about her. He asked her if she had a mentor when she was young. She said, "Maybe, only one, her name was Sister Xavier." The sound of the rushing river filled the night almost too much, the deafening roar against the nocturnal silence created a backdrop for their tales. Tom asked her to go on.

"When I was sixteen years old attending Ursuline High School in Santa Rosa, my English teacher was Sister Xavier. I was feeling especially put down in life. Those closest to me, who I looked up to, only had criticism towards most anything I tried to create on my own. And I knew things about the clergy I could never tell that distorted my faith, twisting me inside. Sister Xavier put her arms around me and my writing. She told me I had a natural talent for writing and encouraged me to continue—it was what I needed most. Through high school, as my mind expanded into the coming new age of Aquarius, Sister Xavier promoted and helped shape my work regardless of how far over the edge I went. She was like a light in my teenage life. I soon became one of the editorial staff for the high school newspaper. We began taking what was a straight vanilla publication and moving it slowly into a '60s counterculture school newspaper. Which reminds me of a story.

"My girlfriend Margaret and I were selected to be delegates for a model U.N. forum held at the U.C. Berkeley campus. Sister Edmund was our chaperone for the event. After the forum, we all went to the campus dorms to retire for the evening. Around midnight I began to execute my plan. The day before I'd found an ad in the Free Press advertising a band called 'Country Joe and the Fish.' Margaret and I snuck out of the dorm and walked about five miles to the Golden Chief Bakery dance hall and bar. Passing for 21, we entered the establishment to our wonder. Strobe lights and psychedelic scenes swirled to the acid rock music of Country Joe and the Fish. The next band up was Big Brother and the Holding Company with Janis Joplin. During one of the breaks I walked up to Janis and struck up a conversation. I asked her if she would play for our high school prom. She said she would. Later that night after the place closed, we decided to go with two 35-year-old men back to their apartment for drinks. At their place, we sipped a few, smoked a duby and talked stuff. They were very kind and proper with us. I believe they knew we were under age. We left about four in the morning for the dorms—no one ever knew.

"Back at school we were all excited that Janis Joplin was coming to play the prom. When we explained our intentions, the class president balked at the idea. Thinking it not proper, she squashed the deal in favor of some straight band.

"I remember another story…My girl friend Susie and I had taken the bus to San Francisco; we must have been 18. We were hitchhiking around the city when two older guys in a Volkswagen van picked us up. They took us to their house. Out in their garage they had a music room. Other guys showed up and started playing music. They were trying to figure out a name for their band. We all talked about it, settling for the name, 'Santana.' I didn't realize until years later who had picked us up that sunny afternoon in San Francisco."

Tom asked, "Is Sister Xavier still around?" Mari replied, "Yes, I still see her once an a while, she's a therapist at the Erickson Institute. She helped me when I really needed it. I never forgot her." Tom went on about how wonderful it is that grace provides mentors for us when we need them the most, "Sometimes they are not everything we expect them to be, but they give us a place to ground to and grow when all else seems bleak." Mari continued, "You said something about a second mentor; was that Al? I know you said he taught you how to fly an airplane, but how did you meet him?" Off he went into the past:

"Al Toler is a black man, a Tuskegee squadron fighter pilot during World War II and Director of the PNB Plant Training Center in Portland, Oregon. Here's how we first met. I showed up at center headquarters dressed in bib overalls, a full beard, and long hair down to my waist. As I walked into the building the security guard stood up from behind the lobby desk and quickly walked over to me, 'This is a private telephone company building, may I help you?' I showed the bewildered sentry my PNB ID card and was told to sit in the waiting room. Shuffling back and forth in front of me, the guard made a call on his mobile radio. A few minutes later a message came back instructing me to wait. Perplexed, the guard continued watching me closely until a woman appeared dressed in formal attire. She introduced herself as Mrs. Tanner, Mr. Toler's secretary. She escorted me down the hall to Mr. Toler's waiting room. After about ten minutes a tall black man dressed in a suit appeared. 'My name is Al Toler, you must be Tom Sawyer.' In those days, neither a black man nor a hippie was the stereotypical person you would find working for the phone company. We just stood there looking at each other, recognizing something deep inside, something connected. Both social outcasts, we smiled embracingly, and Al said, 'You'll do just fine.' Al taught me how to fly and to persevere in life; he was like a father to me. And that's how we met."

Because Mari's sister Pauline was one of the first woman 747-jet pilots in the world, Mari wanted to know more about how Tom learned to fly. He continued,

"Al is a by-the-seat-of-your-pants kind of guy. After two weeks of Al's crash-course ground school, he called me one evening and said, "Let's go flying. Meet me at my hangar in Gresham in the morning and we'll fly to Seattle, Washington." When I got there, Al was standing by the hangar door. We wheeled out a tri-prop Cessna 185. Al showed me all the ground checks and explained the details about the plane. He told me to get in the driver's seat. I said, 'I'm not going to fly this, am I?' Al retorted, 'Just do as I say.' Al went over the controls and directed me on the radio communications. Then he started going on about how to taxi to the runway. I was beginning to think he actually wanted me to fly the thing. He explained that there were power lines at the end of the runway and we needed sufficient altitude to clear them or we could be in trouble. I didn't like the sound of that. He twisted a few dials and wrote something on a piece of paper and then, 'OK, Let's go!'

With brakes on, he tells me to rev the engine full throttle, then let off the brakes. As we move down the runway, I think Al is flying the plane from the right-hand controls. But when I look over, I notice he's not touching them. I yell, 'Who's flying the airplane?' Al leans back with his hands behind his head, 'You are.' I exclaim, 'Holy Shit Al, I can't do this.' With a calm, clear voice, he returns, 'Well, I guess we're going to crash.' I look ahead with my hands on the controls and say, 'What do I do?' Al replies, 'Look at your air speed. At 75 knots pull back on the elevator a little, NOT too much or you'll stall out.' To my astonishment the plane lifted off the ground. 'Pull back some more,' Al's voice rings out. Up we went, right over the top of those power lines, missing them by 50 feet. This was my first attempt at flying an airplane."

Mari said, "I would really like to meet Al someday." With certainty in his voice Tom replied, "You will." He continued, "You must have had a second mentor, someone who taught you about Indian ways—you seem to have so much Indian in you?" She said, "I did and it's kind of strange because she is also my mother-in-law. I still call her Nana, which means grandmother." Mari continued,

"It happened when Beto, the boys' father, and I moved to Arizona to live near his mother. We had been living in San Diego. Beto was working two jobs. I was pregnant with the boys and we needed a change. I didn't want to go to Santa Rosa in fear that my parents would find out that I was pregnant—I felt they just wouldn't understand. With some coaxing from Beto, eventually I told them, but that's another story. We picked up, lock, stock and barrel and moved to Arizona. When I met Beto's mom Jaichima, I fell in love with her right away. All things ancient and magic were attractions for me. She was a Huichol shaman, a Mara'akame. We were immediately attracted to each other. Beto went to work as a carpenter. I studied and hung out with Jaichima and Pasqual (head shaman of the Wirarika tribe) and Rutury. She taught me things about the earth, herbs and tribal life. I was fascinated—a deep part of me awakened as we talked. I consider her my second mentor because she could relate to things I was interested in. At that time in my life most people found what I was interested in, quite weird. All these things were going on inside of me before the so-called "New Age" movement. Today these things are accepted and even endeared; back then they were considered strange. Most believed the earth was something mechanical, not something alive."

They continued talking, eventually falling asleep in each other's arms. Early the next morning the boys awakened Tom and Mari by jumping up and down on their sleeping bag. The two lovers walked with the boys to the river for one last look.

Mari said, "Water travels the path of least resistance to the sea—it's chaos, it's entropy; all living things depend on it, if they are ever to reach Mother Sea. Our egos think we are individual, but in reality we are just waves, one wave observing another, all belonging to the water." With that they picked up camp and started back to Ray and Jayne's house. When they arrived they found out that Tom's oldest son Larry was down from Oregon and was staying at Grandma June's house. Tom got the idea of going to the family gold mine.

After breakfast, Bob agreed to take everyone on an all-day adventure to the Red Ledge mine. As legend would have it, Grandpa Max won it in a poker game back in the 1940s, but in reality he was given insider information from the local sheriff and bought it at a secret tax sale. Back in the 1800s the mine was worked by hand, using a steam-driven stamp mill to crush the ore-rich quartz rock into powder. The powder was then placed in a huge iron ball tumbler and the gold was extracted using mercury. Pieces of crystallized gold quartz measuring larger than three by six centimeters had been removed from the mine in its early days. The mine is full of old tunnels that honeycomb a serpentine hillside just outside of Allegany near the little town of Washington.

Bob strapped on his six-shooter, crammed rope, backpacking gear, and everyone else into two vehicles and headed up the famous Gold Rush road, China Grade, toward North Bloomfield out side of Nevada City. This Chinese-built road was the main throughway from the gold fields of Allegany to the trains at Grass Valley. There's a section just before the crossing, on the south fork of the Yuba River, where the drop-off is nearly 1,000 feet straight down along a mile of road. Thousands of Chinese heaved rocks over the cliff into the canyon below until enough rock was built up to form the narrow one-lane road. From the road one can look straight up 500 feet to the top of the cliff and look down 500 feet to the canyon below. Twenty-mule teams pulled ore-laden wagons up this steep incline at China Grade for almost 30 years.

After crossing the Yuba, Bob continued to Lake City and on into North Bloomfield. Bob suggested they stop off at the

Malakoff Diggings. He knew about an old drain tunnel that was built there in 1874 as a base drain for the hydraulic minefields at Malakoff. It was built by hundreds of Chinese using hand chisels and dynamite, boring 8,000 feet through solid granite. The hydraulic mines used huge high-pressure cannon-like water nozzles called monitors that blasted the hillsides, washing away massive gravel mounds, releasing the heavier gold particles in mercury-laden sluice boxes, while the mud and debris washed downstream into the drain tunnel and on to the south fork of the Yuba River.

A half hour later they located Tunnel Road and parked. They walked to an overgrown area near the creek, pushing the brush away until reaching a shoulder-height tunnel leading into the dark. Water flowed ankle deep as they entered a pitch-black passageway to somewhere. Larry was leading the way. He called back, "Dad, you got the flashlight?" The boys were trying to run ahead. Mari yelled, "Boys, wait for Thomas." Tom finally caught up to Larry and gave him the flashlight. They walked for about an hour. In the distance a tiny dot of light, the proverbial "Light at the end of the tunnel," shone like an oncoming train. A few minutes later they reached the end and exited the tunnel into what looked like a panoramic moonscape, a literal gravel desert, that went on for miles. The boys wanted to know what it was. In their minds, they had traveled for hours through a mysterious dark channel leading to the moon. Bob explained, "To get to the gold, the miners tore away vegetation and trees, moving 50,000 tons of gravel per day, turning the entire area into a barren wasteland." The boys were very curious about the gold. They scurried around looking for anything shiny, returning fifteen minutes later with a small piece of petrified wood—not a bad find. Bob announced it was time to go if they wanted to make the Red Ledge before dark. Everyone took the trail above the tunnel and arrived back at the car in 20 minutes.

Once again on the road, they crossed Blood Run to Madres Flats down to Bathhouse Ravine and on several miles to Orleans Flats. Then winding through Wolf Creek and Minnesota Flats to Kanaka Creek, they branched off onto a rutted dirt road toward the Red Ledge mine.

Bob stepped out of the truck and situated his 38 Special. He spun the cylinder several times checking for bullets in all chambers and placed it back in the holster. The Red Ledge is rattlesnake country and was hot, over 100 degrees. Rattlesnakes are "blind" at this temperature. They use infrared to sense the presence of possible enemies. When the outside temperature goes higher than human body temperature, 98.6, they can't warn intruders until it's too late. They can only see a few feet with their eyes and will strike at anything that moves.

Bob gave instructions to "Watch your step" and "Look at the top of the rock you're climbing before grabbing it." The crew stepped out onto the dirt road facing the main entrance to the mine. There'd been a cave-in closing off the main shaft from the road. To the left of the cave-in was a steep incline made of green glossy serpentine rock and mine tailings. Tom had been there many times before. He told the boys to walk close to him. Mari grabbed Jake's hand and Tom snatched Adam's. They all started the twisting climb up the serpentine rock path to an airshaft above the mine. Tom could feel his would-be family tighten up and walk as one unit. Feelings of trust moved between them. The smell of thick pine filled the hot summer air. As they approached the opening to the airshaft the scent changed to a damp musky odor coming up from the sealed shaft 70 feet below. Bob pointed to a piece of serpentine that was shot-gunned with gold-colored metal. The boys got excited. Then he grinned and said, "Fool's Gold. It looks like gold, but it's not. It's really iron pyrite." They didn't care; they wanted to take it home.

Tom dropped a rock down the airshaft. He listened to the thud-echo-bang coming up from below. He was checking for the Rocky Mountain Diamondback Rattlesnake. If they were down there, hopefully he'd hear the telltale rattle of the poisonous vipers. He took a coil of rope from off his shoulder and told Larry to hold on to one end, "Larry, hold on. I'm going down." With complete trust in his son, he began his descent. Slowly lowering his body down the shaft, he disappeared into the darkness 70 feet below.

Tom looks up and sees his sweetheart gazing over the edge with concern. The boys are wide-eyed. Ray maintains the confident look of a sea captain. Bob yells, "Tom, what do you see?" Tom pulls a flashlight from his hip pocket and hollers back, "Tracks, ore car tracks, leading north and south. There's a cave-in from the main tunnel coming back within ten feet of the airshaft. Hold on, I see something." Tom follows the tracks 100 feet or so deeper into the mine to investigate what looks like a black clump attached to a top crossbeam. He hears Mari's voice say, "Be careful." It appears to be moving. All of a sudden, *O my God, it's bats, hundreds of bats all clumped up hanging from an old rotted timber.* The longer he shines the light on them the more they squirm about. The little pig-faced creatures begin screeching. Without warning they bolted like a swarm of bees in the night, almost knocking him down. Circling around for some time, many go deeper into the mine, while others escape up the airshaft. Backing away from the shaft's edge as the winged rats make their exit, Mari yells, "Are you OK?" Tom replied, "It's OK, I'm OK."

He continued deeper into the main shaft until it branched to the right, following the outcropping to another cave-in. Looking up, he saw where miners had worked the ceiling some 100 years ago. The timbers appeared decomposed and wet. He turned and looked down another shaft to the left that dropped 50 feet into the dark with a massive cave-in at the bottom. Adjusting his eyes, he relaxed for a moment next to a fallen beam crossing the ore tracks. A cat-size tunnel rat with beady red eyes scurried down a rotted timber passing near his shoulder, making a screechy-scraping sound as it dragged its tail over the wood and disappeared into the darkness. He began to get the feeling that it was UNSAFE to venture beyond this point.

He stepped around a rusted ore car and followed the tracks toward the daylight shining on the floor around the airshaft. He called up to Larry and started climbing up the rope hand-over-hand until he reached the top and stepped into the daylight.

He put his hands on his knees and breathed in deeply, "The air smells so good up here." Mari and the boys came up and put their arms around him, "Are you all right?" He replied, "Yes, the air's a little stale down there. Parts of the main tunnel don't look safe, but it looks OK around the airshaft."

Mari went down next with Tom holding the rope. It's a leap of faith to have your life held in the hands of another. He could tell she trusted him without reservation—a deepening of the heart that all should experience at least once in their life. She stayed for a few minutes looking around and came back up with a smile on her face. Now it was the boys' turn. Tom went down again and waited at the bottom. Ray and Larry held the rope while each boy descended the shaft. The last 20 feet was wet and steep so Tom met them part way, helping them down. Then Mari came down. They all sat in the light of the airshaft, cuddled together at the bottom, completely content. Then back up they went, one at a time. Everyone took a turn except Bob; he wanted no part in such shenanigans. Coiling up the rope, they headed down the serpentine path to the road below where Bob began explaining how steam-driven stamping mills crushed the quartz from the mine into powder, removing the gold. They got in their trucks and motored onward toward Grass Valley. It had been a great adventure.

The boys had too many questions; Bob thought it a good idea to stop off at the gold mining museum east of Lake City, near North Columbia where he had lived as a boy. After the tour Adam and Jacob seemed to understand the magnitude of what took place 100 years ago and were ready to become miners. From North Columbia they went back to Grandma's house for dinner and spent the night.

The next morning the phone rang early. It was Jane. She said she'd heard from a friend about a quartz mine up Highway 20. Tom and Mari thought that a good idea; maybe they could find some big ones to make healing crystals out of. Mari, Tom, Larry, Adam, Jacob, Ray and Jayne all met for breakfast at Humpty Dumpty's and headed up Highway 20 toward Bowman Lake. After Scott Flats, pine trees towered either side of the road. Continuing for several miles on a gravel road, they turned off on a dirt road at Camp Spaulding and traveled a half mile to an encampment near the mine.

Jayne stepped out of the car and walked up the hillside. She motioned the others to come and pointed upward, "This looks like the place." Passing through pines and underbrush they approached what looked like a cave 100 yards in. There was a problem; someone had roped off the area. Both Tom and Mari got a peculiar feeling as they near the barricade. It was strange, dangerously strange. They contemplated for a moment, sensing the air, then stepped over the rope. The others followed. Mari called for the boys to stay near. As the lovers moved along the treeline a spontaneous bond formed between them.

There was no moisture; the air was crisp with a slight breeze coming at them. Tom could smell canvas and decaying canned food. Up ahead was the back of a tattered army tent with wood and refuse spread around. Beer cans, bottles, and cardboard boxes littered the area. A pair of men's overalls swung back and forth on a makeshift clothesline next to a galvanized washtub. The connection between Tom and Mari increased. Everything Mari was thinking, Tom was thinking—they moved as one to the side of the tent. Suddenly, just when Tom was going to yell out, "Anybody here," a tall man in a dirty blue shirt and black jeans appeared around the corner, standing barefoot in pine needles with a startled look on his three-day-unshaven face. For a moment they just stared at each other. It was like looking into the eyes of a scarecrow. He looked bewildered and half-crazed.

Pointing to the cave Tom began to speak, "We didn't mean to startle you. There's a cave up the hill ..." The man interrupted, "That's my cave. I've been assigned to guard it." Straight faced the man continued, "It's a passageway for extraterrestrials (long pause) inter-dimensional beings." Tom went on, "We understand that there are crystals in the cave. We just came to look at them." Ray and the rest of the group came closer. Walking back around in front of the tent, the man mumbled, "... need to get permission," and went inside. He wrestled around inside scavenging for something. Tom heard what sounded like a clip being forced into a 9mm automatic, followed by the swish-click lock-and-load of a Smith and Wesson.

The man flipped open the front of the tent, almost knocking it down in his attempt to exit, stumbled to one knee, fell back on his hands, and scrabbled backwards. He got up and stood facing Tom and Mari with a pistol strapped to the side of his waist in a semi-drawn position. Tom and Mari smiled. Tom knew exactly what she was going to say. In a calm clear matter-of-fact voice Mari said, "It must get lonely up here sometimes, I'm glad we came to see you."

Somehow those words totally defused the man. Moving his hand away from the pistol, he relaxed his body. Tom and Mari walked toward him with outstretched hands. Making eye contact, they introduced themselves, assuring him they had come in peace. His demeanor softened, a slight glow began to show through his steely eyes as he spoke his next words, "My name is Rally." The lovers figured him to be a shell-shocked Vietnam vet, half out of his mind and lonely. He continued to talk about UFO's and how the cave was some kind of star gate. They let him tell his story without judgment. After 15 minutes of non-stop talk, he eventually gave permission for the group to enter the cave. Rally told his visitors to be careful of demons and walked to the edge of his camp to sit on a cardboard box by the tent.

The first 50 yards of the path were steep. By the time they reached the opening everyone was out of breath. Tom and Larry entered the cave first and walked in about 30 feet. The rest followed. Relative to the Red Ledge this was a small cave. Another ten feet and that was it. They were at the end. A few small quartz formations poked out here and there, but nothing like they had expected. The explorers all sat down in front of the cave, snapped a few photographs and headed back to Rally's camp.

Rally greeted them with a curious look, "Encounter anything unusual?" Tom replied, "No, but we were very respectful; it may be guarded by Indian spirits." Rally uttered, "You think so, maybe that's what it is." He went on, "When you get back to town, find me a woman." Then he proceeded to give a complete description of what "the woman" should look like, with instructions to bring her and food back as soon as possible. Everyone nodded and thanked Rally for allowing them to look at the cave and walked back toward Ray's car.

Tom and Mari were thankful to this tortured soul for providing the backdrop for a quickening that created a synergy between them. Silently, they wished him well and headed off toward their next adventure. The teacher often comes in many disguises—

6

"I've been running.
I got no money, but love.
Good Humor Man do you have a popsicle for me?"

Paper Boy with no change

Water Tower

At 1:00 in the afternoon Tom stood at the edge of Deer Creek Falls, it's 35 feet straight down to the bottom. He looks over the edge at Ray swimming in the pool below and hesitates. The wind is blowing slightly. It's Tom's turn to jump. Boulders and logs protrude out of the water. Too far to the left or not far enough forward is a dead-man's fall. If he belly-flops he could break bones or at the least have the wind knocked out of him; he's going to have to do it just right. It reminds him of the time they carried roof-trusses along a 2x6, two stories in the air—no mistakes. Looking down he begins to chicken out when something comes over him. His senses become heightened by the sound of the falls crashing below. Backing up, he lifts off on one foot, shouting, "What the hell," as he leaps forward, falling slow motion. He feels the water sting his feet as his body breaks the surface and continues to the bottom. It's something the brothers decided to do on a Saturday afternoon. They had been working on Mom's house when Ray came up with the bright idea.

Back at the jobsite Tom packed up his tools in preparation for another motorcycle run to Santa Rosa. He left for Santa Rosa that evening on Ol' Gal, hoping to get to Mari's house in time for dinner.

Slowing down for the dip in the driveway he pulled in, revved the engine twice and hit the kill switch. Mari popped out the side door. They hugged and walked inside.

Mari took him to the side and said, "After dinner, Didi wants us to give him a massage on our new massage table. Did you bring your crystal?"

"It's in the backpack. Should I get it now?"

"No, let's wait till after dinner."

After dinner they went to Mari's room and set up the massage table they had purchased on Tom's last trip to Santa Rosa. The small 10x15-foot room was adorned with East Indian and Huichol artifacts. A picture of an Indian saint hung above Mari's foldout bed. Yellow candles on the altar atop her bureau cast a flickering shadow on the wall. Transcendental music, *Robert Monroe's Green-4,* played softly in the background. The floor was covered with a brightly colored Navajo rug. They knelt together facing the east and said a prayer for the healing of Didi in body, mind, and spirit.

"Tom, would you tell Didi that we're ready?"

From the hallway, "Didi, we're ready."

"Be right there." Didi entered the bedroom, "What the hell is this?"

"We're going to do a crystal healing on you," Mari whispered.

"You're going to do a what?"

"Lie down on the table, face down,"

Didi gave a quick partial smile and groaned as he moved onto the table. Mari placed a thin blanket over his body. Tom guided Didi's head into the face cradle. The Republican realist CEO client was about to receive something far from his customary reality.

"What are you going to do?"

"Didi, just relax, listen to the music."

"We're going to give you a massage, then afterwards we're going to work on your energy body."

"What the hell is that?"

"The energy that surrounds your body. Didi, stop talking and just relax." Mari whispered again.

Mari started rubbing his back and Tom began with his feet. Didi liked very deep tissue work, the kind that would make most people scream in pain. After working on him face-down, Mari told him to roll over. He was quiet and relaxed now. They finished the full-body massage with Mari gently working his face. Then Tom removed the crystal from his pouch, charging it with healing intent with his right thumb. Mari stood at Didi's head, placing her hand a few inches from his bald cranium. Tom began moving the crystal in a spiral motion around the bottom of his feet.

"What's going on? What in the hell are you guys doing?" Didi opened his eyes.

Mari placed a small folded towel over his eyes, "Didi, it's OK. We're just fluffing up your aura."

"My what? It tingles."

"Didi, stop talking and just relax."

Tom began again on Didi's feet, moving the crystal to each chakra, ending at his head.

In a very soft voice Didi muttered, "I'm floating on the ceiling...what are you guys doing?"

"We're almost done."

Drifting in and out, "... but I feel like I'm on the ceiling."

"That's great. Just relax a few minutes longer."

While Didi was having his out-of-body experience, Tom and Mari held hands at the head of the table and said a closing prayer.

"Didi, you can get up when you feel like it. Take your time...there's no hurry. We'll be in the other room."

They left and sat on the couch in the front room. With a puzzled, reverent look Mari turned to Tom, "Who are you?" He knew what she was referring to. He replied, "I'm just a man." She went on, "How could that be possible, my father..." Tom interrupted, "It's more like "Who are we?" It was our synergy acting as a conduit for the energy. I'm no one special, but with you, the love between us attracts a greater force in both of us."

He could tell that she didn't completely want to accept the explanation. She wanted to give him the credit. He went on, "Look, I'm just a man in love. We have to be careful to give credit to the Source." She concurred, but kept looking at him out of the corner of her eye.

A few minutes later Didi came into the front room with a peaceful, bewildered look on his face and continued to go on and on about his unexpected experience. "Gee (as he affectionately calls Noni), come here." Noni came from the kitchen with a dishtowel in her hand and sat on the edge of the coach. "Gee, I was on the ceiling looking down at my body." Noni just smiled and went back into the kitchen.

Tom and Mari excused themselves and went to Mari's room. As they began cleaning up and put things away, Mari said, "I'm not having you sleep in the park tonight, let's see if we can find a room."

"Sounds good to me."

"I know a little East Indian motel on Mendocino Avenue."

"Can I put the motorcycle in your garage?"

"I think so, I'll ask Didi."

Poking her head around the corner, "Didi, can Tom put his motorcycle in the garage?"

"I'm sorry, he can't spend the night; you know the rules."

"No, we're going to stay at Linda's."

"Gee, I'm not dressed, can you pull one of the cars out, Tom needs to put his motorcycle in the garage."

"Thanks, Didi."

Mari explained she didn't want to say "motel" because it would have sounded seedy to her parents, but Linda's was another option if they couldn't find a motel.

While she was packing a few things Tom put Ol' Gal in the garage and grabbed his backpack. They kissed everyone goodnight and headed for Mendocino Avenue. A few minutes later they pulled into the parking lot of the Pelissier Motel. It had been there for years and was now rundown, but clean. They stepped out into the night and watched the bright lights of Mendocino flicker out of sync with the sound of the traffic. Tom's mind was full of memories, or maybe daydreams of walking along the Ganges.

The brass bell dangling on the door rang as they entered the lobby. An East Indian woman dressed in a purple sari with a red dot above her eyebrows stepped out from behind a saffron curtain. The place smelled of incense and tight living quarters. Pictures of the family's guru hung on the wall above the reception counter. Along the wall divider leading to the family's living area, brightly colored cloth drooped next to a glass-beaded doorway. Tom glanced inside. Candles, incense burners, and more pictures were set on a small shrine near the bed. With sincere eyes the woman said in heavily accented English, "May I help you?" Mari replied, "We're looking for a room." "I am very sorry, we just rented the last room and forgot to turn off the sign." Tom said, "*Namaste.*" The woman replied back, "*Namaste.*" It means, "I bow to the divinity within you," in Hindi. Mari looked over at Tom with disappointment. He was thinking, *Looks like another night in the park.*

Back on Mendocino Avenue again, Mari went by the college and maneuvered through downtown past Luther Burbank Gardens onto Charles Street. Tom recognized the street. It was the place where they first met when he attended the Wirikuta meeting, where she walked in barefoot wearing a white summer dress and beaded ankle bracelet. As they continued passing quaint little houses from the 1930s with small manicured front lawns and colorful flowerbeds, Mari said, "This is it. Linda's probably asleep. I'll tap on the window. You wait here. You got a quarter?" He reached into his bib overalls handing her a quarter and watched her walk across the wet lawn to a pane-glass window on the right side of the house. Suddenly a light came on and Linda appeared at the window. Mari talked for a few minutes then came back to the car and got in.

Tom said curiously, "No luck?"

"No, Linda's got a full house, but we can sleep in the garage."

"Cool."

She drove to the end of the block and turned left into an alleyway.

"I'm trying to remember what the garage looks like. Look for an old Plymouth parked along the fence."

"There it is."

"This must be it. There's a side door by the neighbor's garden fence. You got a match?"

Tom rolled his thumb over the lighter, sparking light on the keyhole.

"Damn, it's cold."

"Look for a green rock by the door."

"OK, I got it."

Mari stuck the key in the door and turned the lock. They giggled, "We're in."

"Sweetie, will you get the sleeping bags?"

"You got the keys to the car?"

"Yes, will you lock it?"

Tom came back with backpacks and sleeping bags and opened the side door to the garage. Mari was already making a little nest.

"Look, there's a heater."

"Now all we need is a extension cord."

"There's one."

Tom found cardboard boxes containing old clothes and stacked them on top of each other, building walls around where Mari was making their nest. She found a blanket and placed it over the top of the boxes, making a roof. Zipping the sleeping bags together, she methodically placed it in the nest. They stood back looking at their creation, giggled and crawled in.

Tom whispered, "This is great."

"Do you love me?"

"I love you so much."

"Let's meditate for a few minutes."

She lit a candle and placed it on the cement floor just outside the opening to their little handmade home. It made just enough light. They took off all their clothes except tee shirt and blouse and sat facing each other holding hands. The feeling got stronger and stronger. They remained in silence for a long time until neither could stand it any more. He leaned forward and gently kissed her. Their spirit bodies swirled—magical. Releasing their moistened hands, Tom unbuttoned her blouse, and she took off his T-shirt lifting it over his head. He slowly moved his pointed finger toward her right breast. Her nipples were swollen and erect from the cold. When he came within a quarter inch of her nipple a violet-blue spark jumped to his index finger, creating a flash that lit their faces. They smiled and looked deep into each other's eyes. It wasn't static electricity, they were just holding hands and hadn't moved. It was something else, perhaps the polarity between a female and a male deeply in love? They fell into each other's arms and made indescribable love that night...afterwards talking until the early hours of the morning.

For several months Tom and Mari made many trips back and forth from Grass Valley to Santa Rosa and vice versa, staying with friends as often as they could, or at motels. They helped the boys with school projects, took them on outings and played just for fun—they had become a family. He worked in Grass Valley on the house and would come *home* whenever he could.

When Tom's mom's house was nearing completion, Mari called and said she'd found a place to live in the little accordion town of Cotati. A friend of hers, Pam Zober, had a water tower for rent near the railroad tracks. The top of the tower had been converted into an 8x8 sleeping room with a hotplate and a motor-home refrigerator. There were windows all around. Tom came and looked at it in September around their birthdays. He moved there in October. Mari was taking classes at SSU very near Cotati.

She and the boys officially lived in Santa Rosa with her parents, but the lovers built a nest at the water tower and she would come by whenever she could. Tom took college classes in statistics, biofeedback and yoga with her, studied and got his certification in massage, worked part-time with her as a massage therapist at Dr. Wilkinson's in Calistoga—doing whatever they could to increase their time together. Many weeks went by.

He had very little money. Living on bean burritos and staples that Mari would bring, he had reduced his material possessions to a motorcycle, a cardboard box of clothes, a briefcase containing the patents and business plans for Paratechnology, a 1965 Chevy flatbed truck stored at his long time friend Dave Glass's buffalo ranch in Oregon, and the cabin in the wilderness above the Mosier River Valley, which was now in danger of being sold at auction for back taxes. The motorcycle was in need of repairs again and was now stored at his mother's house in Grass Valley.

It was a bright fall afternoon. Mari showed up at the water tower yearning for a late breakfast at Rafas. After huevos rancheros, she dropped Tom at the water tower before leaving for graduate classes at the university. He waved her goodbye and went inside.

Standing in front of the hot plate, he made a cup of green tea before climbing the stairs to the walk circling the top of the tower. Taking small sips, he leaned against the railing and looked over at the crumbling chicken coops below that marked the era of the 1940s Sonoma County egg industry. He pondered what dreams and hard work must have gone into creating such structures and how we think our dreams will last forever while we're making them.

After cleaning up the "nest," he headed for the railroad tracks. He was a little melancholy and the tracks, for some odd reason, always made him feel at home. The walk did him good. By the time he reached the railroad gate crossing things began to pick up. Feeling like a schoolboy he walked along balancing on the rails, one foot after the other. The air was brisk and clean. He began singing a song as he walked along, "… she was my queen in Calico, I was her barefoot bashful beau, and I wrote on her slate that I loved her so, when we were a couple of kids."

He looked far up the tracks past the Hewlett Packard plant to the university. Talking to himself, he said, "That's where my

sweetheart is." He was so smitten with her. Of course, he didn't
let her know the extent of it, so as not to put a burden on the
relationship, for she cherished the idea of her freedom and he
knew it. She was a no-nonsense lady and would not tolerate
clinging of any sort. As he walked along the rails, singing, he
began picturing himself as a ten-year old boy on his way to see
his sweetheart. Suddenly his right foot slipped off the rail,
twisting his ankle. He fell off the tracks, sliding down a ravine
on his back. He wasn't really hurt, but laid there looking up at
the sky. With his legs uphill and arms outstretched, he chuckled,
remembering the position from a long-ago memory:

I was getting ready to go on vacation. My TAC center
manager took me into his office and asked me where I was
going. I told him I didn't know. He said, 'Listen Sawyer, if we
have a major system failure we're going to send out a helicopter
after you.' I told him my wife and seven-year-old boy had already
left the day before on horseback with a guide named Cowboy
Bill on a 70-mile ride to the coast, some of it on logging roads
and unmarked trails. There would be no way to know where I
was because I was going to track their trail and catch up with
them somewhere between Cherry Grove and the coast. He went
on, 'All right, but call in when you reach a town and Sawyer,
get rid of that broken-down Volkswagen and get a respectable
car.'

This kind of talk about how I should look or be off-hours
made me dislike working for the phone company. In some ways
it made me feel good that I had them by the 'technologies.'
Looking back, I realized that I was sporting a prima donna
attitude and wished I hadn't. Life would soon enough teach me
about the misuse of power.

Back at the farm, I put saddle and gear on Rusty, a young
American Saddle Bred, and headed for Cherry Grove, taking
the back roads, hoping to pick up their trail at Ghost Town.
West of Cherry Grove is an old abandoned resort where the
railroad passed through in the 1920s. Rusty and I passed through
the ghost town and worked our way up Kimber Pass to the top
at Koennecke Junction, an old stagecoach run. At the top of

the pass I found fresh tracks. My wife, my son Larry, and Cowboy Bill, and two pack animals were two days ahead of me. I could see where they had stopped to rest and tie their horses. My wife was on an Appaloosa, Larry rode a Shetland pony, and Bill a Quarter/Morgan. I would have to ride hard and rest less to catch up.

I followed their tracks another ten miles and set up camp at dusk. The next morning early, Rusty and I followed the switchback to the top of a hill. From the knoll I could see they'd picked up a logging road, heading northwest. If I took the trail to the right I'd be able to triangulate their trail, saving maybe an hour.

About 30 minutes into the shortcut I spotted an old log bridge spanning a ten-foot-deep narrow ravine. I got off and looked at the planks covering the bridge to make sure it could take the weight of the horse. Some of these old bridges were built during the Tillamook Burn back in the 1930s and many were rotted. We were 20 miles from the nearest town; it wasn't a place to make mistakes. The planks looked good and we started across. What I didn't realize was that the log beams spanning the right side of the bridge were rotted. We got about three feet across when the right side started to collapse under our weight. Rusty tried to maintain his balance, but was flipped around, falling four feet to the edge of the ravine, landing on his rear (thank God) then sliding another eight feet backwards down a steep embankment to the bottom.

Rusty was upside-down with all fours pointing uphill. My right leg was pinned under the saddle with 1,300 pounds of horse on top. I prayed for Rusty not to freak out. Had he started thrashing around to try to get up, I would have been seriously injured, if not killed. And thank God for the saddle horn or my leg would have been crushed. Turning his head, this gentle animal lifted his neck to make eye contact with me as if to say, 'Well, now what do we do? Are you OK? Should I be afraid?' The communication was much more than that, but I couldn't put it into words. I assured him that we were going to get out of this and to just relax; the worst was over.

Stretching out with my left hand I was able to undo the belly strap, freeing the saddle from the horse just in case he decided to panic and start thrashing around. Then I rubbed his neck, telling him I was going to try to pull my leg out and not to move. That didn't work. My leg was pinned too tightly under the saddle.

The problem was my hip. If I could dig some of the earth away from my hip it would give me room to slide backwards. I started digging with my right hand. It took a long time to do this. Every once in a while Rusty would lift his head and look at me with a bull-eyed look, as if to say, 'As long as you're not scared then it's "all good," but if I sense you getting scared then I'm going to freak.' I kept digging. Finally, I was able to slip my leg out from underneath the saddle. I wasn't sure; I didn't think my leg was broken, but I knew it was hurt. I could walk.

I was afraid to try to roll Rusty over with the saddle on. The way the ground lay, it could have broken his back. After digging out around the saddle horn and other parts, I was able to slip the saddle out from underneath him. Standing at his head, I looked into his eyes and talked, explaining each move I was about to make. Not being able to afford Rusty running off in a panic, I put a 50-foot rope around his neck and tied the other end to a tree. After removing the bit from his mouth I yelled, 'Up Rusty, up!' He thrashed back and forth, rolling onto his right side and stood up. 'Good boy.'

I thought, *If it's broken, it'll be tough going.* Gently removing my pants, I looked at my right leg. It was black and blue from groin to knee, but nothing was broken. After resting for a while I put the saddle back on. We walked along the ravine until the embankment leveled out enough to bring the horse up. I finally caught up with the rest of group two days later, five miles from the coast.

Coming back from his memory, he dusted himself off, walked back onto the tracks and started walking the rail again. A few feet up ahead he spotted a shiny thing lying on a railroad tie. It was a sewing thimble. All happy about that, he reached into his back pocket and pulled out a handkerchief Mari had given him a few days earlier. She could tolerate most things about him, but plugging one side of his nose and blowing snot to the ground was not one of them. He placed the thimble into the still-clean handkerchief and walked on.

Next he found a half-smashed quarter that someone must have placed on the rail. By the time he reached the university he had found a thimble, a quarter, a used lipstick container, a golf ball, a piece of tinfoil and a paperclip. As far as his eternal little boy was concerned, he had real treasure to show his girlfriend.

From the tracks he walked to the pond behind the student rec hall hoping Mari would show up after class. He watched the ducks swimming around, noting the pairs. He loved seeing anything in love—people, ducks—it all fascinated him. Sure enough, there she was coming up the path leading to the pond. She spotted him right off and walked over. With an *I'm so glad to see you* smile on her face she said, "What's your name?"

"I'm Tom, are you free tonight?"

"I don't know you THAT well."

"I've got this terrific place in Cotati?"

"You know I don't like surprises, what are you doing here?"

"Well, I was walking down the railroad tracks and ended up here."

"I can only stay for a little while, I've got one more class."

"Guess what, I found some treasures on the railroad tracks."

Reaching into his jacket he pulled out the handkerchief filled with goodies placing it on the ground, "What do you think?"

Laughing out loud she said, "I wouldn't exactly call them treasures."

"Yes, I suppose you're right, but they must mean something," thinking that she might read them like she reads leaves.

"Yes, they mean you don't have very good taste—just kidding, let's see."

Picking up each piece and placing them near her forehead, she said, "The quarter is about wealth, but it's been flattened.

The lipstick is about your obsession with women, the golf ball is about communicating with powerful people, the paperclip is about doing business, the tinfoil is about life's reflection, and the thimble is about your desire for home and family. But most of all, it means you're in love with me—don't ever let the little boy die."

"O sweet lady, that's so true."

"I've got to run, I'll see you to night."

They hugged goodbye with legs intertwined, ending in a passionate kiss.

Tom picked up his little treasures and headed back to the water tower.

One day on his usual three-mile walk to Cotati for a Rafas $1.75 burrito, he decided to take a detour. Hoping to find a shortcut to town, he turned right off Railroad Avenue onto a semi-country road with 1930s houses amidst modern ones. As he passed the house at the end of the block, a Doberman poked its head over the wooden gate near the road and started barking so fast spittle splattered from its mouth. It startled him at first. Walking on, he paid no attention to it. A hundred feet down the road a feeling made him turn around. Somehow the dog had gotten out and was coming right for him with a killer look in its eyes. It was too late to run. Tom squatted down, watching the wild-eyed canine's flashing teeth approach on a dead run. The dog started putting on the brakes and stopped ten feet in front of him, snapping and growling. Tom watched for a few seconds then started talking to the animal in dog talk.

When he was eight years old, living in Thousand Oaks, kids called him "Dog Boy" because he always had dogs with him and would bring dog bones to school and eat them during recess. In those days he was often seen with strange dogs that were known to be violent.

As he continued talking with the Doberman it began to calm and move closer. He reached his hand out, letting it sniff his fingers. All seemed OK until he stood up and started to walk away. Again the dog became ferocious, threatening to bite. Again he turned and squatted, calming the dog. Repeatedly, every time he would get up and start to walk away the dog would go crazy.

He decided to allow the dog to lick his face. Maybe that would help. He reached out his hand, letting the dog sniff for a bit and closed his eyes. Turning his head to one side he placed his face near the dog's mouth and waited. It smelled his face and hair and neck, then his stomach and crotch. He slowly reached his hand further forward, petting the side of its face and pressing the dog's nose against the side of his cheek. It began smelling his right ear as he petted and praised it, "Good boy." Then it moved its nose to the front of his face and licked him. He stood up, patted his thigh and said, "Let's go." This time the dog followed him as though they were out for a Sunday morning walk.

He was happy to have the dog along. It was his first neighborhood friend. He didn't know anyone in town and was glad to have the company. Following him almost to town, the dog turned around and headed back home.

Tom entered Rafa's through the front screen door, sat at the counter and ordered a bean-and-cheese burrito. Finding it too lonely to eat by himself in the restaurant, he got the burrito to go and ate it as he walked. He loved to eat and walk— something about walking and eating made him feel at home.

Thinking that the Doberman might forget who he was, he walked past the fire station, taking the long way back. Further out Railroad Avenue it turned into country. White Okie houses not painted for 20 years lined the street just before the turnoff to Tom's place. He entered a dirt road dotted with trees leading to his unusual home. Reaching into his pocket for the key, he opened the door, climbing the spiral staircase to the little pane-glass-windowed room at the top of the water tower, and reclined on the mattress on the floor. He stared at the ceiling wishing Mari were there.

He went over details about Paratechnology, thinking. If they could only get funding for the company Mari and he could have a real future, his property would be saved, he could get Ol' Gal back on the road again, the other investors would get a return on their investment and Bob, his mentor, would be proud of him.

He would often walk the railroad tracks looking for date-spikes, and think of the same thing. The Paratechnology stuff never left his mind, except when he was with Mari. When they were together, all was right in the world—the past and the future had very little meaning.

For the next few weeks he lived on hope and love, waiting for word from the Sand Hill venture capital firm about his meeting with Wetek. He had sent the letter he and Mari and Didi prepared using her return address several weeks back and was hanging on for a response.

One afternoon after class, Mari showed up with a letter in hand. She had a smile on her face, "It has a Wetek logo on the corner of the envelope!" Tom thought, *Is this a "Dear John" or an invitation to meet?* Holding it in his hand he said, "Well, this is what we've been waiting for. It's either another hoop to jump through or the end of the road for Paratechnology." Opening the letter with his trusty pocketknife as though he was about to announce the winner of an Academy Award, he lifted out the letter and read it slowly. Mari watched his eyes move down the page. Announcing the news with calm, he said, "It's an invitation to meet; they're interested in the technology and have agreed to use our nondisclosure agreement."

Mari was quite excited; Tom was excited too, but refrained from any outward emotion; he had been on too many roller-coaster rides. Actually he was more excited that she was excited, but that was scary too. He had learned from experience not to obsess over too many "what ifs" and to just go with what was on his plate. He told Mari he needed a few days to prepare for the meeting, and could she make the phone call acting as his secretary and set the meeting in ten days. Not wanting to look too anxious, they waited several days before she made the call. Mari handled it like a pro.

She dressed up and he dressed down. Today was the big day. They would be meeting with Dr. Edmund Sun, Chief Technical Officer, Ph.D. in Applied Physics from the California

Institute of Technology and Dr. Arthur Collmeyer, Ph.D. in Electrical Engineering and president of Wetek Corporation.

They arrived at Wetek's main office in Sunnyvale, California 30 minutes before the 3:00 meeting and waited in the parking lot, going over details and the general approach. Before entering the meeting Tom made up his mind; unless Wetek's offer provided a package that significantly compensated the original investors he would turn down the offer without disclosing Paratechnology's Associative Search Array Processor technology.

It was time. Being careful not to hold hands as they walked across the parking lot, they entered the two-story glass building and introduced themselves to the receptionist. A few minutes later a formally dressed woman appeared, escorting them to a second-floor boardroom. "Would you like something to drink? Dr. Collmeyer and Dr. Sun will be with you in just a moment."

"Coffee for me."

"Tea, please."

She stepped out of the room returning a few minutes later with the drinks. "Thank you." "Oh that's great, thank you."

"Can I get you anything else?"

"Thanks, we're OK."

As she closed the large double wooden doors behind her she said, "It will be a few more minutes."

Tom and Mari spent the next five minutes dwarfed by a long meeting table. The huge mahogany slab stretched out for 30 feet against the backdrop of hardwood-paneled walls and company plaques. They talked about everything but business, mostly dreaming and joking about a possible trip to Oregon. Suddenly the door opened and a slender wiry man entered the room introducing himself, "My name's Art Collmeyer."

"Hello, this is Mari Quihuis, I'm Tom Sawyer."

"Please sit down. Dr. Sun will be joining us shortly."

Rocking back and forth, Dr. Collmeyer went over his company's background and products. Tom liked it that the CEO scientist stirred in his chair displaying an almost autistic nervous high energy. Tom liked to rock too. Mari looked over at Tom silently communicating, *Don't do it.*

Tom talked about Paratechnology's background and reviewed the meeting with Institutional Venture Partners in Menlo Park, then handed Dr. Collmeyer the nondisclosure agreement that Bob Davis' corporate attorney had prepared. Dr. Collmeyer reviewed the document and signed it.

The door opened. Dr. Sun, an intelligent-looking Oriental man, sat down next to his colleague and introduced himself. They got right to it. Tom opened a 20-page document that contained the logic diagrams and state machine architecture (engineer talk for the inner workings of a computer chip) for Paratechnology's ASAP text-search engine, and started explaining in general terms how the search engine could perform a billion string searches per second on unformatted streaming text. Dr. Sun wanted to know how it could perform 128-byte compares against a character stream coming in at 12,000,000 characters per second, in one cycle. Tom explained, "That's core technology, we will not be disclosing it at this time." He then opened the table for discussions regarding a possible deal.

Dr. Collmeyer asked, "What do you want?"

Tom knew Dr. Collmeyer knew that Paratechnology was on the rocks and the best they could do was to try to salvage the technology. Tom replied, "$250,000 plus a royalty license agreement and a consulting contract." Dr. Collmeyer began rocking profusely, "The best we can do is a dollar a chip and a consulting contract." Tom knew the market; this was not going to compensate the original investors and would marry him to Wetek for years. Closing the document on the table Tom looked over at Mari then looked back at Dr. Collmeyer, "I'm sorry, we can't accept that." Dr. Collmeyer replied, "That's the best we can do." He and Mari shook hands with Dr. Collmeyer and Dr. Sun and thanked them for their time.

They were both a little disappointed on one hand, but relieved on the other. If Tom had taken the deal, the investors would have only recouped ten cents on the dollar and the lovers would have been like two ships passing in the night. Tom told

Mari he was really more of an inventor, a project person, than a businessman. Then he told her a story:

"I remember a few years back when we were all meeting with a venture capital firm in Portland, Shaw Venture Partners. I had just spent the week before going over the technology with a panel of senior engineers from Floating Point Systems and Tektronix. They had verified that the technology was both sound and producible. It was a time of celebration. The venture firm was putting on a dinner in honor of the good news. I was the guest of honor, but I didn't know it. I thought they were just happy about the technology. We were at a very fancy restaurant. About 15 people were all sitting at a large banquet table and the food was being served. Someone next to me asked a question and I began rambling on. I wasn't particularly hungry so I continued to have the conversion with my neighbor. Five minutes went by and I looked around—no one was eating. It seemed curious…everyone was looking over at me. I thought, *What are they looking at me for?* I continued to make sketches on a napkin for another five minutes. Then I looked up again. This time Bob Davis was intensely looking over at me with a fork in his hand. I finally got it. No one's going to start eating until I pick up my fork. I picked up my fork and to my astonishment everyone started eating and talking. I had never seen anything like it. I turned red and knew that later I would be getting a reprimand from Bob about protocol. You might say these last few years have been more about education than money."

Now life had something else in store for the lovers.

On their way back, passing over the Golden Gate Bridge they restarted their conversation about spending a few weeks at the cabin on Tom's property in Oregon. He needed to come up with $3,500 to save the property from back taxes and maybe between the two of them they could figure out something. Tom went on, "I have to meet with the investors in Portland to close down the company, and then we could go to the cabin and spend a few days. Would you go with me?" With a big smile on her face she replied, "I'll have to make arrangements with Noni and Didi to watch the boys, but YES." They moved from an almost solemn mood to joy and excitement. They verbally prepared their newfound adventure all the way home—it was Oregon or bust.

They turned into the tree-lined driveway and stopped in front of the water tower, climbed the stairs, took off their clothes and cuddled up in a sleeping bag on the floor. This was the end of an era for Tom and the beginning of something new.

A week later, he made one more try in Silicon Valley, meeting with Vinod Khosla, co-founder of Sun Microsystems at his home in the vineyards, and discussed the technology in front of Vinod's Egyptian-painted garage door. Then that afternoon he met with Nolan Bushnell, founder of Atari at Silicon Graphics, all without success. The ASAP technology applied to a narrow market and that was that. With hindsight, if it had been ten years later, with the advent of the Internet, ASAP would have been a home run.

Exhausted, disappointed and relieved, he wasn't looking forward to the mounds of paperwork and explanations awaiting him in Portland.

A few nights passed. Tom woke up holding his chest. He had had an intense dream, in Technicolor and very real: people were coming after him to take away whatever he had. He made a getaway on a bicycle down a narrow path that ended at a restaurant in the jungle. He was hungry and walked in. No one was in the diner except a man sitting at a corner table. Tom sat down and looked at the menu. It was in a language he didn't understand. Walking over to the man in the corner he asked for help. The man looked up—it was Yogananda, Tom's guru. The master had three eyes; one large one in the center of his forehead. Tom gazed into the third eye of his master and felt motion, a pulling in. He was sucked through a tunnel-like corridor into deep space. Galaxies and solar systems lit up the black sky. He had no body, only awareness of his surroundings. Without words, Yogananda asked, *Are you ready to come now?* Tom replied, *Not yet.* He felt the motion reverse, suddenly waking up in the restaurant. The master said, "Come with me." They walked outside through a side door leading to a terrace surrounded by flowers and green plants. Yogananda pointed to a table. It contained some kind of electrical equipment, something to do with time. He didn't understand what it was, but was fascinated by it.

The master said, "You work on this for a while."

7

"In wildness is the preservation of the world."

Henry David Thoreau

The Hill

Pulling the chopsticks away from her mouth, Mari dips into a blue-and-white ceramic bowl for another morsel of rice. Tom watches her lips open and close with each bite. All of his consciousness has lodged itself in one of the creases in her bottom lip; there he awaits another nibble, another wave of visual ecstasy. She begins speaking; he can only hear faint murmurings until suddenly being slammed back into his brain for word processing, "Tom, Tom, where did you go? I was saying, do you think we should spend the night here?" Background sounds of dishes clanging and conversation flood in, "Oh, yes."

They've been on the road for nearly five hours. Christmas had come and gone; it's January 1, 1988 at the Hi Lo Chinese restaurant in Weed, California. They're on their way to Oregon.

When Mari first walked in, she spotted a red-and-white sign above the cash register, "Rooms for rent upstairs." The wind was blowing, there was snow on the ground, and it was starting to get dark and cold outside. Rather than try for Bend tonight and miss the view along Highway 97, they decided to spend the night in a cheap hotel. It sounded sleazy. Contemplating a fantasy night, they paid the restaurant bill and rented a room. Pausing for a second to watch her skillfully walk up the stairs, he turned and went back to the car.

He brought the suitcase to the room on the left, at the top of the stairs, and knocked on the door. Noticing the wainscoting on the walls and the creaking floorboards, he concluded the place must have been there since the late 1800s. Mari opened the door. He placed the suitcase on the bed, snapped open the latches and lifted the lid. They were going to meet with investors in Portland so they had packed clothes for all occasions. By now they knew each other so well it was difficult to surprise the other. Mari said, "You be the patron, I'll be the prostitute." Tom replied, "This is going to be fun. I think we need a bottle of cheap bourbon."

"Yeah, I saw a liquor store across the street."

"OK, I'll be right back."

Ten minutes later he returned brandishing a pint of Old Harper wrapped in a brown paper bag. Mari was sitting on the bed in high heels, a short skirt and see-through blouse. He folded the bag downward; twisting the cap off, he took a swig and handed it to her. She tilted her head back, swallowed twice, and placed the bottle on the dresser next to the bed. He looked at her and she looked back at him. Several seconds passed as they prepared for the lust fest. Peering into one another's eyes, they started laughing until they climaxed into a belly roar. What was between them was too deep; the matching *samskaras* (behavior patterns from past lives) had released themselves in a burst of absurd humor. Tom walked over to the dresser, put the cap back on the bottle and gently knelt at her feet. Respectfully he removed her high heels and looked up. He didn't see a prostitute, he saw a Goddess. They didn't even bother to take off their clothes. Flipping the blankets back they cuddled in each other's arms and fell asleep.

The next morning they gassed up the Honda and headed north toward Oregon, passing through a spent logging district on the northeast side of Mount Shasta. The view was spectacular. Mari had come this way many times before, on her way to Rajneeshpuram. She loved the chaparral and jackrabbits and he loved the way she said, "chaparral." In fact, he would argue with her, saying, "Are you sure it's chaparral?" just to hear her say it again. There was something about the way she pronounced her words that carried him away.

After traveling 20 miles of high desert they pulled off at Mount Hebron, taking in the view of the northeast side of Mount Shasta rising up from the sprawling desert floor.

Diverse beauty trimmed the road all the way to Dorris, a rual township spattered with jack pine and tumbleweed. Cowboys and used-car salesmen lined the counter at the truck stop café where the lovers gulped down late morning coffee. Just outside Dorris they followed the railroad tracks across a desolate desert passage to the California/Oregon border into Klamath and continued north thru Algoma, Beaver Marsh, Crescent (for breakfast), through the Deschutes National Forest, La Pine and on into Bend where they picked up supplies for the last leg across the high desert.

Tom wanted to take his sweetie to lunch in Sisters. They headed for Hungry Jack's café at the end of the little settlement on Highway 20. As they walked in, the smell of coffee and cigars filled the air. They sat at a booth by the window with the sun in their faces. Tom ordered chicken-fried steak and eggs and Mari her usual, two eggs scrambled and a bowl of oatmeal. Tom profusely shook salt onto his eggs while Mari warned him of the consequences. "My God, Tom, you can see it sparkling in the sun. That's enough." He squinted and began talking about Marcel Vogel and crystals.

A gray-haired man at the counter overheard the conversation and swiveled on his stool, facing them. He wore a large polished agate cowboy buckle on his belt and a Stetson hat with a blue feather stuck in the band. Lifting his head and tipping his hat, he said, "There's a rock shop outside of Redmond that's got one of the biggest quartz crystals I ever seen." After exchanging snake oil and a few tall tales, the old gentleman gave them directions. Tom slopped down the rest of the chitlin' gravy and they drove out Highway 126 in search of the mystery rock shop. A few miles out, huge lava beds stretched off into the distance.

After circling back roads for many miles they finally found the rock shop, out by itself on a long stretch of desert. Inside were lots of glass counters with every kind of gemstone known to man, including petrified dinosaur bones. Behind the counter was a blond girl in her 20s who walked out from the back room looking like she hadn't seen a human for years. She pulled the hair from in front of her face and murmured to herself, "Unbelievable." Raising her voice to an audible level she asked, "You-all need something?" The lovers explained about the old man at Hungry Jack's and his story about the giant crystal. "Oh," she replied and pointed to a tall glass case. The lovers turned around and there it was, the largest single-ended quartz crystal they'd ever seen, standing five feet tall and a foot across. They walked over and stood near the glass. Mari said, "Do you feel anything?" Tom replied, "No, but I wish I could touch it." Tom asked the girl if she could open the case. She replied, "You got $10,000.00?" Tom said, "No." She tilted her head to one side and lifted her shoulders back, "Can't do it." They thanked the girl and continued looking.

The girl stood behind a wooden counter with beady eyes, watching as Mari meandered from one display case to another. Tom thought for sure the girl possessed a shotgun behind the counter because she kept looking down. Suddenly Mari stopped and gazed in at a petrified armadillo-bone necklace garlanded with shark's teeth, then stirred on. While she wandered, Tom had stationed himself in front of a display of Swarovski crystals interspersed with gold nuggets, mint-colored sapphires and unstrung pearls. Mari was curious what had captured him and walked over. On her way an exhibit of antique silver Celtic jewelry ensnared her. Her eyes opened wide as she stared in at crosses, rings and bracelets. She seemed to disappear for the moment in some kind of ancient flashback, then continued to where Tom was standing. Slipping her arm underneath his, she whispered, "We should probably go."

They headed east on Highway 126 and picked up 97 North again for Redmond. Redmond was a redneck town in every sense of the word. The only other town in Oregon more redneck than Redmond was Prineville in Crook County (guns, saddles, rodeo pants, aluminum cans and puckerbrush—home of the Mounted Shooter). Tom was part cowboy and used to shoot a 30-30 Winchester off the back of his trusted horse Babe, so passing through the town made him retell hunting stories hoping they might impress her. Of course it seemed to have the opposite effect; she didn't like the idea of killing anything.

After Redmond they continued on to Madras, stopping for gas where two old men greeted them with gleaming eyes, "Just passing through?" Mari replied, "We're on our way to our cabin in Oregon." Oh, Tom loved that "our cabin" part. He thought she said that just for him. It wasn't like her to talk about things like that. Normally she would have said something like, 'Yes, can we use your bathroom?" Those two old gentlemen were like sages in cowboy clothes. They cleaned the windows, filled the tank, checked the oil and gave the lovers a country smile (a blessing). You could look at these old boys and tell they had crossed many a sea in severe weather and were still able to find land with open hearts.

They passed through Willowdale up Junction 197 to Maupin, Tygh Valley and on into Dufur. The area around Dufur showed ancient seismic geology. It looked like someone had picked up a blanket and shaken it—deep canyons and fissure faults pushed straight up out of the wrinkled valley floor. Mari stopped to pick sage for a ceremony she planned to hold when they arrived at the cabin.

At Dufur, they wound up the hill by Indian Rodeo Coral, pulling the last grade into The Dalles. Stopping for supplies at Fred Meyers, they packed Mari's little Honda with enough food for five days and continued into Mosier, population 239. Passing the post office, gas station, little school and fire department, they drove several miles on a dirt road toward Mosier Creek and stopped in front of Betsy's place near the river.

Tom wanted Mari to meet Betsy, but she wasn't home. Mari looked around. An old faded white picket fence, separating the road from the property, connected to a partially-fallen-down shed that served as a barn for goats. An unpainted shack with a stone chimney, a covered front porch and empty flowerpots lining the walkway sat back 30 feet from the road. On the front porch was a large black-and-gray cat in a rocking chair. Chickens, ducks and geese roamed the yard scratching and picking their way through the snow in search of grass and bugs. Tom began to tell Mari about the first time he met Betsy:

"It was the winter of 1975. We had just finished the cabin and were moving in from the tent. Getting low on supplies, I decided to follow the pass down from Smith Ridge seven miles to Mosier Creek, hoping to make the 14 miles to town before dark. I'd never gone that way before. After making my way down the pass, I crossed the bridge at Tool Shed (a big old tool shed the Highway Dept. stored snowplow equipment in—also known as the last point of 'civilization') and found Mosier Creek Road. There was eight inches of snow on the ground. After walking several miles, I spotted smoke from a chimney a quarter mile away. I approached the house hoping to get my bearings and maybe sit a spell before going on.

"As I got closer I could see an old gray-haired lady by the front porch with an axe in her hand. Her dog growled and she looked up. Looking over at me, she had a goose by the neck in one hand and the axe in the other, 'What chu do'in out here?' She spoke with a Louisiana Bayou accent. I told her I was coming down out of the hills for food and was wondering how far it was into town. She said, 'Ain't chu cold?' I told her it would be nice to warm up by the fire if she didn't mind. Nodding, she went back to what she was doing. She slipped a leather noose attached to a nail around the goose's head, stretched its neck over the oak stump chopping block and swung the axe. She stood up. Turning to look at me, with the axe in her right hand and a headless, blood-squirting, wing-flapping goose in the other, she said, 'Cum on in.'

"As I approached the gate her dog growled. I asked if the dog would bite. She replied again, 'Cum on in.' *What the hell*, I opened the gate and walked along the stone pathway towards the porch. As I approached she said, 'My nam iz Bezzy.' I told her my name and said, 'I'd shake your hand, but it looks like you got a handful.'

'Yu cum set bi da fire and worm up. I boil sum waer. Yu halp mi pluck dis bird.'

'Yes, ma'am.'

'Wel, cum on in.'

"I followed her into the front room and stood by a potbelly stove next to the fireplace. The stove was jimmy-rigged to the chimney with baling wire and rusted stovepipe. She continued into the kitchen. Throwing the goose in the sink, she came back out with the axe still in her right hand and yelled at the dog. Then went back in mumbling to herself. I looked around. Beside me was a tattered couch with an Indian blanket over it and a few dime-store pictures on the wall next to the door. Smoke-stained white curtains covered the fogged pane-glass window. Under the window sat a rough-cut wood round table with books, candles and upturned spectacles. I was beginning to wonder what I had gotten myself into. This time she came out with a big pot full of water in both hands, setting it on the potbelly stove. I felt more comfortable seeing she had laid down the axe.

"She asked me to sit down on the couch. While we were waiting for the water to boil she began telling me stories about when she was a little girl. She was born in 1899 and had lived in the swamps in Louisiana. When she was 12 years old her mother died and afterwards her stepfather starved and beat her, so she ran away and joined the sideshow of the Barnum and Bailey Circus in 1912. She was 13 years old but looked much older, yet she was so tiny she could fit in a suitcase. And that was her act; she worked with the fat lady and the tattooed man as the smallest person alive. They would bring her out in a small suitcase and open it up, and she would step out to everyone's amazement.

"She did this as long as she could, till around 16. Then she met a guy, a 'fella' as she called him, and hopped a train to California where she was raped and almost beaten to death by train guards near Los Angeles. The guy left her. She traveled around doing odd jobs, working the orchards into her 30s. In her 40s, she was able to get work as a riveter in the shipyards at Long Beach and finally worked her way into a secretarial job where she met a man. They were married in 1940; he died ten years later and she took all her savings and moved to Portland, Oregon where she worked as a secretary in a lumber mill. When she was 61 years old she purchased a small tract of land along Mosier Creek and has been here ever since.

"By now the pot was boiling and ready for the goose. She asked if I would get the goose from the sink and put it in the pot. I could tell she was getting tired. I told her the story about building the log cabin up on Smith Ridge as we plucked that goose in a gunnysack out on her front porch. We've been friends ever since. She was a true survivor, a pioneer. In later years, I would come and help her put up firewood for the winter. When she was in her 80s, in 1982, I brought Bob Davis to meet her. He was heavy into circus history at the time and wanted to make a permanent record of her life during the time she was with the circus. She's got to be almost 90 now. I'm not sure how she gets around, but she does."

It was starting to get late and cold and George, Tom's mountain-man buddy, would be wondering where they were. Not wanting to wait any longer, they climbed back into the car and were on the road again. They caught the switchback to George and Maggie's place, pulling the last grade at Wilson Road through the snow. The climb was getting steeper. The front of the Honda began slipping back and forth. Mari reached forward to the dashboard as they slid to the right, slamming into a shallow snow-covered ditch alongside the road. Tom pressed his foot on the gas, the front wheels spun; they were stuck. He switched off the engine.

Stepping out into the crisp mountain air, the smell of ponderosa pine reminded him of the place he used to call home. They took a small backpack with emergency supplies and amiably walked the last half-mile to the Wilson estate. George and Maggie had been caretaking the homestead estate ever since they moved down from Shelton Ridge in 1985. When the lovers arrived at the entrance to the 1,500-acre property, there it was, the Christmas-card panorama of a two-story log cabin with covered front porch and stone steps. Circuit Court Judge Wilson had built it there in 1920 overlooking the Mosier River Valley.

Steeping high through the snow, they moved up the driveway. The dogs started barking and George stepped out onto the front porch brandishing a 50-caliber Hawken. Tom began waving and yelled, "Hey you old mountain man." George leaned the rifle against the window and shouted, "Maggie, Tom and Mari are here." George was halfway down the drive when Maggie and the kids caught up. They all ran toward each other and embraced, walking arm in arm toward the house.

George went on, "We weren't sure you guys were makin' it in tonight."

Tom replied, "We spent a little extra time in Sisters."

"Got a surprise brewing in the back. Where's your car?"

"Stuck about a half-mile back."

"I'll get my rig. Stuck bad?"

"Not bad."

"Got a bear few months back. Maggie made sausage. You can have some for breakfast. You're spendin' the night?"

"If it's OK. I'd hate to go up that pass at night with Mari."

"Don't think of it, got a fire goin' out back for a sweat."

"Thanks brother, it's been a long run."

"Maggie'll make a place by the fireplace, you guys can bed down there."

Mari, Maggie and the kids went inside and warmed by the fire. The front room was filled with Indian artifacts George had collected throughout the years. George Shepard is the only white man allowed at a Klickitat burial. These Columbia River Indians honored him years ago for his bravery, knowledge, and lore of the woods. His easel rested on the hardwood floor next to the window. The knotty pine walls were covered with animal skins.

In 1974, after returning from his adventures at sea in Alaska; Auk Bay, Wrangell, and Kodiak, he and Maggie built a log cabin 25 miles out on Shelton Ridge and lived there in the wilderness until 1985. Their nearest neighbor was Tom and his family, four miles away on Smith Ridge. All their children, Laura, Jesse, and Kelly were born in that cabin out on Shelton Ridge. George would scrimshaw and hunt in the winter, selling his wares in the spring for another year's grubstake. He's an exceptional wildlands artist and storyteller and Maggie, she can hunt and fish and skin a bear with the best of them.

Mari and Maggie went into the kitchen and made tea while George and Tom scrambled for George's four-wheel-drive Chevy pickup, shooting the breeze all the way to the Honda. After hooking up a logging chain to the car, Tom started the motor and George dragged it all the way up the hill. They removed the backpacks and supplies from the car, setting them inside the parlor. Mari and Maggie had taken to each other right off. Tea was ready. They all sat around the stone fireplace and drank tea while George showed off his latest work and told stories about how he had come to find each piece of ivory; long stories about his Alaskan adventures, and swappings from an annual Oregon mountain man rendezvous.

After tea, George took them to the basement to show off the bear hide.

"Maggie skinned him. We saved all the sinew and gut for riggin' and such. Here's the claws."

Maggie removed a newspaper covering, exposing the skin side of the hide. George had made a tanning paste from oak balls, alder ash, urine and salt. Several more weeks of tending would produce a fine hide.

Smiling, George said, "Jesse's been taking care of the fire, the rocks should be just about ready." In Indian tradition the men would go in first, followed by the women. To Tom and Mari, first, last, it didn't matter. Tom and George removed their clothes on the back porch and walked barefoot through the snow to the top of a small rise, each carrying a bucket of water. Jesse was placing hot stones in the sweat lodge with a shovel. The floor of the lodge was covered with tender fir boughs, eucalyptus and sage. The domed walls and ceiling were made from vine maple spars, roofed with canvas and horse blankets. Near the cloth flap-over door, dug into the ground, was a small pit filled with red-hot river stones. George pointed out that you never use wet stones—they must be dry before placing them in the fire, because if they're wet inside, steam will build up and they'll explode.

Tom, George, and Jesse went inside and closed the flap. They sat cross-legged on the floor. It was pitch dark inside. George reached over and slowly dipped a wooden cup into the bucket near the door, splashing water onto the stones. Steam pushed upward in a sudden hiss filling the lodge with moist heat. Then again…and again. It became so hot that the metal medallion Tom wore around his neck began to burn his skin. Even breathing slowly, burned the inside of his nose. George began chanting an Indian prayer and Tom and Jesse joined in. A few minutes later Mari and Maggie entered and sat near the door. They each took turns telling an inner story followed by a prayer. Periodically George would splash more water on the stones. Then they all sat in silence for 20 minutes.

Sometime after the silence, Mari and Maggie left the lodge to prepare for the men. George increased the heat to unbearable, creating a claustrophobic sense that one might not make it out alive. This toaster was used to make peace with fear. Only pride and determination, or bravery, or becoming one with it could get an initiate through the trial.

In true Klickitat tradition, as the men came out one at a time from the lodge, the women poured a bucket of ice water over the top of their heads. The men were not to scream or yell until control re-entered their bodies. Then standing naked in the snow, gazing at the stars, they screamed loud from the stomach, creating an echo in the forest. The experience was invigorating, life-affirming.

After the sweat they all went inside and settled down for the evening. Kelly and Laura had prepared an evening tea and shared their schoolwork and read poems they had written. Mari and Tom curled up in a sleeping bag next to the fire. In true George Shepard tradition, he had to tell one more story before retiring for the evening. Then Tom got up and put a couple of all-nighters in the fireplace. Jumping back in, he pressed his face against the back of Mari's hair, spooning her body; they slipped into slumber.

The next morning everyone was up early except Tom and Mari, still cuddled up in front of the fireplace. Mari could hear Maggie cooking in the kitchen and thought she'd better get up and help her. Tom didn't want Mari to go; it was just too comfortable and anyway the sun hadn't even come up yet. With the kids running around, Mari slipped her clothes on inside the sleeping bag and got up. A few minutes later she returned with a cup of coffee then went back to the kitchen. A couple of sips of cowboy coffee and Tom was ready to go. Mari yelled, "Breakfast is ready." Tom got up. Pulling up the Levis he hadn't changed for three weeks he walked barefoot to the kitchen. Hotcakes, eggs from the chicken coop and bear sausage—what a breakfast. Tom knew that things were a little tight for George and Maggie and offered to help out with supplies, but they wouldn't hear of it.

Maggie said that the bridge was washed out at Tool Shed and they'd have to cross the river on foot. After breakfast they prepared their supplies for the trek and said goodbye. George took the kids to school. Maggie took Tom and Mari eight miles to the end of the road at Tool Shed and dropped them off.

Maggie asked, "When are you coming back down?"

"Six days."

"I'll be here at Tool Shed waiting for you."

"What time?"

"I'll know when you're coming. Stay dry."

"Thanks, Maggie."

They each hugged Maggie goodbye and watched her drive away into the distance. They walked a quarter mile through the snow past Tool Shed and moved toward the river. Sure enough, the log footbridge was washed out. They would have to cross the river by rope. The wind was blowing. It was 20° outside. The windchill factor was 0°. They were about to hike seven miles up a pass to the ridge in a foot of snow. Tom kept telling Mari to be careful not to fall in the water because hypothermia could set in before reaching the cabin and it was over eight miles back to the nearest shelter.

Tom took off his gloves and fastened a rock to one end of 50 feet of coiled rope, then tossed it 30 feet across the river to the other side. It wrapped itself around the branch of a maple tree about three feet up the trunk. He tied his end to an alder tree and stretched the rope tight using a trucker's knot. Mari was to cross first. She took off her 60-pound backpack and set it on the ground. Rigging up a shoulder harness, Tom connected a 50-foot safety-line to her and held the other end in case she fell into the water. The river was running pretty fast—it would be bad if she fell.

Connecting her loop-line, she went hand over hand, reaching the other side without incident. Touching down on the ground, she smiled and yelled, "Now what?" Tom told her to take off the safety rope, tie one end to a tree and then throw the rope back across the river. It didn't quite make it and was carried downstream. She pulled the rope back in, arranging it in a two-foot coil and threw it again. Tom grabbed it before the current could sweep it away. Using small loops of rope he fashioned a quasi-bosun's chair for each backpack, connecting them to the taut rope. Then he connected the safety rope to the loops on the packs and Mari pulled them across the river.

Now it was Tom's turn. Once again she threw the safety rope across. Tom connected up and went hand-over-hand to the other side. Well, almost to the other side. In an endeavor to show off his mountain skills, he lowered himself onto a rock near the edge of the swift-moving water and attempted to boulder-hop the rest of the way. The only problem was, his foot slipped forward on a mossy rock sending him into the river knee deep. It was exactly what he had warned Mari not to do. He found it rather embarrassing, but Mari liked it—she laughed and laughed. Now he was wet to his knees in 0° weather—not good. He could get frostbite, or even worse, lose a toe before reaching the cabin.

Splashing out of the freezing water and rolling up his pant legs, he removed his boots, socks, and pants and stood on an old stump. He then removed dry pants, long johns, socks and newspaper from his pack. He dried the inside of his boots as best he could with a rag before the water froze them stiff, and lined them with newspaper. His pride had been ruffled, but no harm was done. They were now ready to start the seven-mile climb to the top of Smith Ridge.

Confident that no one would bother it, they left the taut main rope at the river crossing for the return trip. They continued up the pass to an old homestead at Little Fawn Spring.

All that's left of the cabin built at the turn of the century is the stone chimney; it burnt down in 1936. Here they crossed a small tributary by boulder-hopping and continue the climb. When they arrived at Bobcat Creek they removed their backpacks and rested before trekking the last leg. Tom remembered when he almost froze to death here and told Mari the story:

"It was in the winter of 1975, February, if my memory serves me right. I had gone down for supplies and was on my way back. It was getting dark. I was almost to Bobcat when a blizzard came up. I could hardly see to walk. I crawled to a snow bank and started digging, packing the snow around me, making a snow cave in the bank, and waited for the blizzard to let up. It didn't let up. I knew I was in trouble unless I could get more packed snow around me. After some work I was able to fashion a spacious cave with enough room to move one foot in either direction. I poked a hole in the ceiling for a vent and one out the side, and started a small fire made from pitch pine that I always carried in my pack. I continued to eat peanut butter and drink, melting snow in a tin cup, to keep up my body heat. I ran out of pitch pine sometime in the middle of the night, and kept slapping myself to keep awake. Falling asleep in the cold is a death sentence.

"By early morning the weather had changed enough for me to begin walking again. When I reached the cabin I could no longer feel my hands or feet. My lips, nose and ears burned. I felt delirious. As my hands and feet thawed by the potbelly stove, the pain was so excruciating I could hardly stand it. Although I still have all my toes and fingers, it gave me a renewed respect for nature that I remember to this day."

After Tom's story they rested a little longer, drank hot tea from a thermos and continued a mile to the top of the hill, passing through an ancient ponderosa pine forest on the west end of the property. They had reached The Hill. Continuing to move up the pass they entered a dense forest of old pines, some seven feet across and 150 feet high. Once they reached the top at Smith Ridge they cut across the southwest meadow near the Pagoda, the onetime home and moonshine still of biochemist

Greg Lock, an old buddy of Tom's from the '60s. As they approached the Pagoda, Mari could see a large stained-glass window fashioned in the form of a cross with a heart in the center, shining from the second story of the handmade cement structure. "Tom, what is this?"

"It's the Pagoda. It was built back in the '70s by an old buddy who lived here for a while. Years later I converted it into a little meditation shrine."

"There's no door!"

"Anyone that finds this spot is welcome to come in and pray. When I was a little boy I used to dream of traveling to India. Climbing high into the Kashmir Valley, I found a shrine in the middle of nowhere, a holy place. I would pretend to meditate at this imaginary shrine."

"Do you think this place is more sacred than other places?"

"For me, yes—for someone else, I don't know."

They went inside and lit a candle on the small stone altar facing the stained-glass window. They thanked the gods of the forest and the God of All for their love and for the journey they had just experienced. Holding hands they walked from the Pagoda under ice-covered oaks and jack pines down a deer trail leading to "Tom Sawyer's" cabin. A few minutes later, there it was, a labor of love, seven logs high, sitting on a knoll covered with a blanket of snow. Each log was 10 to 14 inches in diameter, hand-fitted with foot-adz and drawknife. The wood had begun to crack along the chink lines after 13 winters. Peering through a large pane-glass window in the south face of the cabin, Mari saw a table with three oil lamps; hippie curtains were pulled back on either side with leather ties.

She moved right and stood on her tiptoes peeking in a smaller window. There to her amazement was a cast-iron wood-fired cooking stove and hand-cut wooden counter. To the left of her view, in the center, was the potbelly stove that Tom had spoken so much about. Standing in the snow, they looked over at one another. She looked so happy and Tom was dreaming again, dreaming he would live here with her forever. A part of him knew that wouldn't happen for some time, at least until her children were raised.

Tom walked around to the side of the cabin and stopped.
Mari followed. The wind had stilled to a silent calm and only
the sound of an occasional branch breaking from the weight of
ice echoed from the canyon below. Lifting his arm, he pointed
to the northeast. As far as her eyes could see— only mountain
ranges melting away into the distance. To the north was Mount
Adams in all her glory. To the south was Mount Hood with
cloud streams cascading from her top to the east. Nature's canvas
couldn't have provided a more beautiful day for Tom to show
his lady this wild and wonderful land.

They walked around to the front of the cabin. Chainsawed
steps led up to the front porch. She removed her backpack,
setting it on the porch with a sigh. Turning her head toward a
primitive handmade door, she noticed two large deer antlers
hanging from either side of the entrance.

"Did you kill the deer?"

"No. When my kids Tiffany and Larry were young and we
were all living out here they found them on the ground."

"Someone else killed the deer?"

"No, these are mule deer; every year they shed their antlers
around December and then start growing them again in the
spring."

"I always thought deer had their horns for life."

"No, they shed them every year. When we lived up here, I
did hunt to provide food for my family, but only if we really
needed it. As funny as it sounds, I always made peace with the
animal and said a prayer for its soul before the kill. We felt
thankful that nature provided for us. Some winters were harder
than others."

"You don't have a refrigerator, how did you keep it from
spoiling?"

"Sometimes we'd make a salt brine and smoke it and make
jerky, or in the late fall or early winter after the freeze we'd
hang it in a tree in a gunny sack and saw off what was needed
for the day."

"I've been a vegetarian for years and don't believe in killing
animals."

"Yes."

Turning her head back around she spotted the pond. A hundred yards from the front porch was a frozen two-acre pond. The top of the snow-covered earth-fill dam cut the skyline.

"Is that a pond?"

"Yes."

"Can we go play on it?"

"Maybe. We'll have to get a hammer and test it later. We should probably get a fire going and warm up the cabin before we cool down too much."

Tom undid the lock. He placed his left hand around a carved wooden-pegged handle. Pulling with his right hand on the engraved leg bone dangling from a piece of sinew that disappeared into a small hole in the front door, he pushed open the door.

Inside, Mari looked around while Tom got a fire going in the potbelly. One large room of pleasant proportions, 24 by 20 feet, partially divided by a kitchen counter cut from one large slab of pine, filled her eyes. The wooden floor was made of 2x6 tongue and groove with tin can lids plugging the knotholes; Tom's effort to keep field mice out. On the floor to the right of the counter was a large oval mouse-chewed hand-braided rag rug that extended from the large pane-glass window in the rear of the cabin to the front door. The oiled log walls were filled in with cement and straw along the chink lines. All types of tools, ropes and chains from the 19th century adorned the wall. The only door was handmade from various sizes of carved lumber. Its latch had a bone counterweight connected to a lever with a sinew string—an idea from Buffalo Dave.

The ceiling was unpainted 2x6 rafters with a large center beam hand-hewed from a log, with large wooden pegs in either end. Dated and signed hand-sketches were grouped near the window beyond a wooden foldout table. The lighting consisted of two tall Aladdin lamps, a propane "hisser" and several large kerosene lamps.

Mari walked to the kitchen and stood in front of the blue porcelain wood-cooking stove. To her right was a counter with jars of grains and spices placed along a log beam. A Coleman stove sat just to the right, next to three 15-gallon propane bottles. To the left were pots and pans hanging from nails driven in the log wall. Behind her was a ladder that led to a sleeping loft. The air was stale and cold and held a slight mouse-urine-and-kerosene fragrance that only Tom could appreciate.

On the east wall all types of survival and medical supplies were stashed in small slide-out drawers that went from floor to ceiling. On the west wall was a large bookcase with hundreds of books. Above it, hung by two heavy chains, was a six-foot stained-glass window encased in a frame made from hand-carved 4x4s. Below, sitting on the top log, was a seven-foot bucksaw with wooden handles. Two collapsible handmade chairs made of deer hide and sinew lean against a large rusted milk jug near the door. To the left of the door were jackets and caps hung on nails above a large wooden box containing six days of firewood.

After the room began to warm Tom took off his boots and removed the newspaper stuffing. Tying the bootlaces together, he flung them over the log beam near the potbelly and waited for them to dry. The lovers lay on the floor next to the iron stove wrapped in an Indian blanket, and drifted off to some remote place in time.

Awakened by the sound of coyotes howling, they both sat up on their elbows and listened. First it came from the east near the Worm People and then from the west near Lookout Point.

Tom said, "Sounds like it's coming from the Worm People."

"What in the heck are the Worm People?"

"Oh, they were some folks that tried to live up on the ridge back in the late 1970s. She was a great large lady who could barely walk and he was a tall thin man who packed a Bible and a gun. He carried a Colt 38 Special strapped to his side and would preach fire and brimstone to anyone he saw."

"Why do you call them Worm People?"

"They tried raising worms one year, and somehow the name stuck. They stored a bunch of tires over on their place. The guy tried to convince me that aliens came periodically to use them for fuel for their flying saucers, but I think he had a little business making the rounds at gas stations in Portland. We could walk over and check the place out if you want?"

"No thanks."

"They're not there anymore, they haven't been up for years."

"That's OK. Can we go walk out on the pond?"

"Well, let's go test it."

Putting his newly warmed boots back on, Tom walked to the wall next to the door and removed a hammer from a tool belt while Mari put on her jacket. They walked out onto the porch, glancing at the thermometer on the way. It read 12°. Tom grabbed two six-foot long 2x6 boards from under the cabin and they walked a 100 yards to the pond's edge. He laid the boards next to the waterline and began tapping the ice with the hammer. It seemed OK at the edge. Then he slid the boards out further. Kneeling, one knee on each board, he continued tapping the ice repeatedly until he reached the center of the two-acre pond. He yelled back to Mari, "It looks OK—about eight inches thick."

They played for hours, running and sliding and playing ketch-me-if-you-can. She loved it. Tom asked her if she ever ice-fished. She said she hadn't, but had heard of it. He went on, explaining everything about ice fishing. He had stocked the pond years ago with bass, transporting them up in 55-gallon drums from Fish and Game in Portland. He told her how cutting ice blocks from the pond with a bucksaw in late winter and storing them underground in sawdust provided ice during the summer. She was fascinated. She started talking about how our forefathers must have lived, saying that if American society ever lost "the grid," most would not know how to make it.

It was beginning to get dark and clouds had moved in. They went back inside to make something to eat and found all the water stored in the cabin frozen solid. With axe in hand, Tom went to the pond and chopped a hole in the ice. Filling two five-gallon buckets with water, he carried them back to their little hideaway. He loved to carry water. For him there was something spiritual about it. Thoroughly boiling the water, Mari made macaroni and cheese and they ate dinner that night by oil lamp. After dinner she made tea in an old steel pot on the potbelly and told Tom stories about when she was a little girl.

The massive lid of the cast-iron potbelly stove creaked with a squeal as Tom put another all-nighter on the fire.

He said, "Just think of it, without the warmth from this stove, we would freeze to death this night."

Mari replied, "Out here in the wild, nature seems so unforgiving yet so generous."

"That's so true. If you understand her, respect her, feel her and not take more than you need, she can be very kind and wondrous. If you underestimate her and disrespect her, she can be deadly unforgiving, but that's true of all things that are trying to survive."

It was beginning to happen and Tom knew what it was—he had experienced it many times before. He and Mari were feeling the city and all its trappings peel away. The sounds of animals became more important than television—an almost timeless space had surrounded them.

They slept soundly that night. The next morning after breakfast, they walked to Lookout Point on the northwest corner of the property and looked out across the Mosier River Valley, across the Columbia River into Washington, to the wilderness lands of Mount Adams. The panorama was white with snow-covered pines and firs that went on for a 100 miles. It was an ancient feeling. Below, Mari could see the ridge that separated what Tom called the Kashmir Valley from the pass they had climbed the day before.

Tom began talking about yesterday's journey and pointed out different signs in the forest that tell a mountain man how to survive. The wind on the point was cold; he could hardly get the words out. He turned to Mari and held her hand. Standing there in the splendor like a shy schoolboy he said, "Will you marry me?" She said, "Yes." The icicles hanging from his mustache pressed up against her lips. They turned and looked out over the valley in silence, pondering the future they had just created in that moment. He could feel her thinking, *There's more,* and then she came out with it, "We have to be engaged for six months and you must ask my father." He smiled at the authority in her voice. He was overjoyed. Squeezing her hand, they smiled at each other and kissed again. With in minutes the melted mustache water and saliva froze against their faces.

As they walked back toward the cabin, they passed through what used to be the old garden site. Mari stopped and said, "What was here?"

"Greg Lock and I, with the help of our wives and children and two horses cleared an acre of ground for a garden, 13 years ago. This is all that's left of the log-post deer fence."

"What did you grow?"

"Corn, squash, beans, okra, carrots, celery, eggplant, all kinds of stuff."

"How did you water?"

"We made a siphon over the dam and piped it from the pond. We had such great dreams; we were going to live like it was 1850 forever!"

"What happened?"

"I'm not sure, I think we ran out of projects. Without a project, a purpose, something to get you out of bed in the morning, people go batty. My buddy made a still, after that things went downhill, but it was more than that. It was the age-old problem of people working together for the common good of all and the winters were not exactly easy."

"Do you regret it?"

"Not a minute of it. This land is a place of extremes. You take the 'goods' with the 'bads' and having had that experience… It was a magnificent time; it was bold, wild, dangerous, free, and self-fulfilling. It was the most free I'd ever felt in all my life. But then there's that ancient lesson, 'Freedom's not free.' You have to be willing to work at it."

"How did you get the horses to plow?"

"I found an old man who had a barn full of old horse-drawn equipment; plow, disk and rake, I bought the lot. He told me about an old-timer named Frank who had several sets of harness, singletrees, doubletrees and such. I bought that too. He even threw in a Singer leather-sewing machine from 1859 that his mother had brought to Oregon by covered wagon. It's the one in the cabin by the table. Then old Johnny Kinky sold me an 1869 Studebaker farm wagon that I trained the horses on. Anyway, we used those horses to pull the logs and plow and disk the garden. I can hardly think about it without smiling— the joy of it all. No, I wouldn't trade a moment."

Tom began to shiver. It was too cold to talk. They walked on, leaving the old memories behind and climbed the back side of the dam to the pond. They walked along the top of the dam to a path near the spillway, winding through the oaks to the cabin. Mari noticed the "Welcome" sign made from green painted sheet metal hanging from one of the uprights holding up the porch, and the old rusted-red railroad lamps by the front door. She walked up the first step and paused turning her head from side to side. As she continued to climb, he watched from behind her every nuance—the way the wind caught her hair, the flex of her muscles through her jeans and the sway of her Santa Rosa Roses!

Inside, he put another log in the potbelly and Mari walked around like she wasn't sure what to do. Tom said, "There's some interesting books in the bookcase."

She took off her jacket and walked to the bookcase. Thumbing through the shelves she removed three books; a Time-Life book on women of the Old West, *Little House on the Prairie*, and a Foxfire book on flintlock rifles and folk medicine. Tom went to the propane stove and started cooking rice and beans soaked the night before. As she flipped through the pages of the Foxfire book she said, "You know, we should make something that we could sell."

"Wouldn't that be great? You have some ideas?"

"What if we made screens?"

"You mean like for windows?"

"No you silly, screens like screen dividers."

"I don't know what that is."

She laid down the Foxfire book and picked up the Time-Life book of the Old West.

"Here, see, they used them in the old days."

"Wow, I never knew about that."

"I really enjoy silk painting, and if you could make the wood parts I could paint silk panels to go in each section of a three-panel screen and we could sell them in Tiburon."

"What's Tiburon?"

"It's a place near San Rafael where wealthy people live. I think they would pay a lot of money for a handmade screen."

For the next two days Tom made elaborate drawings detailing the construction and materials needed to build the screen and Mari made beautiful sketches for the silk panels. All the creative juice between them started expressing itself into a dream of handcrafted art. It was very exciting—they were making something together.

It was their fourth day out. They were now feeling that feeling...they saw themselves as living THERE with no one to "Show." Society existed in a distant dream, far away, somewhere else. The only things that provide a sense of era are the stove, the tools hanging on the walls and the kerosene lamps. There are no cities, no roads, no hospitals, no schools, no airports, no restaurants—it's January 7th, 1888; they would need to make do until spring. Mari said, which was not like her to pretend, "We have enough to make it 'til spring?" Tom smiled. He knew she had the fever. It's a wondrous feeling. For some, it can be scary at first and for others it comes like a long-lost friend. Mari went on, "I could live here forever." In the backs of their minds they knew it was pretend, but maybe...

Suddenly, Tom's ears perked up. Mari wanted to know, "What is it?" Putting his fingers to his lips he walked over and picked up the 30-30. Cocking the lever, he put one in the chamber and slowly let the hammer back to "safety." He could hear the crunching of snow off in the distance. Someone or something big was coming up the canyon towards the cabin. Mari said, "What do you think it is?"

"I don't know, it's either a big elk or someone on horseback, moving fast." They both scrambled to the pane-glass window and looked down the path toward the Pagoda. A few minutes later—there was George coming through the frozen fog on horseback, riding full-out with a grin on his face. He looked like a wild man, a mountain man just in from a rendezvous, with his Cole Younger black overcoat, saddlebags, rifle, and coonskin hat. Making the turn in front of the cabin he howled and hollered, "Hey you old mountain man." It's what they've called each other since '75. Tom put the rifle down next to the milk can and opened the door, "What you doin' up here? Come on in and sit a spell."

George replied, "You got a fire goin' ?"

"I'll put the coffee on, you come warm those bones."

Mari was amazed. She had never heard anything like it. Those two old mountain boys threw one-liners back and forth for ten minutes; they were in their element and loving it. George tied Red Shirt, an Arabian-Thoroughbred, to Yellow Ribbon. Yellow Ribbon is what Tom calls the oak tree out front that holds the pipe-bell he put there 13 years ago. Mari started the coffee going. Slapping the side of a Kodiak can, Tom opened the lid and filled his top lip with chew. George rolled a tailor-made and lit up.

George took a deep drag off his cigarette and announced in a loud voice, "Got some news, storm's movin' in tonight. You guys going to be OK?"

"How big?"

"They say maybe two feet, maybe more."

"It's OK by me. What do you think, Mar?"

By now the lovers loved the isolation and being snowed in for three weeks sounded just fine. What better excuse than "snowed in." Mari grinned and said, "All right with me."

Tom said, "That settles it then, we're in for the long haul."

George replied, "Do you want me to get a message out for you?"

Tom answered, "Tell Maggie we still want to try to hook up at Tool Shed in two days. Let's see, that'd be the 9th. If we don't show, you know we're staying in. If that happens, you could get a message to Mari's parents. Oh, also call Bill Smith at HGW, tell them we're snowed in and all right, and will be in Portland as soon as we can. Here's the numbers."

Tom and George started talking about the old days. Mari was very interested in the whole subject of living off the land. In fact, it was a dream of hers that she had never gotten a chance to fulfill after having the boys. Really the boys were her life now, and she did all she could as a single mom to care for them, but this was a holiday, an adventure. She knew that they were in good hands with Noni and Didi.

George was going on with the story about the time a bear came and sat on his tent in the middle of the night, almost breaking his ribs, when Mari interrupted, "How did you guys meet?"

Tom began to tell the story:

"It was in the fall of 1976. I heard a chainsaw running over on Shelton Ridge three miles out. It went on for several days. I got curious and started heading down the dirt road that can only be driven in summer and fall. After pulling a steep grade at Terry's pond, I followed the road to the right. I reckoned the chainsaw sound had been coming from further down on the ridge the day before.

"There, set back from the road was a log cabin. I could see smoke coming from the chimney and opened the truck door. Before I could walk ten steps the front door opened and a woman stepped out holding a shotgun. She kept it pointed at the ground, but I could tell by the way she held it, she knew how to shoot. I told her that I was her neighbor over on Smith Ridge. She told me that George wasn't home, but he'd be back tomorrow. I got the gist of what she was saying; I should come back when George was there. She was friendly and all; however, my instinct told me she was no one to mess with. I thanked her, got back in the truck and headed for home.

"The next day George rode up to our cabin on horseback with his son Jesse, carrying a broken singletree. He introduced himself and we put on a pot of coffee. I asked about the singletree. He said he broke it pulling logs with his horse Duchess, a Morgan-Percheron.

"I told him the story about my Morgan-Quarter Horse Babe, who loved to pull. How one day I was pulling logs up from the canyon behind the Pagoda and stopped Babe to clear the run—we were going to hit a stump. After rolling the log to re-adjust the path, I leaned Babe forward taking up the slack on the tugs. Then I told her GO. She lunged forward. Just at that moment the log rolled back in front of the stump. She was in full motion when the log caught the stump, snapping the singletree like a pretzel. I spent the rest of the afternoon fashioning a new singletree.

"It gave us something in common all right. I told him we could fix it if he wanted. Together, from an oak branch, with foot-adz and drawknife we made a new singletree. We put the old swivel hooks back on and set new wedges on the ends—it was a fine job. Having made this gesture of friendship created a bond between us that has never been broken to this day."

After a few more stories about fishing holes and fires, George said, "I'd better get on down the hill before the storm moves in."

Out front George reached into his saddlebag and brought out bear jerky and smoked salmon wrapped in a paper bag, and said, "For the long haul." He mounted Red Shirt and trotted out 20 paces. Turning his horse to face the cabin he yelled, "You take care of that pretty lady," and rode off, disappearing into the snow.

8

*"Dance like no one is watching.
Sing like no one is listening.
Love like you've never been hurt
and live like it's heaven on Earth."*

Mark Twain

The Way Home

Tom was repairing one of the deer-hide chairs with sinew when Mari walked over to the window, "It's snowing." Stretching his back, he opened the cabin door and walked out onto the porch, "Sure enough. Come out here Mari, it's so beautiful." It was a frosting-snow coming down ever so lightly. It absorbed all sound, producing a calm, an almost a numbing calm. They stood there in awe for several minutes just watching. Breaking the tranquility, he began to speak, "This is a very ancient and sacred thing. It is a time when spirits can manifest themselves more easily. The crystalline structure in the billions of snowflakes falling, gives them a place to manifest, like the hundres of thousands of dots making up a television screen."

Back in the silence again he whispered, "Let's go walk."

"OK, will you braid my hair first?"

"I love to braid your hair."

She sat down on the bench Tom had carved from solid pine years ago. Placing her hands on her lap she leaned her head back onto his stomach. She looked up, rolling her eyes back to meet his and said, "You got a rubber band?" He could never say enough about her wild dark hair and when the snow frosted the ends, her hair frizzed out like static electricity. He reached for a box next to the lamp and pulled out a small thin piece of leather, "Would this work?" Mari nodded and smiled. He gently brushed out her hair, parting it in three groups. Slowly, with reverence he began weaving the strands. Finishing the last interlace he wrapped the leather tie around the end, "There, you look like an Indian princess." She smiled and kissed him on the cheek.

They put on warm clothes and grabbed their walking sticks. Tom had made a walking stick for her from a pine branch he'd gathered from the Kashmir Valley that morning. Tom's stick had three notches on it. Mari was curious, "Why three notches?"

"It means; past, present and future."

"Then why does my walking stick only have one?"

"Because you are in the present, you haven't yet created a long past and are only beginning to create a future. In time, when you take the initiation you'll get another notch."

"What initiation?"

"Spending a day and a night out there in the forest with the animals, armed only with a knife. No food, no water, no shelter, no matches—you gather and create all you need from nature, facing any fears that may come. The next morning you come back a changed person and for that you get the second notch."

"And what about the third notch?"

"We can talk about that later. Let's go before the weather changes. I want to take you up by Indian Rock near Widow Maker."

"What's Widow Maker?"

"Just Come."

From the cabin they walked about a mile through the snow to a great ponderosa pine tree and stood near its edge. He pointed at the tree, "See how some of the large branches about 50 feet up have died and are covered with ice, yet they're still connected to the tree?"

"Yes."

"That's why they call it Widow Maker."

"What do you mean?"

"A tree like that can drop those heavy branches at any time. To stand under it, is to tempt fate. That's why they call it Widow Maker. Don't ever stand under a tree like this one—nature will not honor your innocence. There are times when you put yourself in harm's way to test yourself, but you do it on purpose. Shall we sit under her a bit?"

He knew that to do something in the face of real fear is courage. Mari said, "For what purpose?"

"For the act itself."

Without hesitation she walked under the tree. He followed. She put her arms around the tree and hugged it and he did the like. For several minutes they gazed out into the endless blanket of snow. Tom grabbed her by the hand and walked out from under the great tree. Holding hands they lifted their arms into the falling snow and thanked nature for all that is Hers. Then they walked to the edge of the canyon by a large rock overlooking what Tom called the Kashmir Valley. "This is Indian Rock."

"What a view…"

"I love it here. Do you know how to get back to the cabin from here?"

Mari looked around. The snowfall had covered their tracks and everything looked the same.

"No."

"When walking through woods you've never been in before, always stop every so often and look back so your mind can take a picture of what it looks like on your return. Pay attention to tall trees that stand out; this is especially true in snowfall. Notice how those trees look. Each one is different if you look closely."

She bent over and drew a heart in the snow, "Thank you for showing me these things." Within a few minutes the heart disappeared. They both smiled and walked on.

Tom pointed across the valley. "See that ridge over there? If you follow the ridge down two miles you'll find a gravel road leading to a massive rustic A-frame dwelling. Not far from the A-frame is a small camp shack. A true mountain man named Fred Harrison lives there."

He began telling her the long version:

"He's the only one left who lives all year round out here. Alone, he raises cattle out on that ridge. He built a huge A-frame north of the main pond all by himself. He was one of the few that survived the Bataan Death March. During the march from Mariveles in 1942 over 70,000 prisoners of war were bound, beaten, or killed by their captors. Some were forced to dig their own graves and were buried alive. More than 20,000 died before they reached the concentration camp at O'Donnell some 100 miles away. Along the way Fred kept picking up fallen comrades, pushing them on. Some were bayoneted when they fell from exhaustion. Out of the survivors, one in three later died from malnutrition and disease.

"Fred's an incredible man. He talks with a high squeaky voice, but don't let that fool you—he's awesome. Whatever he says, he does. One day I stopped by to see him. He told me he was going to gravel his road from Lee's Pond to the Leaning Tree. I said, 'How you going to do that?' He said, 'One shovel at a time.'

"I came back a week later to find him shoveling gravel out of the back of his old Ford pickup. I said, 'Fred, where'd you get the gravel?' 'Up by the lookout.' 'Well, that's six miles out,' I said. He replied, 'No problem, I got nothing but time.' I helped for a while, but was having trouble keeping up with the old man. It took him seven months; he graveled two miles of road, by hand, one shovel load at a time.

"Now mind you, nobody lives in that A-frame. He built it for his wife, who promised to come and live with him out on the ridge if he'd build it. Well, he built it, to her surprise, but she never came to stay—just a visit now and then.

"To tell you what kind of man he is: One day he was working on his roof 30 feet up, and tumbled backwards. He slid down the roof to its edge and dropped another ten feet to the ground, breaking three ribs and puncturing a lung. So what did old Fred do? Coughing up blood, he crawled on his hands and knees to his pickup and drove to the first cattle gate. Now any ordinary man would have driven right through the wire gate on his way to the hospital, but not old Fred. He gets out of the truck, opens the cattle gate, drives forward, stops, gets out, closes the gate, gets back in his truck and drives to the next cattle gate. He had to pass through three cattle gates before reaching the main pond, then drive 45 minutes on a dirt road to the hospital. When he arrived they wrapped him, X-rayed him, gave him pain medicine that he refused, and told him he had a punctured lung and would have to stay in the hospital. He told them 'b-u-l-l-shit' and drove back to the ridge and laid up in his cabin for several weeks, taking mountain herbs and such. One month later he was back up on the roof swinging a hammer, at 76 years old."

As they walked back toward the cabin Tom stopped under a large oak tree, "Do you know that this is my favorite kind of tree?"

"You told me that before."

"Well, I didn't tell you this. When I was a young boy living in Thousand Oaks, I would go off by myself and sit under oak trees at night, especially on a full-moon night. I didn't quite understand it at the time, but I was having a yearning to sit quiet, to meditate. I knew others would think I was weird, so I never spoke of it. The way the branches zigzagged reaching into the night sky made me feel protected. The silhouette at dusk, the touch of the moss at her trunk, the strength of her wood and all the little animals that lived in and around her. To lean back against an oak in the tall grass and look up through her branches to the stars, put me somewhere—somewhere that I couldn't explain to anyone else, except maybe you. You remind me of the majestic oak."

Mari replied, "What is it about you? I can't tell if you're trying to merge or flatter me. Don't flatter me or you do me an injustice. If this is, just because it is, then go for it."

"What do you mean?"

"Become one spirit. Isn't that what love is? The merging of spirit."

"My desire *is* for us to become as one, like the left and the right hand connected to the same body—pulling the cart together."

"You know this path is not for everyone. When people get too close, ego gets scared."

"I have surrendered to the path. When I look at you I see God being a woman. I see God being everything around us including us. How could anything be without God? God is everything. One could pick a guru, a flower, a mountain, a thought, a dream, or a way—as the path. There are many paths leading to the same source. In this time you are my path, my teacher, my karma, my highest guru."

"Then why have you picked me over any other woman?"

"If we were infinitely conscious of God then we would already be one with each other, but we're not. It is your *Maya* (confusion) and my *Maya*, our combined *Karma* (law of cause and effect) that makes us teachers for one another. I may not find enlightenment in this lifetime, but deep inside of me I know we will take each other part-way there."

With that Tom took out his pocketknife and carved a heart on the tree. In the center he carved an *Om* (source of all being) symbol, and below it he carved the words, "Mari + Tom."

The lovers turned away from the tree and walked hand in hand toward the cabin. The feeling of being lost in the wilderness with the snow falling all around set the moment for each next step into the snow.

Back at the cabin, after dinner Mari cleaned the oil lamps. Her long thin fingers wiped the carbon from the inside of the glass chimneys while Tom read her a story from Whitman's *Sea of Grass*. "...these prairies as a sea of grass wherein appeared no island..." Suddenly she interrupted, "Tom, tell me how you came about building this log cabin?"

He began near the beginning:

"In the spring of 1973 I had been working the farm in Cornelius, Oregon by day and the phone company by night. We bought the farm in 1969 and had been running a small

Class B goat dairy, milking 26 goats morning and evening. We had restored the old six-bedroom farmhouse and by now had settled into a routine. My boss came to me and told me, 'I'm moving you to days.' In my protest at being moved to the day shift, I would come to work wearing my farm clothes. Getting up at 4:30 AM to milk and then being at work by 7:30 left me no time to change clothes, or so I rationalized.

"After seeing the movie *Jeremiah Johnson* that spring, while walking through the park in Portland it hit me. No, wait there was something that happened before that. I was sent out to work on a bank Centrex in the commercial district of downtown Portland. It was after-hours for the bank. I was wearing a pair of worn-out bib overalls with rabbit skin sewn to the butt when I knocked on the glass door to arouse the guard. The guard came to the door and said the bank was closed and told me I should move along, NOW. I told him I worked for the phone company and was there to analyze problems with the bank's Centrex. He didn't know what a Centrex was, so I said, PBX? He didn't know what that was either. For him, I didn't compute. He thought I was some kind of nut. I tried showing him my PNB identification, but by now nothing was going to change his mind. Perception was reality. I walked to the nearest phone booth and placed a call to my manager stating that the guard would not let me into the bank building and what did he want me to do? My boss said he would call one of the bank executives and call me back. Fifteen minutes later the phone rang. In a weary voice my boss said, 'Go back to the bank, show the guard your ID, he will let you in—and Sawyer, come see me in the morning.'

"The next morning he proceeded to chew my ass about my dress. It wasn't the first time either, but for some reason it really affected me. In those days I thought that how someone dressed had nothing to do with intelligence, responsibility, or one's station in life. I thought anyone who thought that way was basically full of shit. With this fresh on my mind, I was walking through the park and it hit me. I would sell the farm, quit the phone company and move to the wilderness. Everything clicked at once; my hermit mentor Rudy, the oak trees from my childhood, and the movie *Jeremiah Johnson* all converged on me in the same moment. There was no doubt in my mind as to what was about to happen—I was dropping out.

"By the spring of '74 I had quit the phone company, sold the farm and was living in a tent with my wife and two kids on 80 acres near the Mount Hood Wilderness Reserve along the Columbia River Gorge in northern Oregon; nearest town Mosier, population 239, 22 miles away on a dirt road, no electricity or running water for 17 miles. We carried water to our campsite from a two-acre pond situated 100 yards from the cabin site and cooked around a campfire for six months while building the cabin. In those days, there wasn't even a road for the last three miles. I must confess, I never felt so alive as in those days, living around the campfire. Up at sunrise, to bed at sunset.

"Although the property was free and clear, we had reduced our possessions to a handful of tools, horse-drawn equipment, a rifle, two horses, two dogs, a few blankets and an old beat-up Ford pickup. All we had to do was get the cabin built before winter—and of course somehow make enough money to get a winter grubstake and pay the taxes on the land. I had started a small business that employed twelve people in Portland the year before. We manufactured ESS test equipment for the Bell System, and Robert Kohler ran the day-to-day operations in my absence. In the back of my mind I was counting on the business to provide, but it didn't matter—somehow I knew we would make it.

"We lived like *Wilderness Family*. It seemed to come so natural. Everyone had their chores and when it came time to pull and set logs we all worked together. One afternoon, I think it was late summer, we were two logs high on the cabin, and a Volkswagen van came rumbling up over the south pasture. It was my old buddy Greg Lock with his sweetie Susan and her little girl Erin. He had served in Vietnam and had just got back from living in South America. He had gone to school to be a biochemist and had dropped out of a Ph.D. program to get back to the land. He wanted to know if he could live and work on our land. I showed him a spot about 200 yards from our cabin site, under an oak tree, and told him he could build his home there. They set up a tent and started building a cement house. He got bags of cement from Red's Trading Post in The Dalles and we packed water by horse and gathered sand and gravel from the creeks. Greg helped me log and I helped him gather sand. It seemed to go well.

"I remember one day we were logging on the north face of the canyon bordering the BLM. It was steep, and very dangerous work. What neither one of us saw, was the log teeter-totter. A 100-foot windfall was lying across the top of a six-foot stump. Several logs were piled around the butt of the windfall. We had cut into a standing 150-footer, notching it to fall due north. But as it came down it twisted and started falling northwest. As it did, it came down onto the high end of the windfall, which acted like a teeter-totter. All the logs that were lying over the end of the teeter-totter became airborne. It began raining logs. Logs and branches fell all around us. There was no place to go—we just stood there with our hands over our heads and watched the whole thing play out in slow motion. It was a miracle no one was killed that day. Huge pieces of timber came within inches of where we stood. We were serious at first, then we started laughing.

"Another time Greg chopped the back of his hand with an ax and was trying to sew it up when I wandered into his camp. I ended up finishing the sutures. Moments like this brought us close together.

"Once I had spent the day preparing a log with a foot-adz. Pulling the 30-foot log to the cabin site with Babe, I was ready to place it on top of the existing structure. Several times in the past I had gotten Greg to help me with this part. But he seemed so busy trying to get his place together before winter, I thought I would do it by myself; it was something I had done many times before. By now the cabin was seven logs high. With the help of the horse I was able to get the log up OK, but before I could set the corner wedges, one end rolled back off. The 3,000-pound log struck me between my neck and right shoulder, compressing my spine. I dropped to my knees in pain. The backs of my legs went numb. Being a young man, I was up and back at it again within a few hours; however, that injury would temporarily cripple me in later years.

"Right around Thanksgiving, the cabin was finished except for the roofing. It was so cold that when I tried to nail the rolled composition roofing to the plywood sheathing, it broke like glass. We had to heat the roofing by the woodstove and get it up on the roof before it froze. The day we finished, it began snowing. We had made it by the skin of our teeth.

"Everything was ready for winter; food canned, wood chopped, beans, rice and potatoes put up. We had books, a washtub, a potbelly stove, a wood cooking stove and a list of winter projects. What I didn't know about was a thing called 'cabin fever.' Isolated for months on end, waiting for the spring thaw can drive a person crazy. Winter is not without pain. It's like being seasick; some get it worse than others. It's a type of winter depression; come spring, it's wiped away, forgotten like the pain of birth. Joy and exuberance fills your being when you hear the sound of birds and other animals waking up from their long winter sleep.

"That winter, mounted police rode in 25 miles, in two feet of snow, to see if we were still alive. We greeted them with coffee and homemade cookies and told stories about living in the wild. It was a welcome break from the winter routine.

"We lived out here three winters before splitting up, but that's another story. My younger brother Ray helped for a month and David Glass from the buffalo ranch helped too. And that's how we came about to building this cabin. There are a thousand stories, but that's the gist of it for now."

Mari thanked him for the cabin story as she finished the last lamp. Walking to the pane-glass window she pulled the curtains back and stared out into the snowfall. As he joined her at the window, she slipped her arm around his waist and said, "Do you think we're locked in?"

"Maybe, if it snows all night."

"The only thing is, I think Noni is going to worry."

"Don't worry, we can always get out, it's just a matter of how much work it's going to be. You and me, we can do anything."

She smiled and kissed him. They made a little nest near the potbelly and drifted off.

The next morning Tom awoke to the smell of coffee and hotcakes on the griddle. Mari, wearing her field jacket and hiking boots, was preparing pancakes with real butter, powdered milk and strawberry jam. The fire had burned out during the night and the cabin was freezing, "Tom, wake up, would you get a fire going?" He walked barefoot to the chopping block next to the potbelly and began splitting dry pine into small slivers with his special kindling ax made in 1867. "That smells good. What's it look like out there?"

"It's still snowing!"

"After breakfast we'll cut some firewood to replenish the stash and make a test walk."

Soon the fire was roaring. The stovepipe was glowing cherry-red. The potbelly huffed and puffed like a locomotive coming down the tracks. Mari announced, "Breakfast is ready," as she walked toward the potbelly, placing a ceramic dish on the floor. Tom said, "It's getting red. I better turn down the damper." Closing the damper with one hand, he reached into a straw basket hanging from the beam next to the stove and grabbed two forks. Sitting cross-legged next to each other they ate from one plate and drank from the same cup.

After breakfast she started cleaning up while Tom cut firewood. There was three feet of snow on the ground and it was still snowing. With the woodbin full they began going through the check-off list: Pitch pine, dry matches, ax, water, jerky, chocolate, blanket, first-aid kit, candles, peanut butter, rope…their backpacks were ready. If they were going, they would have to go soon. Mari wanted to go to the Pagoda before they left. Tom thought that a good idea, they could have their test walk. Stepping off the porch into the snow, they sunk to their crotches. Mari's legs were longer than Tom's; it was a little easier going for her.

At the Pagoda, Mari took out the smudge stick she had made from the sage during their stop in the desert near Dufur. She lit the stick waving it in the air by the altar and began saying prayers in Spanish. They sat in chainsaw-carved chairs in meditation for several minutes. Blessing the land they walked back to the cabin and warmed by the fire. In less than a quarter of a mile, their legs had gotten cold and wet. Tom said, "Mari, take off your pants." He picked up a bottle of cooking oil from the kitchen counter and started rubbing oil on her legs. After putting her long johns and pants back on, he wrapped the outsides with plastic bags and newspaper. Allowing for a bend at the knee, he fastened the whole thing with electrical tape and she did the same for him.

Wearing caps, jackets, oiled boots and gloves they said goodbye to the cabin and headed out. Tom wanted to take a short cut down the saddleback at Lookout Point to Bobcat, saving about a mile. Each step consisted of lifting each leg to almost waist height, lifting it forward, placing it in the snow and sinking back waist-deep again. They would have to walk like this for seven miles down the pass to the Mosier River crossing near Tool Shed. Fortunately most of it was downhill.

They walked across the pond and down the backside of the dam by the old garden site. Then picking up the trail, which only Tom could see through the fir trees, they continued down to Lookout Point. There they stood for a few moments—the 150-mile view was spectacular. Just getting this far hadn't been easy and the thought of walking another six-and-a-half miles through almost waist-deep snow seemed impossible. The wind was blowing. They cuddled together for another icy wet kiss. They took the ridge trail to the right looking to the east over the Kashmir Valley then bent around to the west and connected with Saddleback. At 2,600 feet they needed to stop to rest. Tom found a large ponderosa pine tree with boughs close to the ground. With his pack-axe he cut several wide boughs, laying them out under the giant tree to sit on. Mari said, "It must have created hardships living up here in the winter?"

Tom replied, "Well, it wasn't always easy, but there was something wonderful about getting through it. I remember one time:

"Greg Lock and I dragged a 50-gallon propane canister five miles from the Leaning Tree at Deer Fork Pond to the cabin, through three feet of snow. It took us part of the day and into the night. By the time we arrived at the cabin our hands were numb and bloody from pulling on the rope; we only had one pair of gloves between us. There was something about completing that together. When we finally got the canister down to Greg's place we just stood there in a daze and started laughing. There is something about going through hardship with another human being that brings souls close together, even if it's just for that moment—it's the kind of thing you take into another lifetime.

"Another time I was coming back from Portland in our four-wheel-drive Toyota Land Cruiser, heading up Highway 84. There was snow and ice on the road. Just the other side of Bonneville Dam a hitchhiker was standing almost frozen in the snow. All he had was a daypack and a small case in his left hand. He kept waving me down with his right. He looked like something the cat dragged in, which somehow made me feel comfortable about stopping. I pulled over and asked him what he was doing way out here in the middle of nowhere in the cold. He said he was freezing. He hopped in. I asked him how far he was going. He said he was trying to get to Coeur d'Alene, Idaho. I told him I was only going as far as Mosier but at least it would get him another 60 miles closer. I could tell he was happy to get out of the cold. Once he started to thaw out, he began shaking all over. As we continued, the snow got deeper with pockets of black ice. By the time we rolled into Mosier the wind had picked up and it was beginning to get dark. I told him that I felt bad about letting him back out into the cold. He asked me where I was going. I told him I was headed for my cabin about 20 miles out, way out on a ridge in the wilderness. It was 22 degrees out and the wind was blowing, I couldn't just leave him there. I looked over at him, sizing him up and said, 'I'm going in, but I won't be coming out for at least three days.

You're welcome to stay a spell.' All he said was, 'OK.' Then I started wondering what my wife was going to think about me bringing home a stranger.

"We passed through Mosier and started climbing into the mountains. About five miles out, off the paved road, I could tell we weren't going to make it in all the way, even with the big knobbed tires I was running. I told him we would probably have to walk the last five miles in the snow and if he felt uncomfortable about that, I would take him back to Mosier. He just said, 'Let's go.' We continued for another 15 miles to Leaning Tree. Looking down into the canyon I could tell that there was no way we would make it across the creek at the bottom and up the other side. We began walking. After about two miles the snow was so thick you couldn't even tell there was a road. The last three miles were through the forest in the dark. The sun had set and it was really starting to cool down. I kept thinking 'This guy is brave; he has no idea where I'm taking him.' He would glance over at me once in a while, checking my expression. I talked to him now and then to help him feel comfortable; he would just nod.

"On we went until finally we saw the kerosene lights of the cabin showing through the windows. I saw a slight smile come on his half-frozen face. I entered the cabin and told my wife we had company. Actually she was pleased—she hadn't seen another human being except for the kids and me for quite some time. Our visitor didn't say much. He took off his backpack and placed the small case he was carrying by the potbelly stove and started warming himself. My wife made up a nice dinner and we all sat around the table. I asked him what he was going to do in Coeur d'Alene. He just said, 'Music,' and kept on eating. He ate like he hadn't eaten for a while. When his plate was empty he didn't ask for more. My wife asked him if he would like some more. He said, 'Yes, ma'am.' She heaped up his plate again.

"After cleaning his plate he went over and picked up the small case he'd carried in, and untied the rope that held it closed. As he lifted out a small stringed instrument, I asked what it was. He said, 'Dulcimer.' That's all he said, just 'Dulcimer.' He began to play and sing the most beautiful songs I've ever heard. He was truly a gifted musician. Not an ordinary musician, but world-class. Maybe even slightly savant, because his communication was quite awkward. His music was incredible— he communicated to the world through his music. I could tell he was not used to being around people and perhaps had come from the Ozarks. He spent three wondrous days with us saying hardly a word—playing music for his room and board. He was a gift from the Universe, the kind that blows in on a cold winter day."

Mari said, "Tell me one more." Tom told her he would, but they needed to start moving again or they would get cold.

"My son Larry was about nine years old and we did 'most everything together. I needed to get into Portland to take care of some important business and Larry wanted to go with me. It was the middle of winter and there was two feet of snow on the ground. I wasn't sure a nine-year-old could make such a journey, but he really kept it up so I told him he could come. I told him he would have to walk down the pass to Tool Shed.

"Back in those days there used to be a bridge across the Mosier River. It washed out in the storm of '81. I explained to him once we got to Tool Shed we would have to walk into Mosier, then hitchhike up Highway 84 into Portland—some 100 miles. He said he wanted to, but what does a nine-year-old boy know…or a 30-year-old, for that matter. We started at sunup and didn't make the 22 miles into Mosier till almost dark. His little legs just wouldn't go anymore and I had to carry him piggyback the last four miles. We had to hit the highway before dark or the chances of getting a ride would be tough. We stood underneath the overpass at Exit 69 for some time. The sun was starting to set and I knew we'd be in trouble if we didn't catch a ride before dark.

"In those days I carried a portable CB radio in my backpack just in case. I started talking over the air on Channel 19, the trucker's channel. 'How about that westbound trucker, you got a copy on old West Virginia?' That used to be my handle. I pressed the transmit button and tried again. Out of the static came back, 'This is Snake Bite, eighteen wheelin' out of Idaho headin' to Portland town westbound on 84. We got a copy on you. What's your 20?" I replied, 'Hey good buddy. This is West Virginia. Me and my boy are standing under the overpass at Exit 69. We need a ride into Portland, over.' Back out of the static, again the trucker roared, 'I'm ten miles out of The Dalles headed your way. Stand by, I should be there in about five minutes. This is Snake Bite, we're going 10-10.'

"Five minutes later here he came. A big old eighteen-wheeler, pulled by a Peterbilt tractor, hauling two trailers loaded with pipe. Larry and I started waving and jumping up and down. The trucker pulled on his horn twice and started downshifting. I bet it took him almost a half a mile to stop that rig. Larry and I climbed in. Larry went back in the sleeper and I rode up front. About 30 miles from Troutdale the black ice started getting bad—I could see the reflection on the road. But old Snake Bite, he didn't slow down. I figured he knew what he was doing. At 50 miles per hour, suddenly the truck-tractor jackknifed on the ice and the whole cab swung left, pointing straight at the chain-link center divider. I thought we were going in, and all those tons of pipe he was carrying would follow right on top of us.

"Snake Bite was cool, like it had happened to him hundreds of times before. The truck continued to go straight down the highway being pushed by the trailers, but the cab was still pointed at the center divider. Snake Bite calmly reached down and tapped the trailer brakes twice. The cab whipped to the right and straightened out. He looked over at me, smiled and pulled on the air horn, and yelled out over the roar of the diesel, 'You got a westbound trucker. It's gonna be all right.' Larry was asleep and never knew what happened. We finally rolled into an industrial part of Portland about 10:00 that night. It was another adventure, a father-son thing. You would have had to been there."

Tom reached over with an outstretched hand pulling Mari up from the snow. They continued down the saddleback to Little Fawn Springs, stopping north of Bobcat for another rest, and took turns rubbing their faces with snow. He scraped the snow off a stump, making a place for her to sit down near a tributary feeding the river. She watched the icy water run in from above then looked over at him with puppy-dog eyes and said, "Would you tell me one more?" Tom replied, "We should be getting along. If we miss Maggie we'll have to walk another 12 miles into town." Mari pressed her lips together and looked away. He thought, *What am I doing? What's the big deal? Your sweetheart wants a story, lighten up; you're running on Divine time. Go with what is.* Then he replied with a big frozen smile, "OK, one more short one." She turned with a schoolgirl smile and he began:

"Before we built the cabin, our camp was under the oak tree out in front of the cabin site. Late fall was coming on and the air was beginning to get cold. My wife would bake bread in a little rock oven I built next to the fire-ring, and at night we would heat rocks in the oven before putting out the campfire. We had just bedded the kids down in the back of the tent and moved several heated stones inside to warm us for the night. No sooner had we lain down than the wind started to pick up. The sides of the tent began to flutter with each gust. The wind was coming up from the east and that usually meant bad weather.

"The week before I had cut and installed 14 roof trusses for the cabin. I had just finished installing the last one that day. With the ridge beam in place on top of them, I tied each end with rope from the ridge-beam ends to stakes on the ground. The wind continued to get stronger. My wife yelled out, 'I think we're going to lose the tent!'

"We both crawled toward the back to protect the children, when suddenly a gust ripped the tent from its stakes. I could hear the wind screaming through the trusses and the kids crying. We placed more blankets around the kids and I went to check the ropes holding the cabin roof. The wind was so strong I could hardly walk upright. The trusses made an eerie singing sound as the wind squealed over the timbers. When I reached the north rope to check the stakes, all of a sudden the rope snapped. Trusses began splitting along the top log and fell one upon one other like dominos. I went back to where my wife and the kids were. We managed to get them into our battery-dead Ford pickup and tied blankets over the windows. We all huddled together like that till daybreak. We had lost one precious week and winter was coming on fast. We all worked long hours and just finished the cabin roof one day before the snow fell."

The story seemed to open a can. Mari wanted to know more about what it was like for my wife and the kids. Tom replied, "We better go." They continued down the pass. After about a mile he stopped and said, "I think it's hard on a woman living out here," and became quiet again.

By the time they reached the draw near the river crossing, it was 3:00 PM. They were both tired and wondering if they'd missed Maggie. Tom pulled a pair of binoculars from his backpack and looked across the river, "No sign of tire tracks. She hasn't come yet."

"What if Maggie doesn't show?"

"Fortunately the road has been plowed—we'll walk as far as Betsy's and hope she's home, but Maggie will show. Whatever Maggie says she does. Something would have to be really wrong for her not to show up."

"How will she know we're here?"

"I don't know. Maggie has a seventh sense."

Mari had strong legs and seemed to have done fine. However, after seven miles of high-lift marching Tom was walking bowlegged, like he'd been in the saddle for two days. The wind had picked up and was blowing snow in swirls. It began to snow even harder, insulating all sounds around them except for the rush of the river below.

They walked closer to the river. Pulling on the main line still in place from their trip in, he felt it taut and secure. The snow blew directly in their faces. Squinting to see the rope, they moved to the river's edge. Removing Mari's backpack, Tom connected the safety and loop lines to her body and repeated the instructions for the hand-over-hand technique.

He told her not to release too soon; the snow covering the river's edge was an illusion of solidness suspended over the water. She began to cross. He knew if she fell and the loop-line didn't hold, she would fall submerged in the water—he would have only minutes to pull her to shore with the safety-line before her heart stopped.

Hand over hand she made her way midway; her feet dangled and moved about as if on an invisible bicycle. Her weight made the rope bounce as she traversed the next boulder rising up from the rushing water below. *Another ten feet and she'll be on the other side.* In a knuckle-tight grip, she paused for a moment and spun her head to see if Tom was still there. He was readying himself in case she let go. Her face was determined. She looked back at the bank and continued boulder to boulder to the other side, stepping past the snow-covered river's edge. She turned and waved. He took a deep breath and waved back.

After attaching the packs to the mainline he connected the safety-line and signaled her to pull. She pulled the packs across without incident. He would be crossing without the safety-line connected to another human. If he fell in the water, however, his body weight would release the main line; it was looped around a branch and tied to the safety-line, providing a way to pull himself to shore. Connecting his loop-line, he began the crossing—this time, no shenanigans.

Halfway across an abstract thought sped through his mind, *I have boarded a train, I'm waving to you everywhere.* He made it. They danced around in the snow, laughing and throwing snowballs at one another.

Tom pulled both ropes across the river with the safety line and rolled them up. Suddenly they heard the crinkling sound of tire-chains on snow. They had just finishing coiling the last rope when Maggie drove up.

Maggie stepped out of her four-wheeler smiling, "You made it."

"How did you know when we were coming?"

"I could feel you guys coming down the ridge."

"You got the magic, Maggie."

"You ready? Throw your gear in the back."

Spinning her rig around in the snow they headed toward town. She pulled the last turn at Betsy's junction; double-clutched the downshift, and slid sideways. Rotating the steering wheel to compensate for the side-drift, she sped up the hill with a grin on her face.

That night the lovers stayed at George and Maggie's and left, ever grateful, the next morning. They crossed the Columbia River on the steel bridge at the town of Hood River, entering the state of Washington and headed east on Highway 14. Tom wanted to show her the Stonehenge at Mary Hill. Near a castle-like chateau with formal gardens overlooking the Columbia River Gorge is a 6,000-acre ranch, where a full-scale replica of England's famous Stonehenge sits overlooking the river. During the turn of the century, railroad magnate Sam Hill built the castle and Stonehenge for his lover. In 1926 Hill invited Queen Marie of Romania to live at the castle. Rumor has it they were lovers until his death in 1931.

After visiting the castle they drove three miles further east along the river and turned onto a dirt road. Parking the car near a burned-out brick building, they went on foot toward the river. Up ahead they could see blocks of carved stone forming a large geometric circle. The energy was strange—a weird feeling moved over them; that feeling you get when you can't believe your eyes. There it was, an exact replica of Stonehenge.

As they entered the circle of monoliths, Mari began to beam. She loved the intensity radiating from its geometry. Tom removed the camera from his daypack and started snapping pictures. She looked like a child priestess, young beyond her age. Some past-life memory was altering her appearance. It was spooky seeing her face change. She motioned him to come stand by her. He began to vibrate, but was unable to match her energy; she had gone beyond what he was capable of. Sensing his inability to keep up, she turned with a compassionate gaze and kissed him between the eyes, grounding him in a shower of love.

She reached into her pack and pulled out four scarves: one purple, one green, one white and one black. Holding the purple and green scarves in her right hand and the black and white in her left hand, she began spinning in the snow. With her eyes rolled skyward, she twirled and laughed like a child at play—full of life. Clouds of warm air puffed from her mouth into the cold.

Her hair was wild and sparks twinkled from her eyes. She walked toward the cliff's edge, surveying the Columbia River 100 feet below. Her eyes followed the river to the other side, a mile across. Standing there she stared off into the distance. Tom thought, *What grace has brought me to such a woman, how is it that I feel so honored even to kiss her feet?* Just then, the crunching-ice sound of car wheels coming down the road broke their enchanted silence. Turning away from the river she slipped her arm under his and walked to the Honda.

They crossed the river again to the Oregon side at Biggs Junction and continued west toward Portland along the Gorge, which Tom considered one of the most beautiful places on earth. After traveling for several hours through the river canyon, that over thousands of years had cut its way through 80 miles of Cascade Mountains, producing the highest density of waterfalls per mile in the Northwest, they stopped at Multnomah Falls. Legend has it, as the moon was rising up over the trees on the other side of the river an Indian maiden jumped from the top of the falls, falling 620 feet to the pool below, sacrificing herself to save her village from disease.

Tom watched Mari as she passed the "Do not go beyond this point" sign. He hung back to take photographs of her ascent toward the thundering mist at the base of the falls. The air was cold. The churn of the water plunging into the pool produced a fresh earthy ozone odor. Suddenly the wind changed, sending a mass of water in her direction. The waterfall was breathtaking. She stood on a large boulder near the base, stoic, in a restorative trance as the mist enveloped her body. For a moment she disappeared. Tom became concerned that she had been swept into the churning pool underneath the boulder. The wind shifted again. There she was, still standing, drenched from head to toe with a big grin on her face. Tom grabbed a towel from his backpack and ran toward her. He dried her arms, face and hair, and escorted her to the car. Looking around for other humans, she crawled into the back seat, stripped naked and put on dry clothes.

Several miles down the highway, they stopped at the Troutdale Truck Stop for a late lunch, a change of clothes, and general cleanup. In Portland they entered the downtown area stopping off at HGW first, then on to meetings with Shaw Venture Partners, Norwest Venture Capital Management, and the law firm of Stoel Rives. When Tom's involvement with Paratechnology, Inc. was officially closed, they headed for the buffalo ranch to rest and mend from a battery of meetings that he wished could have been different.

Thirty-five miles west of Portland near the little town of Cornelius is where David Glass (a bovine podiatrist and long-haul trucker), had developed a fine herd of buffalo over years of breeding. David had been an old friend of Tom's since 1969, when Tom first moved to Oregon from LA.

Driving down a country road, passing farms and orchards, the lovers turned onto a dirt road edged with an overgrown picket fence leading to the buffalo ranch. They pulled in next to David's work shed and shut off the motor. Tom leaned his head forward on the steering wheel and closed his eyes. Lifting his head from the wheel he read the wooden sign over the ranch house door, "No Sunday Trading" and said, "Mari, it feels so good to be out of the city."

Getting out of the car, they passed through David's shed on their way to the back door. A glint of light shining from a harness buckle hanging next to a wooden beam caught the corner of Tom's eye. "Mari, look how David does his stuff." All types of unrelated things were piled up in corners on top of old buckets and such. From the rafters hung different sorts of tools, spools of baling wire, wooden spoons, assorted block and tackle, ropes, chains and barrel hoops. On one workbench were jars of nuts and bolts and several sizes of rusted coffee cans filled with nails and screws. On another bench were gears, sprockets and grinding machines. Next to the door was an acetylene tank and welding mask. David arranged gadgets and what-have-you's in an order that only he could understand, forming unconscious virtual art.

Tom did his special knock on the back door; no one was home. Fingering the key from its hiding place he turned the lock and opened the door. Memories flooded in from the time when he lived there with David, Laneka and Bud. The country kitchen was brightly painted, with various knickknacks and framed photographs of girls David once loved. On the wall next to an old-time refrigerator was a trucker's calendar with a naked lady up front. The lovers went into the front room and sat on David's handmade couch next to the woodstove. Tom reached over and touched the stove; it was still hot. He figured David was not far off. The walls of the front room were paneled in scrap barn wood, with Indian artifacts hanging about, which David never spoke of. In a glass case were Indian skulls and bones from some long-past dig in New Mexico. In the bathroom was an antique bear-claw bathtub. Different-size tubes and pipes wound around from one fixture to another, bypassing the failed old plumbing in the 100-year-old farmhouse. Next to the tub was a wooden box filled with clean towels and a good supply of Hustler magazines.

Tom put another log in the stove and the lovers fell asleep cuddled up on the couch. An hour later they were awakened by the sound of a slow growling voice, "Brother Tom!"

"Brother David! Where's Bud and Laneka?"

"They're bringing in the groceries."

"David, this is Mari."

Standing in the hallway carrying a bag of groceries, with a gleam in his eyes, David's slow rough voice rumbled like a cowboy just off the range, "Hello, Mari."

"Can we give you a hand?"

"Sure."

David is a man of few words. He only speaks when necessary. Tom and Mari went out and greeted Bud and Laneka, David's twelve-year-old daughter. While talking about the trip up, they helped unload a month's worth of provisions from David's diesel truck.

That night after dinner they all sat around the fire and told close-call stories. Tom told the one about when he was almost killed at gunpoint in a raid by a bunch of rookie cops on a gas station in East Portland. David told about the time his truck jackknifed in the snow on a run down Zigzag on Mount Hood, flipping upside down, burying itself six feet deep in snow on the edge of a cliff, cutting off all oxygen to the cabin until a passerby dug him out two hours later. Bud talked about his days as a lobbyist in Washington D.C. and Mari told her story about the time she was almost raped by the Federales in Mexico.

Mari glanced over at Tom with that *I'm getting tired* look.

Stretching his arms above his head, he said, "David, is there anyone upstairs?"

"Nope, that's your room."

"Where you sleeping, Bud?"

"I'm still out in the Airstream, I like it out there."

Tom looked over at Mari, "Hey sweetie, I'm ready to hit the rack. Are you?"

Mari smiled, "I'm ready."

Bud poured another cup of coffee and David, Tom and Mari climbed the rickety stairs. David's room was next to Tom's and they've got this longstanding tradition of saying goodnight like *The Waltons*. After cuddling up with his sweetie Tom reached for the string hanging down from the wall lamp attached to the sheetrock and said, "Goodnight, David."

"Goodnight, Tom."

Mari said, "Goodnight, David."

"Goodnight, Mari."

Tom put his mouth near Mari's ear and whispered like a cowboy, "Goodnight, darlin'." Turning her head to meet his lips, they kissed and drifted off into slumber.

The next morning everyone was up bright and early. There were chores to do and Tom and Mari wanted to get in on them.

David said they could feed the buffalo corralled in the stockyard across the road. Mari was very excited; she had read about buffalo in wildlife books and Indian stories, but had never seen one up close and personal. Tom knew the routine from when he lived there and was excited to show her. As they walked out the back door David said, "Tom, be careful about getting too near the fence, there's a mean one in the herd. We call her 'Mean Mama'; she'll try to gore you through the fence."

"OK, just pitch some hay? Did you want us to grain 'em?"

"Just hay 'em, I'll grain 'em later."

Mari and Tom walked across the road to the stockyard where 12 buffalo stood breathing into the cold morning air. Billows of condensation puffed from their great flexing nostrils as they snorted and stomped in anticipation. The cantankerous shaggy-maned animals horned each other away from the feed bins. Weighing in at over 2,000 pounds each, most stood six feet tall at the shoulder, seven feet long, sporting a three-foot tail that could raise a welt on the side of a man's face in one lash.

The lovers gathered flakes of alfalfa from the barn and piled them high in a cement-coated wheelbarrow next to the door. Tom pushed the wheelbarrow while Mari held the top of the stack. As they approached the stockyard fence, Mean Mama stepped forward to within two feet of the wire. She had a hazardous look in her eyes. Even Big Jake the bull stayed clear of her.

So as not to cause a fight, Tom took some flakes to one end and Mari to the other—they both pitched over the fence at the same time. The lot scattered into two groups. Mean Mama smacked her mother Connie in the side with her horns and proceeded to eat. Stomping, she began thrusting her head from side to side, flashing her horns. She made it known that she would eat her fill before the others got any. Tom and Mari went back to the barn for another load of alfalfa, this time creating two more piles, then again until six piles of alfalfa lay on the snow-covered ground.

Now that the herd had calmed down, Mari wanted to know if she could reach through the space in the split-rail fence and touch one of these majestic animals. Tom told her if she was careful, she could pet Connie without any problem, but to be very alert for jealous Mean Mama. They walked over near the loading ramp where Connie was eating. Mari stuck her hand through the fence and touched Connie's massive neck. Connie didn't seem to mind the touch at first, but her eyes started to widen. Tom whispered, "Mari, move your hand back toward her shoulders where she can't strike you with her horns." Suddenly, as Mari began to move her hand away, Connie flipped her head to one side just missing Mari's arm.

Mari looked over at Tom, "Doesn't she like me?"

"It's not that; she's wild and not used to human touch. She was just warning you. Where you had your hand, if she wanted to, she could have hurt you. Try gently placing your hand near her shoulder." Mari had to reach up to touch the back of Connie's shoulders. Connie was a little nervous, but all in all, quite happy with this position. She still looked around from time to time, checking the situation. Mari said, "She's so wonderful. I love her."

"She can sense that. That's why she's letting you touch her."

Mari went on, "Buffalo are the spirit of the plains. You know the book you were reading me, *Sea of Grass*; it all comes to me now just touching her."

"Remember that book you had me read you at Salt Point when we were first going together?"

"*White Buffalo Woman!*"

"Yes—now you've touched your spirit in hers."

Mari stood there caressing this gargantuan beauty in silence—something wonderful was happening. After a few minutes, Mari moved her hand away and stood back from the fence. "Tom, it's hard to believe that only a hundred years ago 60,000,000 buffalo roamed the plains and by 1900 there were only 1,000 left. David said there are around 30,000 now, but what a tragedy of man's stewardship of the earth; imagine, 60,000,000 buffalo."

It was 6:45 AM. Mari put her arms around Tom and they walked back to house. In the kitchen, Tom looked over at David, "Mean Mama is a mean one." Dave nodded, "She'll be hamburger by the end spring." Tom poured a cup of coffee and cleared his throat, "Mari and I are engaged to be married." Everyone cheered. Interrupting, he continued, "I still have to ask her father." They all started laughing and patting him on the back. After breakfast and dishes they said their goodbyes to David, Laneka and Bud and hit the road once again.

Mari wanted to see Tom's old farm before heading south. Turning off onto a gravel road they continued up Dickson Mill Road for several miles. After the bend, they pulled over and looked down into a sprawling valley. Off by itself was an old two-story farmhouse painted yellow with white trim, with 90 feet of covered porch on two sides. The old barn was still standing. Mari said, "Tell me about the farm?"

He looked a little sad. Memories of his children growing up there, his first wife, the people that came to live with him, the country parties, the horses, goats, sheep, peacocks, chickens, guinea hens, ducks and geese, the dogs and his pet raccoon, all flooded into his mind. Mari said, "Are you OK?"

"Yes, just a lot of memories." For Tom it was like looking back into another lifetime; he had traveled too far to return to the past. Mari said, "If you feel up to it, tell me a few stories." He began with a smile on his face:

"We had just moved into the house; it was pretty run down. I was out back digging a garden on the east side of the barn with a shovel. I noticed a man watching me from the farm up above our place. He just stood there on his porch watching for the longest time. After a while I stopped looking up to see if he was still there and continued my work. After about an hour I saw a tractor coming down the road next to our property. I said to myself, 'If only I had one of those.' The tractor continued down the road and suddenly turned into my drive, making its way up the berry-bush-lined road to the back of our farm. Driving right up to the garden site, the man pulled back the throttle on the tractor to talk over the sound of the motor, 'I was watching you work that shovel, would you like a hand?' I told him I would, and thanked him. He positioned his D6 Caterpillar over the garden site and lowered the 12-foot-wide disk to the ground, and in three swipes the garden was ready to plant. I couldn't believe it. In less than three minutes, he did what would have taken me days. He stepped off the tractor and shook my hand, 'Hello, my name's Andy Pearson, I'm your neighbor. I've got the farm up above your place.' This is how people were back in those days.

"See that big tree out there behind the woodshed to the right of the house? There used to be a tire-swing there. I would push the kids on that swing almost every day.

"The barn was built in 1898 and the house in 1901. We just moved in and started restoring the place. The house hadn't been lived in for 12 years and was rundown. Many of the windows were broken out, the porch had collapsed on one side, the electrical and plumbing were shot and the roof was in need of repair. We paid $19,000 for 13 acres with the barn and house, which was situated on an 80-acre parcel. We had the run of the land. Anyway, I was going into town to buy electrical supplies to start rewiring the house. Of course I didn't know anyone and had just met Andy. I arrived at the local hardware store and walked in. They had 'most every thing I needed and the man waiting on me was very friendly. Remember, I had just moved up from LA and was used to the way people treated each other down there. I asked what the total came to. He said $376.40. I only had $200.00. I told him I would have to put some things back. He asked me my name; I said Tom Sawyer. He giggled and said that he hadn't seen me in town before. I told him I had just moved up from LA and bought the farm next to Andy Pearson. He said, 'You know Andy?' I told him the story about the tractor. He said, 'Any friend of Andy's is a friend of mine.' and told me to take the stuff and pay him the difference the next time I was in town. I was blown away and thanked him profusely. It wasn't so much for the electrical parts as it was for his trust. I felt such a feeling of belonging and love—I wasn't used to being treated like this—I thought I'd died and gone to heaven.

"Some of my old street brothers from when I ran a halfway house for parolees out of Soledad Prison came to the farm to live and work. One of these was named Flip. He got his name one day when he nodded out on reds in our tree house in LA and fell six feet onto an electrical wire. The power line caught him around the stomach and bent him in half. He hung there momentarily, then flipped upside down, falling another 10 feet to the ground, landing on his back. From that day on we called him Flip.

"A street brother named Bill Mathews came up from LA to help me work on the house. He brought his wife and two kids and they ended up living at the farm for a while. He was a very good artist, but not too good at carpentry. I asked if he would like to make a wooden cover-box for the electrical panel I had just installed on the side of the house. He said he'd love to. He spent hours building the box, like an artist would—he made a labor of love out of it. When he finally hung his cover box on the house, painting it white with colorful flowers and birds, he came and got me. When I turned the corner to look at it, I could see that it wasn't straight up and down with house. It was crooked. He was so proud of his work and grateful that someone trusted him, I didn't have the heart to say anything, and in that moment something far greater than a straight box took place between us. The box is still there just the way he made it.

"We had a goat dairy, milking 26 head morning and night. My six-year-old daughter Tiffany used to help me milk. My wife started making goat cheese and I did deliveries of milk and cheese. One of my stop-off points on my little dairy route was Bill Unger's picker camp/hippie colony. It was my favorite stop. Most of the cabins had dirt floors swept clean by beautiful hippie girls, and children running about in the main yard. Carol was one of my regular customers. When I entered the camp, I asked for her and was directed to a small building attached alongside her house. It just looked like another doorway entrance. One of the people standing there said she was in there and to just knock. I went to the door and knocked twice. Kicking the door open she said, 'Yes, what is it?' There she was sitting on the shitter, naked as a bluejay with a smile on her face. She said, 'Oh, Tom, you got some milk for me.' I was speechless.

"We got a peacock and two hens. I thought they were so beautiful. He would spread his feathers out and dance for the hens. Around dusk, he would start screaming. He sounded just like a woman getting killed. One evening the Sheriff drove in. He said the neighbors a quarter mile away had called—they had heard a women screaming for help. I told him we had peacocks. I'm not sure he believed me.

"It was around noon one day, because we had just finished lunch. I heard the sound of glass breaking upstairs. I ran out the back door and looked up. The peacock had moved on to the next window. Apparently he had seen his reflection in the glass and started fighting with himself. He was jumping up, flipping his feet forward and slamming the window with his spurs. Of course, the glass would break and cut him, making him even madder. Then he went to the next window. He took out three windows before I could get on the roof with a broom and shoo him off. I sold the peacocks the next day.

"My fondest memories of the kids.... My six-year-old son Larry and I would jump in my old battered Ford pickup and tend the fence lines, resetting posts and stretching wire. I had made a wooden broom-handle toolbox for myself, and a miniature one for Larry. He had his little hammer and pliers and we would walk the lines hammering down loose nails.... I loved to swing my little girl, Tiffany, on the tire swing, seeing her fly, her excitement and the way her little arms barely reached around to hold on.... In the winter the whole family would slide down the hill on cardboard and make snow bricks with a shoebox for our annual igloo.... Tiffany loved to play in the snow. Sometimes she'd sneak out the back door and run barefoot in the snow in her pajamas, chasing the dog.... Tiffany would get up early in the morning before anyone else and take every piece of clothes from her drawers, trying each one on, modeling to her reflection in the window.... Tiffany fell off the haystack and bumped her head. Flip brought her back to consciousness by putting hot peppers in her mouth—she cried for hours....

Larry climbed onto his tricycle, rode down our dirt driveway and fell, cracking his head—blood was everywhere…. The things we watch our kids go through as they learn to walk in life. I would take them both over my shoulders and carry them up the stairs for their bedtime story; we called it, 'Sack of potatoes.' It almost makes me cry thinking back to those days.

"I had taken classes in LA on shoeing horses. So I put up a little sign down at the feed store in Cornelius advertising myself as a farrier. People would trailer their horses up to the farm and I would trim and shoe them. One day a man brought up a pair of Percherons. I told him I had never worked on draft horses. He started talking about pulling with horses. I had a déjà vu. After he left I kept having daydreams about going to town in a 'surrey with the fringe on top.' I ended up buying two Morgans, a breed that had been used to pull stagecoaches in the old days. I bought an old Studebaker hay wagon, 1907 model from Johnny Kinky's barn and trained the horses to pull. Later, after I felt sure of the horses I would harness them up and pull the kids around the hills for miles on a flat piece of plywood. It was their favorite thing to do.

"Our water supply came from a spring up above the west pasture feeding the cistern down by the house. I used to dehorn goats and trim their feet. One day a man showed up with two goats for dehorning. After doing the job, I told him I would trade him for the dehorning if he would help me carry up the new spring lid that I had made the day before. The lid weighed 200 pounds. We had to carry it a quarter mile to the spring. I had to set my end down three times before reaching the spring; he never set his end down. His name is David Glass. We have been friends ever since.

"At one time, there were five families living here. Most of them had come up from LA to escape the city. We all ate around one large table—I felt like a father to them all.

"I used to enjoy picking pieces of gravel from the driveway and hitting them with a plastic baseball bat into the pasture below.

"I had just put soybeans in the pressure cooker, placing it on the stove to cook. I asked my buddy Flip, a recovering heroin addict, to watch it while I took a shower. I told him he needed to watch the stove; if the little rocker on top of the cooker stopped rocking, remove the cooker from the stove right away. He must have spaced out because when I turned the water off, I couldn't hear the rocker puffing back and forth anymore. I yelled, 'Flip!' Just as I did, the whole thing blew up like cannon fire. We spent days picking beans out of every imaginable place. There were beans stuck to the front room ceiling!

"One summer day we were all in the kitchen canning wild blackberries picked from along the driveway. Someone suggested planting comfrey in the east pasture. I said, 'There's no way to get water out there, and even if we had a pipeline from the spring, there isn't enough water to feed a crop.' Then I got the bright idea of drilling a well. It came to me in a flash; we would use a posthole digger. I rigged up an eight-inch auger connected to ten-foot lengths of three-quarter inch galvanized pipe, allowing us to add new sections of pipe as we went. We built a derrick from 30-foot lodge-pine, forming a tripod to pull the pipe from the ground. I based it on a catch principle I'd seen when working in the oil fields in Ojai, called an 'elephant's cunt.' We made a large handle so four people could turn the auger. After weeks of spare-time work we hit rock at 65 feet. We had five gallons a minute, not enough water to sustain a crop.

"It sat like that for a couple of weeks. We were about to cap it off and call it a day when Lynn Harrison, another old buddy from LA, dropped by. He said, 'Why don't you dynamite it? If it's a big boulder then nothing will happen—if it's a small one it might blow it away and you can start digging again.' It all made good sense. Back in those days, if you had a farm deferment you could just walk in and buy dynamite; farmers used it to blow stumps. I asked Lynn how many sticks, and he said, 'Eight should do it.' I purchased eight sticks of dynamite with 15-second waterproof fuses and detonation caps—a bit of overkill. We tied the sticks together with twine and attached the bundle to a potato-sized rock. Using an ice pick, I slowly punched a hole in the end of each stick and inserted the caps and fuses. It makes my hands sweat just thinking about it.

"Out in the pasture at the well site, we lit the fuses, dropped the bundle down the hole and ran like hell. A hundred feet away we fell to the ground laughing like I never laughed before. We waited and nothing happened. We waited and waited and then Lynn wanted to walk back toward the well to see what happened. I said, 'I don't know about that.' We got within 20 feet of the well when BOOM, the ground shook and out of the well came a perfect cylinder of water 40 feet high and eight inches around. It just stood there in mid-air for some time before falling to the ground. We laughed so hard we peed our pants. Too bad, there was a big boulder at the bottom; we never did get any significant water out of that well.

"Andy and I planted a joint crop of alfalfa in my west pasture. Alfalfa back in those days was going for $35.00 a ton. I spent many fond hours plowing and disking the field with Andy's D6 Cat.

"About the second time I had borrowed the Cat, I was pulling logs up from the creek near the back of the farm. I had several logs attached to the back. I was following the fence line on one side and a tree line on the other. The road narrowed and I was trying to be careful. I looked to the right and noticed the Cat had picked up a strand of downed fence wire in its right track and was neatly rolling it off the fence. Putting the Cat in neutral, I jumped off, and cleared the wire, checked the logging chain and the position of the logs; everything looked good. I got back in the seat, leaned back and thought, 'I feel so powerful driving this thing.' I put the Cat in gear and let out the clutch. Unbeknownst to me, the smokestack had caught a large fir branch and had bent it way back. Just as I was thinking how cool I was, letting out the clutch, the Cat moved forward releasing the branch. It sprung back and hit me square between the eyes, knocking me off the cat. I was dazed; it almost knocked me out. I looked up to see the Cat going up the road by itself. In a few minutes it would be taking out Andy's fence—final destination, Andy's house. I got to my feet and ran to catch up with it. I climbed up the back and over the seat just in time to keep it from going through the fence. I sat back in the seat, wiped the blood from my face and stared out across the valley listening to the idle of the motor, thinking—I really wasn't all that cool."

Tom paused, took a deep breath and put his arms around Mari, "There are too many stories to tell and not enough time to tell them." They got in the car and headed for Beaverton. There they picked up the freeway and drove nonstop to Ashland, except for a quick lunch in Eugene. They got a little motel room near downtown Ashland and started contemplating dinner.

They looked at each other with that look and started grinning. Mari said, "OK, I'll dress up and you dress down." Mari entered the bathroom. He could hear her opening her cosmetic bag and setting things on the sink. Then came the snapping sounds of a suitcase opening. He remained lying across the bed with his arms hung over the edge. After a few minutes she stepped out dressed in a black mid-length Moschino skirt, black fashionable G.D.B. shoes, shoulder-cut top that accented her collarbones, and a white pearl necklace. He wasn't sure how she had achieved what she did with her hair—she looked like Jacqueline Kennedy Onassis.

Now it was his turn. He looked over with a smile while dragging his old sea bag into the bathroom. A few minutes later he returned dressed almost in rags—a faded brown and red shirt held in place with a safety pin at the collar, with torn sleeves and grease-stained holey Levis. He had a canvas junkyard jacket slung over one shoulder. His boots were crusted with dried mud from the buffalo ranch and his unwashed matted hair hung down past his shoulders.

They both giggled with approval. She looked like she had just stepped out of a Porsche in front of the Statler-Hilton Hotel; he looked like he had just crawled out from underneath a bridge embankment on the LA River.

They proceeded to find the classiest restaurant in town; some place that required reservations would be good. Mari thumbed the yellow pages, found just the right place and called for reservations. Before entering the restaurant they strolled the promenade where passersby gawked in disbelief. Several very proper ladies had gathered near the corner. As the lovers approached, there were stares and whispers coming from the crowd. Tom said, "Mari, let me give you a piggyback ride." Mari hiked her skirt to her waist and jumped up on his back with her arms around his neck. He galloped like a horse past the onlookers, turning the corner toward the restaurant. Gently letting her to the ground, she straightened her skirt. He planned to enter the restaurant first just to see what would happen, and then she would come in after a few minutes and grab him by the arm, announcing that she had made reservations.

Tom entered the door of Restaurant Chateaulin, regarded as one of the Pacific Northwest's premier French restaurants, located next to the Oregon Shakespeare Festival Theatres. The ambiance seemed relaxed and charming. The maître d' stepped forward. His smile was upbeat at first then shifted. It all happened in slow motion. It took the maître d' a couple of seconds to make sure he wasn't seeing things, "Can I help you?" Tom said, "Yes, I have reservations for 8:00."

"Your name?"

"Tom Sawyer."

"I'm sorry, you must have the wrong restaurant."

"Is this Chateaulin?"

"Yes."

Just then another couple entered through the front door dressed to the nines and did a double take on Tom. The maître d' immediately sat them at a table, glancing back at Tom from the dining room with a *Please go away* look. Tom stood in the entrance rocking back and forth. Mari was watching him through the frosted glass door. He stood there for almost ten minutes before the maître d' walked back, "I'm sorry, the restaurant is full." Mari made her move. She opened the door, stepped up next to Tom, slipped her arm under his and said, "We have reservations for 8:00—Mari Quihuis." The maître d's jaw dropped in wondrous disbelief. He smiled almost trance-like at Mari, "Oh yes, one moment." He picked up the reservation list and started thumbing. His face locked up in curiosity—he dared not ask. Very politely he said, "This way, please." The dining room was very romantic with white tablecloths, crystal glassware, burgundy carpet, fin-de-siècle etched glass partitions and polished wood. The walls were covered with prints of Paris.

It turned out to be a great experiment in human behavior. The dinner was exquisite; the people were friendly. Everyone in the restaurant was curious. The primary look on women's faces was one of compassion; *She must be treating this poor soul to dinner.* Almost every man in the place was taking turns looking, first at Mari then at Tom with a bewildered look, *How did he ever get a woman like that?* Tom wondered the same thing himself.

9

*"When I am with you, we stay up all night.
When you are not here, I cannot go to sleep.
Praise God for these two insomnias
and the difference between them."*

Mevlana Rumi

Valley of the Moon

It's early. Tom has just returned to the water tower from his morning walk. He's been out gathering eucalyptus leaves by the railroad tracks. He boils them down on a camp stove under the oak tree out front; extracting oil he believes will be a new body-lotion he and Mari can sell. Sitting with his elbows on the picnic table that doubles as an outside kitchen and office, he felt discouraged by the idea and went inside. He sat down on the toilet, and stared at the photos of Mari plastered to the RV-refrigerator door three feet in front of him. He loves to look away feeling her eyes still on him. He was ready to do something, but the right idea just hadn't come yet. Pulling up his red suspenders, he put on an overcoat and walked across the field near the abandoned chicken farm, heading for the railroad tracks. Halfway across the field he stopped and looked back at the water tower. Noticing the morning sun flashing off the windows at the top, he glanced off into the distance…he was running out of money. He had to do something or lose the log cabin property to back taxes.

Ol' Gal and The Hill were about all he had left. Since his children had spent their formative years growing up in the wilderness there, he wanted to make sure that someday they would receive their legacy. And how was he going to marry Mari without a job? He had spent the last three weeks hunting for software engineering work in Santa Rosa as well as Grass Valley, putting in applications at several firms; nothing seemed to pan out. Reality was setting in.

He continued his morning ritual along the tracks, hoping to find some little jewels that might make Mari smile. Approaching the bend he looked down the tracks and watched them narrow into the distance. Two stray dogs were playing near a drainage ditch to his left. The wind blew the grass back and forth like waves in the sea, reminding him of his farm in Oregon. That's when it hit him; he would have to go back to Oregon to find work.

That afternoon he went with his sister, Theresa, to a belly-dancing school and purchased a purple-violet silk dress from India with a butterfly belt from one of the instructors. He carefully wrapped it in newspaper and gave it to Mari. She wanted to know if the gift was clothes. He didn't know it at the time, but she hated for anyone to buy her clothes and told him so as she opened the package. Slowly removing the paper, one page at a time, she exposed the silk cloth lying underneath the black and white newsprint. To her surprise, she loved it. She pulled the dress close to her body and spun around, smiling like a child.

Ever since their return from Oregon, they had been working on the screen-divider envisioned at the cabin. The idea was to create decorative screens and sell them in Marin, making their living together through art. Tom had all the walnut wood cut and had finished the sanding. Mari had completed the hand-painted silk panels they would mount in the three walnut frames. Over the next few days they fulfilled the first part of the dream and finished the assembly. Tom even had a brass plate engraved that said, "TOMARI 1988" and fixed it to one of the legs. They had three weeks of work, plus materials, in the project and were hoping to get $1200-1500. They had a grand time going from shop to shop in Marin, but the most they were offered was $600. As much as they would have liked to continue the dream, it wasn't going to work. They discussed it, and as painful as it was, Tom would have to go to Oregon to find work or lose the property.

He moved his possessions from the water tower into Mari's bedroom closet at her parents' house and said his goodbyes. Hoping for good weather, on February 11, 1988 he packed a few provisions and headed for the buffalo ranch on Ol' Gal. David & Bud were going to put him up at the ranch until he found work. He planned to get a small grubstake by selling his '53 Chevy coupe and the one-ton flatbed truck stored at the ranch.

He made the trip in good time, and with fair weather rolled into Cornelius, Oregon the next day. Once settled in, he began making phone calls to all his old high-tech connections. Certain he would find work, he began dreaming how he, Mari and the boys were going to live on a farm in Oregon with horses, sheep and all kinds of animals. Maybe he would even have a dog again. Through his associates, he hoped to get in the back door of a software firm, but unemployment was high everywhere. He began to get disheartened. He sold the car and truck which brought him up a little, but that wasn't going to cover the back taxes and it certainly wasn't anything he could begin a family on.

He was missing Mari badly—he stumbled off the curb onto a "white line," so to speak. The next day he wired what money was left to Mari's bank account and called her on the phone. It was Valentine's Day. He confessed his departure from the straight and narrow—she told him not to bother to come back; she would return the money. After three days of phone calls and promises of "never again," she took him back. So elated by her forgiveness and the prospects of being together again, he did what he had hoped he wouldn't ever have to do. He called his mother in Grass Valley and asked to borrow enough money to pay the back taxes. She understood, and told him not to worry; help would come when he really needed it. With most of the grubstake in Mari's bank account and the property covered, he saw light at the end of the tunnel. Something good was going to happen, but he was going to have to work for it. On February 19th, homesick and somewhat optimistic, he left the buffalo ranch for Santa Rosa.

After a long two-day run on Ol' Gal, he pulled up in front of Mari's house covered with road grime and grease spatters from the motorcycle's faulty chain-oiler. She must have heard the bike turn the corner, because she was standing in the driveway with a most interesting look on her face. Her left eyebrow was lifted, as if to say, *I'm not too sure about you,* yet her mouth was smiling from ear to ear. They were elated to see each other. The last week had been an ordeal that tested the glue binding them together. She gave him a verbal warning, punched him in the shoulder and threw her arms around him. He felt every road-weary muscle in his body relax—home again.

Mari told him to take a shower. He hadn't bathed since he left. She laid out clean clothes on the bed and afterwards they sat on the front room couch, cuddled up in each other's arms. Didi approached in a businesslike manner, "Tom, and how was your trip?"

"It was long, but the weather was pretty good."

"Did you find work in Oregon?"

"No."

Mari leaned over and whispered in Tom's ear, "Are you going to ask him?" Didi wore hearing aids in both ears and couldn't quite make out what she said, but by his body posture, Tom could tell he knew that something was up. Tom sat straight up, cleared his throat and said affectionately, "Didi, I would like your permission to marry your daughter." Didi's eyes got all big, "What the hell you asking me for, she's 37 years old with two kids?" Tom swallowed, took a deep breath and replied, "Well, I'm asking for your blessing." Didi yelled, "Gee, can you come in here?"

Noni's voice rang out from the kitchen, "Be right there." A few minutes later she showed up, "What is it?"

"Tom wants to marry Mari and is asking for our permission!"

Noni looked shocked and stammered for words, "W..e..l..l, we should talk about it, later." Noni looked at Mari and then over at Tom with a slightly worried gaze, then turned and went back in the kitchen. Mari looked at Didi and said, "How do *you* feel about it?"

"Where are you going to live?"

When Didi asked that question, it became apparent to Tom that the worried look on Noni's face was about the boys. *Would her grandchildren be moving away?* Tom answered Didi with respect, "I'm not sure. I have to find work. I hope to find work here in Santa Rosa." The game show *Jeopardy* was just coming on and everyone settled into the program—nothing more was discussed that evening.

Tom spent the night in the park and returned to the house the next morning. When he knocked on the side door, Mari answered and told him, "Go into Didi's bedroom and sit on the bed, Didi wants to talk." Tom became puzzled and frightened—he felt like he was going to the principal's office. She repeated, "Go ahead, it's OK, he just wants to talk." Tom entered the door off the hallway leading to Didi's office/ bedroom/inner sanctum. With an unshaven face and the blankets pulled up to his waist, wearing a V-neck T-shirt, Didi lit up a Pall Mall and bellowed out as though he were calling a meeting of a board of directors, "Tom, please come in and sit down." Tom looked around and didn't see any chairs, so he sat on the edge of the bed as Mari had instructed. "Did you rest well?"

"Yes."

"After breakfast I'd like to take you to the company warehouse."

"OK, what did you have in mind?"

"I'd like to show you around."

"OK."

After a 30-second silence Tom said, "Was there anything else?"

"NO, go get some breakfast and I'll get dressed."

After breakfast Tom and Didi drove to the company warehouse in Didi's brand-new Cadillac. Stepping out of the car Didi stood by the door and lit up another Pall Mall. Taking a deep drag off his cigarette he began a documentary narration of how the company was founded and his involvement in its creation. He told Tom that when he worked for the railroad he got involved with computers and soon developed an accounting program that saved the railroad thousands of dollars. Higher management took total credit for his work without giving him a dime. He quit the railroad and during this period, his family began to go hungry. One day after coming home from job searching and finding no food in the house, he swore to himself that his family would never go hungry again. He decided to get involved with a wholesale grocery business that was just starting up in Los Angeles. By taking the innovations he had created for the railroad and applying them to the wholesale grocery business, he was able to bring a significant contribution to the newly formed start-up. And as CEO, over the last 20 years, he had been able to grow the company to a $400,000,000-a-year operation.

Didi walked toward the massive warehouse. Pulling a set of keys from his right pocket he opened the door. It was Washington's Birthday and only one man was on duty. As Didi approached, the man snapped to attention, addressing Didi as, "Mr. G." After a formal introduction, Didi asked Tom to look over the warehouse and asked him if there was something he wanted. Tom looked around the football-length facility stacked with every kind of grocery item imaginable, but didn't ask for anything. He felt as though he were being interviewed for a job. As the conversation continued it became clear that Didi was giving his blessing for the marriage. Woven in between the lines were bits of hope; hope that Mari and the boys would not be moving away. Although the conversation went on for some time they never spoke directly of this.

Keeping in mind how painful it would be for Noni, Didi, and Pauline if he moved the boys out of town, Tom kept looking for work in Santa Rosa. He put in an application as an embedded systems engineer at a company called Weightronix near the Sonoma County Airport and left the next day for Grass Valley.

He became troubled by the dilemma. If he didn't find work in Santa Rosa, marrying Mari would cause great pain to her family, yet he needed to find work if he were to marry her. He loved her boys and knew he would bring them up as his own.

In Grass Valley he put in an application with the Grass Valley Group as a design engineer and waited for the phone call which never came. Following a lead in the newspaper he found a temporary job as a software consultant, programming in "C" for a small marketing firm in a newly-formed commercial area near Grass Valley, and moved back in with his brother Ray.

Finally, after a tremendous amount of soul searching, Tom was prepared to move Mari and the boys to Grass Valley, but prayed that somehow he would find work in Santa Rosa.

Mari called three weeks later; she wanted to take him to a temple up in the mountains above Cazadero. That weekend Tom flew in on Ol' Gal just in time for Croatian dinner. He slept underneath the oaks in a nearby field and woke the next morning in time for waffles.

He was curious about where they were going, not that it made any difference; he just liked to watch Mari during her explanations. She had learned from childhood to be very precise with information and it gave him an excuse to gaze at her, as if he were listening to every word. He was always interested in what she had to say, but was even more interested in observing the way she held herself so royal-like when providing information. But most of all, he liked to watch her lips. There was something about her eyes and her lips that carried him away.

After skim-listening for ten minutes he said, "How far did you say it was?" Mari replied forcefully, "T..o..m, didn't you hear a thing I said?" He just stared; he loved seeing her get all "CEO." Sparks jumped from her eyes, her elegant long neck elevated. She stood erect. Lifting her left eyebrow, she placed her hands on her hips, and retorted, "Is there something wrong with you?" He calmly replied, "No, you said about 30 miles." Secretly inside he was smiling, thinking, *My God, you're beautiful.*

The plan was: they were going to go to Odiyan, then on to lower Salt Point on the coast, and spend several nights in a campground. After packing up all their gear they headed out in Mari's car for Cazadero. On their way they passed through Forestville and the Korbel Winery. On the outskirts of

Guerneville Mari slowed down and said, "Keep your eyes peeled for a road on the right called Old Cazadero Road." A hundred feet later Tom yelled out, "There it is."

Turning off Highway 116 onto an old country road that wound up into the mountains, they crossed Mission Creek and continued past the little town of Monte Rosa. Passing through redwood trees and rolling green meadows, they continued their way up the hill five miles, to a plateau that looked out over a small valley to the west. Mari pulled over and got out. "Smell that air...I love it here. We have to cross a creek up ahead. I hope the car can make it." Tom replied with a quote from Gandhi, "What we can do, we will try to do." He didn't care if they had to carry the car across the creek, every moment with her was its own reality—he didn't care from one moment to the next as long as she was there.

They continued down into a sleepy little green valley. The smell of black oak, Pacific madrone, alder, and moss scented the air. Arriving at the creek, Tom got out of the car and grabbed a stick lying near the road. He walked to the water's edge and waded into the middle of the creek. Pushing the stick down into the water at midstream, he marked the depth with his thumb, looked back at Mari and smiled. She was wondering what the heck he was doing. As he walked back to the car, he told her to "pop the hood." He pushed the stick down to the ground next to the engine and said, "Looks like we can make it." He wanted to make sure that the water level, once they entered the stream, wouldn't flood the distributor cap; it was marginal. He waved her on. The car entered the water. Halfway in, the wheels began to slip. Tom yelled, "Hold it." Knee-deep in water, he started pushing on the back of the car as Mari slowly let out the clutch. That did it. They were up on the bank and rolling down the other side. Mari stopped and Tom jumped in.

He started to sing a silly song from his childhood:
"Puff and Toot,
Puff and Toot,
Puff and Toot's his name,

Puff and Toot,

Puff and Toot,

Little choo-choo train.

We'll see cows and horses and chicken chickarees,

We'll be gone all summer so let's be on our way,

We're off to the country, off to the country, Oh what a lovely day."

Turning her head, jaw-dropped, she placed her lips together and grinned, "What a lovely song."

Passing through the tiny lumber town of Cazadero, they continued up Tin Barn Road into sheep country. Hundreds of sheep grazed the grassy rock-laden plain of the western Cazadero plateau. After driving 12 miles on a dirt road, something began to appear in the distance. As they continued up the hill, it got bigger, and brighter. It was huge. It looked like a flying soccer the size of a football field slowly lifting off the ground. Tom looked over at Mari and said, "What is that?" She kept her eyes ahead; a smile appeared on her face. She knew something he didn't know. Another 50 yards and there it was in full view. She stopped the car and got out. Following her every step he repeated again, "Mari, what is that?" She lifted her arms into the air and said, "Odiyan." They climbed a big rock and sat shoulder-to-shoulder with legs crossed, looking down into the next valley. Mari began to explain. "Tibetan Buddhist monks along with Odiyan's founder Tarthang Tulka, originally from Eastern Tibet, came here to this valley ten years ago and started construction of the main temple. No outsider is allowed in, except by special invitation. The main temple dome is made of gold leaf. Inside there are 108,000 carved statues of Buddha circling the inside wall on ten miles of shelves; at the center is a ten-ton prayer wheel, the largest in the world." Tom was speechless. They sat there for quite some time saying nothing, just gazing at the wonder.

After surveying the temple grounds, they spent the next four days walking the beach at Salt Point. Every seagull was a messenger. Every wave that hit the sand became a memory.

These sounds would literally ring in Tom's heart in the years to follow.

A few days later he returned to Grass Valley and continued working, depositing as much money as he could into Mari's bank account, keeping a little savings on the side for the wedding ring she didn't know about. In their minds they were already married and for the time being, they would have to live apart.

Tom put in another application at Grass Valley Group as a hardware/software engineer and continued working part-time for the marketing firm. Sometime in April, Mari and the boys moved from her parent's house to a house on Neo Street in Bennett Valley near Santa Rosa. The stage was set; now he only needed to find work in Santa Rosa and they could begin settling into family life. After several weeks of missing each other, Tom called and suggested that they go on a gold-panning trip to the Mother Lode.

There they were again, off on another adventure. If they could have afforded it, they would have wandered the planet for years, never feeling lost. After several days of camping and drifting through the minefields of Allegany they came upon a sign alongside a dirt road, pointing down into a canyon. It read "Kenton Mine Lodge." Mari said, "What do you think it is?" Tom replied, "Not sure, but maybe they've got some food. You want to check it out?" The road wound down into a steep gorge bordering the river near Minnesota Flats. They weren't sure what they'd run into, but "what the hell," down the road they went. Chaotic rock formations paved the road a quarter mile in, trees lined the way to two large splintered posts with strange markings. Across the top was a sign that read "KENTON MINE."

They continued under the sign. To the left were two rusted-out vintage cars, old mining equipment, and what was left of a wooden sod wagon. To the right several buildings along the river appeared abandoned. They parked the car by the river and walked over to one of the buildings. Stepping up onto the porch, Mari looked in the windows while Tom kept a lookout on the road. Turning, she stumbled on a broken step, scratching her knee as she fell to the ground. She looked up at Tom running towards her, "It's no big deal, I'm alright."

"What's in there?"

"Beds. This must be part of the lodge or bunks for miners."

"There's a road branching off to the left, you want to follow it?"

"Sure."

Not too far in they started seeing large piles of firewood, a fresh chainsaw, cans of oil, and rusted 55-gallon drums heaped up near an old log building. They pulled the car in front and shut off the motor.

Tom cautiously stepped out of the car and walked up the cement steps to the front door and knocked. A thin elderly man appeared at the screen door, followed by a sweet, heavyset older woman. Tom said, "We saw your sign up on the road and thought we might find something to eat." The old woman replied, "We're not open. The season hasn't started yet." Mari walked up the steps behind Tom, saying, "Oh, OK. Sorry to bother you. We were just looking for something…" The old man interrupted, "What do you think, Mother? Come on in, we can figure out something."

The lovers opened the screen door and walked in. In front was a long wooden table, the kind of table that had served a thousand meals, food-stained, rustic, but clean, with wooden chairs all around. Each chair was different; some had cushions and some were just plain wood. Most of the backrests had missing uprights, but were still functional. To the left was an old piano. Above the piano was a gun rack with two rifles; a shotgun was leaning against the piano bench. To the right was a potbelly stove. The kitchen was partially visible through a serving bay cut in the logs. A large muscular man with his shirt off walked in from the kitchen to the far side of the table, picked up a set of barbells and began working out. Mari and Tom looked over at each other, mentally saying, *Kind of strange.*

The man kept pumping iron and flexing his biceps, occasionally looking over at Mari, then back at his swollen muscles. The old man walked in from the kitchen and introduced the bodybuilder, "This is Ernie. He helps out around the place." Ernie's face turned shy as he continued to show off his massive muscles and wipe sweat from his brow. Ernie looked like he hadn't seen a woman in years. He looked to be in his late 30s, but had the persona of a teenager. He seemed to respond to the old man's looks, which made Tom feel more comfortable.

Coming in from the kitchen, the old man turned to Tom and asked, "What do you and the missus want to eat?"

"Do you have hamburgers and a salad?"

"Mother, do we have fixin's for hamburgers?"

Mother yelled back from the kitchen in a high-pitched voice, "NO."

"What do we got in there that we can fix these kids?"

Mother replied, "We got duck and T-bone steak."

The old man said, "How's that, roast duck and T-bone."

Tom looked over at Mari with a smile and said, "That sounds great."

Mari whispered to Tom, "Like, is this for real?" Tom asked the old man how much it would cost for such a meal. The old man replied, "You pay after." Tom tried again, "We just want to make sure we have enough money." The old man repeated, "You pay after." Tom looked at Mari and answered, "OK, I would like the steak and Mari would like the duck." The old man asked the lovers to sit and went back in the kitchen while Tom and Mari watched Ernie lift weights—it was kind of like watching TV with the sound off.

The old man came back in with two kerosene lamps. He set them on the table and smiled as he adjusted the flame. Then walked back into the kitchen. A few minutes later it all began to happen. First the salad with some exotic balsamic vinegar dressing, followed in courses by miner's soup, cooked potatoes and carrots smothered in butter, glazed roast duck flavored with orange sauce, marinated T-bone steak cooked to perfection, and Mother's hot apple pie; all unbelievably delicious.

While Tom and Mari ate through each course, Mother and Father returned to the kitchen for cleanup. During apple pie they came out and sat at the table and told stories while Ernie continued to lift weights. Tom asked if Father played the piano. Father got up from the table and leisurely walked toward the piano. He picked up the double-barrel shotgun with a curious look and slowly placed it in the rack above the piano. Turning with a grin, he sat down and began playing a rinky-dink saloon song. After a few minutes, he lifted his hands from the keyboard and the piano continued to play. Father turned with a little-boy grin, "It's a player piano!" They all laughed, even Ernie. Mother asked Mari if they'd be spending the night. Mari replied, "We have to get back to town." Mother looked a little disappointed. Tom asked, "How much do we owe you?" Father looked up at the ceiling and said, "$25." Tom pulled two 20s from his wallet and handed them to Father, "Please keep it, that was a wonderful meal." When the lovers opened the screen door, heading for the car, Ernie glanced over with a sad look on his face. Mother and Father walked down off the porch and waved the lovers off. They waved until they were out of sight.

That night, back in Grass Valley, Tom removed a small bottle from his backpack containing the black powder (iron pyrites and gold dust) they had collected during their days of gold panning, and dumped the contents into a large spoon. He removed another small bottle containing mercury, adding it to the black powder. Stirring the contents, he poured the mercury off into a woman's nylon stocking. Twisting the sock, the mercury popped out through the other side and fell back into the bottle. He reversed the sock and scraped what was left into a small metal spoon. Holding the spoon away from his face, he heated the spoon with a lighter. A poisonous puff of white smoke dispersed into the air. What was left in the spoon was gold! Between the two of them they had panned less than $50 worth, but having those days together was worth more than all the gold in Nevada County.

Mari went back to Santa Rosa the following day. For the next few months Tom continued to work for the marketing firm, taking time off here and there to go with Mari on little adventures. In late May he received a phone call from Grass Valley Group to come in for an interview. Several days later they called to say that the company was looking for someone with a stronger background in analog design. In a way, he was relieved, but on the other hand he knew he had to find something stable before he and Mari could marry.

In the meantime, Mari had purchased two new possessions. She called him on her new phone and told him that she had also bought a wedding dress. He was elated. On June 2, 1988 she graduated summa cum laude from Sonoma State University with a degree in clinical psychology. It was on that same day that he slipped a modest but beautiful solitaire diamond engagement ring on her left hand. Now it was official; they would be married in July. The families were rejoicing—everyone heard wedding bells ringing in the hearts of the two Gypsy lovers. Two weeks later Tom went with Mari to her family's annual gathering, spending a week with a clan of 20 or so Croatians. Each one, in their own way, blessed their coming together. Even though Tom hadn't found work, that weekend the two lovers stood near Vernal Falls on the Mist Trail at Yosemite and made plans for their wedding. It would be a traditional Huichol wedding with vows of their own choosing.

On June 26th they purchased the wedding license and began making formal plans. The following week Mari left for a weeklong retreat in the mountains of New Mexico with her ex-mother-in-law and spiritual teacher, Jaichima. Upon Mari's return, all had provided their blessings, and preparations for the wedding were to begin. A dear friend of Mari's, Gale, who lived in the western mountains outside of Healdsburg, provided a place for the "isolation."

On July 12th Mari and Tom were separately taken blindfolded into the forest. The landscape was steep and full of oaks, with tall dry grass on either side of the path leading into the woods. Mari carried a bedroll tied together with rope over her right shoulder. Her friend carried a canteen filled with water. A slight breeze blew the tops of the grazing land, now home for rattlesnakes, wild boar, deer and coyotes. Holding the hand of her trusted female friend, Mari continued the climb. The sun was hot, baking the top of her black hair. Another hundred yards and the smell changed from musky oaks and dry grass to a sweet pine smell. She knew they were entering the forest. The temperature began to drop as they walked under a canopy of trees on the north face where the trail leveled out. Her friend started skipping. They both began to giggle. Her friend reached down and picked a Lazy Susan, placing the bright brown-and-yellow flower in Mari's hair, "Oh Mari, you look so beautiful. Not much further." Mari smiled, following deeper and deeper into the woods. They playfully strolled for another 15 minutes. "We're here, Mari. Let me take your blindfold off." Mari turned and held her friend's hands. "Do you think I'll make a good wife for Tom?" Her friend replied, "Oh Mari, you're so lovely, you'll make a wonderful bride."

"No, that's not what I mean. Will I make a good wife? I'm afraid of my shadow self."

"We all have that to consider. The love between you two is strong."

"That's what I mean. Tom loves me so much, I never want to hurt him."

"Remember that you will mirror each other and your mirrors will not always be clean. When your mirror is dirty, he will not see himself in the same way as when your mirror is clean and visa versa. A deep, committed relationship is the eagle's path. You will learn quickly about your strengths and weaknesses. Conscious marriage is one of the highest forms of spiritual evolution. It tests every aspect of the spirit."

Mari sighed and commenced laying out her bedroll. Trees in the small but beautiful meadow surrounded her. She had no idea where she was or how to get back if something unusual were to happen. A thought passed through her mind, *Night will come soon, I'll be alone in the dark.* Throwing a kiss goodbye, she thanked her friend and lay down in the meadow looking up at the northern sky.

Tom was led in another direction. He was taken blindfolded to the top of a high ridge that looked down onto a ravine to the left of a small grotto near an abyss. Rather than sleeping out in the open on the ridge, he made his camp in the trees near an old fir stump, which would serve as a bench in the days to come. His guide and friend read him words from Meher Baba:

"Love is different from lust. In lust there is reliance upon a sensual object and consequent spiritual subordination of oneself to it, whereas love puts one into direct relation with the reality behind the form. Love is equally different from greed, which is jealousy. Greed is possessiveness in all its gross and subtle forms. It seeks to appropriate persons and gross objects, as well as such abstract and intangible things as fame and power. In love, the annexation of another person to one's individual life is out of the question, and there is a free and creative outpouring that enlivens and replenishes the being of the beloved independently of any expectations for the self. The paradox of greed, which seeks the appropriation of another object, in fact leads to the opposite result of bringing the self under the tutelage of the object. Whereas love, which aims at giving away the self to the object, in fact leads to a spiritual incorporation of the beloved in the very being of the lover. Human love is tethered by these limitations of greed, jealousy and anger."

Then Tom's friend went on with his own words, "And if you didn't have at least one of these you wouldn't be here on this planet. Love does not hurt, only these things hurt. In human love, the duality of the lover and the beloved persists, but in Divine love, the lover and the beloved become one." And with that he hugged Tom and waved goodbye.

Each betrothed was given a location far from the other. They were allowed only a blanket and slept on the ground or among the trees. Each would remain fasting in the forest for three days and three nights with only water. No visitors were allowed, except a few appointed people who would come under the direction of the Shaman Jaichima to give advice about partnership and guidance to the spirit of these lovers. Only men could visit Tom and only women could visit Mari.

On the third day, Jaichima and Vicente Rutury came and blessed them both separately. Then they were taken individually to a home outside of Santa Rosa where they were dressed in formal attire for the wedding. Mari wore a long white wedding dress and Tom a light blue tuxedo. They were not allowed to see each other until the actual ceremony began. From there they were taken up into the mountains above the Valley of the Moon east of Santa Rosa and made to stand far apart from each other near a large oak tree in the middle of a meadow.

Two weeks before, Mari had hand-sewn wedding scarves from instructions given her by Jaichima during the New Mexico retreat. Mari had made a white scarf with red trim for Tom and a white lace scarf for herself.

Each wearing their scarves, they looked over at one another for the first time since their seclusion. Despite being light-headed and dehydrated from the fast, they were so happy to see one another again. Mari's father stood next to her and Tom's mother stood next to him. Mari was wearing a pink rose in her hair and holding a large bouquet of brightly colored flowers in her left hand. Her right arm was under the arm of her father. He wore a gray silk suit and gray tie with a yellow rose pinned to his lapel. They truly looked distinguished together. Didi stood tall and proud; Mari was happy that her father was giving her away. Tom's mother wore a blue and white dress with a pink corsage; she stood in contrast, like a beautiful Gypsy woman against the landscape of rolling hills and oaks. Mari and her father and Tom and his mother walked toward each other, stopping at the base of the large oak tree, three feet from one another.

A few minutes later Jaichima and Vicente joined them. Jaichima was dressed in white with a medicine bag over her shoulder. The bottom of her dress was embroidered with red and blue geometric Huichol designs. She wore a large brightly embellished hat with tassels; dazzling feathers garlanded the top of her head. In each hand she carried feathered prayer sticks. Vicente wore light traditional Mara'akame shaman clothes; he carried two human bones, each clustered with tiny bat wings, in his left hand and a gourd rattle in his right.

All the relatives were there on both sides of the family; some had traveled more than 1,000 miles. Wirikuta people, Rajneesh sannyasins, street people, Buddhists, mountain people, friends, and several of Mari's old lovers formed a circle around the oak tree—about 250 in all. Breaking the circle, they lined up one after another, forming a spiral around the lovers. Each held a small candle with a ribbon, prepared days earlier by the bride and groom. Jaichima began the wedding ceremony, speaking mostly in Huichol with a few English words thrown in here and there. Then Vicente spoke, again mostly in Huichol. The chants and whispered words connected the two lovers through the spirits of the ancestors and ancient earthly pasts.

Vicente lit a candle and handed it to Tom. Then Jaichima lit a candle and passed it to Mari. Tom and Mari touched their candles together mingling the flames back and forth. Together they lit the candle of the first person on their left. That person, in turn, lit the candle of the person next to them and so on, until all 250 candles were burning in the spiral of friends and family. Two Wirikutas, Howchi and Ulu, beat leather drums as Jaichima and Vicente continued to chanted sacred words during the lighting. After all the candles were lit, the drums became quiet.

Tom turned to Mari and began to speak: "You are my *sadhana* (my spiritual practice)." Mari replied, "You are my beloved partner on the path. Take the first step." They each walked a quarter turn in a circle and faced each other.

Tom said, "Let us walk towards the Light together."

Mari replied, "Remembering we are free, offering love and acceptance."

"Take the second step."

They walked a quarter turn and faced each other.

Mari said, "Learning that which we could not learn alone."

"Take the third step."

Again they walked and faced each other.

"The place where all things meet. Take the fourth step."

Once more they walked and faced each other.

Tom spoke, "With joy in my heart, welcome home."

Mari whispered, "Welcome home."

Then their twin boys handed rings to the bride and groom. The lovers took turns placing the ring on each other's finger while gazing into one another's eyes. They were then given beaded rings that they wore on their right hands. Jaichima placed the prayer stick over Mari's heart and spoke in Huichol, doing the same to Tom; she took a corner of each of their scarves and tied them together in a knot—and with that, she pronounced them man and wife.

They kissed a long kiss. Suddenly the drums started up again. They began walking through the spiral formed by their friends and relatives, with their twin boys following behind. Adam carried a four-foot-tall blue-and-pink Huichol wedding cross and Jacob carried flowers, followed by Tom's children Larry and Tiffany and Tom and Mari's parents. As they walked in procession through the spiral, different ones spoke out giving blessings.

They were married on July 16th 1988, in the Valley of the Moon, in the mountains east of Santa Rosa where an isolated green valley trimmed by a river meanders into the plains below. On a full moon night the river is lit with a mystical shimmer. The place is said to be inhabited by the spirit of the moon/sea Goddess, Mari-Anna-Ishtar. It is said, walking the river at night, some have encountered gnomes, divas and wood nymphs playing on the banks in the moonlight.

Ironically Tiffany, who had come from Oregon to see her father wed, met a boy named Curt at the wedding. She didn't return to Oregon for ten years. Later they married and had two children.

That night, after the reception, Tom and Mari came home to their house on Neo and slept for two days. Noni and Didi watched the boys while the newlyweds set off on their honeymoon adventure the following day. Their first stop would be Blayney Hot Springs in the John Muir Wilderness area, along the South Fork of the San Joaquin River.

Outside of Fresno, they took Highway 168, climbing 7,000 feet to the Kaiser Pass. Then up Forest Service Road 4S01, a notorious road that winds up to 10,000 feet. It is a one-lane road in many areas and moves along sheer cliffs with no guardrails. There were times when they had to back down the road to let downhill traffic get by. Once at Lake Florence, they acquired wilderness permits from the ranger station and rented a ride across the lake from a fisherman in a small boat. The lake was calm and clear, almost sapphire blue. The fisherman let them out on a huge granite outcropping near the north shore. Massive trees jutted out through sheer rock high above them. The air was hot with the sweet smell of pine. They unloaded their gear and waved goodbye to the fisherman. Tom remembered the look on Mari's face; it was one of remoteness and respect for unseen forces in nature.

There were no roads from there, just miles of trail into the wilderness. They headed north, not quite sure how to get to the springs. About a mile up the trail, they came across an old man with a pack mule and asked directions. He said if they continued to follow the trail nine miles up, they would be close to the hot springs, but he wasn't able to explain what landmarks to look for.

Mari looked so cute from behind. Tom watched her walk. She wore brown hiking boots, white socks, bare legs up to the bottom of her large white boy's T-shirt that hung just below her cute little round bottom and pink underwear that flashed as she walked, and a large blue backpack with a sleeping bag attached at the top. Around her waist she had tied a narrow flat piece of purple cloth that hung just past her knees. When she walked, it swayed back and forth with the rhythm of her hips—if Tom were a fish, she was a finely-tied fly. After walking the trail for five miles, they decided to set up camp near the river.

They found a grassy meadow with purple wildflowers a hundred yards from the water. Tom never said it, but he was thinking, *Out of Alice in Wonderland.* He wanted to walk holding hands with Mari through that field of flowers, forever, never to return.

Throwing a rope high onto a branch of a large pine tree he strung the backpacks 20 feet up in the air. It was bear country and they needed to be careful with their food. They set up a one-man/two-lovers tent and built a small fire ring out in front. He cleared the grass down to the ground about five feet around the ring, while she gathered firewood. After the camp was set up they walked to the river and jumped in. It was 90° in the shade, but the water was ice cold. They screamed as they scampered naked into the water.

The river was crystal. Tom waded over near a beaver dam and was looking around when Mari showed up with a camera. She started laughing and taking pictures of his tattooed body. He yelled, "Mari, give me that thing, let's take your picture!" She ran off giggling. He chased after her, splashing through the water. She was laughing so hard she wet her pants. It was easy as pie getting the camera from her; she wouldn't stop laughing. He started taking pictures of her as she ran. She started putting on poses as he continued to click the shutter. She yelled, "Don't use up all that film." He kept clicking, running out the entire roll. Holding the camera in the air, he said, "Oops, it's all empty." She started splashing water at him. He ran for the tent laughing and yelling, "You're going to get the camera wet." They both ended up in the tent.

That night they heard rustling around their food packs up in the tree. By the time Tom got there with the flashlight and a metal pot to bang on, nothing was there and the packs looked OK. The next morning when they took their packs down, one side of the food pack had a two-foot slash in it, top to bottom. The pack was made of heavy canvas that could barely be cut with a knife. Tom had hung the packs too close to the tree trunk and a bear had climbed the tree, taking swipes at it in the middle of the night.

The next morning they got an early start and had been walking north about three miles when they came upon a log cabin, actually more like a log home with horses and corrals. They knocked on the door; a woman with long gray braids answered. Mari did the talking. "Good morning, we're looking for Blayney Hot Spring?" The woman replied, "Come in." The lovers entered. The woman started telling her story, going on for half an hour. Apparently she hadn't seen anyone for a while. She ran a small horse-packing outfit called the Muir Trail Ranch and was extremely helpful and friendly.

After telling her story she pointed toward the river, "You're almost there. Just walk in the direction of the river from here, cross the river and on the other side around some tall grass you'll find the springs. But be careful—one of the holes is scalding hot. It's marked, but put your hand in first. Last year some guy simply jumped in without testing for the temperature. He didn't come out alive." The newlyweds made their way across the meadow to the river. Once on the other side, there it was, just like the woman said, a tall thick grass area near the river. They took off their clothes and danced around. Testing the water with their hands, they slowly slipped in. It was hot, but wonderful. Someone had built a trough that mixed the scalding hot pool with the cold water from the river to create a just-right temperature.

They spent several days roaming meadows and camping along the river before making their way back to the landing at the granite outcropping on the north shoreline of Lake Florence. They had scheduled a pick-up for 3:00 that afternoon. The boat arrived on time. As they were going back across the lake Mari's hair was flying in the wind. She looked like a Greek Goddess. Tom started taking pictures. It was an incredible moment.

From Lake Florence they headed south, eventually making their way to Santa Barbara on Highway 1. There they spent the day wandering around Mari's old alma mater visiting all her old haunts, especially the coffee house she frequented back in university days, those days when every man's head turned to catch a glimpse. There she told him the story of when she was hitchhiking and was picked up by a man who took her to LA. That same man picked her up again hitchhiking in New York and again hitchhiking in France. She considered those her most significant coincidences, but never understood their meaning.

Continuing south, they stopped in Oxnard to visit Mari's *Teta* Mary (*Teta* means aunt in Croatian) and then to Newbury

Park. He took her to see where Rudy 'the hermit' lived before he passed away. Rudy's old shack was still standing. His little workshop had mostly been picked through; a few old Model 'A' parts remained scattered here and there. The rusted gas station thermometer still hung skewed over the front door. Only the ghost of Rudy rocking in a chair on the porch, carving on a wooden cane remained in Tom's mind.

Everything had changed. They walked back out to the road and drove higher up into the hills. Turning the bend by the chinchilla farm, the streetcar house and Grandma's cabin were still there, but the people had all changed. They stopped in front of Grandma's cabin. Tom looked out over the valley and remembered seeing his dog Oojie getting run over by a Helms truck near the bend in the road. It was the first time he had ever seen something die that meant so much to him. The memory was awful, and somehow activated other childhood memories. He grabbed Mari's hand and walked around behind Grandma's cabin. Looking down McKnight Road, he remembered taking turns one summer day, coasting down the hill in a small metal wagon with his friend Johnny and flipping over near the bottom of the then-graveled dirt road, sliding the last 20 feet on their bare backs and picking scabs off each other for the next month. He remembered sitting on the back porch with the sound of flies buzzing about his face, and the squeaking sounds of the screen door, and the churning of the wringer washing machine where his mother washed clothes.

Suddenly a man appeared at the back door. He had a curious look on his face. Tom said, "I used to live here years ago. Would it be OK if we look around?" Staring back at the married couple the man paused for moment in thought, and then said, "How long ago? I've lived here for 20 years." Tom replied, "I was a little boy. This used to be my grandma's place. I used to sleep upstairs. Do you think it would all right if we looked upstairs? I would love to look out through the pane-glass window into the valley one last time."

The man concurred and began walking up the rickety outside stairs that Tom had climbed a thousand times before. The memories became strong: he could smell the kerosene stove that "once upon a time," heated the cabin. As the man opened the door at the top of the landing the hinges made the same squeaky sound they had made 35 years ago. Everything seemed smaller than Tom remembered. To the left was where his grandpa's bed used to be, who had died before he was born; it was where his 18-year-old hero Uncle Larry had slept. The rumbling sounds of Larry and his buddy's hand-choking a Model 'A' jalopy in the driveway played in Tom's mind like a ghostly record.

It was in this room that his uncle passed down to him a bow and quiver of arrows. The moment poured through Tom's soul; to the boy and his uncle it had been a recognition-of-manhood. He remembered how honored he had felt and how that act had shaped his life.

Tom grabbed Mari's hand again and walked toward the closet next to where Grandpa's nightstand used to be. He turned to the man with a big grin on his face he said, "I know this seems unusual, but do you mind if I look in the closet?" The man nodded and Tom opened the closet door. He got down on his hands and knees and crawled to one corner. He placed his face on the floor and kept it there for the longest time, looking through a small hole into the past. Lifting his head from the floor he looked back at Mari and said, "It's still here." Both the man and Mari said at the same time, "What's still there?" Tom replied, "When I was a little boy, my uncle Larry drilled a hole in the floor in the corner of this closet that looks down into the bathroom below. One day Larry showed me his secret and told me never to tell—to this day I have never told anyone." Then Tom started laughing, "Look for yourself." The man went into the closet and looked down the hole, "Sure enough," he said, "I'll have to tell my wife." Mari's look changed from one of concern to a smile. They continued into the next room where Tom used to sleep. He stopped in front of a large pane-glass window to the right of the door and stared out to the valley below, drifting off into another memory. After several minutes of silence Mari said, "What are you thinking about?" Lifting his arm he pointed to the east end of the valley and replied:

"I'm remembering when my friend Dave and I hiked into Salto Creek Canyon. We were 13 years old and had followed the creek to a small cave about a quarter mile in. As we explored the cave we found a two-foot-wide hole poking up through the ceiling in the top of the cave. Pretending we were Indians, we built a campfire and started making up stories about the tribe that had once inhabited the area. The fire started burning low and I went to gather more wood. By the time I returned the fire was almost out. I started blowing on the coals to get it going again. Suddenly a large spark jumped from the fire, then another. I jumped back. Then all hell broke loose. It wasn't the coals popping. It was gunfire. From somewhere up above the canyon, someone was firing into the opening in the ceiling of the cave. Bullets were coming down the chimney, spinning around, hitting the campfire and bouncing off the walls. The pace picked up—it sounded like a machine gun.

"I took off my T-shirt, stuck it on the end of a dead branch I had collected for firewood and began climbing the hill to the right of the opening of the cave, waving it in the air. I looked back at Dave—he was in disbelief, almost frozen. We climbed 50 feet up to where we could see five teenagers rapidly firing rifles from the ridge above. We yelled and waved our white flag. As suddenly as it began, it stopped. By the time the teenagers crossed the creek to our side we could see their faces. They wore looks of terror, thinking they had killed someone—explaining that from above they had seen smoke coming up out of the rock, and thinking it was something natural from the earth, it would make a good target. Everyone learned something about themselves that day."

Tom dropped his arm and thanked the man for allowing him to reminisce on his property and walked back to the car. The lovers continued to stop here and there bringing up little moments from Tom's childhood. Except for Uncle Ted and Aunty Fay's place, most everything had changed.

When Tom was around ten he spent a summer at Aunty Fay's. Ted taught him about construction and flying 'fog fishing' and how to drive a boat and Fay taught him about kindness and family. Fay's father, a blacksmith, taught him how to throw his hip joint out of the socket for a beer. In those days young Tom had a crush on Aunty Fay and wanted to marry her.

They stopped at Earl's place. The house was no longer there. Earl was Grandma's old boyfriend who back in those days had pet raccoons and could fart on command. He could even fart the first couple of bars of Yankee Doodle. Of course he had long since passed away.

From Earl's place they went to Bobby Mander, one of Tom's old roaming buddies, whose father used to sit out on the porch of their silver paint-peeled trailer, half-snookered playing the banjo, tapping his wooden leg to the music and singing out of tune. The trailer wasn't there anymore and word had it, Bobby was doing time for holding up a gas station.

From there they took a back road across Hidden Valley, passing over the mountains to Coast Highway 1 at Malibu near the ocean, destination Lake Shrine.

Tucked away in a small ravine near the spot Sunset Boulevard meets Pacific Ocean Boulevard, near the sea, is a ten-acre site called Lake Shrine that contains a large round spring-fed lake, framed by natural hillsides and surrounded by lush flowers of every type. It has rushing waterfalls, fountains, and statues dedicated to all religions. White swans glide across the lake near a lacy fern grotto surrounded by lily pads. A peaceful, mystical energy permeates the area. Mari stood by a circular bed of red-and-white flowers in front of the Gandhi Memorial in a long white dress and red top. In that moment she took on the look of a sacred *deva* (nature spirit). Her golden-brown eyes glowed; something deep inside her projected itself to the surface of her outer being. Standing there in front of the 1,000-year-old Chinese stone sarcophagus near the shrine on the west side of the lake, the only place left on earth where one can visit the ashes of Mahatma Gandhi, Tom watched her transform into Divine Mother. Both blown away by the moment, they found a little wooden deck in a cove near a waterfall, and began meditating in silence. Just as they were coming out of their silence a man approached from the shore.

He introduced himself in a cheerful mellow voice, "Hello, my name is Turiyananda. I saw you two meditating—you looked so wonderful together. I live here at Lake Shrine with a few other monks. I'm a renegade and don't fit in real well with this conservative bunch. When I was young I spent a lot of time with Master Yogananda. He has since left his body and my body is getting old and I too will be leaving here soon, but I want to tell you about the Valley of the Gods. I hope you can go there someday." He removed a pen from his pocket and began drawing a map on a folded piece of paper; "It's very near Mexican Hat, by the Arizona border." This saintly older man was familiar and authentic; the lovers listened with deep reverence, searching for hidden meaning in his every word. They knew in that moment that someday they would go to the Valley of the Gods.

From Lake Shrine they went to Pershing Square in downtown LA where Tom used to shine shoes. He told her how he and Skip Spindler used to scoot across a 12-inch pipe ten stories in the air between the Church of the Open Door and the Biltmore Hotel. And how they once purchased suits from the Goodwill and pretended to be senator's sons at the Statler-Hilton, where they would impress the maître d's with their newfound status and raid the hors d'oeuvres.

Further south, they stopped in Inglewood to visit the street where Tom spent part of his growing up years, 50163 West 111th Place. The street was no longer there. A high school football field had replaced it.

They headed east towards the Grand Canyon but decided at the last minute to stop off in Las Vegas and take in a show. They rented a cheap room on the outskirts of town and walked to Caesar's Palace. After watching David Copperfield they returned to their room for the night.

Mari decided she wanted to play strip poker. She told Tom that the loser would have to jump up and down on the bed naked. The game began. Soon Mari was winning. The only thing he had left on was a sock on his left foot and underpants. Mari said, "I'll give you a chance to catch up; if you win this next hand I'll take everything off except for my left sock and underpants, but if you lose you have to take all your clothes off and jump up and down on the bed." Tom exclaimed, "Can I deal?" Mari replied with a Cheshire-Cat smile, "Of course you can." He carefully shuffled the cards, slapping the deck down on the table for the cut. She lowered her head, lifted one eyebrow and touched the deck leaving it pat. He dealt out five cards each. Mari asked for two cards; Tom said he was keeping his hand pat. He had a straight and thought for sure it was going to beat her possible three-of-a-kind. She smiled and said, "Well, lay 'em down." He sat up, cocking his shoulders back, "Bet you can't beat these." Flipping her hair to one side, she laid down her hand, and said, "Start taking 'em off." She had a diamond flush. Tom removed his left sock and underpants. Mari started giggling, "OK, jump up on the bed." He leaped up on the bed thinking, *This is not so bad.* With a huge smile she said, "OK, start jumping." He began doing jumping jacks until he realized that a certain thing was flopping up and down as he jumped. He became embarrassed and stopped. Mari exclaimed, "No, no, continue jumping." He started up again. She went into an uncontrollable belly laugh, rolling on the floor and pounding her fists to catch air before the next wave of laughter hit. As he continued to jump, he kept muttering, "Mari, this is not fair," which made her laugh even more.

The next morning they set out for the Grand Canyon. After spending a few hours walking around the rim, Tom talked Mari into taking a 45-mile shortcut across the desert on a dirt road marked "No Trespassing, Indian Reservation," on their way to Arizona. They got lost somewhere in a barren region along Manami Creek just off the reservation. Tom spotted an unmanned Forest Service lookout tower and climbed it. Mari was beginning to get a little short. He needed some good news; after all, he was supposed to be a mountain man. From the top he could see a road ten miles to the east. They took a compass reading, jumped in Mari's Honda and head east across the desert. Thirty minutes later they hit the pavement and turned right. Hoping the road was taking them in the right direction, about 15 miles down the highway they came across a small Indian outpost/gas-station/rock shop just north of Wupatki. They were on Highway 89, headed toward Flagstaff, on their way to Sedona. Mari was happy again and Tom had made several points for being a good navigator.

After meandering four states, they ended back at Neo where married life would move them downstream to their next rite of passage.

10

*"There's no emptiness in the life of a warrior.
Everything is filled to the brim."*

Carlos Castaneda

Neo

Six months later. The lovers have settled into their proper suburban Sonoma County home and are fixing up the place, working mostly at night and wandering during the day. While job-hunting, Tom spent several months developing a hare-brained idea. He wanted to build a magnetic perpetual motion machine and Mari helped him create some of the models, which eventually disproved most of his theories. Even though the venture turned out to be mostly blue-sky they surely had fun.

One afternoon while turning the corner from their daily walk, it dawned on them; the neighborhood was silent and correct. Occasional cars passed without a glance. No one waved. Passersby peeked intermittently with guarded smiles. Most stayed within the bounds of their 1970s remodeled homes with their perfectly landscaped lawns, reflecting safety over any display of culture or outward expression. Except for the latest new age-hippie-bikers that moved in three houses from the corner, Neo was a savagely peaceful scene that had hardly changed in 40 years. The mind had its place, the street had its place—people tried not to look at each other. The contrast reminded Tom of when he lived in a little fishing village on the northern coast of Antigua—in the midst of their terrible poverty everyone smiled and said, "Good morning."

At 5:35 AM, the sound of a newspaper hitting the front porch lifted Tom from his warm spoon-snuggled position next to Mari. Sitting up on one elbow he looked out the window through the trees into the backyard and stared at the foothills just beginning to silhouette in the dark of the morning. He's been tossing and turning and hasn't slept all night. Today is the big day. He's got a job interview over by the airport at 7:30 AM. Glancing over at Mari's brown-olive Croatian face, he rolled over and gently kissed her ear and whispered, "I love you."

In the bathroom he splashed cold water on his face, stinging his eyes. Bounding for the shower, he emerged singing "You Are My Sunshine." Standing on one leg, he dried off while a recurring thought passed through his mind, ...*we really need this job, but how will I survive leaving Mari every day?* Soon the smell of coffee and frying bacon moved him down stairs. Zombie-like, they ate their breakfast from plates on the floor while Tom laced up his boots.

For almost a year they had been together day and night— never away from the other. He approached this next passage with trepidation. Fear of being away from his sweetheart and "could he still perform in the corporate world," had haunted him.

After breakfast, out in the garage Mari stood beside him in front of Ol' Gal. Stroking the seat, he threw one leg over and grabbed the handlebars. Speaking out loud to his motorcycle he said, "Where are you taking me today, Ol' Gal?" Mari pressed her lips together, tilting her face slightly to one side, as if to say, *I'll miss you.* Locking onto her eyes, he pressed his right thumb down on the ignition switch; the cranking sound of the engine erupted into coughs and sputters followed by a loping roar. The smell of exhaust fumes filled the garage. Stepping off to open the door, he wheeled his idling mistress to the street. Underneath his jumpsuit he was wearing a white shirt, tie and brown slacks. The only things giving him away were his slightly scuffed motorcycle boots. In the street, in front of God and everyone, Mari kissed him as though he were going off to war. She yelled over the sound of the motor, "You always have to kiss me goodbye because we never know what the Universe has in store for us."

He headed north on 101. For 15 miles the cold blew across his face creating a permanent speechless smile. On Airport Boulevard, bearing west, he leaned back into the throttle and glanced upward at a Lear Jet on its final approach. He muttered to himself, "Someday I will learn to fly again." Flying on the ground as best he could, 90 in a 45, he banked into the corner near a large corporate building and downshifted, squealing the back tire in defiance of the world he was about to enter. Several blocks down on the right sat a large, almost windowless building with sprawling lawns and security gates. He stopped several blocks from the building and chained the motorcycle to a tree next to an abandoned army base. Removing his jumpsuit, he brushed his hair in the side mirror and walked towards a white two-story office building that took up the entire block. As he approached the building, he noticed a large granite marker in the center of the lawn, NCI–WEIGHTRONIX. He walked around the corner of the lawn and followed a cement walkway leading to two large mirrored-glass doors where he straightened his tie, tucked in his shirt and took two deep breaths. Pulling on the door to the right he heard a click; it was locked. He tried the door on the left. As the door opened, a woman talking on the phone behind a large wooden-paneled reception desk motioned him to sit down on the leather seats near the guard station.

After a few minutes she hung up the phone and said, "May I help you?" which sounded more like, "What are you doing here?" Tom said, "Good morning, I'm Tom Sawyer, I have a meeting with Mr. Brazis at 7:30." She replied, "Yes, what's your name?" "Tom Sawyer," he repeated. With an *Oh sure* sound in her voice she answered back, "One moment please." After picking up the phone and nodding at the guard, she spoke again, "Mr. Brazis will be with you in about 15 minutes." Tom began leafing through some of the journals on the table in front of him. A well-dressed man passing from one of the adjoining offices, walking fast, glanced over at him and continued out the front door. Several minutes later a tall friendly-looking gentleman appeared, "You must be Tom Sawyer, I'm George Brazis."

"Nice to meet you."

"Let's get you a visitor's pass."

Mr. Brazis walked Tom to the guard station and secured a laminate with VISITOR printed on it, number 7239, then said, "Come with me."

As they walked side by side down a long polished-linoleum hallway, Mr. Brazis stopped for a moment and said, "How do you like riding that Harley?" Tom became stunned and stuttered out of balance. He thought, *How could he know I ride a Harley? There's no way for him to know that. He's either psychic or they must do one hell of a background check.* They began walking again. After a long pause Tom broke the silence, "How do you know I ride a Harley?" The gentleman grinned, "Because I'm your next-door neighbor. I live in the house next to you on the right. You can call me George if you like." A thought passed through Tom's mind, *All those hot summer nights with the windows open.* He and George politely giggled and turned into a private office. George seated himself behind a glass-covered wooden desk and motioned Tom to sit down. They spent the better part of an hour going over Tom's background and qualifications. Then George gave him the Cook's Tour of the facilities, introducing him to several engineering management types before seeing him off at the front desk.

Tom fired up Ol' Gal and headed home. On the last street he gunned the engine and turned the corner onto Neo. There was Mari; she had heard the sound of the motorcycle coming and opened the garage door. He stepped off Ol' Gal and hugged her like he had been gone for months. She said, "How did it go?" He replied, "Guess what?"

"What, you got the job!"

"No, I don't know yet."

"Well, what?"

"The guy that interviewed me..."

"Yes?"

"He's our next-door neighbor."

"Oh no." She rolled her eyes, almost blushing and continued, "You know, those hot summer nights."

"That's what I was thinking."

"Well, we'd leave the windows open!"

"So?"

"Well…he probably heard."

"I think it's going to be OK. He smiled a lot!"

Mari slapped him on the shoulder and walked him arm-in-arm into the house.

Two weeks later Tom went to work at Weightronix as an embedded systems software engineer. Now life began to get full—fuller than they liked. Soccer for the boys, the lovers' everyday basket-lunch meetings at the Weightronix park bench, Tom's tooth-grinding performance-anxiety sleepless nights, their missing each other, the boys' homework, doctor bills, all the stuff of a full-on family commitment began to replace the previous year of sweet requited love.

They embarked on a new ritual. On Mondays after 6:00 PM they would not speak to each other. It was their silence day. They would write notes back and forth gazing into each other's eyes. Regardless of what trials came up they weathered the storms knowing the depth of their love could withstand anything…until one day, a year later, Tom came home from work.

As usual, he turned the corner gunning the motor in expectation that Mari would have opened the garage door and would be there waiting to greet him. The garage door was closed and Mari was nowhere in sight. He stepped off Ol' Gal, opened the garage door and wheeled the motorcycle in with the engine still idling. After a couple of revs on the throttle he shut off the motor and walked toward the side door. Something seemed strange. He opened the door with a smile on his face, ready to embrace his sweetheart— and saw the love of his life sitting cuddled up on the couch with another man. He placed his hand over his heart and backed out, slowly closing the door behind him. In the garage, he walked in circles, not believing his eyes.

He thought, *What happened—how could this be, is this some kind of test?* His heart was pounding—nothing seemed to make sense.

After gathering himself, he placed his hand on the doorknob and slowly opened the door. The man was still sitting on the couch. Mari had moved to the kitchen sink and was doing dishes. The look on her face was one of disappointment. After looking Tom directly in the eyes, she began, "Tom, you remember David—he was at our wedding."

"Yes."

"He stopped by to say hello. David, why don't you show Tom the slides that you brought back from India?"

David was a local anesthesiologist and an old friend of Mari's. They had met when she ran the Rajneesh meditation group in Santa Rosa years ago. Mari went on, "Show Tom the pictures of Babaji's cave."

David opened his briefcase and began going through photos.

"Here's one of the trailhead leading up to Baba's cave in the Himalayan Mountains near Dwarahat."

A few photographs later Tom began to relax. He walked into the kitchen and stood by Mari. Speaking in a low voice, he said, "Are you OK?" She replied, "I think so, are you OK?"

"I think so."

The disappointed look returned to her face. Tom turned and looked over at David sitting on the couch, then turned, looking back at Mari, "Can we talk in the other room?" She placed the dishtowel on the sink and walked quickly into the front room. She began whispering and then suddenly changed her voice back to normal; "You silly, what's wrong with you? Just because I'm cuddled up with someone else doesn't mean that I don't love you. He's like a brother to me. I'm a Rajneesh and we express our love openly. I'm confused. Are there rules, because I'm married? Does it mean I shouldn't love my friends?"

"Yes, I mean, No but…"

"I didn't say 'want', I said love. I'm going to drive David home, you can come along if you like."

"I'd like to go with you."

Again the disappointed look came over her face. She motioned, "Let's go."

David packed up his photos and they all climbed into Mari's little Honda.

When they arrived at David's house, David climbed out from the back seat and turned toward Mari. He leaned forward and gave her a long kiss goodbye through the window. The kiss lasted a little long for Tom's liking and he began to feel painfully jealous. David waved goodbye to both of them and disappeared through the front door.

All the way home neither Tom nor Mari said a word. Tom's jealousy had created a huge gap between them. They both felt a distance not experienced before now. Mari went upstairs and lay on the bed in the dark. Tom went to the garage and sat on his motorcycle for several hours. He pulled a small pad from his pocket and wrote these words:

"Please don't teach me anything you can't do yourself. I'm frightened and don't know what to do. I love you dearly, Thomas."

He took the note, folded it into a tiny square and started upstairs. Mari was sitting on the bed, a queen-sized futon mattress on the floor covered with green and purple blankets. She had been reading by candlelight when Tom arrived at the doorway. She looked up and said, "Come sit beside me." He walked toward her with his arm outstretched. Holding the tiny note in his hand, he opened her palm and placed it there. She smiled and read the note, hugging him. She held him like a mother would a child. They sat there in silence and watched the candles flicker. After some time, Tom uttered, "What are you reading?"

"Oh, something that St. Paul wrote to the Corinthians. Here, you read out loud."

He picked up the book and began to read, "Love is patient and kind; love is not jealous or boastful; it is not arrogant or rude. Love does not insist on its own way; it is not irritable or resentful; it does not rejoice at wrong but rejoices in the right.

Love bears all things, believes all things, hopes all things, and endures all things."

The reading had a profound effect. It was as if they had just watched a passing storm and the sky had become clear again.

As time went on Tom realized that if he were to be complete with such a soul as Mari he would have to give up his Oregon-boy ideas of *You are mine and no one else can have you*, as her love expanded far beyond the normal household idea of matrimony.

When she walked into a room, people were in awe; they gravitated to her like bees to honey—not even knowing why. She was not a person of great success or stature; she was a person of immense value. Regardless of age, gender or culture, people could feel that secret something she held inside of her. Something ancient. Something that emanated consciousness continually searching for itself beyond flesh and blood.

With the glass slightly cracked, but not broken, they started going on weekend trips together: sometimes with the boys, sometimes by themselves. They traveled well and simply enjoyed being on the road together. He would drive; she'd lean back with her bare feet on the dash of the little Honda, running off to some unknown destination. Any time Tom could get away from work, they were off to somewhere. Death Valley was one of their favorite destinations; Albany Sauna outside Berkeley was another. They loved to walk the Berkeley campus and supplement themselves with culture by strolling down Telegraph Avenue. Everywhere they went they held hands or had their arms around each other. They had become a nucleus, maybe almost one: together, with the freedom to reach out at any time. They had become real buddies.

On the twin's 13th birthday, they took them to the cabin in Oregon for their Rite of Passage, performing a secret earth ceremony and trials taken from primitive ways.

One sunny afternoon on Neo, Tom was playing "grass ball" with Adam and Jacob in the front yard, a game they had made up. Mari was sitting on the porch in the shade watching all her children play. Adam had just beaten Tom and it was Jacob's turn to challenge the winner. Tom took his position beside Mari on the porch and they were watching their boys play when the phone rang. It was Mari's old Rajneesh friend Jane. She told Mari that Dhiravamsa (the Thai Monk that Mari spent several years traveling around Europe with) was putting on a two-day retreat workshop in Grass Valley near North San Juan. Mari told Tom that she wanted to go. For some reason Tom wasn't jealous of Dhira and agreed to go on the outing with yet another ex-lover. That weekend they packed up a few things and headed for GV. Tom felt badly for Dhira because he knew how close Dhira and Mari had been in the past. Mari told him not to worry; Dhira was a monk and was supposedly beyond such things. On the drive over Tom asked Mari to tell him about Dhira. Mari had a way of being brief, only providing the essence.

"I met Dhiravamsa at a Vipassana retreat in Santa Cruz in 1978 and we fell in love. He taught me much about Vipassana, which I'm grateful for. We traveled throughout South America. I helped him with English and set up his foundation here in America. After establishing our home in Santa Rosa, we traveled to Europe and spent time at Chapter House in England. I loved him. I still love him and am thankful for the way he was with the boys. We still keep in touch, but only as dear friends. He hurt me and I hurt him. I ended up leaving Dhira and going to India."

Tom and Mari finally arrived at the five buildings that made up the little gold-mining town of North San Juan. Passing near the old cemetery, they stopped at the Chinese restaurant for directions to Baboo's place, where the retreat was being held. After discussing the instructions on their handmade map with the cook, they were off again. They finally found the turnoff near the South Fork of the Yuba River. Traveling for several miles on a dirt road they reached Baboo's place, reminiscent of a 1960s commune—several old restored houses with wooden covered porches, wood heat, a windmill, and solar energy. What looked like a large chicken coop with a redwood exterior had been converted into a retreat center.

After touring the houses and chatting with old friends of Mari's, they entered the retreat center and took their places on meditation cushions lining the newly polished hardwood floors. The scent of Nag Champa incense filled the air.

After what seemed like a half hour, Dhira entered the room. He was smiling, dressed in an orange robe. Everyone stood and bowed and returned to their cushions. Tom looked at Dhira in the midst of his discourse. Tom may have been projecting, but there seemed to be a sadness about him that only Tom knew about. After the discourse they sat in silent Vipassana meditation for an hour while a woman on the left talked to herself and cried throughout the session. A bell rang out signifying the end of the meditation. Dhira put on rock 'n roll music and everyone began to dance as though they were celebrating something. After a few songs, a woman entered and walked over to Mari, whispering something in her ear. One of the boys had been hurt—they returned to Santa Rosa that evening.

Jacob and Adam had been playing football inside Noni's house. As Adam ran with the ball, Jacob shoved him, sending his arm though a corrugated glass window. Adam received 17 stitches in his right arm.

A few months later Tom and Mari were out working in the yard. Every year they would have a garden. Tom had made a hole with a little swinging door in the fence so they could walk down the creek behind their house. After "work" they would often sit on the bank with their arms around each other and dream new dreams.

Mari had planted corn, tomatoes, squash and just about every kind of vegetable that one could think of. Most of the seedlings she acquired from the Farallones Institute in Occidental, California where they bank organic heirloom seeds. She asked Tom if he had ever heard of putting crystals in a garden to help the plants grow. He said he had never heard of that, but it sounded good.

Then he brought up Marcel Vogel and his work with plants and crystals. He reminded Mari about his connections with Marcel Vogel through Dr. Ron Mann and how he had attended a Psychotronics seminar with Dr. Vogel at Portland University back in the old days, which eventually led to Dr. Vogel making a tuned crystal for him; the one he used on Mari's father.

Dr. Vogel was IBM's top research scientist and Mari wanted to meet him. A few phone calls later, Tom took time off work and arranged an audience with the master of crystal technology. They arrived in San Jose and weaved their way around a complex of high-tech buildings to the back of Psychic Research, Inc., Dr Vogel's research laboratory. Entering the building they were immediately greeted by Jennet Grover, the institute's laboratory director. She said it would be a few minutes; Dr. Vogel was finishing an experiment. Jennet gave them a tour of the lab, and showed them Marcel's electron microscope. She began explaining the doctor's background, "Among his 128 patents, he invented the colored phosphorus for color television, the magnetic medium used in all audio- and television-recording tape and computer hard drives, and liquid crystals used in every portable computer screen in the world. I know you have questions regarding plants."

Mari asked about his work with plants. Ms. Grover continued, "He was able to duplicate the Backster effect using plants as transducers for bio-energetic fields that the human mind releases, demonstrating that plants respond to thought. He used split-leaf philodendrons connected to a Wheatstone Bridge, a device that compares a known resistance to an unknown resistance. He learned that when he released his breath slowly there was virtually no response from the plant. When he pulsed his breath through the nostrils as he held a thought in mind, the plant would respond dramatically. It was also found that these fields, linked to the action of breath and thought, do not have a significant domain to them. The responsiveness of the plants to thought was also the same whether eight inches away, eight feet, or 8,000 miles! Based on the results of the experiments, the inverse square law does not apply to thought. This was the beginning of Marcel's transformation from being a purely rational scientist to becoming a spiritual or mystical scientist."

Soon Dr. Vogel joined Tom and Mari and started showing Tom some photographic plates of what looked like quarks from a linear accelerator. The doctor explained that the images were actual thought forms taken with a special camera. Tom and he continued with some technical discussion about Fourier Transforms. While talking with Tom, he turned and noticed Mari. That ended that discussion. A level of excitement came over the doctor as he gazed at her. In a loud voice he said, "Young lady, please come with me, I'd like to run some tests on you." He put one hand on her shoulder and they walked over to an Omega 5 resonance-testing device. He took a small sample of blood from her finger and placed it in the machine. Numbers appeared on a digital readout. The numbers must have meant something unusual, because he commented, "Very high, you understand what most people don't. I would like to make a crystal for you."

Mari asked questions about her garden and plants in general. Dr. Vogel told her that all plants respond to the vibrations around them. He cited studies showing that classical music increased the growth rate of corn while rock 'n roll music decreased the rate.

Three weeks later, Mari received in the mail a six-sided double-terminated five-inch-long quartz healing crystal from Marcel Vogel. This helped dispel some of the conflicts she had with her father over her worthiness. Her father based his opinion on "success"—she was a person of "value."

In the summer of '89 Mari and Theresa, Tom's mystic sister, performed a marriage ceremony for Larry, Tom's son and Kimmie, Larry's newly-found sweetheart. They were married on an isolated beach in a Celtic ritual, by wind and fire, where masters moved on trails set in times not many remember, when lovers became one in the mist of it all. Larry and Kimmie stayed for several days at Neo, then ventured out, honeymooning at uncalculated locations, as they made their way back to Oregon.

A few weeks later Tom and Mari decided to go on one of their flip-a-coin for-directions motorcycle adventures. After securing the boys with Grandma Noni, they headed for Highway

12. It was a time in their lives when flowers and green meadows meant more than progress. The scent of the road, the serendipity, the wind on their faces, that's what they longed for. Tom back-shifted at the corner near Calistoga Road squealing the back tire. Mari was leaning back into the sissy bar with her feet on the upper foot pegs, bending her long elegant legs at the knees, reminiscent of a gynecological position. She leaned forward and grabbed his helmet with her right hand, pulling his ear back to her lips, "Let's flip a coin here."

He yelled, "OK, tails we turn left, heads we go straight."

As Ol' Gal idled at the red light, Mari reached into her vest pocket, pulling out a penny with her left hand. Spinning it into the air, she caught it forehanded in midair, shouting, "Calistoga Road."

Tom yelled back over the roar of the engine, "Let's do it!"

Off they went, winding their way up a country road. When they arrived in Calistoga it was 98°, perfect riding weather. As they rolled through the town Mari removed her vest, revealing a sleeveless see-through top. Yelling at Tom over the engine, she said, "Let's get something to drink." The mixed smells of restaurant food and spas created a touristy tang in the air. They stopped in front of a health-food store for fresh-squeezed carrot juice, Mari's favorite. She liked to read labels on containers and began wandering about the store, picking up this and that. He watched her, as he always did, with amazement. She glanced up and caught him staring and hip-swayed out onto the sidewalk, letting the screen door bang behind her. By the time he opened the door, she was already sitting on the bike with her long legs stretched to the blacktop, lifting one eyebrow. That meant, *Have him washed and brought to my tent* or *I'm ready to go.* Priding themselves on knowing what the other was doing without verbal communication, they loved not talking, watching for body language and intuitive signals. To an outside observer it seemed as though they could read each other's every thought.

Tom already going through the gears, Mari waved at her friends who ran the glider port at the end of town. After miles of winding road they arrived in Middletown. She pulled out another coin. If it were "heads," they would be going to Stonyford, a little town in the middle of nowhere, 30 miles on a dirt road southwest of Redding. They had found the place a year before on a motorcycle run up Highway 49 to Sierraville. Stonyford consists of a church, a tavern, and a country grocery store. Or "tails," it was Harbin Hot Springs, a place Tom knew nothing about.

Mari grabbed for the coin as it spun through the air; she missed. It fell to the ground and bounced "tails" side up. It was settled; they were going to Harbin Hot Springs. Tom turned left at the signal off Highway 29 and headed towards the mountains. Winding through the hills for nearly three miles, passing cows and farmland, they veered left at the fork and followed the road to what looked like a gatehouse.

Over the sound of the engine idling, Mari said, "It's Japanese style!"

"What the hell does that mean?"

"Everyone is naked."

He gave Ol' Gal two revs and hit the kill-switch. Mari lifted her right leg over the sissy bar like a veteran biker and strolled towards the gatehouse. He watched her shadow as she walked— his only duty was to follow her. He didn't know it, but she was leading him into a land less traveled. He was silent. He kept thinking, *What if I become aroused, how embarrassing.* Soon he relaxed, after remembering swimming naked in the Yuba River.

Two people were already standing in line at the gatehouse. The lovers held back as they waited with their arms around each other, staring into the distance. Knowing the answer, Tom broke the silence, "Have you been here before?" Mari replied, "Many times. I used to come here in the '70s, don't you remember? This is the place I told you I would take you someday."

"Oh yeah, this is the place?"

"Back in the old days, we'd put a donation in a can. Now it costs $7 a night to sleep on the deck."

"What's the deck?"

"You'll see."

He was like a 9th grader entering high school on the first day. She did all the talking at the gatehouse while a half-naked blond lady with a German accent took down pertinent information: driver's license, phone number, license plate, address and age. After stretching her neck to see the motorcycle the lady replied, "Dat vill be furty-tu dowlars vor tree nits." Mari translated, "Tom, it's $42." He reached into the backpack and handed her two 20s and a five. Mari looked up and winked—normally she handled the money and he liked it that way.

At the motorcycle she instructed him to follow the dirt road up the hill. They passed by an iron gate in the shape of a dragon and stopped at a building on the left. Mari said, "This is the office and I'd like to check it out." It was for his sake that she was stopping; she wanted to walk by the naked people in front, to see what his reaction would be! As he passed by two large-breasted ladies standing near the porch, a sense of freedom and fear culminated into a single flash—it was no big deal.

Mari gathered some pamphlets from the front and slid back on the bike. "Tom, go up to the top of the hill by the gazebo. We can park up there." Idling slowly, the hollow guttural sound of the Harley broke the almost pin-drop silence of the surroundings. To the left was a bazaar with exotic clothes and trinkets from the Far East, modeled by their attractive merchants. At first he tried not to look, then Mari said, "Oh look Tom, isn't she a gorgeous creature?" Almost falling over on the motorcycle, he stuttered, "A-a-a-h?" Mari laughed a big belly laugh, pinched his ear and said, "Lighten up you silly, we're here to relax." They parked the bike and took their zip-together sleeping bags, backpack and rolled-up blanket off the front fender. Mari dug around in the saddlebags for a book while Tom hung the helmets off the mirror and gawked. Past the gazebo to the right was a health food restaurant; to the left of the restaurant was a yoga studio. He gazed over, trying not to look at the naked fat man sitting on the bench. Mari picked up on it right away. "Now don't be prejudiced, I can tell he has a beautiful soul." Pointing with his finger Tom said, "What's that down there?"

"That's the movie theater and behind the restaurant is a health food store, that's where we're going next. Let's leave the stuff here."

They began walking toward the restaurant. All of a sudden Mari got big-eyed and detoured down a dark hallway to the right stopping in front of a small piece of paper tacked to the wall, "Oh Thomas, *Easy Rider* and *Annie Hall*. I love Woody Allen. OK, that's it, we're going to the movies tonight." She kissed him and grabbed his hand like a schoolgirl rushing onto the dance floor. Pulling him down the steps at the left of the yoga studio, she continued on to the back of the restaurant and turned quickly inside a little side entrance.

Tom peered in through the partially-open screen door held by the hand of the goddess, "Thomas, come in, it's OK." He looked around at the bananas and packaged foods as the door squeaked shut behind him. She immediately started selecting items from the shelves, placing them in a plastic Safeway shopping bag (which she saved for all occasions) and walked toward the register. A tall thin man with a salt-and-pepper beard, wearing a hematite necklace, stood in back of the checkout counter. He had begun ringing up the items when a woman wearing a white wraparound skirt and no top walked in asking for directions. Swimming on the Yuba was one thing, but a topless lady with big breasts in a grocery store was another. Tom tried to pretend that it didn't bother him. Mari leaned up against him. Cocking her head to one side she smiled and said, "T-h-o-m-a-s, is there anything else we need."

"Not that I can think of."

Handing the man a $20, she grinned and giggled, "OK, let's go over to the kitchen."

He followed her across the grass where statues of goddesses adorned the green lawn in front of a large brown-and-white restored 1880s hotel/boarding house. The fragrance of flowers filled the air. Everywhere he looked were floral gardens, flowerbeds mixed in among the shade trees and stone walkways leading off to hidden grottos; a mysterious place of beauty, just outside normal reality. Awestruck, he sat for a moment on a small wooden bench and began unlacing his scuffed boots. Tying the laces together, he flipped them over his shoulder, one hanging in front and one in back. They continued to walk off the lawn onto a narrow graveled road. He closed his eyes; the stones pressing against his feet reminded him of Antigua. For a second he was standing on a cobblestone walk near Rummer's Run on the bay of Parham in Antigua. An eager tug from Mari's hand opened his eyes, sending him rushing back into the moment. Straightaway a woman passed in front carrying a small child. To the right an Olympic-size swimming pool with children splashing about caught his eye. A large redwood deck appeared on his far right with a myriad of people lying spread-eagle on towels, basking in the sun. Then it really hit him; everyone was NAKED.

Quickly he moved his gaze away from the scene, grabbing Mari by the skirt. For an instant he became a child in fear of being separated from its mother. She moved the groceries to her left hand and put her arm around him, "You OK?"

"...Yes."

"See those steps? They lead up to the hot pools. Beyond that is the inner chamber. The water is real hot in there. Above that is a cold-water pool and meditation area."

"OK."

"Here's the shower and changing room, it's co-ed."

"OK."

She quickly turned and walked up the stairway leading to the second story of the building over the changing room, exclaiming, "This is the community kitchen."

"OK."

Reaching the top of the stairs she said, "You have to have shoes on to go in here. I'm going to try to find a refrigerator before they're all taken, I'll see you inside." Squatting near the door on one knee, he began lacing up his boots when suddenly a young woman in her 20s wearing a miniskirt-length T- shirt opened the door. Startled, he looked up directly into a patch of light blond hair. For a moment he couldn't believe what he was looking at. Slowly he raised his eyes to hers, and she smiled and darted down the stairs.

He opened the door timidly and peeked in. Straightening his shoulders, trying to hide his shyness, he entered with a brisk walk as though he had some direction in mind. The kitchen was packed with people clanging about. The pervading smell of cooked vegetables and tofu filled the air. The only direction he had in mine was Mari. He spotted her by a long row of commercial stoves talking with a lady and quickly walked over. "Oh, Tom, let me show you where I put the food." Grabbing him by the hand, she walked over to a large stainless steel refrigerator, "See I put our name here on the door." She opened the door and continued, "This is our box in case you want something to eat later." She may have not known, but he had no thought of ever coming here without her. As she closed the massive steel door, fog formed along its edges. She turned and walked toward a large window next to the dining tables and looked out, "See the swimming pool?"

"Yes…"

"Beyond that is the little smoothie shop. There's a trail there. It will take us to the deck. That's where we're going to sleep." Tom peered out the window into a vast courtyard of naked bodies, replying, "How are we going to get there?" Expressing her growing impatience with his childishness, she uttered, "Let's go get our stuff."

They walked back to the motorcycle, gathered all their belongings and headed back up the gravel road to the gate near the main hot pool. People were strolling about in the sun, going here and there, some looking into the distance, others at each other. She guided him past a crowd near the swimming pool. Pausing at the smoothie shop, she said, "We can come back and get some coffee." To her it was nothing more than a Sunday stroll through the park; for him—well, he would never be the same. They continued up the trail overlooking a compound of massage parlors and staff buildings. Below that, expanding out into a sprawling valley surrounded by majestic mountains, were the community gardens.

Mari spoke softly, "Here we are." Promenading over to the railing surrounding a large wooden deck built into the hillside, she whispered, "Look out there. There's over 1,000 acres of trails. I hope you feel like walking?" Tom didn't say anything. He stood near the edge looking down to the ground 30 feet below. He turned, to catch the glimpse of a man in a yoga posture standing on one leg with the other lifted to his forehead, naked! Swiftly he turned his gaze to the trees in the distance above the dressing room 100 yards away. For a moment he thought he was seeing things, but there in the oak trees among the manzanita was a woman squatting naked with long blond ratted hair. She started running from tree to tree, talking to someone nobody else could see. At first she appeared very animal-like, then he saw her lifting her hands as if in prayer and running to the next tree doing the same thing. Pointing, he turned to Mari and said; "See the woman in the trees?" Mari looked up from her unpacking and said, "Yes, I've seen her here before. I think she lives here. She prays to everything and is refreshingly wild. If she sees you looking at her she will come up and give you a hug, but don't be alarmed. She's quite innocent."

After building a little nest near the corner of the deck Mari began taking off her clothes. Slipping her skirt over her knees she looked over at Tom with one eyebrow raised, meaning, *You do the same.*

Compensating for his shyness he flipped his underwear off the end of his foot, catching them in his right hand. He turned toward Mari and said, "Bet you can't do that." She laughed. It was something they did at home every night, but here it seemed hysterical to her. They walked down the trail past the smoothie shop, past the swimming pool, to the outdoor showers. Wrapping her arm around his naked waist she ushered him into the shower next to the co-ed changing room. They took turns washing each other, then proceeded up the steps to the hot pool. Mari led the way, merging into the steaming waters. Neck deep, she moved to the back corner of the pool under the fig tree. Tom read the sign mounted on the wrought-iron railing surrounding the pool, "SILENCE AREA, PLEASE NO TALKING". They hugged, wrapping themselves around each other. Mari whispered, "Will you float me?"

Tom was watching the couple in the middle of the pool doing something that looked like floating. The man, in his 50s, balding on top with a long white beard, had his arm under the back of a lady in her 30s, supporting her to float on the water. His left hand was under her head; her arms were stretched out, with her breasts fully exposed above the water. They were moving slowly back and forth across the pool as if dancing. Tom whispered back, "Is that floating?" Mari replied, "Yes. They call it Watsu. It's very relaxing."

Tom lifted Mari up by the middle of her back. She stretched out horizontally across the water and they began to move about the pool. After a few moments of making sure he wasn't going to let her head drop below the waterline, she closed her eyes and drifted off into a trance. They glided around the pool for 15 minutes then she slowly lowered her feet to the bottom and stood up, "Tom, let's go into the inner chamber. It's hot, 114°, so go in slow." She walked down the steps to the inner chamber, slowly submerging herself. He watched the expression on her face, and then entered. It took his breath away. He felt pinpricks all over his body. Neck deep in the water they moved to the corner and turned facing each other next to the goddess shrine.

He looked across the tiny chamber, catching a glimpse of the woman he had seen earlier running from tree to tree in prayer. She was very old, yet there was something about her that seemed very young, maybe ten years old. Her long gray hair was all ratted together and she had no teeth. She saw Tom looking and began to move toward him with her arms stretched out, greeting him like a long-lost friend. He tried to move around behind Mari, but it was too late. The woman put her arms around him, pressing her naked body up against his. Suddenly he relaxed. She looked him in the eye raising her hands in *pranamah* and said, "Bless you." Then she did the same to Mari. She blessed them both as she climbed the stairs. Turning into the passageway on the left she moved out of sight. Discharging any thought that she might be jealous, Mari looked at Tom and said, "See, I told you, wasn't that wonderful?" He replied, "Strange at first, but yes, she's all heart. Is she what the Hindus call a *mast*, someone who's in a state of Divine Madness?" Astonished, Mari looked at him and replied, "Yes."

After the inner chamber experience they walked up the rock steps to the cold pool and plunged in, exhilarating every cell in their bodies. They sat for a few moments near the Quan Yin shrine and rang the bell-chimes before returning to the deck. That day Mari took him to all the little grottos and hidden trails winding through the mountains—he had lost all sense of self-consciousness.

Instead of cooking that evening, they ate in the restaurant. Later they attended the movies where they lay on blankets to watch the film. The movie-house was an unusual place; made in tiers. Each tier is seven feet deep, dropping three feet to the next tier. Large cushions fill each tier—everyone brings their own blankets.

That night after the movies, snuggled in their sleeping bag, they watched the stars and satellites move across the sky. Mari had drifted into dreamland; Tom was so moved by all the wonder he couldn't sleep. He slipped from the sleeping bag without waking Mari and roamed through the night toward the sauna. It was 2:00 AM. He didn't figure anyone would be there. He walked up the cedar steps and opened the squeaky outer door. Opening the inner door he noticed that the place was full of people. Both cedar tiers on either side of the dimly lit room were filled. He squeezed in next to a woman sitting by the door. The air was hot and dry and smelt of perspiration.

Then it began. Moaning, moaning that he had only heard through the walls of a cheap motel. It began slowly, first one person, then another, until the whole room was filled with the sound of orgasm. Sporadically it would stop like crickets in the night and begin again. He found himself being aroused by the energy. It contrasted with his own ideas about monogamous sexuality, something that he had known since childhood. He became confused, thinking, *Mari is up there asleep and I've walked into a fringe event without her, something's wrong.* He left the sauna and returned to the deck. Tip-toeing to the nest, he climbed back in the bag, startling her from her slumber. Groggy, she whispered, "Oh, Thomas, where were you?"

"I went to the sauna."

"How was it?"

"Well, OK I guess."

"What time is it?"

"The clock on the wall by the pool said 2:30."

"We better get some sleep."

"I have to ask you about something?"

"Can it wait till morning?"

"…I guess so."

"What is it?"

"Well, you know the sauna?"

"Yes."

"When I went there, there was a whole bunch of people."

"Y-e-s…"

"They were all moaning like they were having sex."

"Oh, I know what that is. There's a group from San Francisco; they do psychic sex. I've seen them up here before. Did you get aroused?"

"A little, it was hard not to."

"Are you all right?"

"Yeah…"

"It's all base chakra stuff. I suppose we all pass through there on our way to somewhere else, just don't get stuck there. It's the quicksand along the spiritual path. Cuddle up next to me, let's go to sleep."

"It's OK?"

"It's OK."

That morning they got up and made breakfast in the community kitchen and soaked in the pools till noon before returning to the deck. They both fell asleep on a blanket on the deck. When Tom woke up Mari was gone. He panicked for a moment, then realized she had probably gone back to the pools.

The experience of the night before not only clarified that he only wanted one woman at a time, Mari, it also woke up his dreaded friend Jealousy. The thought of her being in the pools without him didn't go down well. He figured he'd better get his act together before walking down there, because he knew she would have none of it. He was able to calm his thoughts and go on toward the pools.

First he checked the swimming pool—no Mari. Then he went to the sauna; she wasn't in there. He walked past the changing room. Out of nervousness he stopped at the drinking fountain and began gulping water from the faucet. A woman with a water jug came up behind him and waited for him to finish. When he turned around there was Mari in the hot pool, being floated by some guy with a ring in his ear. For a moment he thought, *It seems OK.* Then the guy lifted her body up, pressing her breasts against his and slowly swirled through the water. Her eyes were closed and completely relaxed.

In that moment Tom's heart began to pound uncontrollably. He thought, *Here it comes, my own worst enemy. How am I going to control this? I can't blow it here, she would never forgive me.* He figured if he got in the water and watched for a while maybe he could put some understanding around it. If he'd just face the fear it might get better. It made it worse. He was able to control the rage, but his own sense of insecurity was attacking his heart. She hadn't even opened her eyes. Observing how pathetic he was, he left the pool without a scene. She had not known he was even there. Had it been ten years earlier, he would have physically attacked the man.

Back at the deck he began walking in circles trying to calm himself. Then he started for the pools again, *This guy is going to pay.* Moving across the deck he saw the fat man he'd seen the day before sitting on a bench. The man noticed Tom's rage and looked back at him with compassion. There was enough medicine in that look to keep him from his destination with disaster. He looked again at the fat man with fierce eyes. Again, the man returned compassion. Thoughts passed through Tom's head, *How does he know how I am feeling? He seems to know something about me.* There was enough emotional inertia left in Tom's gait to carry him off the deck to the path, where he paused in a pinnacle, life-changing moment. If he turned left, he would be going for revenge. If he turned right, it would take him up the hill into the forest.

Instantly something bubbled up to the surface of his consciousness, from a place deeper inside than the rage. Perhaps it was his love for Mari and who they were together. It seemed to happen in a flash—he turned right and ran up the hill. Once deep in the forest the rage and tears gushed to the surface. He found himself blindly throwing his fist into the trunk of an oak tree. He cried profusely, slamming his knuckles, again and again, against the bark until blood flowed down his arm. He slowly sunk to the ground at the base of the tree and watched himself watch himself. After a few minutes he returned to the deck and lay down on the blanket with his eyes closed, hoping no one would see him. He lay there for quite some time.

When he sat up, the fat man was still sitting there on the bench in front of him. The man clasped his hands together across his lap. Without a word he continued to gaze at Tom with compassion, as if to say, *I hope you feel better.* This time Tom took a good look at the man; he emerged like Ho-Tai (the big, fat Chinese god of happiness), a Bodhisattva. Compassion emanated from his big belly. Tom looked back. The man did not lower his gaze. They were together in a moment in time, and every redneck notion seemed to vanish from Tom's being. Without a word the fat man rose from his bench and disappeared into the forest.

Just as Tom was beginning to think about what Mari was going to think when she saw his hand, she appeared. At first she didn't notice and began talking about the Watsu instructor who had floated her in the hot pool. Tom looked down at the ground, ashamed of himself. As she bent over to pick up the towel, she noticed, "What happened to your hand?" He told her everything; how he felt at first, how the fat man helped him without words, how he hit the tree. Disturbed at first, she softly said, "You silly boy, let's go wash that off."

They spent one more day at Harbin roaming about the countryside, in love again, forever.

11

"Do not go where the path may lead,
go instead where there is no path and leave a trail."

Ralph Waldo Emerson

The Lost Coast

It's 5:04 PM, October 17, 1989. Tom's at work, Mari is home by herself and the boys are with the grandparents watching the *World Series*. Mari has just begun to fold clothes on the bed, with Flavious the cat. Flavious jumped off the bed and started pacing with big eyes. All of a sudden the house groaned and began to shake. Waves rolled across the floor throwing Mari against the dresser. The sound of cracking sheetrock echoed everywhere. Mari made for the stairs and ran to the backyard through the patio door just in time to see the entire back fence lift into the air and come back down again. Repeatedly, waves curled the ground pointing trees in slanted directions. Not knowing when it was going to stop, she moved away from the glass window by the steps and ran out into the back yard, where she watched the house wobble and suddenly become silent.

Tom was at his computer terminal in the lab at Weightronix. Without warning, the sound of a freight train rumbling through the concrete tilt-wall-constructed building echoed through the hallways, rocking his chair from side to side. He knew. This was not his first time, having grown up in LA. He looked over at Bob, the engineer working next to him. Bob was still trying to enter characters on the keyboard. As Bob continued to make more attempts to strike the correct key, his chair swayed to and fro. Tom yelled out, "Bob, It's a earthquake, I'm outta here!" Tom tried to stand and was thrust forward, falling to the floor. Bob had fallen backwards over his chair. They both stood and ran for the door. Bob kept saying, "Aren't we supposed to stay inside under a doorway?" Tom responded, "You can stay if you want, but I'm out of here." They both cleared the exit to the parking lot in time to see cars being tossed into the air. The blacktop rippled like a blanket shook from one end. It continued, wave after wave. Out of the 600 people working there, most had already gone home. All Tom could think about was Mari and the boys, *Are they OK?*

Adam and Jake were in front of the television set at Noni and Didi's when the TV screen went blank and rocked like a boat. They both stood on the couch and yelled, "Cool, what's going on?" They thought it was fun. Didi yelled, "Dammit, get away from the damn window and get under the door jamb." The sound of their grandfather's voice blurted out from the bedroom as the house wrenched and swayed back and forth.

Tom tried to make a phone call, but couldn't get through. He got in his car and drove straight home, flinching at every overpass. When he arrived, Mari was in the front yard talking with neighbors. She said she had talked with the boys and everyone was OK. The epicenter had been at Loma Prieta, about 100 miles away.

Six months prior to the earthquake, while walking home from one of their weekend breakfasts at Coco's, Mari crouched down by the tulip tree near the school grounds and motioned for Tom to sit, "Tom, we have to come up with a realistic down-to-earth dream so we can work together." He agreed and they began dreaming.

Now, when you get two dreamers dreaming together, some really far out stuff comes up. They concluded, "We will become flying photojournalists." Tom would get a pilot's license; she was both a journalist who had helped write a New York Times bestseller and an amateur photographer, and Tom—well, he'd fly the airplane.

They both enrolled in ground school at SRJC and Tom started flight training at Let's Fly several weeks later. Through another set of coincidences, his boss at Weightronix, Gene Katz, ended up being his flight instructor.

The 7.1 Richter scale earthquake had a profound effect on Tom and Mari's psyches. Now it was time to get serious. The event had stunned them both and Mari wanted Tom to quit work more than ever and be at home with her and the boys. She never did like the idea of him working away from the house, especially now after the earthquake.

On October 18, 1989, one day after the earthquake, he soloed with Mari waving him on and completed his single-engine private pilot's license on August 15, 1990. Their dream was coming true. Now all they needed to do was find someone who was willing to pay them to have so much fun and they would be together forever!

She attended a class on how to market oneself as a journalist and began hanging out with a friend who had done it before. Nothing seemed to pan out. They had the training and the credentials—now what?

Somehow the dream of working together was so powerful, they started pretending they were on assignment and began flying here and there. One weekend afternoon they flew to Mendocino for lunch and toured the town. They visited several restaurants, masquerading as writers for a gourmet restaurant magazine. They even had conversations at the table that would have encouraged any eavesdropping maître d' to bring them only the finest. And when they made the short-run power take-off at the postage-stamp-size Mendocino airport, buzzing the trees at the end of the runway, any onlooker would have said, "Yep, they're flying photojournalists all right."

They spent a lot of time sitting together on the back porch dreaming their dreams. Things started looking better financially with Tom's promotion to project leader, so they went out and bought a brand new 1990 Isuzu Trooper for all the newly-planned land adventures. They started traveling as much as possible on the weekends. Whether in the Cherokee by air or the Trooper by land, Mari would always ride with her bare feet on the dash and he would play with her hair.

Tom had some vacation time coming so they decided to put the Trooper to the test. Objective: find the Valley of the Gods, the sacred place that Turiyananda had told them about at Lake Shrine. First they would need to find Mexican Hat, a little settlement near Four Corners in Utah. It was good weather and they rolled into Mexican Hat the next day. Traveling northeast out of Mexican Hat on Highway 163, they turned north onto a dirt road. A small sign attached to a galvanized pipe near the road entrance said, "Valley of the Gods, Off Road Vehicle Recommended." As they entered the valley the scenery took their breaths away. Thousands of rock formations jutted hundreds of feet into the air; shades of red, brown, and yellow mixed in majestic combinations, hallowed, forbidding in some ways, influencing their imaginations to wonder off onto occurrences that might have happened 1,000 years ago. They stopped by a large monolith rising 300 feet high. They stood at its base looking up. An occasional powder-white cloud passed by. The sky was opal-blue, the air was hot and clear and smelled of sage.

The sand around them had increased since their last stop and living plants were becoming rare. Separate basalt formations towered against the clean and polished white sand, which caught the blaze of the sun like tiny diamonds. Further on they sat in meditation for several hours on a stretched-out blanket at the base of a monolith. Mari poured tea from a thermos into two Yosemite cups and they ate bread.

Driving another ten miles deeper into the valley, they began to feel the presence of "something," but couldn't see what it was. It became overwhelming. The sensation continued as they moved along the valley floor. A déjà vu was presenting itself. The feeling was about to take them into another dimension, when Tom suddenly reached over and touched Mari's leg, causing her to jerk her head around with big eyes, "Mar, see that sign up ahead? Let's stop. I want to see what it says." Mari snarled, "When we're in that state, warn me next time before you touch me." She brought the car to a stop in front of a small wooden sign three feet high held in the ground by a wooden stake. Tom leaned his head out the window. The writing appeared hand-painted with a bad brush; letters contrasting against dark-brown splintered wood spelled out, "Steak Dinners

One Mile Ahead." They both looked at each other in disbelief. Tom liked it.

They hadn't seen another soul in 20 miles and were perplexed but curious. Tom went on, "I can't believe it, here we are out in the middle of nowhere and there's a restaurant! What do you think?" Mari replied, "Let's check it out." After about a mile the road bent to the left, and there it was, sitting up on a knoll. It looked like someone's old rundown ranch house, but it was the only place around and the distance seemed right. Tom uttered, "This has got be the place." They pulled up in front and walked up a long chain of broken concrete steps to the porch. Tom swung open the door as though he was walking into Danny's Steak House and then it began.

As they stepped inside, to the right was a cowboy with a handlebar mustache, dressed in chaps, half asleep on the couch with a gun strapped to his waist. The man grabbed for his six-shooter. Having trouble pulling the gun from its holster, he started yelling, "B-E-T-T-Y, B-E-T-T-Y." Suddenly, a barefoot woman ran from the kitchen straight toward the front door with a potato in one hand and a butcher knife in the other. By now the cowboy had removed his gun and was calmly pointing it toward the front door. Tom started talking fast, "We saw the sign down the road, it said, 'Steak Dinners.' We're very sorry. I think we have the wrong place."

Everyone took a sigh of relief. The cowboy holstered his gun and the woman lowered her knife and started talking, "Rusty, I keep telling you, we need to take that sign down. Hope we didn't give you too much of a scare?" Mari replied, "We're OK. We're sorry for walking into your home like that." Tom piped up, "Yes, I saw the sign. I thought it was a restaurant, I apologize for just barging in like that."

After making their introductions and exchanging addresses, Betty invited the lovers to sit down for tea. Come to find out, Betty taught school on a nearby Indian reservation and Rusty minded the farm and took care of the horses. Betty invited them to spend the night, and the next morning Rusty saddled up four horses and they all rode out through the Valley of the

Gods. Promising to write, the lovers headed for Goose Neck and camped along a 2,000-foot ravine for a couple of days.

They spent several more days and had a string of back-road adventures before arriving home, where things began falling back into the grind again. Tom could tell that Mari was beginning to get uneasy; it was time for another road trip.

In the summer of 1990 they decided to take Ol' Gal on the annual "Redwood Run." They would need enough supplies to last three days. Tom spent the day changing the oil, checking the engine and frame and polishing the chrome. She was ready to go. Mari put provisions in the saddlebags and they were off on another adventure, headed north up Highway 101, where 5,000 bikers would meet and party at French's Camp along the Eel River for three days.

Mari had a thing about riding the motorcycle at 75 miles an hour on the freeway. She motioned Tom to get off the freeway at Steele Lane onto Old Redwood Highway. Winding around every back road north, they finally ran out of blacktop and were forced back onto the freeway north of Windsor. Going through the gears on the onramp, they merged into a pack of 20 motorcycles headed north. As the wind increased, he could feel her body tighten again. He backed off the throttle to 55 and moved into the slow lane. As much as she loved to ride in the pack, she hated being on the freeway. They watched the pack pull away at 70 and disappear out of sight.

Not long after that, a carload of biker chicks in a lowered '63 Chevy pulled up in the fast lane next to Ol' Gal, giving the lovers thumbs-up. The blonde in the back seat rolled down the window and yelled, holding out a black-and-white wife-beater T-shirt in her right hand, flapping in the wind. Tom backed off the throttle, reached out with his left hand, grabbed the T-shirt at 50 miles an hour, and passed it back to Mari. The occupants of the car cheered and pulled away. Tom yelled back to Mari, "What's it say?" Leaning forward, yelling in his ear at the top of her lungs, "North East Harley-Davidson Motor Company, Wangaratta, Australia."

They got off the freeway at Cloverdale onto a two-lane country highway and waved at a small group of bikers lined up along the roadside. He could feel the muscles in her arms relax. Most of the pack had gone on to water at the Hopland Brewery. Thirty miles later they pulled into Hopland. More than 1,000 motorcycles had lined both sides of the street. Tom backed the bike into the curb near the tavern, revved the engine twice, and hit the kill switch. Mari slowly got off and walked toward the corner. He followed. She swayed across the street to the Hopland Hotel and disappeared inside. Tom watched Ol' Gal from across the street while Mari went in for something to drink. Shortly she returned, handing him a communal cup of hot mint tea. They stood in a mass of rumbling chrome, breathing exhaust fumes until the tea was all gone. Gazing at the street, they saw it was mostly filled with rich yuppies dressed in biker Halloween costumes. There were few in the crowd that actually lived the life, and for the most part, the day of the outlaw had passed. It was then that Tom realized, even though he was tattooed from head to toe, he too had joined the ranks of the weekend biker.

They pulled out of town with 100 other motorcycles. Mari loved the sound and the muscle of riding with the pack. As they hit the first turn, Tom leaned into the corner; Mari wrapped her arms around his waist and pulled him back into her chest. Kicking his boots to the front pegs, he gunned the motor through the first corner and leaned back. It was right then, that it began to happen. He could feel her every thought and feeling, and she the same with him. He could feel the wind in her face, the front tire gripping the blacktop, the roar of the motor and the presence of everything around him. For a moment, they became a singularity going down the highway; he and she and the motorcycle had become one thing. Blinding flashes of sunlight snapped through the trees creating strobe effects that sent them both into an autonomic region where no one was driving. It was as if the trees and the white line were steering. For a moment, Zen had taken over.

This had happened once before when they were on a country road on the back side of Mount Shasta. Tom saw a deer up ahead by the side of the road. As the bike moved forward everything went into slow motion—smells intensified, the feeling of oneness expanded to include even the deer. As the deer leaped forward, it passed in mid-air across the front fender, clearing it by three feet. At 50 miles per hour, the handlebars brushed the deer's hind legs as it made its descent, clearing the clutch lever by a few inches. The entire event was in slow motion. No fear was present. It was as if everyone knew ahead of time exactly how it was going to play out. Call it conscious grace. Call it being in the zone. It was a perfect moment.

Tom recalled what went through his head while the road was driving itself, *A meadow opened up into the sky, I saw Mari there in a field of flowers. My ego ceased to be. She was silhouetted against the backdrop of rolling green mountains. Her dark hair hung forward against a white dress, I could see nothing more. I walked with her forever, never to return. I knew then that we were inseparable, destined to twin until death. It made me smile inside.*

They continued north for 60 miles, rolling into the little settlement of Piercy. Five thousand motorcycles were lined up in a mass of screaming engines and smoke. To the right, as they passed the turnoff to French's Camp, biker chicks on the back of a flatbed truck pulled their T-shirts up over their heads, flashing the incoming pack. The party was about to begin. To the left was a bazaar of zigzagging longhaired bearded bikers and their mamas slopping down beers and checking out the color. Tents along the roadside containing biker crafts and paraphernalia spilled out onto the two-lane. A long line snaked down the street to the entrance of a makeshift tattoo parlor. High levels of testosterone expressed through powerful engines and screaming tires played out to the crowd. The smell of burning rubber…exhaust fumes blurred the big belly of a biker as he bent over to pick a cigarette butt out of the dirt.

The lovers looked down toward the Eel River, the scene expanded—there was a red and white bus with blue writing, "Live to Ride and Ride to Live" spray-painted on the side. Thousands were gathered around a makeshift bandstand. Hundreds of blue and green and white tents filled the valley next to the river. Even the presence of the Highway Patrol failed to calm the swarm. Tom and Mari parked Ol' Gal near a hot dog vendor and mingled through the crowd to watch two bikers arm-wrestle for a pair of women's underwear. A large Viking biker with a full beard and long hair, wearing a red short-sleeve shirt, engineer's boots and leather vest, sat on his bike flashing his tattoos while eating a bowl of chili. A blonde-haired mama in sunglasses, next to him, gawked with her arms crossed. The sign above his head said, "No Lead, Gas $1.28, Eat Me."

Tom hardly ever told Mari what to do, but this time he told her to stick close. In response she spun three times with her hands over her head then grabbed him by the arm and ran to the center of the crowd. They milled about bouncing from one strange scene to the other until they wove their way in behind the tattoo tent. She yelled into his ear, "I've got to find a bathroom." Tom pointed to a long row of portable outhouses lining the road. She said, "No. I'm going to the woods. Will you come with me?"

They disappeared from the multitude and were soon several feet into the forest, 50 feet from the noisy highway. Near a redwood stump, she cleared the leaves, pulled down her pants, and took care of business in private. Tom walked a few feet away and watched a host of crazies moving about like a swarm of bees through the trees. He turned back in time to see Mari wiping herself with a fallen branch. She motioned for him to come over, "Tom, I don't want to stay at French's Camp to night."

"That's OK with me."

"Do you think we can find a camp further north?"

"I don't know."

They walked back through the trees to the horde, weaving their way around to Ol' Gal. Tom started talking to a guy in a black-and-white muscle shirt next to the Coke machine, asking if he knew of a place to camp away from the crowd. The man looked puzzled, and took another puff from a joint suspended on an alligator clip, "You're not partying here?" Tom smiled, "We want somewhere private." The biker dropped what was left of the roach, grinding it into the dirt with the tip of his boot and smiled back, "Try north, a place called Benbow. You'll see the turnoff ten miles up." Tom looked back at Mari. She was leaning against someone else's motorcycle. He quickly moved toward her, "Don't lean on anyone's bike. If some biker mama sees you leaning against her man's bike, there could be trouble."

They meandered through the tents till dusk checking out the scene. At dusk they fired up Ol' Gal and headed north. Just as they pulled out of Piercy, a biker with a chick in pigtails riding on the back, wearing a pair of men's underwear tied around her head like a bandana, almost sideswiped them as they pulled onto the highway, yelling, "Long may you run."

That night they slept in the campgrounds at Benbow, then headed north the next morning for the Avenue of the Giants, a 20-mile stretch of Highway 101 lined with 2,000-year-old redwood trees. An hour later they stopped at a roadside café for breakfast. Mari peeked in through the checkered-cloth-lined windows, observing an old man sitting next to a logger at the counter eating bacon and eggs. The chalkboard menu on the front door spelled out the special for the day, "Spotted owl and eggs, $4.95." Mari responded, "Do you think we should eat here?" Tom replied, "It's cool, anyway I'm hungry." They sat at a small table near the front door and ate Denver omelets. Just as they were finishing, a big muscle-bound redneck who had obviously had beer for breakfast came over to the table on his way out the door, "How do you like that Harley?" Tom replied, making strong eye contact, "It's good weather. The road's been good to us." Mari piped up with a hint of sarcasm, "We're enjoying the beauty of the TREES." The man looked at her, then back at Tom with steely eyes. For a moment Tom thought, *Oh shit, here we go.* The man broke his stare and continued out the front door, letting the screen door slam behind him. He paused to look at Tom's bike before climbing into an old beat-up pickup. With his left arm hanging out the window, he looked back at the lovers through the café window and flipped them the bird. Continuing to look back, he pulled away slowly, and weaved down the road out of sight.

That day the lovers rode up and back through the Avenue of the Giants, spending the night again at Benbow. The next morning the weather turned cold. So they headed south pausing at a rest stop south of Willits. Mari put a flowered dress on over her Levis, then Tom's dirt-colored junkyard jacket. She fastened a red-and-white bandanna around her head and re-laced her boots. She looked like a bag lady with sunglasses. Tom loved it. When they arrived home that night they heard on the news that there had been three stabbings at French's Camp and two had been killed on the road. Mari was glad they'd stayed at Benbow, making their own Redwood Run through the Avenue of the Giants.

During the next several weeks they spent weekends with their boys fishing off the rocks at Bodega Bay. They mostly talked and dreamed of a family business where they could all be together.

The following weekend Mari wanted to take Tom to the river for a picnic; she wanted to collect stones for a grotto she was building in the back yard. He could tell she had something on her mind. It was Saturday morning and the boys had spent the night at a friend's house. Mari packed a picnic lunch and they drove to Cazadero and walked along the river in search of rocks. They gathered around 100 football-size stones and put them in the back of the Trooper.

After the work was done, Mari placed a blanket under a tree near the water by a sandy beach. They lay down beside each other listening to the sound of the river and the insects buzzing by. Suddenly, Mari rolled over on top of Tom and told him to spread his legs and put his arms out. She fashioned her arms over the top of his arms, palms touching, and placed her legs on top of his legs, ankle to ankle. Lifting her head she kissed him and scooted downward, placing her head on his chest.

She began to speak.

"I remember when I was 16, I had a guitar. My girlfriends Susie, Janet and I used to make up songs to Beatle music and performed at our Catholic high school. We used to walk in the cemetery in the early morning and watch the sunrise. We wrote for the high school newspaper and designed clothes and jewelry and put them in flower-power shops in Berkeley. I read about Timothy Leary and Alan Ginsburg and made out-of-fashion clothes that would be 'all the thing' three years later. I felt condemned by guilt to fashion myself to live in a box prepared by the previous generation. I grew up thinking no matter how excellent I was I would never be good enough. I was bright, artistic, and creative to no avail. No matter how good I was, I was the rebel in the family. I had a tremendous need to step outside the line. You pay a price for that."

Tom interrupted, "You know you probably came into a family that would provide that kind of pressure so you could break out of the mould. You're a pioneer."

Mari rolled over on her side on one elbow and continued, "The boys are 14 now—what I'm saying is, I'm concerned about the boys. They have my charm and use it to their advantage. They have a gift, and like me, they're not sure about the significance of it. I'm afraid when it runs down they'll be lost. I feel lost, lost to this corporate work-a-day thing that we are doing. You go to work, I stay home, and the boys are off with their friends. We are all like ships passing in the night. We have to find a way to make a living and be together. I don't want to live like this in the corporate do-good world of my father's, there's got to be another way. Let's pray that something good will happen."

Tom cleared his throat, "Maybe we could get a job writing for *National Geographic* or start a massage business together?" Mari retorted sharply, "Come on Tom, that's all we do is dream. We need a job where we can all be involved with each other and still make a living."

Tom continued, "When I was a boy, I had a paper route, shined shoes and collected bottles. I always wanted to be a shoeshine-boy—it was my dream. The thing is, nowadays there isn't really work for kids, and they become lost and don't develop an early sense of self-worth. Most everything is given to them. They have no purpose, except to find pleasure; work is something that parents do. Usually the mom is forced to work just to make ends meet and children suffer for that. I know, I'm preaching to the choir. As far as the boys, they love us, even though friends are a big deal... Those boys have charm, yes, and they enjoy people. They also have a spiritual side and I think that's in the cards—they will always be provided for."

Mari still feeling strongly, replied, "Yes, that may be, but what I'm talking about is us as a family and as individuals. I don't think that I can go on like this much longer. I love to travel, you love to travel, the boys enjoy being on the road; we are all adventurers crammed in a box. My spirit is getting squashed. I'm going to go to the car and get my medicine bag, let's do a ceremony here by the river."

When she returned, they prayed by the river, asking for guidance and help. Not knowing exactly what to picture, they knew Divine Mother would provide the way.

A few weeks later Tom met a guy named John at work. They were like brothers in spirit. John left Vietnam in 1974 and stayed in a Buddhist monastery in Japan for two years before returning to the United States. One day he told Tom about a desolate stretch of beach on the northern coast that extended for 25 miles along a wild and forbidding area, ending at a place called Shelter Cove. If he and Mari ever wanted to hike it, John said he would show them the entrance. He called it the Lost Coast Trail.

It was perfect timing. That night while sitting on the back porch at Neo, Tom mentioned the trail to Mari. She loved the idea; it put her boxed-in demons to rest. It was September. Tom arranged to take off work from the 17th to the 22nd. They would have six days to hike the 25 miles, celebrating their birthdays somewhere on the trail.

That Sunday, they took highways and back roads while John and his wife Cathy led the way. Tom and Mari followed in the Trooper to the mouth of the Mattole River on Light House Road. From the road the river grew wider cutting its way to the ocean. Sixty-foot log timbers stacked like giant twigs in riffles, lined the flats on either side of the river. Beyond, blue-green breakers crashed and foamed at the mouth of the river making its transition into sea.

In the midst of this magic, John and Cathy stepped from their car and kissed. They all sat huddled in a circle on the sand and remained quiet for some time listening to the seagulls. John and Cathy smiled. The lovers grabbed their packs and waved goodbye. John drove the Trooper to Shelter Cove and left it there in a parking lot near Black Sands Beach.

Tom and Mari started trekking that night, south over dark sand, each carrying 60-pound packs. Their feet sunk into the soft sand for a quarter mile, making the walk difficult. Moving closer to the water's edge they found firm wet sand and continued two miles to the western point, rounding the bend near the Punta Gorda lighthouse ruins. Crossing a creek feeding into the ocean from the north, they saw wildflowers crammed into the gulch in the descending valley. The magic was beginning. Looking out to the horizon they could see the curvature of the earth. To the west, the sun shimmered off the waves. The smell of salt sea air filled their nostrils. Routine had vanished.

Mari walked slowly around the lighthouse. She walked closer, observing the blue paint flaking from the tower that once guided ships to safety. Grass on the hillside around the structure was deerskin brown, the sky powder blue. Above the sand line they continued for another two miles, following an old jeep road along the coast, and made camp near some large rocks inhabited by sea lions. Just offshore was a gully that provided fresh water and refuge from the wind. Packers before them had built a shelter made of driftwood and rocks. A sign carved from wood sat in front of the shelter. It read, "The Hyatt Regency."

They would spend the night here in this wild heavenly place. Taking off their packs after hours of trudging through the sand, they lay down beside each other on the dry earth and looked up at the dusking sky. Tom turned over to Mari and said, "I don't need to 'never' go home. I'm already here." She smiled at his English and picked up a handful of sand, "Time runs through my hands."

They arranged their sleeping bags in their tent in a small meadow, built a small driftwood fire, and walked toward the water. The surf broke along the beach with such force they could barely hear the cry of the seagulls passing overhead— rushing to find their nests before nightfall. From the riverbank not far from where they camped, a flat creek meandered down to the sea and forked halfway along the coast into a small bay. Holding hands they watched the sun blaze yellow and then red as it sank into the sea.

They wandered the beach until the sky turned black speckled with stars. Twenty feet away from the surf the night had become alive with frogs and crickets. As they followed their footprints in the sand back to the eastern tip of the gulch, where they had made their camp, the night had become filled with nature's orchestra. The present century had passed away. They could no longer tell it was 1990.

More tired than hungry, they cuddled in their zip-together bag and listened to the waves crash in the distance. Tom tried to point out stars in the sky—an attempt to impress her, even in this exhausted moment. Mari rolled over and kissed him tenderly, "Good night sweetie." Tom whispered in her ear, "Good night', I love it here." The dream, the dreamers and dreaming had become one.

The next morning they awoke with ferocious appetites. Mari whipped up the few eggs they had brought into an omelet made with dried seaweed she had gathered on her morning walk. Lifting the wooden plate closer to her mouth she took a bite and looked up at Tom, "Did you dream last night?" A little startled by her insight he rambled on, " Y-e-s, it was intense— I was driving in my old '63 Ford truck toward the river. We were living in Portland on the east side. As I approached the river, the ground began to shake, deep fissures formed 100 feet down in front of the truck. I put it in reverse and backed up as the ground collapsed in front of me. People all around were screaming in panic. There was a stranded man behind me asking for a ride. I told him to jump in and we continued in reverse. We were both looking through the windshield at the city in the distance, when the entire city burst into flames at the bases of the buildings. All of a sudden every building in the Portland skyline exploded falling to the ground in slow motion. I couldn't believe my eyes. Someone was yelling from down below, 'There's a battleship in the harbor.' I continued back to the house. Lightning was striking all around us. You were standing naked in a pool of water. I picked you up over my shoulders and carried you away and then woke up."

Mari continued eating her breakfast without words. Then she stood up and looked midway out into the sea, "Do you think something's going to happen?" Running his hands through her hair he replied, "No sweetie, probably just some old stuff bubbling to the surface. Did you have a dream?" She stared across the meadow for a few moments before replying, "Not really, nothing I can remember. Let's get our stuff and head on."

They continued along the beach for a mile. Cliffs began forming on the left and the beach narrowed. Mari pointed, "Look, there's boulders along the base of those cliffs going out into the sea."

"Yeah, if the tide comes in, we'll be trapped between the cliffs and the water."

"Do you think we can make it? How far before we reach land again?"

"According to the map, it can't be more than a mile—let's try it."

"Wait, let's flip a coin."

"OK, "heads," we go on, "tails," we try to find another way."

She flipped a quarter in the air, letting it fall to the sand at her feet. It came up "heads." They continued on, jumping from boulder to boulder. The wind started blowing, making it difficult to maneuver with their packs. Tom stopped about a half mile in, "Mari, look, I think the tide's coming in, we're going to have to hurry. I can see up ahead, the cliffs fall back into a gulch, we'll be safe once we get there." Walking, running, jumping with all they had, they continued until the last 100 yards.

The tide had come in and they were forced to work their way along the base of the cliff. The last 50 feet, they were within a foot of each other, face-to-face, hand-over-hand up against the cliff as the breakers pounded them from behind. Suddenly they both slipped and were pulled into waist-deep water. The next wave crashed, thrusting their bodies back to the base of the cliff. They tried to climb the cliff in vain and were again sucked from the rocks. The current moved them south, toward the beach ten feet away. They tried to stand and were shoved to their knees by the next wave. Their packs were soaked. They continued on hands and knees to the beach and lay in ankle-deep foam moving back and forth around them. They had made it through. Mari stood in the wet sand and spun in circles lifting her hands into the air. Her soaked hair flew out straight as she danced. Fortunately they had packed most everything in plastic bags.

Once in the meadow away from the rising tide, they built a fire and put their bedding out to dry. Dancing around the fire they chased each other like little children, giggling and hollering into the valley, celebrating yet another close call. Sea lions, cormorants and pelicans were offshore accompanying the lover's private festival. Tom ran to his pack and broke out a collapsible fishing pole, baited the hook with dried anchovies and began to cast into the surf. Mari stood by his side. They fished for an hour and caught two sand perch. She cooked them on sticks over the fire. The catching, the cooking, the eating—it was total.

A day and a half in, they could no longer tell what era it was. A strange welcome feeling surrounded them; they were finally together without time.

They continued for four more days, exploring canyons, walking in meadows of wildflowers, following streams to the sea. About halfway, they built a great bonfire on the beach with driftwood and seaweed. That night they celebrated their birthdays in the magic of the night sky.

They had not seen another soul for five days. Walking along Black Sands Beach near Shelter Cove, they spotted their first manmade objects. The modern world rushed in like a vortex, snapping away at their primordial moment.

12

*"With dreamful eyes my spirit lies
under the walls of Paradise. Drifting."*

Thomas Read

Paradise

Fog has rolled in over the valley. The grass in the field out back is wet with morning dew and the alarm is about to go off signaling another day on Neo. Tom will kiss Mari like he always does and wake up the boys for school. Mari will get up and make breakfast and attend to her art projects and massage clients. The boys will go to school and Tom will spend the rest of the day at work. They don't know it yet, but today is a special day; it's Monday April 29, 1991.

Tom was in the lab at Weightronix when a page came in over the loudspeaker announcing he had a call on line three. He went back to his desk and picked up the phone. In a studious voice, he articulated, "This is Tom." The melodious voice on the other end echoed, "This is Mari," followed by a tiny chuckle mocking his businesslike ambiance. His whole persona softened, "Oh, how are you sweetie? Everyone OK?" Mari replied, "Yes. I didn't want to interrupt you, but a man named Bill Smith called this afternoon, it sounds like it might be important. He wants you to call."

"Really, wonder what he wants?"

"He left his home number, do you want it?"

"No, I'll call him tonight."

"Who is he?"

"We were involved in a startup together years ago. He's on the board of Arawak Corporation. I haven't talked to him in some time, he's a good guy."

"Oh, OK, I'll see you tonight."

That evening Tom called Bill Smith back. He found that John Mariani was looking for someone to run the utilities operations at Jumby Bay and wanted to know if Tom was interested in the position. Jumby Bay is a world-class resort based on its own island off the north coast of Antigua in the British West Indies. John Mariani, owner of Banfi Vintners and self-made billionaire, owned the controlling interest in the island. Tom told Bill he was interested, but would need to discuss it with Mari.

Sitting on the back porch Tom broke their traditional Monday night silence, "Mar, how would you like to go live on an island in the Caribbean?"

"Was that what that call was about?"

"Yes, Bill Smith wants to know if we would be interested in working at Jumby Bay."

"Is that the place you told me about?"

"Apparently they're having troubles. They're looking for a new utility operations guy."

"Well, tell me about it?"

"I don't have any details yet. I need to contact a man named Paul Zuest who's President of Arawak. What do you think?"

"Why are they calling you?"

"Remember, I told you I worked there years ago as a engineering consultant. It all started in 1983. I used to go down there on and off over the years, guess they're looking for someone who's had experience on the island."

"What about the boys?"

"We all go together or not at all."

"Would we be together?"

"Yes, you could help me, we would all live on the island together, we would be working and living in the same place, it's a whole different world."

"Where would the boys go to school?"

"I don't know, we'll have to do some research."

They were both in shock over the reality of the idea. "This could really happen," she said, as she stared out at the clothesline Tom had built in the backyard. Suddenly an ear-to-ear smile appeared on her face. The smile told him everything he needed to know.

On May 7th Bill Smith arranged for Tom to call Paul Zuest in Antigua. During the phone conversation they discussed Tom's history with the island and Paul requested that Tom send a resume to a man named Percy Fiedtkou at Jumby Bay.

Mari and Tom discussed the whole thing with Noni and Didi. They appeared to be happy, but reluctant that their grandchildren would be so far away.

Through a series of phone calls, Paul and Tom agreed to meet at Mari's aunt's house in San Francisco for an informal interview. Her aunt *Teta* Neve lived in a posh flat near the Palace of Fine Arts and was pleased to host the occasion. Tom picked up Paul at the airport and they spent the afternoon discussing responsibilities of the job, conditions in Antigua, and the boys. During the discussions, Mari took Tom to the side and wanted to know what the prospects would be of visiting the island before committing. He thought that was a good idea, but considered it as a point of negotiation, best saved for when they started working out the details. Tom and Paul began negotiations by fax on June 13th. On June 22nd Tom and Mari flew to Antigua for a four-day, all expenses paid, look-see.

They flew to Florida and picked up a small airplane bound for Montserrat, an island in the French West Indies. After a short layover they boarded again for Antigua. On the final leg of their flight, Mari asked Tom how his experience with the island all began:

"I was working as a consultant for Intel Corporation at the time and they had asked me to assist on a project called Palm Guard in Oregon. Palm Guard was funded by a group of Canadian bankers that wanted to create a paperless monetary society. They were developing a device to scan the palm of the hand for positive identification. I was asked to come in and help with the microprocessor development. The CEO of the company was Robert J. Davis, former CEO and co-founder of Tektronix, you remember me telling you about that. Anyways, at the time, Tektronix was Oregon's largest employer, with over 22,000 people. One afternoon he called me into his office and asked if I would take a few days off to help re-program a microprocessor for a sewage treatment plant in the Caribbean. It took me by surprise and I wasn't even sure I heard him correctly. I told him that microprocessors were my area of expertise, but what about the Caribbean? He began telling me this fantastic story.

"'When I retired from Tektronix, my wife, Jonnie and I bought an island in the Caribbean off the coast of Antigua. I built a deepwater harbor and restored an old 16th-century estate on the property. We lived there for 12 years. It became a secret hideaway for celebrities who wanted to get away. Jonnie grew tired of the island so I gave it to my stepson Homer Williams and came back out of retirement to work here at Palm Guard. Homer started developing the island into a resort and last year he put $20,000,000 into restoration and new development. Here's the deal. I'm not totally clear on the situation but what I understand, there's a sewage treatment plant near the estate house that is not operating properly and they feel the microprocessor is at fault.'

"Again he asked me if I was interested. I told him I was very interested, but could he provide some specs on the system. He said that wasn't likely and if I accepted the offer, I would need to be on a plane the next day and I would only have three days to complete the task. I told him I would do it. He ended the conversation with, 'More later.' The next day I met with Homer Williams at his office in Portland and scratched out a few more details before boarding an airplane at 10:00 PM.

"After a 14-hour flight I landed in Antigua. I was to take a taxi from the airport to a place called Crabs Marina and catch a boat for Long Island, two miles off the coast of Antigua. The boat was supposed to meet me there at 2:00 PM. Traveling several miles down a dirt road from the airport, I arrived at

Crabs around 1:30 PM and waited. Two o'clock rolled around and no boat. So I drank rum at a little outside bar at the marina and continued to wait some more. Three o'clock—still no boat. I asked the bartender if he knew about a two o'clock boat going to Long Island. He told me, 'Anytime now, mon.' I felt relieved knowing at least I was in the right place. Four o'clock, still no boat. I asked again. He laughed as he explained, 'Two o'clock, mon. Dat means sumtime in da afernon, it cud be two, tree, four; relax mon, it well cum.'

"Sure enough, 4:30 rolled around and there it was approaching across the water. I ran over to the 40-foot motorized catamaran and said to the guy driving, 'Is this boat going to Long Island?' Over the sound of the motor, he laughed and replied, 'Ya mon, it's da only place it go. You Tom?' I said, 'Yes' and jumped in. As we approached the island I felt as though I were entering another dimension—it felt like Fantasy Island. We docked at a large harbor where only two other boats were moored. I stood on the bow and gazed toward what looked like a castle with expansive lawns and pathways that seemed to go on for miles, cutting into tropical jungle.

"I disembarked and walked toward the castle. Except for a few cottages to the right, it appeared to be the only semblance of civilization. When I arrived at the expansive steps, a tall Antiguan man moving kitchen equipment that should have been moved by three men, looked over at me. I asked him if this was the estate house. He nodded and disappeared inside.

"I needed to find a guy named Larry Ables and his brother Paul. According to Homer they would be easy to spot; they were the only two Caucasians on the island and the main contractors for the project. I wandered the island asking people where I might find Larry Ables; they would point off in a direction without saying anything, then I would go there. I did this for about an hour, until the last man I spoke with pointed to a building by the sea on the north side of the island. There, near a sidewalk being poured with new concrete was a tall white man. He spotted me and came over, 'You must be Tom Sawyer.' I replied, 'You must be Larry Ables,' We both laughed and walked to a large gazebo not far from the construction site. He picked up a walkie-talkie and radioed for his brother and three beers. Soon his brother Paul arrived on an electric cart with three Jamaican Red Stripes.

"We all sat around a table sipping cold beer and Paul began to speak, 'OK, we have 200 men working the island right now, but the subcontractors responsible for the infrastructure walked off the job in a contract dispute. We have a sewage treatment plant still in the container up at Cottage 8, the desalination plant isn't working, the main pumping station is down and the sewage treatment plant at the estate house is going crazy. You have three days; I want to know right now if you think you can do it?' I thought to myself, *What's he talking about? I came here to fix a computer chip in an already existing sewage treatment plant.* But I didn't say that, I just continued to listen. He continued, 'Look, Homer has floated a $10,000,000 note with the bank and the resort is supposed to open in four days. If we don't open the resort on time then the bank is going to call the note. To make matters worse, if you think you can't do it then we need to call off the press and the VIPs right now or the reputation of the resort will be ruined. Can you do it?'

"I asked him if we could walk around and look at the equipment he was talking about. He said, 'We can do better than that; we'll ride.' We all jumped into the electric cart and toured the areas in question, then drove back to the gazebo. Sitting at the table, I don't know why I said this—it just came out of my mouth. I raised a Red Stripe to my lips and took a swig. Putting the bottle back on the table, I replied, 'Give me 35 men, five walkie-talkies, an electric cart, lights 24 hours a day, two backhoes and a D8 Caterpillar and I think we can do it.' Larry replied, 'Are you sure?' I said, 'Yes.' Larry went on, 'All right then, you got it, whatever you want, you got it.' I really didn't understand the magnitude of what I had just gotten myself into. It all seemed like a dream. It wasn't until the next morning that it began to dawn on me.

"I had been up all night thinking. At first light I walked to the harbor and looked back toward Antigua. Taking in the sea and the birds flying overhead, I gazed off in the distance across the water; I could see a barge being pushed by a large seagoing tug. I couldn't make out what was on the barge. As the barge got closer it hit me. On the barge were two backhoes and a D8 Caterpillar. I was floored. My stomach dropped to my knees. I couldn't believe it. Right then I realized, this was all for real. I thought to myself, *What did you do? Do you really think you can pull this off, do you understand the significance of what you just told those guys and what's riding on the whole thing?*

"We worked for 36 hours straight, around the clock. With a bunch of good men, and a whole lot of luck, bubble gum and baling wire we were able to get the island operational a day an a half ahead of schedule. Towards the end there we were getting creative—we ran out of washers and started drilling holes in quarters to finish the job.

"The next day the VIPs started arriving and the press came in, and Long Island Resort was given a five star rating. I ended up staying on the island for two months writing maintenance procedures and getting things right. In Portland I was celebrated as a hero. In truth, the job seemed to happen beyond me. Obviously, I was there physically, but magic was pulling the strings.

"I am the son of a plumber. And that's how it all began. Over the years they've called me in for emergencies and consulting contracts now and then, and that's basically it."

Mari asked, "So how did John Mariani end up with the island?"

Tom continued, "After Homer's development, one year later Long Island became the number one resort in the Caribbean. Rooms cost up to $2,000 a day, all-inclusive, and they also sold parcels of the island to the rich and famous. Later Homer sold 70% of Arawak Corp. to John Mariani, who renamed the island Jumby Bay, 20% to a Japanese consortium and held 10% for himself."

Mari replied, "I feel like we're on a 007 mission. Tell me more. Did you have a girlfriend?"

Tom was a little shocked by the question, but thought it was a good one, in that Mari had made it a point to introduce him to all her old boyfriends. "Not really, I pretty much stayed with the work. There *was* a girl I admired, I was secretly in love with her, but that was years ago."

"Well, is she going to be there?"

"I don't know."

"What is her name?"

"Her name is Corina."

"Tell me, how did you meet her?"

"She was working at Long Island as a secretary. Her father, Malcolm Edwards, who was head of the Telephone Company in Antigua, and I worked together on an undersea cable. Routinely a cement barge used to dock across the bay from the island. Once during a low tide it reversed its engines, sucking up Long Island's communication cable into its props, stretching and breaking the cable in several places along the cable's two-mile run. The next day I was following that cable in pitch-black water, diving at 60 feet, so I could only stay down for 30 minutes at a time. Malcolm tended the boat while I moved along the bottom, hand-over-hand, following the cable until I'd find a break. I would then send up a marker buoy and Malcolm would note the location.

"This continued for some time. It was so dark in the water I couldn't see my watch, but I figured it was time to ascend. As I pushed off from the bottom I got vertigo and for a moment I thought I was falling or being sucked backward. The only thing that kept me from panicking was watching the bubbles. I knew bubbles went up. As I rose from the bottom a few feet, the water cleared and I could see my depth gauge, so I decompressed at 30 feet and continued on up. Malcolm was right there for me. On these dives I learned to trust him and we spent many days together working the island. He was somewhat of a father figure for me. I very much enjoyed his company."

Mari said, "Who's Malcolm Edwards?"

"Oh, that's Corina's father."

"I see. Well, that's an interesting story, but you didn't tell me much about Corina…what's she like?"

"Oh, yeah. She was in her early 20s, slender, educated in England, no nonsense, and very beautiful."

"Do I need to worry?"

"No sweetie, I think she's married now."

"And how do you know that? Is that supposed to make me feel safe?"

"What I mean is —"

Mari interrupted his attempt to clean up what he had stumbled into and started laughing, "You silly, I'm just teasing you for all the times you ribbed me about my boyfriends."

"Oh, OK, I thought I was on trial there for a minute."

Smiling, she started again, "I could tell you're excited about coming here, I just wanted to make sure it wasn't about another woman." Then she started laughing again.

Tom got serious and continued, "I love coming here because I love the people and believe that's why I've been successful. If the people like you, then they want you to succeed. If they don't like you, then it will look like all kinds of things are getting done, but in reality, nothing is getting done. That's the way it is."

Mari went on, "Do you think they'll like me?"

Tom answered, "NO—they'll love you."

Mari smiled and put her head on his shoulder for the rest of the flight.

He woke her just as the jet was making its final approach to Antigua in time to capture a view of Jumby Bay from the left windows. A few minutes later they touched down at Antigua's Bird International. As they walked down the staircase from the Boeing 707, they were hit by a blast of hot musky air and diesel fumes. Tom took a deep breath; fond memories rushed in. After clearing customs, they walked to the main lobby and spotted a man holding a sign, "Mr. and Mrs. Sawyer." Hundreds of Antiguans moved about wearing bright colors, a few flagging down cabs, others greeting loved ones, some looking for tourists to connect with. The man took Tom and Mari to a black Foster

Jonas cab and opened the door. Carrying two small backpacks, they climbed in and slid the door closed.

The cabbie drove at 60 MPH on the wrong side of the road, eight miles to the top of a blind hill past the US Air Force Station, down a tiny side street by the sea leading to the docks. The smell of hot raw sewage and diesel fumes breezed into the open windows. South of the docks they merged with a stream of foot traffic making their way from Shell Beach to the main road near the Beachcomber Hotel. The cab stopped in the middle of it all. They grabbed their packs, maneuvering amongst brightly dressed women and barefoot children to a graveled covered dock jetting out into the ocean at Shell Beach. The wind picked up. The smell of the salt air got stronger as they made their way to the end of the dock. They stood there listening to the sound of water splashing against pilings. Scores of colorful paint-peeled boats lined the cove. Staring out across the sea to Jumby Bay Island in the distance altered Tom and Mari's reality. They looked into each other's eyes as repeated thuds of moored craft slapped against one another. Sand gleaming deep under the boats along the dock took Tom back to memories lived there years before.

Ten minutes later the sound of a speedboat approaching from across the bay broke their trance. Peering closer Tom recognized the driver and smiled while the boat reversed its engines and docked alongside the boarding ramp. It was his old friend Bird. Tom introduced Mari as they helped her into the boat. The two men greeted each other like long past brothers. Mari sat down, but Tom was still standing when Bird revved the engines, flipping him backwards into the seat. Bird spun around with one hand on the wheel grinning from ear to ear. Tom smiled back and yelled, "Ya mon."

As they sped toward the island the swells settled and the waves became choppier, slapping the bow into the air. Mari looked back to watch the dock disappear behind her. Now the island showed clearly, half a mile away, and in the distance they could hear the crash of the surf breaking along the reefs near the island's west dock. A hundred yards inside the reef Tom started pointing to different parts of the island. Swinging past the cape, west of the estate house, he showed her the sewage treatment plant that had gotten him there in the first place. She wasn't particularly impressed.

They landed at the west dock by the Beach Pavilion and were greeted by a German man named Werner. He introduced himself as the Food and Beverage Manager and put on the complete performance with a cabaret of sight and sound, the full tour with champagne and caviar. Tom knew then that Warner figured they were guests and was not wise to the purpose of the visit.

They were taken to a quaint cottage near the Estate House. After a short rest they snatched two bicycles from a communal bike rack and toured the grounds, following the main road that circled the island. As they approached the east shore Tom stopped near an expansive villa with a Spanish-tiled roof and tennis courts. "Mar, see this place, it belongs to Roland Franklin, the most prominent corporate raider in the world. On a little further is Robin Leach's; you know, *Lifestyles of the Rich and Famous*, and then around the bend is Lord Sainsbury's new place, he's one of the richest men in England." After they left Lord Sainsbury's Tom fell back to watch Mari pedal from behind, then piped up again, "Let's go back around this way and ride out to the northwest point, I'll show you John and Henry Mariani's place. Their swimming pool disappears into the sea."

Tom spun around and headed to the beach. They walked to the ocean near the point at Pasture Bay. It was sunny, the beach secluded, the water emerald-blue and clear, soft and warm, a slight easterly breeze blew Mari's hair from her shoulders. They experienced peace and privacy, something that Mari had always yearned for. Beckoned by the magic they bicycled back along lush pathways lined with flowers and tropical foliage. As they passed near Pond Bay House a symphony of wild birds disturbed the silence.

They stopped near a round rock planter about 20 feet across and Tom began to talk again, "Mar, see this planter. The men I worked with built it. Most people don't know it, but buried underground just inside the wall is a time capsule. It was signed by all of us. We had a bronze plaque made that covers the top of the capsule dedicating the opening of the resort in 1983 to Bob and Jonnie Davis."

As the lovers rode to secret places Tom knew, Mari asked a thousand questions. He enjoyed her asking questions— somehow it made him feel he was important in her eyes. They continued to the top of the hill and looked back at the red-tiled roofs dotting quaint green rolling knolls that climaxed into the sea. Soon they arrived at their cottage and stepped onto the veranda. Mari ignored the wicker chairs with flowered cushions and sat on the steps. Tom sat next to her knee to knee. The scent of oleander and bougainvillea hung in the breeze. They sat for some time with their heads touching. Then she broke the silence; "I've never seen anything like this place. Let's go swimming." They put on their bathing suits and walked to a white sand beach west of the Pavilion where the water was warm and crystal blue; it was like stepping into a sapphire.

That night they ate at the Estate House restaurant in lavish luxury; it was an international affair of French, Italian and native cuisine. Seven courses were served with world-class wines from Montalcino, Strevi and Gavi, Italy. They sat at a white cloth-covered table near the veranda overlooking the sea and listened to the crickets and night frogs while two waiters, just for them, provided anything they might desire.

The next morning Tom met Paul Zuest at the Beach Pavilion for breakfast while Mari toured the island with Ted Isaac, the island's General Manager. Ted made Mari feel comfortable about the boys' education by suggesting they attend school with his son.

That afternoon Tom arranged a boat to Parham, a small fishing village on the north coast of the Antigua where he once lived. He wanted to introduce Mari to his old friend and right-hand-man, Buck White.

Motoring into Parham Sound their boat reversed its engines, gently touching the dock. They walked down a slippery wharf and ambled by a line of small wooden fishing boats to a gravel road leading to the street. The water splashing against the dinghies in the harbor reminded Tom of his life in Parham.

Parham was the first place the English settled when they arrived in 1711 and contained much of Antigua's long-gone history. Near a 300-year-old cobblestone wall an old man lifted a pint of dark rum to his lips. They nodded as they passed and continued to the street.

Turning the corner they saw a row of brightly painted tin houses mixed in among the English and Portuguese 16th-century ruins. Some of the small houses were built inside the ruins; others perched on the hillside overlooking the sea. They continued down the cobblestone road to a two-story white wooden building. The second story was living quarters and had a veranda that stretched around one side. Below was the drinking establishment they were about to enter. Banana, plantain, and mango trees spotted the grounds leading to the sea. Tom turned to Mari, "This is called White House. It's a tavern, but not to be confused with the White House Tavern down the road. It is customary that a stranger, entering an establishment, announce and introduce themselves to the proprietor."

As they entered, a man with a monkey on one shoulder looked over and continued out the door. They walked to the bar and pulled out a stool, "Hello sir, this is my wife Mari, I'm Tom Sawyer." The man spoke back, "How yu go? How you cum to this village?" Tom replied, "*Iry* mon (Antiguan for 'Real good, man'). I used to live here years ago when I worked at Jumby Bay." The man said, "Ya mon. Yu like someting to drink?" Tom replied, "Two Red Stripes please." To the left of the bar, four older men slapping dominoes on a makeshift wooden table looked up. Tom continued, "I used to live up above your establishment in the bungalow above the bar." The man replied, "I heard of you, long time ago, maybe ten." Mari said, "You used to live here?" Tom replied, "Yes, upstairs."

Thanking the proprietor they grabbed their Red Stripes and walked outside to the covered entrance facing the street, where they watched children playing in the road as brightly clad women carrying baskets on their heads passed by. Tom went on, "Living at Jumby Bay is like living at Disneyland. It's like putting in a quarter and going on a ride—life is choreographed. Here in the streets of Parham, life is real."

Mari looked down the cobblestone street, watching a bird peck a dry piece of bread, "What was it like, living here?"

"I love it here. I was the only white man in the village of 400 people. I love the people here and they seemed to love me. I would play ball with the children in the street, go to the community market, play dominoes with the old men and walk barefooted everywhere."

Mari exclaimed, "Barefooted? You seem like such a tenderfoot!"

"Buck White taught me. One day we were walking on a sharp gravel road leading to the sewage treatment plant at Jumby. I noticed Buck was carrying his shoes. I asked him why he wasn't wearing his shoes. He said, 'Because I enjoy it.' From that day on I went barefoot, even while dining at the Jumby Bay Estate House restaurant. In the old days, Homer used to dance on the tables like Zorba the Greek with the Antiguan help to steel-drum music and we all laughed and had fun. Back then, when the resort first opened, there was a spirit in the air. Not only was it a classy place, it had heart and was full of life. I think that magical combination established Jumby Bay's reputation. But today, it's much more reserved.

"Eventually my feet got used to it and I could walk anywhere. Somehow it made me feel connected with the people. They nicknamed me 'Tattoo.' After a while everyone gets a street name. I wonder what they'll call you? Buck White is really Walcott Joseph. In the slave days names were given to identify their owners. Anyway, most people in Parham didn't wear shoes.

"At that time most people didn't have radios in the village. There was a man that lived in a shack on the hill. He had some big speakers and would play music for the whole village, kind of like a disc jockey. If you needed candles, you went to so-and-so's house, if you needed clothes mended you went to another person's house and so on. Everyone had a skill or merchandise and operated out of their homes. Most everyone went to the community well for water. It's where people got the news. There was laughing and singing going on all over. In the United States if you walk down the street singing and dancing people look at you funny. Here it's lovable and enjoyed. In the USA if you say hello or good morning to a stranger, inside they're asking, *Who are you and what do you want?* Here people say, 'Good morning' from their hearts and you feel it.

"Life here in the village is sometimes difficult, always spontaneous, inventive and full of joy. It's an adventure to live here. It's a blessing to live among these people and they have taught me much about my own nature. But I can tell things are changing. Since my last trip here, I see that people are staying inside more and competing among themselves, thanks to TV. Anyway, what do you think about living here if we take the job?"

"Let's walk around some more and check it out, it feels good to me."

They continued towards the village well. The old well was gone, replaced by a faucet poking out from a cement slab in the square. Hand-in-hand Tom and Mari continued, passing a small group gathered by the well. Behind them were two men butchering a goat. They waved. Some waved back, others just smiled with curiosity. Down a narrow side road, they came upon two older gentlemen walking on the same side of the street. When the men got close enough to notice they were white, the men walked to the other side of the road and waited for the lovers to pass before re-entering the street.

Mari wanted to know why they did that.

Tom told her, "Antigua had a long history of slavery, clear into the 1920s. These men were taught by their parents that if you see a white man walking in the street you have to clear the street to let them pass. It's terrible what happened here during the slave days. Someday I'll take you to the Parham Estate House. It belonged to the governor at one time and then later to the overseer of the village. I'll show you the dungeons where they chained the strongest men for breeding purposes. What the white man did to these people for power and greed was unconscionable. When I used to live here I had to tell the men

I worked with, not to call me Master or Sir. It took a long while before they accepted that."

They continued to the White House Tavern. Tom told Mari to wait on the porch while he went inside. He poked his head in and yelled, "Has anyone seen Buck White?" A big man near the pool table put his stick down and walked toward Tom, "Wa yu white mun wan wit Buck White." Tom replied, "He's a friend, I used to live here at White House." The man snapped, "Buck's na here." Tom said calmly, "Does he still live in Parham?" The man replied, "Me show yu." He went out to the street and pointed toward the police station. "Go pas dare up da road til yu se iron picket fent." Tom thanked the man and after zigzagging through the village they found the house with the iron picket fence.

They walked to the door and knocked, but no one was there. Mari commented, "The man at the White House Tavern, was he friendly? I couldn't tell. He was a big man!" Tom replied, "Yes, he was just shocked to see white people in the village. It's hard to tell if this is the right house or if Buck's coming back soon. Let's go, we'll try to come back later."

Tom went on, "Once while I was working at Jumby when Homer owned the island; we were trying to move a large stone. Three men could not lift it and could barely move it with levers. I told them to go get the backhoe on the other side of the island. Someone said, 'Go get Big Mon.' I said, 'Big Man, who is Big Man?' Off they went—a few minutes later they returned with the largest human being I'd ever seen. He was six foot six with arms bigger than my legs. Someone said, 'Where do you want it?' I pointed. Without a word Big Man crouched in front of the stone lifting it to his waist. He carried it eight steps and dropped it with a thud. I couldn't believe it; it was the most awesome thing I ever witnessed.

"There was one other incident that moved me deeply. We needed to clear rocks from a meadow near the sugarcane mill by the Estate House. Buck suggested that we get the Rastas. Not knowing who they were, I went on Buck's word and the next morning 60 Rastafarians showed up on the island. We told their leader what we wanted done. He walked to the center

of the field and all his men circled around him. He raised his
right hand in the air and yelled, 'A ba ya habi tu' or something
like that. In unison they all yelled back, 'A ba ya habi tu.' As
they worked they all sang together. What would have taken
normal people three days to finish, these Rastas moved in one.
It was a spiritual experience."

Mari and Tom set off for the corner where kids were playing
basketball on a makeshift court in the ruins of a cement-slab
building. Mari said, "Let's watch the kids play, you know the
boys would love to come here and play basketball." Tom said,
"Yeah, they'd love it here." They watched the kids play for a
short time and then Tom asked Mari if she wanted to see St.
Peter's Church. They hiked up the hill and walked around the
old church building, peeking in the windows. The ceilings looked
like the wooden ribs of a boat turned upside down. A small
sign out front said, "St. Peter's Church, built 1711, rebuilt after
the fire in 1840." Tom suggested they go to a church service
when they come back to Jumby. Mari looked over at him with
smiles and said, "When we come back to Jumby?"

They walked back to Buck's, but still no one was there.
Tom looked at his watch. It was time to go. He removed a
Motorola two-way from his belt and radioed for a boat to pick
them up at Parham dock. On the way to the harbor he started
telling her what was in his heart:

"When I lived here almost ten years ago there was such a
sweetness here; indescribable. Here they live in poverty, yet
they have so much heart and grace. There's a sense of
community here." Pointing toward Jumby Bay Island he
continued, "There, only a boat ride away, they live in all their
opulence and wealth, yet inside they have lost the innocence
and joy that nourishes the spirit. I prefer to live here and work
there." Mari agreed.

It would be a half hour before the boat arrived. The lovers
lay down on a small covered wooden bench at the dock, listening
to the seagulls cry and the water gently splashing against pylons.
The smell of fish and diesel drifted in the hot afternoon sun.
They lay there without words, cuddled together watching the
water cast its flickering brilliance into their eyes. It was a moment

never to be forgotten, a moment like the one at Rudy's and at the telephone booth at Salt Point. It transcended all else around them—it was a perfect moment.

Back at Jumby they ate dinner on the beach with Robin Leach and some of John Mariani's entourage, listening to steel drum music into the night. The next morning Tom met with Don Tate, Director of Real Estate Development for Jumby Bay. They drove to the new construction sites throughout the island and Don welcomed Tom to the team.

That afternoon, Mari told Tom she wanted him to take the job and they would all move to Antigua. Tom met with Paul Zuest that evening and signed the necessary papers. The next morning they flew back to Santa Rosa, California; again forever changed.

13

*"We must all obey the great law of change.
It is the most powerful law of nature."*

Edmund Burke

Forever Changed

Back in the USA things seemed to move faster. They notified family and friends. The next day they joined the Goslovich clan for several days at Yosemite and then traveled to Mariposa where they met up with Tom's mentor, Al Toler. The following day Tom turned in his written resignation to Weightronix, Inc. and said goodbye to all his work buddies. They leased out the house on Neo and started boxing things up. In the midst of it all, on July 16th, their wedding anniversary, Tom gave Mari a large gold necklace, which she immediately returned for a small gold necklace with two hearts. On July 22nd Virginia and Alan Harrison threw a bon-voyage party for the lucky lovers headed for the West Indies.

After tons of preparation, storage lockers, paperwork and shipping, they arrived back in Antigua on July 25th with their boys. They put up at Pond Bay House overlooking the sea for two weeks while Tom scoped out the job and Mari looked for less posh accommodations in Parham. Adam and Jacob moved into the scene like ducks to water.

On the third day of their arrival, in the afternoon, Tom was to report to Percy Fiedtkou, the company's Human Resource Manager. He was escorted in by Executive Secretary, Corina Edwards! Mr. Fiedtkou was on the phone so Tom sat in a chair in front of his desk. Mr. Fiedtkou, a muscular olive-skinned older man, had worked the bauxite mines as an engineer in his youth. There was something about him that Tom couldn't put his finger on, something different than most. Tom sat there for almost a half hour while Mr. Fiedtkou made phone call after phone call, occasionally rubber-stamping documents on his desk. He did this as if Tom wasn't there, never making eye contact. Tom watched everything the man did, never saying a word, just a fly on the wall. Hanging up the phone from his last call, Mr. Fiedtkou stamped a few more papers with a forceful thud, went to a filing cabinet, pulled a folder and sat back down. Lifting his head to make contact for the first time, his eyes snapped open looking directly into Tom's. He didn't say anything for several seconds, then pronounced with proper British pomp and circumstance, "Mr. Sawyer, welcome to Jumby Bay."

Tom would be Chief Engineer and Vice President of Operations. Forty-three people would report directly to him. From higher up came his first assignment. He was to be the hatchet man, laying off the Maintenance Manager and three other people in the department.

As they were parting Tom asked Percy if he was Antiguan. Percy replied, "No, I'm 100% Arawak Indian from Guyana." Then he proceeded to tell Tom long stories about his days in the mines of South America and his travels in search of gold along the Amazon River.

Mari got the boys enrolled in school at the Christian Brothers Catholic School in St. John's. Each morning, Adam and Jacob took the boat to the mainland and caught a bus for school. On the weekends they'd go by boat to Parham and play basketball all day.

Mari and Karen Tate, the Marketing Executive's wife, started hanging out together during the day while Tom was working. After two weeks, they still hadn't found a place in Parham. In lieu of their little home in the village, they made tentative plans to move to an ivy-covered cottage on the hillside near the Tates with a birds-eye view of Jumby Bay, but a few more weeks would have to pass. Every weekend they went to Parham in search of a place to live. Soon Tom discovered that the word had gotten out on how much money he was making and had filtered back to the landlords in Parham. In the past he had rented the two-bedroom bungalow above the White House Tavern with its lovely veranda overlooking the streets of Parham for $35 a month, utilities included, but now even rundown places were going for $900 U.S. and up.

He spent the next couple of weeks evaluating construction sites, engineering new hookups, ordering equipment, reorganizing people and departments, creating budgets, meeting with port authorities, accountants, department heads and putting out personnel fires. Except for top-level meetings Mari went with him everywhere, acting as his personal secretary. She loved showing up at construction sites dressed in skimpy California attire. Tom was so proud to be with her. She was beginning to take on the persona of a Jackie Kennedy. She was that way, a chameleon; if the situation required she could sleep under a bridge one night and the next, be dancing in the ballroom of the Statler Hilton. When they weren't playing on the beach with the boys, they would spend the evenings consolidating budgetary reports for John Mariani.

It had been almost a month since they shipped their household belongings and the container hadn't arrived yet, somehow it was "hung up in customs." What that meant, was, someone needed to get paid, but it all worked out. The lovers knew how to live out of a suitcase. On August 4th they were having lunch at the Beach Pavilion Bar. A waiter named Durham whom Tom knew from years ago, who spoke perfect Kings English, began speaking *Bewee* (Antiguan patois) because he knew Tom liked it. He asked if they were going to J'Overt (pronounced jew-vay) Mornin'. Mari said, "What is J'Overt Mornin'?" Durham replied, "Dat's where yu jump up in da street fro nite til da sun cum up." Mari said, "Tom, have you been to J'Overt Mornin'?" Tom replied, "No!" Mari went on, "We should go!" Tom said, "Where is it?" Durham replied, "Me show yu, St. John's, a bunch are goin' yu can cum wid dus."

"All right," Mari said with delight.

That afternoon they took a boat to Parham and joined a bus full of Antiguans bound for St. John's, the capital city. Everyone was laughing and telling stories. Children were running from one end of the bus to the other. Just outside Parham the bus stopped to let a herd of goats pass and several more people climbed aboard. When they arrived in St. John's people had already started to gather. Trucks had lined up on the street with rum and beer and steel drum bands were everywhere. By evening thousands had gathered in the streets, dressed in bright colors. In Antigua, when people stand in line, even for the post office, it's different than in the US; there's no unspoken two-foot rule. People stand in line squashed up against each other, complete strangers, talking and singing and moving about. It's a holdover from the slave days when slaves were forced to pack the line as tight as possible.

Tom and Mari lined up behind the Jumby Bay truck. Their 15-year-old boys fell in formation next to them. Tom was pressed into the back of an Antiguan woman; Mari into him, and some Antiguan man behind her and the line went on for about 200 people more. The truck started to move. People began walking and jumping-up to the music blasting from huge speakers mounted on the back of the flatbed truck. Tenders on the truck continually pitched rum and beer into the crowd. Hundreds of trucks drove through the streets of St. John's that night, all singing and dancing to the music. They did this all night until the sun came up the next morning, J'Overt Mornin'.

When the sun rose, the lovers and their twins found a little flowerbed to lie in, in the middle of a traffic circle in downtown St. John's. Sleeping off the celebration, they laid there cuddled up in a Widdy-Widdy bush until 8:00 AM. When they awoke, cars were zipping through the traffic circle, surrounding them like ants. Tom radioed Jumby Bay for a cab, "Come to Corn Alley by Silston Library, downtown."

Back at Jumby Bay, sitting on the patio overlooking the sea at Pond Bay House, Mari wrote the following letter to her family back home,

"Looks like we're going to stay at Pond Bay House a few more weeks or at least until our shipment arrives. Life's a challenge. We're in Antigua, ten days according to the calendar, but surely it's been a few months. Those last few pressure-packed weeks in Santa Rosa seem a distant past as we rest and eat and walk around this dream-like place they call 'Paradise.' The boys and Tom sleep soundly this afternoon—just tried to wake them for lunch unsuccessfully—we were up most of the night for 'J'Overt Morning.' Dancing in the streets from 2:00 AM until 9:00 AM following the Jumby Bay truck laden with giant speakers and drinks. It was good fun, not crazy scenes like you see in Mardi Gras movies. This land is remarkably safe and gentle and they even party like members of one big family. Many women have children with different men so everybody seems to be a cousin, uncle, half-sister, nephew, etc., of everyone else. It makes it tough for the Antiguan working at Jumby Bay in a supervisor's position because he's expected to order his own relatives, and we all know how difficult that is! Ha, Ha.

"I'm sitting out on my deck overlooking the sea. All the rooms and cottages have remarkable views of the turquoise and jade reef waters surrounding us. The boys and I have taken up sailing in little Sunfishes. After we master (!?!) that, I want to try windsurfing. The kids have tried water-skiing, but I haven't yet. A mama duck's walking by with four little brown chicks. Lots of birds here and lizards. Brown pelicans, laughing gulls and mourning doves and a hundred I don't know the name of. Everything is geared to the guests' comfort. Soft sheets and big fluffy robes—enormous towels and spacious rooms with daily replenished bar. Tom and I have our own room that has a shower overlooking the sea, that's probably larger than our bedroom will be when we move to Parham Village on the mainland of Antigua.

"We've looked at a few houses—found one we may take, but it's being remodeled and may not be done on time. We're supposed to move around the 15th of August, although we'll ask to stay longer if necessary, at least until our container arrives. We've been given two rooms at Pond Bay House, laundry service, and free all we can eat and drink, but I'm ready to either get a job here immediately or get away from Jumby Bay. I'm in a Limbo somewhere between staff and guest. This is one of those positions I'm not good at – where you have to worry about saying and doing the 'right thing.' I'm sure I'd be digesting these seven-course meals a lot better every evening if we were paying the $1,500 a day, and my children's and my actions were not a reflection on my husband's work performance.

"Everyone seems to like the boys, guests and staff alike. They're gaining weight and quite brown already. The boys are about average height here. After years of slave breeding these people are big, buff and beautiful. Some of the men look like professional football players, truly immense and powerful looking. The women are very beautiful – graceful and warm.

"Management is mostly white. The Antiguan general manager is a personable guy—looks like a Boston Celtic (about 6'5") and is good with the guests. The personnel manager is an Indian (of Arawak descent) from South America. He's a twin, but his brother lives in Brazil or Venezuela. The lady who runs housekeeping is an Antiguan and daughter of the Prime Minister or some bigwig in Antiguan Politics. The president, Paul Zuest, is Swiss. He managed the finest hotel in the world (the Hotel Bel Air in Beverly Hills) before taking this job nine months ago. Werner, a German, also here nine months, is the food and beverage manager – worked at Donald Trump's Taj Mahal before coming here. He's a character. The boys get a kick out of him.

"The first few days we were here Tom sussed out a tremendous workload of things in the utilities that need repair. Now he has to work to get a budget to implement the changes. Because of the war in Iraq the tourist industry suffered greatly internationally. People are starting to travel again, but this is the slow season, and the resort will be totally shut down (as it always does) in September and October for maintenance (hurricane season). We haven't had any storms, but last week before we came there was an unusually intense lightning storm that downed the microwave tower on the mainland linking Jumby Bay. Everything has greened out because of the rain that came with the electrical storm and the island's much more beautiful than when Tom and I first came four weeks ago to check the place.

"Anyway, because of the bad season the chief financial officer is feeling very tight-fisted and Tom fears he may not get the budget he needs. The boiler for hot water to our room is broken at the moment, which in this warm weather is not a serious problem but is typical of the infrastructure here. Everything to do with water, sewage, power, and transportation seems to break down regularly. Pipe will be laid and then joined with improper pieces or adhered with an adhesive that's not supposed to be used with water. Fire hydrants will be buried, or not have the right pressure available. Pumps for lift stations break down, sewage sometimes overflows and on and on. Lots of work for Tom ahead. He's creating an office today.

"Word's out that I do massage and they're considering it; a French acupuncture doctor comes twice a week. Charges $100 for a massage, but they feel he's not around enough and nobody likes him that much or his work. I haven't seen him yet. As soon as my massage table arrives on the boat, I'll ask to give some of the management's wives a session so I can fire up some enthusiasm for my work here.

"Went and met the Christian Brothers' administrator at the boys' school. I liked him! While the boys and I were talking with him, the gardener at the school accidentally tore up a water line while doing some grass clearing with his machete! A few minutes later, the electricity went out. Brother said it happens all the time. I have an electric clock in my room that's running about twenty minutes fast because the electric flow isn't right. Everybody's thrilled that Tom's here. The Antiguans that worked with him when he was here six years ago remember him well and genuinely like him. Management hopes he can solve some of the perpetual problems. People have reminisced about little kindnesses they remember from when Tom was here before. The general feeling is that 'Tattoo-man' has their best interests at heart. It's going to be interesting to see how management reacts to Tom wanting more money, more rights and training for the workers.

"Saw the hawksbill turtle nesting the other night. They've come up to one beach, Pasture Bay, here at Jumby Bay for centuries to lay their eggs (about 200); an endangered species.

Adam and I saw one in the water when we were coming back on a boat from the main island. Two college girls spend every night doing research, counting and observing them.

"The boys and I are in the water every day – we're all three chocolate colored now. Never got a bad burn—boys are peeling a little on their backs, but look good! Tom's looking very dapper; the Laundry Ladies keep his clothes pressed (I never did) and he looks years younger now. We miss our computer and when it arrives, it'll be much easier to write. Love, Mar."

The next couple of weeks, Tom and Mari and a crew of Antiguan men worked at getting utilities in for new construction, along with the normal day-to-day operations. Their container still hadn't arrived so they moved from Pond Bay House to the ivy-covered cottage overlooking the sea.

On August 27th Noni and Didi arrived; they missed the grandkids and thought Jumby Bay would be a great vacation. Tom made arrangements—they would only have to pay half the resort price. Mari obtained food from the mainland for their meals at the cottage. It was a great reunion. The following is an account in Didi's words:

"We arrived in Antigua on time. After collecting our baggage, we had to go through Customs. This turned out to be quite an experience. While we were waiting a young girl came up to us and asked if we were going to Jumby Bay Resort? We told her we were. She then proceeded to give us instructions about which taxi to take to the boat landing and said she would contact Jumby Bay by radiophone to come and get us. In the meantime it was our turn to go through customs. We piled our baggage and a box, which Mari and Tom left behind in Santa Rosa, on the counter. The customs officer asked what was in the box. I told him it was my friend's package that they forgot to take with them. He then ordered me to open the box and show him the contents. We were going to originally mail the package but because we decided to go to Antigua at the spur of the moment we saved the postage! I tell you this because we did such a fine job wrapping, we couldn't get it open. Finally someone handed me a penknife to cut it open. When at last I had ripped the package apart the Customs Officer looked at me in a most dejected manner and asked me if I was bringing any additional things to my friends. I said no and he passed us through.

"We took the cab, 1950 Volkswagen and headed for the boat landing. The road was full of potholes and very eerie darkness prevailed as we arrived at the landing. The boat was waiting for us but none of the family was there to greet us. I spoke first and said hello. The response was a mumbled 'Hi mon'— this was my first introduction to what was to become a much used salutation during our ten-day sojourn in Jumby Bay, Antigua. The boat ride was most enjoyable because tropic winds had a cooling effect in an otherwise very humid and hot environment. It reminded me of Sinatra singing 'The Summer Wind.' We arrived at Jumby Bay about fifteen minutes after leaving the boat landing. Much to my dismay there was no one to meet us at the dock. One of the men on the boat loaded our bags on a golf cart and drove us to the main building. At last a friendly face appeared in the darkness, it was Mari with that wonderful WELCOME grin. I must confess I immediately relaxed and felt secure in the knowledge that we had arrived safe and sound.

"Mari and Tom took us into the fancy bar on the second floor and introduced us to some of Tom's co-workers. I asked where the boys were. Mari said they were across the way watching television. So we went across the way to say hi. When they saw us, each rushed to kiss us hello. They overwhelmed their Noni with kisses and hugs and I received my share. All of us returned to the bar and partook in drinking some beverages. About midnight we left the bar and rode in the golf cart to their home on the island. When we arrived we were greeted by a cat that the family had adopted, about fifty lizards of all types and colors and a great number of moths and mosquitoes. Because of our tiredness we didn't care about bugs, lizards or anything else. We just wanted to go to bed. Tom and Mari were very gracious to give us their bed and they slept on the floor.

"The next morning we got up, took showers and by 8:00 we walked to the Beach Pavilion for breakfast. What a surprise.

An entire buffet of fruits, juices, toast, biscuits, croissants, cereals, hot entrees and many other delicious choices. When I told the boys that I was very much impressed with the cuisine, they informed me that the buffet was just the beginning. Adam said, "Didi, after you finish with the buffet you order your main dish, from the waitress." And to prove to everyone that I followed Adam's advice I gained six pounds during our stay. After a fulfilling breakfast we walked around the Beach Pavilion to look at all the sights. A beautiful sandy white beach bathed occasionally by a small wave of crystal blue Caribbean Sea, greeted us. 'Wow! This must be what paradise looks like!' I whispered to myself only to have my thought interrupted by Jacob saying, 'Didi, do you want to go water skiing?' Pointing towards the dock where some of the guests were putting on water skis, I asked Jacob 'How much does it cost to hire the boat?' 'Nothing,' he said, 'You just ask them and they let you know when it's your turn.' This is when Mari told me that for $1,000 (US) per day per person all facilities, food and rooms are included, a very expensive Paradise.

"It was lunchtime and Tom joined us. He informed us that he had a busy morning and was hungry so we all had a terrific lunch. I tried every food on the buffet and for my main entrée I ordered pork chops—they were delicious. I must tell you that their chef was a master. Everything I ate from the buffet tasted wonderful.

"After lunch we returned to our villa via bicycles. The bikes are left in various places around the island and anyone can take them and use them for transportation. You can imagine my surprise the first time I came looking for my bike and it was gone. I told the boys my white bike was stolen. They both laughed and told me, 'No, Didi, you just take another one.' I guess I should have figured, notwithstanding the $1000 per day, no one could get off the island with a stolen bike anyway.

"Back to our villa we went. My muscles, which I hadn't used for 40 years, were really tight from my bike endeavors. The boys suggested we go for a swim. My pride would not let me admit that I was exhausted and would rather take a nap. So reluctantly I said, 'Sure, let's go.' A quick change and I found myself back on the bike headed for the beach. When we arrived I could hardly stand with my aching muscles. I immediately jumped into the water and to my surprise it felt like entering my bathtub. The water was mercifully warm and very salty. It was so salty little effort was needed to float. I remained in the water for 30 minutes and was rewarded by a tremendous relief of the pain in my muscles.

"Coming out of the water I felt very thirsty. The boys were relaxing in their lounge chairs so I suggested that we go to the bar and get a drink because I was very thirsty. Mari had warned me about dehydration because of the heat. Jacob said he would go and get me a beer. I thought what a nice thing for him to do for his grampa, so I said, 'Great, get two beers so you don't have to go back a second time.' I had no sooner uttered my words than Jacob handed me a cold Heineken laughingly. He informed me that right behind our lounges was a well-stocked portable bar. They had been drinking 7ups while I was in the water. For $1,000 per day I was sitting in the lap of luxury. We continued to swim, sun, and drink for the rest of the afternoon. Noni and Mari joined us for the last two hours before supper, which was going to be an ON THE BEACH BARBEQUE..."

Eight days later Tom arranged with Hans, Jumby Bay's water sports manager, to take the 40-foot schooner out for a day's sailing and snorkeling near Bird Island as a bon-voyage for Noni and Didi. The grandparents stayed ten days before returning to Santa Rosa.

Mari had become deep friends with Meg Hoyle and Michelle Zacks, the biologists on the island from the Georgia Sea Turtle Cooperative, part of the Institute of Ecology at the University of Georgia. They had spent two years working on the hawksbill turtle project on Jumby Bay. They lived in a remote part of the island and were without electricity much of the time. Tom had power installed to their little concrete house in the jungle on the southeast shore. The "Turtle Girls," as everyone called them, started eating dinner and taking showers and shared in everyday household chores at the lovers' house. They were a godsend for Mari. Already she had grown weary of how unreal "paradise" could be. It was good for her soul to have some real friends.

One afternoon while Tom was finishing up budgetary work at the office, Mari sat on the front porch of her new cottage overlooking the sea. Wondering when their household shipment would arrive, she spotted over-ripe bananas on the ground. She laid them out on the front porch; within five minutes 20 canary-like birds called "Banana-keets" were feasting. They made a wonderful racket until there was no bananas left. The day before, a beautiful carob-crested hummingbird had come into the house and for the next five hours it flew around inside trying to escape. Finally it lay exhausted on the floor and Mari picked it up and set it free.

Little lizards with puppy-dog faces came into the house regularly to eat the cat food set out for the surrogate cat Bebe. Depending on the background these lizards change colors, matching the environment like chameleons. "Familiar? It's what we're having to do," Mari contemplated. Skin-burning poisonous Buddha-like cane toads, her favorite, lay in the low light and bellowed deep bass sounds. Two days ago the boys had found a black-and-white baby sheep and brought it home. They had to keep it secret because if the locals found it wandering, they would eat it. The place was beginning to feel like a family affair. In the eyes of the resort, Mari became a housewife, even though she was Tom's constant companion in work. She knew it could take several months before she received a work permit from the government to do her massage. Tom secretly made plans to convert one of the duplexes near Bond Bay House into a day spa for Mari's work. The dream was beginning to manifest.

On September 18th Mari gave Tom a handmade card that said, "Happy Birthday. I love you Thomas for where we're at, out on an adventure set in an instant by us. I'm not sure where it climbs, but it doesn't matter as long as we have time. I love you, Mar."

Tom had finally let the maintenance manager go and had appointed his longtime friend Buck White to the position. Buck's motto was, "We can do it together."

On the 20th, Tom gave a little card to Mari that said, "Happy Birthday Sweetie. We are like left and right arm. I could not carry on this without you. I pray things come about soon so you can practice your craft once again. We are converting the Pond Bay duplex into a day spa for you. I love you wife, Tom."

That afternoon a power emergency came up and they were not able to spend the day sailing to Parham as planned for Mari's birthday.

At the house she sat on the front porch and wrote in her journal,

"For some strange reason I keep remembering. I don't remember much. That's what worries me. And interpretations' judgment worries me too. It's a matter of taste for most people and I seem to find my greatest joy in the 'universal maybe.' That's why I indulge in the fuzzy so much and like to go a rambl'in. I remember songs—poems a bit. O Johnny O's. What I don't remember is things, memories, thoughts and feelings from long ago. Whatever was I thinking in my 20s? I remember the furniture in Cecil's apartment. The big white overstuffed couch. Pillows. All the books in floor-to-ceiling dark oak cases that matched the windows and floorboards. The lectern with either a TV or typewriter on it. Mostly a typewriter—My God, nobody had a PC then. I remember the claw-foot bathtub where I found a crab floating in the water and spent a fascinating hour checking pubic hair for more. A young twenty acne-prone intellectual lady walked in eyeballing me and I realized half-consciously she was a lesbo.

"A writer—I remember standing with Lothario. Lotho fixing breakfast in the kitchen; My domain? Still at an age when I got flustered if a whole bunch of guests showed up for dinner. When and how did I get over that! Another half achievement half noticed. I remember Lotho breaking up mushrooms into the eggs scrambling. I'd never seen that before—supposed to chop them in neat little slices. I still mostly knife'em, but have been known to break a few. And walking in on a long-dark-haired beauty in bed with Cecil. What a nut. I don't remember a lot about how I was shaped and what has created these all-pervading feelings of shame that plague my mid-back especially. I don't remember."

After writing in her journal she wandered to Pasture Point and walked topless on the beach. As she walked near a deep tide pool, she noticed a large school of gray fish, ten to 14 feet long lying on the sandy bottom slowly moving back and forth; hundreds, she thought. She became amazed and pondered what it would be like to be there with them. She put her top back on and ran back to the road by Lord Sainsbury's villa hoping to find someone. Just then Buck White turned the corner in his electric cart. She told Buck about the fish she'd seen and asked if he knew what they were. He told her he thought they might be nurse sharks mating. Buck followed her back to the water. He told her, when they're schooled like that, they're mating and somewhat harmless and any other time, very dangerous. Buck waded in first, with Mari following not far behind. She came within a foot of a large muscular nurse shark slowly moving back and forth in the water. Buck told her not to touch. She stood there, waist deep in water, in awe of the animal's power. Feeling no past, no thought of future, just an incredible sense of presence, she became elated and couldn't wait to tell Tom.

Tom finished up with his emergency and returned to the house, not to find Mari anywhere. He noticed Vernon, Jumby Bay's exterminator, spraying the plants in the back and asked if he'd seen her. Vernon nodded yes, then no. Tom walked back to the porch and there in the distance was Mari. As she got closer he could see she was glowing. A vibrant smile appeared from ear to ear. She looked like a walking sparkler. Tom said, "What is it sweetie? You've done something wonderful. What is it?" Mari replied, "I just swam with the sharks!" and began telling him the story. Tom was so happy. That night they went to Franklin's Point and sat on the dock watching the moon rise from the sea in the east, splashing their legs back and forth in the warm water like children.

On the 28th of September Mari got up in the middle of the night to go to the bathroom. As she made her way in the dark she banged her right breast into the edge of the partially opened bathroom door. Not thinking too much about it she returned to bed, but the thud had woken Tom. He asked her what happened. She said she was clumsy and banged into the door and told him to go back to sleep, it was OK.

The next morning Tom noticed a silver-dollar-size black and blue welt on her breast. He said, "Sweetie, is that what you did last night?" Mari replied, "Yes, I hit it on the edge of the bathroom door." Tom said, "Let's look at that...maybe we should get some ice on it." He went to the kitchen and came back with an ice pack. Mari continued to ice it throughout the day. That night it looked like it had gone down some, but she had whacked it good. They watched it for several days turn into a dark hematoma. They were concerned, but figured it would go away.

Time passed and Mari finally got permission from the government to work at Jumby Bay. It was all set; she would be the massage therapist for Jumby Bay and the plan for converting the duplex into a day spa was finalized. She would be working on people like Vidal Sassoon, Princess Di, the president of AT&T, all the movers and shakers of the world. John Mariani sent a man from his accounting office in New York to review Tom's new budget. After his survey of the situation he granted Tom the necessary funds to upgrade the island. Then he mentioned the possibility that, after Tom finished his contract at Jumby Bay, he and Mari would go to Italy to work on a 15th-century castle that John Mariani was planning to restore into a Balsamic vinegar operation. Things were beginning to look up.

Gerry Grady, a longtime buddy of John Mariani and CFO for Jumby Bay was asked to step down and Tom took on his duties with Ballast Nedam, the Dutch construction company on the island. Including Ballast Nedam's operations, Tom was now responsible for 250 men with an annual operating budget of $12,000,000. Things would become busy. Tom and Mari and Hans, the chief engineer for Ballast Nedam, had dinner together that night. Tom told Mari, "There's something about Hans that I respect; he cares about the quality of the work and about the workers."

Finally, with the help of Marjorie Nedd-Sullivan, Jumby Bay's Procurement Officer and Tom's comrade-in-arms, and some political nudging from Flora Jacobs, who was related to the Prime Minister's family, the container arrived with all their belongings. They hadn't found a place in Parham Village yet and decided to gather a few things from the container to make their house on the hill feel more like home.

That night they had a "the container's here" celebration. They invited the Turtle Girls, Buck White and Tony who has worked at Jumby Bay since he was a small boy, for dinner and dominoes. Tony was famous with the boys for his infamous quotes, like, "Sometimes the 'pussy' will refuse you." After dinner, Mari told Michelle, one of the Turtle Girls, how she had slammed her breast on the door. Mari and Michelle went into the bedroom and Mari showed her the wound. Michelle said she thought it had been too long and felt Mari should see a doctor.

The next day Mari made an appointment to see an Antiguan doctor in St. John's. He suggested that she go to the United States for further testing. The next day Mari left Jumby Bay for Santa Rosa. Tom and the boys stayed on.

14

"Should the whole frame of Nature Round him break,
in ruin and confusion hurled,
He, unconcerned, would hear the mighty crack,
and stand secure amidst a falling world."

Joseph Addison

Free Falling

The sun has just risen at Jumby Bay. The sugar-white sands of the island's west coast are beginning to sparkle with first light. From the east, mourning doves "hoo" above the faint sound of diesel generators carried by the wind and drift through the open window of Tom and Mari's ivy-covered Caribbean cottage overlooking the sea. Tom, awakened by the rustle of palms, rolled over and touched Mari's side of the bed like he always did when she was gone—she left three days ago for the United States. He kissed the boys goodbye on their way to catch the boat for school and was walking across the grassy meadow to his office when he noticed a small piece of tarpaper blowing in the morning breeze. The paper curled and twisted into the air, passing by the old sugar mill ruins near the road. It continued across the grass to a jasmine tree and rested for several seconds on a branch surrounded by pink flowers. He began to wonder...how was it being guided? Was it the wind or the shape of the paper or was it just destiny?

Last night Tom got a call from Mari. She had made it safely to the U.S. and was awaiting results from a mammogram. He keeps thinking of her constantly. He's going to be working with a crew today. The main waterline servicing the island has broken near the Bone Yard, and a myriad other tasks lay in before him.

Paul Zuest left for Italy a week ago and Tom is in charge of the island. Two nights ago a Jumby Bay boat, on the night run to Antigua, ran over a small wooden fishing boat gathering crab pots near Davis Harbor. Fortunately, the old fisherman wasn't killed and was rescued with minor injuries. Tom kept thinking in terms of Mari's compassion. He arranged to get the old fisherman first aid, and fed and transported back to his home in Parham. He tried to get funds set aside to replace the old man's boat, to no avail. *What rights does a poor fisherman have?* Tom was beginning to feel the heart of Jumby growing cold. In the old days, Homer would have bought the fisherman a new boat and taken care of his family while he healed.

All this ran through Tom's mind as he continued past the jasmine tree that a few seconds earlier had held the tarpaper in its flowers. Suddenly, two Antiguan men arguing near the harbor caught his attention. He changed direction and moved non-stop toward the dock. As he approached he spoke out, "Are you all right?" Both men turned and stopped talking. It was Bernard, a supervisor on the maintenance crew and Joseph, a plumber from the marina. Bernard said that Joseph had dropped a pipe wrench into the harbor. Joseph started to explain that he was working on a pump when the wrench slipped from his hand. Tom put his arms around both men and walked them away from the scene.

He began to explain, "As hard as we try, sometimes accidents happen. Most accidents can be prevented if we think ahead." Bernard didn't want to give it up. Tom went on, "Bernard, you've been here since the Bob Davis days, what, 20-some years now, let me tell you a story."

And Tom went on:

"Mr. Davis gave me a book to carry on the airplane from the United States to Antigua. I was supposed to deliver it to a certain attorney when I got there. He explained to me there were only three books like it in the world. One was at the Smithsonian Institute, one at the University of Texas and I carried the third one. The book was hand-scripted around the turn of the last century, a very valuable book; it was called the *The History of Antigua.* I wrapped it with some other books so as not to arouse customs, placed it in my backpack and boarded a plane at Portland, Oregon. Homer had given me his VIP card and told me when I arrived at the Denver airport, I could go to the VIP lounge and relax during the layover. I left my pack with the book in the overhead compartment of the airplane figuring it would be OK; I was coming back to the same plane in two hours anyway.

"I went to the VIP lounge and when I returned I found that the plane had left without me. At first I couldn't figure out what had happened, then it dawned on me—Denver was one hour ahead, and I had forgotten to set my watch ahead! I went to United and they said 'No problem, we'll have someone take your pack off the plane when it arrives in Miami and you can pick it up at Baggage Claim when you get there.' I was relieved. When I arrived in Miami the book wasn't there; somehow it had gone on with the airplane to New York.

"They were having real problems at Jumby. The reverse osmosis plant was down, the undersea pipeline had broken near the army base and the water barge from Barbados was not due to arrive for three weeks. The island was without water, so I had to continue on to Antigua without the book. When I arrived I put a trace on the bag with the airport officials in Antigua and continued to Jumby. Each day I took a boat back to the airport to check the status of my pack. On the fourth day they said the pack was in Miami and wanted to know if they should send it to Antigua. I told them I was returning in three days and to hold the bag in Miami. When I arrived in Miami, I went to the Baggage Claim department and gave the man my claim number. He went back and looked. When he returned he said there was no such bag and perhaps I should check with New York. I was frantic. I asked him to please check again. He went back for a second look. After what seemed like an eternity, he turned the corner carrying a small dark blue pack. He set it on the counter and I looked inside. The book was still there! Think of all the anguish I caused myself and everyone else because I wasn't thinking ahead.

"When I gave the book back to Mr. Davis in Portland he said to me, 'If you're not making mistakes, then you're not learning anything, but the difference between a wise man and a not-so-wise man, is a wise man doesn't continue to make the same mistakes over again.' Now Bernard, schedule a diver, retrieve the wrench and let's go on with the day."

Everyone smiled and went back to work.

Around lunchtime, Tom took a break from the pipeline to eat at the worker's canteen. Now that Mari had gone, he had been eating with the Antiguans. He was at the table with Margery when he received a call on the two-way to come to the office, "Tattoo, your wife's on the phone." He ran to the office. He returned 15 minutes later with a solemn look and began to speak, "Margery, see that man over there, he loves what he's doing and doesn't like to go home." Pointing to another, "See that man, all he can think about is women." Pointing to another, "And that man, he doesn't work for money—he's only interested in praise. It seems so odd to me that I can read these people, yet I have no idea what's going to happen to Mari. They want her to have a lumpectomy." Margery replied, "She's going to be OK." Tom went on, "I know, but she seems so scared or maybe it's me that terrified. I just wish I was there with her." Margery continued, "Don't worry Mr. Sawyer, she'll be coming home soon."

Ten days later, Tom received a call from Mari, "Hi sweetie, the surgery went well. I'm a little scared and so sorry about having to be here. I got the results back from the doctors this morning. It's confirmed, I have breast cancer." Tom was speechless. Then he spoke, "Oh sweetie, I wish I was there to hold you." Mari went on, "I'm not sure what to do, but I know we'll all be together soon. I'm seeing several oncologists for more opinions and am beginning to do research. I was frightened before but somehow felt relieved when they told me. I went into a state of bliss; it's lasted several days now. I don't know how long it will last."

Tom got a temporary leave of absence and he and the boys left for the United States on November 7th. Mari and the grandparents and Mari's sister Pauline met them at the airport. Tom recalled,

"I walked towards her in the airport. I'd been chewing gum the whole flight; I was so nervous. The boys ran ahead and put their arms around their mother. She kissed each one and looked up at me. She was so beautiful, so innocent, so vulnerable—childlike and radiant, as if nothing had happened. We all held each other. Inside I was crying. It was as if she held me from a place inside her, deeper than I'd ever experienced; in the midst of her sorrow was a love far beyond anything known to me."

Tom and Mari and the boys set up temporary quarters at Noni and Didi's while Mari healed from her lumpectomy, but soon the general feeling was, "we all need some space." To make matters worse, their house on Neo was still leased out and the lessee wouldn't give it up. After a month of living with the grandparents they moved to a small trailer by the railroad tracks north of town. They spent most of their time seeing doctors and doing research. Mari consulted with one of Stanford's top research oncologists and came to the following conclusion. The type of cancer she had (infiltrating ductile carcinoma with metastasized lymph gland involvement) was slow-growing and would not respond well to chemotherapy, and if she had radiation she stood the chance of damaging a lung. Her prognosis was perhaps five years of life. According to the doctors, she would have four to five years of fairly normal life—then death would follow.

She made a conscious decision to forgo both types of conventional treatment and searched out alternative medicine. She said, "Why should I take these treatments and be miserable for the remainder of my life, then die anyway." She had always been a seeker; now she would be doing it for her life.

Their container finally arrived from Antigua with all their household things and life at the trailer soon took on a gypsy feel. Mari wanted to go on a Vipassana retreat in the mountains. The reality of her condition began to set in and they both felt the need to deepen. The boys remained with the grandparents and continued school in their previous district, while the lovers set out on the road once again.

At the time, Tom was calling Jumby Bay every day and ran the operations remotely with the combined help of Buck White and Bernard Charles. The day after Christmas he contacted Buck White and said he would be incommunicado for ten days and could they run things without him? Buck said, "Together we can do it." Buck's famous words set the lovers out on their next journey.

Two days later they left for the Sierra foothills south of Yosemite. They would be spending the next ten days at the California Vipassana Center in complete silence watching their minds do what minds do. Tom was taken to the men's compound, a rough-planked non-insulated wooden building on the north side of the property with one toilet, cold water and no heat. After group orientation, he laid down on one of the top bunks and thought about Mari. He wondered where they would put her. The exposed wooden studs gave his quarters a concentration-camp appearance. This is where he would sleep for the next ten days.

Tom had been given instructions by the headmaster: "There will be no talking, no sound-making of any kind. Every action will be done mindfully. The men will eat separately from the women. In fact, the men are never to come in sight of a woman except at the meditation hall. Women will sit on one side of the hall and men on the other."

Dusk had arrived and the temperature continued to drop. Tom had just wrapped himself in a woolen blanket on the bed when the bell rang out. It echoed off the surrounding hills, signaling it was the men's turn to eat. He followed the designated path through the forest to a campsite, where monks had prepared oatmeal, vegetables and hot tea. This would be his diet morning, noon, and night. Each man took a bowl and cup. Tom squatted near the base of a tree mindfully eating his gruel when suddenly a shooting star streaked across the sky. He stopped watching his mind and noticed the cold had made his whole body stiff. It was time to go. As he walked back the sound of crunching leaves overrode the gentle pounding in his chest. Whatever the process, he had become keenly aware of the silence.

At his bunk, he pulled the covers over his head and waited for the 4:00 AM bell. He could hear other men rustling about trying to get warm. In an atempt to clear his mind, he went carefully over each stud in the wall, first counting each one and then mentally examining the texture. It had already begun. His mind was trying to find a place to land, something to keep it busy. He analyzed one of the splinters on the bedpost and figured it contained a trillion atoms. He counted all the ceiling joists and re-engineered the roof structure and vowed not to drink tea again at night.

He was jarred from a half-slumber by the morning bell and followed the path leading to the meditation hall, carrying a small maroon meditation cushion gifted him by Mari. Women entered from the north door and men from the south. Perhaps 100 in all mindfully found their places on the floor, women on the right, men on the left. Tom watched from the corner of his eye for any sign of his sweetheart. He was too far forward in the hall; *She must be behind me,* he thought. After taking the lotus position he sat up straight on his cushion and concentrated on his third eye (an imagined eye in the center of the forehead).

From the front of the hall the headmaster spoke, "Concentrate on the end of your nose, let your mind go, do not try to control it. If it drifts away, gently bring it back to the end of your nose. This is your first exercise. Just be the observer and watch what the mind does, but do not judge it. Do not judge it if it drifts away and do not judge it for what content it might come up with. Just merely be the observer. That's what Vipassana is, creating the observer and eventually realizing that the observer is the source of all being; the source of consciousness."

All kinds of thoughts began to manifest, '...would Mari be OK? What did the gauntlet ahead look like? What of my job at Jumby Bay?' Worry thoughts were the first to appear. Then came the fantasies, followed by regrets, and a list of accomplishments and failures. He kept bringing his mind back to the end of his nose, only to have it drift off again a few seconds later. At one point he switched to Kriya meditation, watching the energy moving up and down his spine. There he could be for long periods without conflict. Kriya had been his practice for many years.

Tom had drifted off into the future when suddenly he was startled back into his body by a resonant chime ringing out through the hall. The master broke the silence and assured everyone that if they could only concentrate on the end of their nose for a few seconds, then they had done well for the first attempt.

As Tom was leaving the hall he caught a glimpse of Mari going out the door. His heart fluttered.

They continued the same practice morning, noon and night, sitting in meditation 14 hours a day. Each day he positioned himself in the back of the hall hoping to catch sight of Mari. Even the prospect of seeing the back of her head was purely wonderful.

On the ninth day, as he followed the path through the woods from his noon meal, he noticed a roped-off area running through a large manzanita bush by the compound. The rope stretched along, tied to a pine tree, and continued on, following an imaginary line through the bushes. Nearby was a sign staked in the ground; "DO NOT GO BEYOND THIS POINT." He watched a fluffy gray squirrel come down from the tree next to the rope and scurry across under barricade. All participants of the Vipassana retreat had been given instructions to stay within the boundaries marked by rope. He cleared his mind and pondered, *Stepping over the line, that's what I've done all my life.* Knowing that if he got caught, he'd be asked to leave, he searched his soul again.

Without hesitation he reached up with his right hand, lifted the rope and darted for the clearing next to a large oak tree. He continued to a spot overlooking the valley. Now he was alone— a renegade gypsy sitting on his heels, balanced by the tips of his toes. How peaceful it all felt. All his life he had had trouble following the rules and wondered why.

He contemplated, *It's not that I'm such a bad person, I love people—it's boundaries that scare me. When I look in someone's eyes and I see a sign that says "KEEP OUT," it makes me feel unloved. And when I see eyes that lead deep inside to a luminous hallway, I feel loved. I'm glad I came here.* Carefully, with a slight grin on his face, he passed over the demarcation, back into the land of rules.

On the tenth day, everyone had gathered in the meditation hall for the final reflection. The master requested that the meditation be one of solemn determination. They were to sit without moving a muscle for three hours. No changing position. No clearing of the throat. No slouching. Tom imagined sitting on a blue lotus flower in the midst of a great clear pond. He placed ethereal flowers at each chakra along his spine. Moving his awareness slightly above his head he looked out onto a peasant's meadow of green grass. There he watched Mari in her 20s gathering flowers in the fold of her dress. Each placement of her feet, the bend, the careful collection, the holding of the hem exposing her legs as she walked to the next flower overrode any other thought that might have intruded. This transcendental state carried him through the next three hours without attention to body or mind. Suddenly, the tiny ring of the bell permeated the hall like a mighty gong signaling the end of their ten-day stay. All rose and walked to the courtyard. They were now allowed to speak their first words.

Tom approached Mari; a minute smile came upon her face. She was still not back in her body. Her eyes glistened with awareness, clear and deep and full of life. She spoke so softly a butterfly could have perched on her lips without being disturbed. The sound of her voice resembled the slow rustling of silk paper: melodious, inside, as if timeless. Her body seemed to glow with simplicity. Her first words were "Home is where we are, what's our address?" Tom just smiled—it was so like her. He held her gently. Then they wandered off holding hands toward the men's compound. He gathered his things and then they went to where Mari had been staying. As she walked in the doorway of the women's compound, she hesitated, looking back, and vanished inside; another picture, another moment for Tom.

A few minutes later she appeared.

There were no vocabularies to describe how beautiful and brilliant she looked. Without words they walked to the car and got in. Tom put the keys in the ignition and looked over at Mari, "Did you have heat?"

"Yes, I heard that the men had no heat."

"It's true."

"Were you cold?"

"No, you warmed my heart."

"What are we going to do? Shall we wander to the end?"

"It's your words, 'Home is wherever we are.'"

On the drive back up Highway 49, Tom pulled onto a side road and drove to the end of a densely wooded lane just to see what was there. Nothing was there; it ended in a clump of trees opening into pastureland that went on for miles.

As they sat there looking through the windshield of the Trooper, Tom began to speak.

"I have a feeling following my heart, not knowing where it will lead me. I was attracted to this road because it called me. It might seem silly, but it has something to do with a Model A Ford, like Bonnie and Clyde. We have money in the bank and nothing but the open road. Are you steering?"

Mari replied, "Not really, I feel it too. You know, you need to make a decision about Jumby Bay."

"What's there to make, I'm with you—we need to be here now and your family and the boys would feel better, too. We need to be here to explore the possibilities. As soon as we get back I'll call Paul Zuest."

"I'm so sorry all this has happened, I know it cut your dreams short."

"Not really, you may find this...I draw my meaning from you and the boys, if not there—then here."

"Stop it."

"It's true."

"Are you hungry? Let's find a little place to eat."

They stopped at the Crystal Falls Restaurant in Oakhurst near Highway 299, an older building looking on to a boulder-filled pond surrounded by woods. During dinner on the deck, a woman carrying a black case kept walking back and forth. Mari was curious and asked what she had. The woman handed it to Mari and then began telling her the story of a single mother.

Mari opened the case. Inside was a silver flute. The woman said it had belonged to her mother and she wanted to sell it. Mari looked over at Tom with that look and gently replied to the woman, "How much do you want for it?" The women replied, "$300." Mari smiled and looked at Tom again. He reached into his back pocket, drew out three $100 bills from his wallet and handed them to the lady. Mari smiled and the lady replied, "God bless you," quickly disappearing from the deck.

They continued up Highway 49 to Angels Camp and spent the night in a cheap hotel on the outskirts of town. It was their first night together after having been separated for ten days.

Except for the cancer they were on top of the world. They had a good sum of money stowed away in a Swiss bank account, medical insurance, and nothing but time together. The reality of Mari's cancer really hadn't set in yet, not in the sense that she was walking *The Green Mile*. She didn't feel any different and had no physical symptoms except for a small scar on her right breast. It was as though they were on another perpetual honeymoon.

When they arrived at Tom's mom's in Grass Valley they were vacillating about Jumby Bay. Neither knew if leaving the island was the right move. They went for a walk in the woods and prayed for guidance. Still no feeling of correct direction came. They were in a quandary. They thought of flipping a coin and then gave up on the idea. Pausing near a barbwire fence stretching though the woods they began to go through the logic.

Mari said, "I feel really bad that we are having to leave Jumby Bay. I love Antigua. It's all I can do to bear the idea."

Tom replied, "Don't feel bad, it's not your fault. It's just the way of things. I want to walk with you wherever you go. Where you lodge, I lodge."

"You know this body will not last. When I was a young woman I knew I was going to die of cancer. I told Beto when we were first married."

"Whatever our destiny is, I walk with you. As much as we would both like to stay in Antigua we have to be here so you can receive treatment. Your parents are worried and I think the boys need to be close to their friends and the grandparents."

"I have a knot in my stomach about leaving Jumby."

"Me too. I think it's the security and the adventure—maybe it's just the security, but we've got to stay here."

"It's like something is dying, maybe because it was such a big dream come true."

"It's like the monkey that stuck his hand through a chain-link fence to grab an orange and couldn't pull it back through the hole. In order to free himself all he needs to do is let go of the orange. You think?"

"I have to be sure you have no bad feelings about leaving Jumby?"

"It would have been fun at Jumby, going on to Italy and all that stuff, but that's not possible. Without you, it would be like wearing sunglasses on a dreary day."

"I wasn't thinking about you going without me."

"I know; that would never happen. I would be miserable in Paradise without you. We need to be here and I could not be without you. There's no choice really; I need to call Paul Zuest. We will walk this new path together. With clear and open heart, I have no regrets."

"OK."

Tom made the call to Paul Zuest on his mother's phone. He thanked Paul for his patience while they sorted out Mari's prognosis and treatment, and regretfully resigned. Mr. Zuest accepted Tom's resignation and arranged for him to overlap by phone until a suitable person was found to replace him. When Tom hung up the phone he looked over at Mari. They were both feeling the same thing. It felt like someone had kicked them in the stomach.

By the time they arrived in Santa Rosa the next day, they were vacillating again. Mari wanted Tom to call Mr. Zuest back and work out an arrangement so that in case she got better, they could return to Jumby Bay. Tom called, but Mr. Zuest had already found a candidate, an old buddy from the Hotel Bel Air, and wasn't interested in the idea—and that was that.

Back living at the trailer, they spent weeks walking the railroad tracks together. In between seeing doctors they went to garage sales. Mari stuffed rags in the cracks around the windows of the trailer and added all her touches like plants and flowers and pictures of Indian saints. Time passed. They found a little hole-in-the-wall café about two miles up the tracks and went there almost every day for breakfast.

In March they left for Oregon to see several doctors in Portland, then retired to the Hill with a group of friends and planted 2,000 ponderosa pine trees before returning to Santa Rosa.

More time passed. One afternoon there was a knock at the trailer door. It was one of Tom's old buddies from Oregon, Dr. Norman Easley. He wanted Tom to develop a software program for natural medicine. They discussed the details and Tom told him he'd think on it. Mari thought it was a good idea because Tom could work at home, but Tom didn't think the timing was right. He decided they should have time to search out a treatment before settling into a project.

In June, Tom could tell that something was brewing; Mari seemed to be getting angry over little things and was more quiet than usual. Tom asked what was wrong and she exploded, "All our things are in storage. The boys are living at my parents. I have cancer. We're out of our home. Our dreams have crumbled and all you can do is try to love me. We need to do something." Tom was speechless, and then he replied, "What would you have me do?"

"I don't know. That's the problem. My friend Jane Eldridge has a massage workshop next week at Harbin Hot Springs. She wants me to be one of the instructors. It would be good for me to get away."

"Did you want me to be there?"

"I think I need some time away to sort out these demons in my head. I'm angry at the world for taking so much away so fast. You act as if nothing's wrong. All you care about is me and I'm dying."

Tom replied, "You're not dying. You're a long ways from dead. Don't you think it's important that we be together?"

With fire in her eye she snapped, "You JUST don't get it, do you? I need some time apart. Yes, it is 'us' that's dying, but it's also 'me' that's dying. I'm boiling inside like a volcano and I need to take care of it."

"I'm not sure what to do?"

"Didn't you say the cabin roof was in need of repair?"

What she said was beginning to hurt Tom, and he thought perhaps she was right. This was the first real conflict they had ever had. He responded, "I could build a porch or a woodshed, but that could take a month. Are you all right with that?"

"Yes, I'll be all right. I just need some time."

"OK."

The next day he packed up a few things, gave Mari a kiss goodbye and headed for Oregon. Two days later Mari left for Harbin Hot Springs.

During the 28 days he spent on the Hill in the wilderness, he kept a daily diary of what happened:

"Today is Friday, May 15, 1992. I met George at his ranch outside Mosier. He made me breakfast, eggs and sausage omelet. We went to the Bunk House and talked about our childhoods, heart to heart—he has proven to be a good friend. I headed out for the Hill about one o'clock. Just before leaving, George showed me an old cowboy trick for finding which way is north. 'Take a grass stalk and place the stem vertically in the middle of your "hand-dial" watch. When the time is between twelve noon and two o'clock position your watch so the shadow cast by the stem points at two o'clock. Then the shadow will be pointing true north.' I checked it with a compass at 22° deviation. It worked! On the way in—every bit of nature is in full spring— it's so beautiful. Coming down the road from Apple Tree Pond I ran over a pointed branch and blew the left rear tire on the Trooper. I changed the tire and moved on. It's funny, just before the blowout a voice in my head said, 'Go around that, you could puncture a tire.' Just as the thought came through—

"poof" went the tire. I should have slammed on the brakes and checked the road. Oh well.

"I spent most of the day unloading the car and cleaned the cabin. The mice have done a real job. I miss my sweetheart Mari and it's only the first day. I walked out around the side of the cabin to hang up a blanket so the wind could dry it. There in the middle of the path that goes down to the Pagoda lay a diamondback rattlesnake. This time I listened to my voice and looked down—I would have stepped on her if I hadn't. I went in and got my walking stick and asked her to leave. It crossed my mind to shoot her because she was so close to the cabin. I hope she got my prayer for her and she leaves the area and makes her house further down the hill. This was a test for me to be in a position of power and yet be compassionate at the same time. I'm happy with my decision. At 7:00 I went to the Pagoda for prayers, ate dinner, rice, then went for a walk up the road to Widow Maker. On the way I walked through a beautiful meadow of violet and white flowers that looked like trumpets. I call these flowers 'Mari Trumpets.' Turned on the CB at 8:00, but did not make contact with George. I'm in bed getting ready to read. My friends the mice are checking around to see what new things I may have brought—8:45—Goodnight my love—it's a full moon, my chest is tight and I miss you—to have the one you love beside you means so much to the spirit.

"**Day 2:** Last night I dreamed of Mari; a snake was trying to get her, I risked myself to save her. I woke this morning feeling better. I was rinsing beans I'd soaked the night before and was getting ready to pour maple syrup on the oatmeal when I heard, 'Hello, anybody home?' It shocked me. I thought, *A human voice way out here!* Two ladies have bought 80 acres three miles down the road next to Fred's. Heather is a computer person and her friend Lois is an attorney. They asked me to attend dinner with them next Saturday at 5:30. I tested the sun on the roof to find a good location to attach the photoelectric panel. Spring has brought out many animals. A lizard has brought a baby with her; he's about an inch and a half long—sort of cute. Many different kinds of birds and ducks came into the pond today and swam for a while. Everybody is busy building homes and nests. For a moment I saw this as a dance. Today has been emotional for me as the city starts to leave me. I went to the Pagoda for meditation and cleaning, afterward a wave of emotion came to me. Thoughts of brother Greg—I spent time going over my life. I've always dreamed of being close to God, to be a helper in some way. I realize that every day is a new beginning.

"I was walking down the road towards the cabin and another memory came up. I remember walking this very road carrying food and supplies and my kids running up the road yelling, 'Daddy's home, Daddy's home.' I started crying. The mosquitoes are out searching for food and the coyotes are singing again tonight. I think of how much I miss my sweetheart. I tried George again on the CB at 8:00 to 8:15 and was not able to get through. It's getting dark…it's time to light the lamps. I looked at the gun beside the bed and the picture of Gandhi; they seem so opposed. I could have duck for dinner, but it was not in my heart to take one. They were a pair, male and female. Perhaps I'm just not hungry enough. They were symbols of Mari and me. I love them. They were so beautiful together—so I continue to get beans and rice routinely. Returning to simple life is painful in some ways, but it feels like the right direction. The only thing missing in my life is my loved ones—they should join me shortly I hope. Even though Mari is not here, some part of her spirit must be, because there are times when I think she is in the cabin, waiting for me to return from my walks. Goodnight Mari—sweet dreams to you. I thought of Theresa today and how I'm so glad she's my sister.

"**Day 3:** I dreamed about a snake again last night trying to get Mari—I'm not sure what this all means. I'm starting to develop a routine in the morning—oatmeal, dishes, clean up— then on to some task I've created for the day. It's the third day and I feel spacey. I got the frame made today for the PV panel, I hope to hook it up tomorrow before batteries get too low. Still having tightness in my chest throughout the day. I believe it's anxiety and being lonely—this is to be expected till the city wears off.

At 11:30 AM two elk, a doe and a buck, came to the pond. They went into the water up to their shoulders. I watched them from the front porch thru binoculars. They stayed for about 40 minutes then left with a thunder. It was a nice surprise. More new birds are coming in today; the oak trees are in full bloom. Woodpeckers and Baltimore orioles have arrived. A small silkworm stopped by to say hello, flying on his magic invisible string. I had beans for dinner then went for a walk up the road past the Worm People. I sang as I walked, calling for God to appear to me in some form. As I was walking back to the cabin thunder started, just a passing thunderstorm.

Besides thinking of Mari, the big event of the day took place as I started to walk to the car. This time she warned me with her rattles. She was coiled and ready to strike with her head raised high, hissing. I jumped away from the sound—it was so automatic—just my body moved. I didn't know until a few seconds later how close a call it had been. I stopped and talked with her again—that she must find a different place to hunt. I went inside and got the fishing net and threw it on her. She became entangled and I picked the net up with a stick and carried her 100 yards below the pond next to the forest line. She was so big, four and a half feet, that she caught herself in the loops of the net and could not back out. I could see that she was caught permanently. It was starting to get dark. I ran back to the cabin and tied my knife to a wooden spoon then ran back to her. She allowed me to cut the loops in the net with surprising cooperation. She was now free and scurried off into the tall grass. I thanked her for warning me and we seemed to part as distant friends.

I tried to reach George again tonight, but the skip is bad—couldn't get through. My friends the mosquitoes are singing to me again tonight. The critters are making their routine run in search of food. A little wind tonight, the loft window is banging...I need to fix it tomorrow. I'm not sure why I'm here. It's almost like a drive, like the urge for animals to migrate. But

I miss my sweetheart. I can hardly stand it. I know that something good will come of this. Goodnight—love to the Croatian lady. Today while I ate my beans I paused between bites, and the next bite I could taste your lipstick on the spoon as though you stopped by and took a bite. I hope you are well and full of love.

"Day 4: I dreamed last night that Mari and I were going to school together. Mom was there. I should write dreams in the morning...I have forgotten most of it. I'm using about five gallons of water per day for cooking, washing and drinking. I eat oatmeal for breakfast and beans for dinner—so far so good. I woke this morning feeling a little stronger than I did yesterday. After breakfast it really hit me—I'm the only one out here, Fred has gone back to Portland, no other humans for 20 miles. I feel tight in my chest, although I can breathe easier today. Sometimes I feel like I need to yawn but I can't.

"I finished the solar panel today, put it on the roof and wired it to the monitor circuit I put together. In the process I thought the terminal should be soldered, so I hooked up the inverter (12v to 115v) to the battery and plugged the soldering iron into the inverter. Then I noticed I had wired the inverter with the polarity reversed, burning out a $160 inverter in one stupid mistake. I'm a little spacey. I need to check my steps more closely than normal. It was a stupid mistake and I feel terrible. After getting the solar charging system hooked up and seeing it work, I feel much better. It's difficult making things from scratch without proper tools and materials. I went for prayer and meditation today, asking God to give me strength and for a healing for Mari. A storm is passing through again tonight—it's very windy. I've been drinking four to five cups of water—more than normal.

"I walked up the road again today and stopped at Coyote Pond, and then down the canyon towards Shelton Ridge. I found a great rock that is good to sit on and meditated. Coming back to the cabin I saw 'Mari Trumpets.' I reached down and touched one and as I did I spoke to my sweetheart telling her how much I love her and sending her healing love. I've been asking for forgiveness for so many things. When you get quiet like this so many things come to you. I feel the forgiveness a little at a time. I truly wish to become a *Satyagraha*, someone who uses the power of love and example to make change, rather than forcing change. I walked today and reminisced of it in my past and in the future. I realized how much I've slipped, but having gained some small portion of wisdom from my slippages, now it's time to take two steps forward. God is my only true happiness. When I'm in touch with God then I have something to share with my loved ones.

"Tried George again tonight, but skip is still bad. Need to change transmission time to 10:00 AM—skip is quiet then. A bird is using an old nest on the front porch; we're starting to become friends. I miss the company of Adam and Jacob; when I see the roof it reminds me of how much fun we had. Mari, for this I can't thank you enough—being here has been enlightening, more so than a retreat, because of the aloneness— it's so powerful. God bless you and keep you in the heart of the Divine Mother—Goodnight my love. I'm noticing when I see the virtues in other things (animals, plants, people) my virtues become more magnified.

"**Day 5:** Last night I dreamed about an old friend from Weightronix, Mike Skoogs and shoes. I went to a school with Mari. We were in the cafeteria after hours and a black man came up to me and asked what I was doing. I told him I wanted to fly to McDonalds for a hamburger. He said I should jump down the stairs. Three black ladies dressed in cafeteria uniforms were standing at the bottom waiting for me to jump. I said I would not jump. A man came from around the corner and put a gun to my head and pulled the trigger. I died, but was still conscious. I asked him why—he said, 'Just for fun.' I went to find Mari. A man came up to me and asked if I would take a letter to his deceased son since I was already dead. I said I would, but I needed the date when the boy was alive. I put the letter in my pocket and went to find Mari; I found her with Moses and the boys. I was sad because she could not see me. She stood by a phone booth so I went inside and started tapping Morse code on the glass, 'M' 'a' 'r' 'i' – 'T' 'o' 'm'. She heard me then I could see that she saw me. We held each other and I cried. I cried so loud I woke up.

"Went to Hood River today and helped George log, thinning pine on the south canyon. The carburetor on the chainsaw needs some help, maybe I'll work on it tomorrow. I picked up supplies in Mosier, went to the ranch, met George's dad and ate dinner there.

"**Day 6:** Went to town and spent part of the day hauling logs with George to my cabin for posts for the new porch."

While Tom was going about his business in the wilderness, Mari decided to leave the workshop at Harbin Hot Springs in the middle of the night and head for Oregon. She promised Jane that she would return on Friday and continue working as an instructor for a series of retreats that Jane had planned. She drove the 900 miles in one day and arrived at the cabin around 3:00 in the afternoon to find no one there. Tom was helping George haul logs and it wasn't till 4:00 that Tom arrived on the Hill.

"**Day 7:** Spent most of the day cutting and hauling logs with George. Mari my sweetie has arrived from Santa Rosa. It's hard for me to believe she is here in flesh and blood. We discussed our feelings towards each other—all is well. She knows something I will not be able to fathom in this lifetime, she has secrets that await fertile ground—things I hope to learn someday. She looks so alive and beautiful—it's hard for me to get into the moment knowing she will leave again in a few days, but I am thankful for this time with her. We both know, but we have wandered off into some strange corridor where cancer does not exist, a place of slight denial. She looks so well it's hard to believe anything's wrong. We spent the evening walking in the meadow near Bear Rock basking in each other's light, the light that is lit by the presence of the other. It will be hard when she leaves again.

"**Day 8:** Mari and I have been peeling logs with a drawknife most the day. We have been thinking about using the logs to build a woodshed. We walked four miles through the Kashmir

Valley to mountain man Fred's place and had dinner, then walked back in the dark taking the short cut at Bird House.

"**Day 9:** George stopped by with a load of 2 x 4's. Gerry Higgins stopped by and Bob and Heather. Lots of visits today. Mari and I worked the logs again today. Mari's working on the logs peeling them with a drawknife. I'm getting the feeling we should concentrate on the porch and save the idea of a wood shed for later. The porch does not block the view of Mount Adams and would provide for wood storage underneath, because the end of the cabin is so high off the ground. The bird on the front porch had her babies this morning. Three little ones hatched out. A three-and-a-half-foot-long rattlesnake dropped by to say hi; he was under the Trooper. Mari spotted him and we shooed him off. I'm writing this sitting on a stump on the backside of the cabin watching her cook dinner through the window. I cut kindling this afternoon and she's cooking some elk meat George brought us. I look forward to lying in her arms tonight.

"**Day 10:** Mari and I went to Hood River. We decided to put the porch on the west wall rather than build a woodshed; wood can be stored under the porch and it won't block the view of Mount Adams. Mari stripped logs and I took measurements for the new porch. We mixed cement and poured mid-cabin footings. After, we drove to Twelve Mile and visited with Tepee Steve. Saw Don and Sharon and looked at the wood-fired sauna. Mari would like to build a log sauna on the hill near the picnic area—we have put logs aside stacked behind the cabin for this future project.

"**Day 11:** Mari barked logs again today and I set footings for the new porch. The Higgins brothers stopped by and returned the ladder. In the afternoon Mari and I went to Hood River to find the lumber store closed for Memorial Day. We stopped and looked at some houses for sale. Mari thinks she might want to live in Hood River. The Hill is too far away from town for the boys to go to school. We looked at an old church that has been converted into a home, very artistic. She really likes the place. Back at the cabin, a thunderstorm passed overhead about 6:00 PM. Several strikes hit the ground about five miles away then one hit within 200 yards—it literally shook the log walls. Mari made an excellent dinner for us tonight with fresh supplies from town. Lamps lit, we're in bed reading, wonder what the future holds for us.

"Day 12: Went to Hood River again today and picked up lumber, we sang songs the whole way. We measured and placed footings into their final positions. I love it that Mari is here with me. I know she will leave soon—it makes me a little sad.

"Day 13: We got a lot done today: poles are up, runners in place and we started on the floor joists. Later we went to the Pagoda for meditation. She's leaving tomorrow to fulfill her commitment with Jane. I will miss her dearly—she needs the time and I accept that—I don't understand it, but I accept it.

"Day 14: Went to The Dalles with Mari. We had breakfast in town, washed our clothes, then bought her a new pair of shoes. Talked with Larry on the phone; he just finished recording more of his music. We folded clothes together, then said goodbye. She left in one direction and I in another. As she drove away I wished her faith, love and happiness—I could feel her as we parted. I really enjoy working together with her on the porch and lying down beside her—seeing the beauty in her eyes. I worked from 12:00 to 5:30 on the porch; got all the floor joists in. Went for a walk around 6:00. I feel weak—I forgot to eat. I opened a can of beef stew and lay down—I feel much better now. One thing I noticed is while Mari was here I felt no shortness of breath, when she left I could feel it slowly come on again. I lit two sandalwood incense sticks for Mari and I—Goodnight, going to bed to read master Yogananda's book.

"Day 15: Dreamed last night about a store called 'Survival and More.' They had everything from flintlock rifles to water jugs to first-aid kits, fire starters, kerosene lamps and a book section; you name it, it was there. Today I worked five hours on the porch. I was getting the feeling that I had to hurry up and finish the porch, because I want to see what it looks like when it's done. Got the interconnection completed today between the old porch and the new. I thought about my sweetheart and hoped she made it safely to her retreat tonight. I wish for her that she would see the Goddess in her heart.

"After dinner I went to the Pagoda, a coyote called me there. I meditated and thought of Krishna. A little squirrel came and sat by me while I was meditating. When I turned my head to say hello, he ran off—I guess I scared him. I was wishing he would stay. Today I feel better. I went for a walk and sang songs to my beloved masters, wishing that a divine spirit would appear to me in the forest. The wind is blowing again. A deer came to the pond while I was eating dinner on the front porch. Some clouds passed over today; they were dark and when they moved across the sun they turned red. Found a dead gray racer snake on the road, some one must have run over her. I think I'm going to have to take down the antenna and clean the connections. Fixed the tomahansa chair today. Will fix the old school chair tomorrow. It's getting dark, time to light the lamps—goodnight my love.

"**Day 16:** Larry and Kimmie and my grandson Damon have showed up. I forgot it was Saturday. Larry helped me with the porch. We all went for a walk in the afternoon. George showed up later and helped too. They all left around 6:00. It's so amazing when people are here and then they leave—as they go down the road, I watch the dust till I can't see it no more, and all of nature's silence floods in around me.

"**Day 17:** Got up at 6:30, had bacon and eggs, then went fishing at Terri's Pond and swam for a while. Spent the afternoon putting on the decking for the porch. It's 89°. Followed the Honeysuckle to Smith Ridge and went swimming at Bobcat Noose. Went to Nez Rock and looked out over the valley, a sight to behold. When I see the silhouette of the night sky against the tree line I can't help but think of Mari—I know I knew her in ancient times. Walking back in the dark brings me to myself; I rely on faith and whatever knowledge I may possess to get me back safe to the wood stove.

"**Day 18:** Worked on the decking, got a little more than half on. Wind is blowing hard this evening. I was just finishing up for the day and went to move more boards for tomorrow when a large gust blew in and with it came on the run a buck deer in velvet—he ran right past me as though I was not there. He came within 20 feet of me on the run—so beautiful was he. I stopped for a minute to watch him; it was magical. Went for an evening walk and thought of Mari and how nice it was to hear her voice in the wind. She seemed pleased with her work and I could hear love in her voice. Love is Faith. I feel the presence of Master this evening. I walked to the edge of the Kashmir Valley and thought of all the great ones that roamed our earth in the past. And perhaps even this beautiful valley. It's 9:45; wind is still blowing hard, it's time to read and sleep.

"To Mari: Dressed by the sight of a flower I hear her voice smiling with those Bhagwan eyes. Therein lives a Goddess, child of both moon and sun. It is important that she stares off into the distance in three-dimensional dress, to sit on a rock and watch her hair blown by the wind. From that loving peace of blue and gold and pink, where water reflects her true nature. O child of the Anasazi wishing to stand nearer to God, can you hear me? Remove the veil and you'll find love's presence. Look deep into her eyes and you will see Green *Tara's* peace—she is about to discover. A looking glass, small bowl and sunlight waiting to be used by the beautiful lady, once so charming, still so charming—when I looked into grandma's eyes. Why is she so many things to me? Did I know her before—beautiful lady won so long ago in a whispering gallop? I ride towards my Father with her by my side, O magical lady, how could I be so honored with you as my wife. I feel so peaceful tonight; a single presence surrounds me—goodnight sweet lady, goodnight.

"**Day 19:** Fred came by to tell me he found Don Pittman dead in his pickup truck this morning up on Shelton Ridge. He died of a heart attack. The grass is turning brown; the sweet smell is everywhere. Something is starting to shift; I feel bad about Don, yet today is the first day that I have had no loneliness. There is a peace about me. I'm finally happy just being here with myself and the animals. Animals are coming closer. They don't feel threatened by the man with the large mustache. I hope to finish the decking today. I can start on the ceiling joists tomorrow. It's 5:00 and I'm going to rest a little, it's staying light till 8:30 now. After meditation I went for a walk to the meadow near the Kashmir Valley. I stood there motionless for ten minutes. A deer was walking right towards me; I didn't move a muscle or blink my eyes. She walked right up to me—I could almost touch her. She caught my scent and lifted her right front leg, like a dog pointing, then walked curiously away, looking back every few steps. Goodnight all, I love you, goodnight.

"Day 20: Today I felt very strong, got the deck completed. Running out of fresh water and need to go to town. Worked on the decking till 6:30 then drove to Mosier. Fred was coming up the hill at Lee's Pond with a load of pine at the same time I was going down the hill. I backed up the hill, when Fred got to the top we visited for awhile. I got to Mosier before the store closed. I called Didi's to get Harrison's number; Didi seems like he needs a friend. I called my sweetheart; she sounds good to me. I read her the poem I wrote last night and told her about Larry's new song 'Time passes me by and you're not here with me.' Headed back to the Hill and stopped off at Beagle's, found out that they're friends with Blind Jerry. They invited me for dinner, didn't get back to the cabin till 12:30. Unloaded and went to bed, very tired tonight.

"Day 21: I'm very tired today—missing Mari again. I'm having a hard time getting started. Worked for about four hours on compound cuts for the ceiling joists. Cleaned up. Went to meditation and short walk. Wind has been blowing hard all day. Working in the wind seems to drain me. I hope tomorrow is a better day. I think the town trip threw me off a little. Tomorrow supposed to go to a mountain man rendezvous with George, but I don't see how I can go—still need to get the porch done. Having trouble breathing again; seems like I have to yawn, but I can't. I know it's anxiety about missing her. Need to ground with God and nature. Here I get to find out just how connected I am…not doing that good. Feeling better now that I'm writing. Made navy bean soup like Mom used to make when I was seven, it tastes just right. Goodnight.

"Day 22 – 24: My dad's birthday. According to the grapevine, Ernie Kuck died and his estate has logging rights on 6,000 acres. A bank holds the estate and plans to log off 2,000.

Left for the Free Trappers mountain man rendezvous in the mountains. No one is allowed in the camp with anything newer than 1870. All fires must be started with flint and steel or bow, all rifles are flintlock and dress must follow the era. Water must be in skins, no plastic jugs. Had a great time. Still missing Mari. George told the story about the time a bear sat on his tent in the middle of the night.

"**Day 25:** Back on the Hill again, George is helping with the porch so we can get the roof on for winter. Boys said they would not be able to come up and help. I can't count on getting another trip before winter. Hope to finish before next week. It will be good to be back with Mari. I pray for guidance. There's something Mari said that keeps going through my head, 'It's better to die serving others.' I'm here to recharge and ready the place and I hold on to her words like a jewel—they allow my spirit to come back to the city and survive the craziness there. Right now it seems like the grandparents, the boys, Mari and I are going in different directions for different reasons. I find this hard to bear. When and if the shit hits the fan I feel we will all pull together. Right now I feel to be of service is the only thing worth doing. It may be a little altruistic, but is what I hold on to.

"**Day 26:** Today I got up very early and started on the porch ceiling joists. Got all joists up. George showed up about 10:00 AM with supplies, generator and skilsaw. Things should go much faster, no more cutting by hand, although I feel like I'm cheating. Still getting a little pain and trouble breathing—I can't believe being away from her can affect me like this. I hope she understands that I must finish. I wish she could be here. She's putting together a massage practice for us in Santa Rosa, hope to get a little building downtown. We may not make a lot of money, but we should be able to make enough to live on and more importantly we will be working together and be of value to others. What we give from our hearts now is what we will use to build our house later. I wish she could hear my heart. I love her, and what is it? I miss my wife and friends—Love, Thomas. The coyotes are singing again tonight. Most of us say one thing, do another, and think another. What we say, do, and think should be the same so that we are in harmony. What will come of this country? Goodnight my love.

"Day 27: Woke early this morning. Today I'm working by myself; I had to use rigging to hold endplates for the roof. Got all the endplates up including the old porch connections. All sheathing is cut and nailed down. Just need to put up rolled roofing to complete the porch. Hope I have enough roofing nails. Worked from 8:30 AM till 9:00 PM. I'm shaky—need to eat. Should be able to get roof on tomorrow and Friday is cleanup. I wish Mari were here. There is a beautiful pink ring around the moon tonight. The sunset was as though I can see the spirit of the earth. Even with all my pounding, many deer came to the pond at sunset.

"Day 28: The day started out like most days. I was sitting on the new porch eating my morning oatmeal when a squirrel dropped by to say hello. There were many deer around the pond last night. I started calculating if there was going to be enough roofing material. I started thinking I would have to go to town for another roll, and then I remembered there was a roll in the cabin. Carrying those 90-pound rolls up the ladder is a new and old experience. I worked from 9:00 AM to 7:30 PM without stopping. I guess I should eat more because I'm looking a little thin. About 4:30 a strong wind came up, 60-70 miles per hour. A major storm was coming in, I could see it in the distance—it looked scary. Continued to work on the roof. Things kept blowing off. I had just come down to pick up some roofing that blew off and a gust blew the ladder over—good thing it happened while I was on the ground. I kept thinking that the oak branch over the porch would break in the wind and hit me. Well, it never did – just a thought.

"Mari is constantly in my mind today. Hoping she is well and has peace of mind. I'm so looking forward to coming home and starting our massage practice. The wind is blowing so hard it's lifting the rug inside the cabin up four inches with each gust. I gave up on my sunset walk tonight. A little sadness has come over me realizing that tomorrow I leave the Hill, and on the other hand I'm excited about seeing Mari! The porch is all complete. I'm very happy the way it came out. It really looks good. Now we have almost 60 feet of covered porch around the cabin. Tomorrow I clean up, and leave for Santa Rosa—home of my Santa Rosa Roses. Somewhere between the cracks in my predicaments the light shines through; God bless this nature and God bless my family. Goodnight."

Tom left Oregon the next morning. When he arrived at their trailer in Santa Rosa, Mari was there, waiting for him with a note that said,

"That's Thomas. There's a man with laughing eyes—he listens to me then forgets what he heard so I have room to change. I told him he was beautiful and he is—does he remember to fill the cracks in his bones? When we were little, we used to pretend we could fly. I had my umbrella and jumped deep into a black rain puddle. He went to the cockpit of a 727, I got wet; he was freed. After all the wash is done and everything is in a pile, it all looks the same. But I know which buttons are his and I love them because they've been close to him. I miss him too much so I cut it off. Home is where we are. What is our address?"

Their reunion was like a stretched rubber band—letting it go, aimed directly at the heart. They re-fused like two inseparables, bound together in love.

15

We spent them not on toys, in lusts, or wine,
But search of deep philosophy, Wit, eloquence, and poetry;
Arts which I lov'd, for they, my friend, were thine.

Abraham Cowley

Successive Approximation

It's a beautiful summer day in July, Mari's in the lead. On the way home from breakfast at CoCo's they jump the fence at Meadows Lane and cut across the field behind their house. She's 25 steps in front of him and he always plans it that way. Stopping for a moment, pretending to notice the bicycle tracks cutting across the high grass, Tom gazes at her in the distance. He's become fascinated by the distinct sway of her hips. Beyond her, the skyline cuts through rolling hills and massive oak trees lining the ridge. As he watches her walk away, a dry hot wind swirls her hair to one side. She turns and looks back, as she always does, "Come on, you slowpoke, I know what you're doing." He smiled and jogged to catch up. As he approached her, he realized that all around him was beauty—because she was there. He wondered what his world would be like without her. Letting the thought trickle down through his worn-out boots, he picked up the pace.

They have just moved back into their house on Neo. With the boys settled in school, the lovers opened a massage practice out of the house. Soon it evolved into an office and massage room in an old Victorian downtown. Tom made a hand-painted sign and hung it over the front door, "Green Mountain Clinic." They stayed busy, working mostly with people who had injuries from automobile accidents. It was nice because they could make their own hours and Mari enjoyed the work. They continued for about a year, until Mari felt it was too much. They went back to running the business out of the house on Neo, seeing a few clients a week. Tom set up a room upstairs and started doing software consulting for a company designing a rule-based diagnostic system for natural medicine.

One warm summer night in August, Mari lay naked on the bed except for a tiny white slip around her waist, doing the bills when Tom walked in. He removed his boots and Levis, letting his underwear fall to his ankles. Lifting his right leg, he kicked his foot upward flipping his size-34 Hanes high into the air, catching them in his right hand while exclaiming, "Bet you can't do that!" She broke into laughter and looked up. Smiling, she said, "Come on, you silly, help me put stamps on these letters." Climbing onto the bed beside her, he began licking envelopes. "Well, how's it looking?"

Her right hand held a piece of white paper with itemized figures, "Not too bad, but I noticed this doctor bill is not being covered by our insurance, what's up with that?"

"Gee, I don't know, maybe I better get in touch with Jumby Bay."

"I paid all the premiums, I can't figure out why they wouldn't cover this."

Two weeks later they found out that their medical insurance had been canceled. The insurance policy was through the Caribbean Hotel Association and when Tom left Jumby Bay they made payments to the association through Jumby Bay. Mr. Fiedtkou, the HRD manager at Jumby Bay, told Tom the association had picked up a new insurance carrier and there had been a clerical error, and since it had already been filed, it couldn't be reversed.

It was later rumored; when the association changed to the new carrier they dropped persons with terminally ill conditions. Since the carrier and the association were based in Puerto Rico, United States insurance laws no longer applied, leaving them without coverage. They began to rely more on family and friends to navigate the financial river and watched their savings dwindle.

One warm afternoon Mari came back from the mailbox smiling, with an envelope in her hand. They'd received a letter from Rusty and Betty, the people they'd made friends with in the Valley of the Gods. Rusty and Betty had moved and wanted the lovers to come visit.

In September for their birthdays Tom and Mari left for Arizona in search of Rusty and Betty's new place, somewhere in the remote desert wilderness outside of Flagstaff.

Several days later they arrived in Arizona and found Spur 171, a long dirt road heading out across the desert. Tom turned off onto a gravel road and continued five miles, stopping near a decline that led into the foothills. Next to the road was an orange flashing sign set on a sawhorse in the middle of nowhere. It said, "Danger—Flash Flood Area—When Rain Is Present—Do Not Go Beyond This Point."

A few drops had fallen on the windshield, but not enough to turn on the wipers. Tom thought for a moment then continued. Mari was hesitant and wanted to turn back. He convinced her it was all right as they made their way through what had now become an eight-foot-wide dry creek bed, snaking from side to side along a slot canyon with walls 40 feet high. The rain increased and was now pouring so hard the wipers couldn't keep up. Tom put the Trooper in four-wheel drive and continued on, hoping to find a place to turn around. The water rose to the axles. About eight miles in, the water had risen over the bumper and Mari was not happy. The adventure had become scary. Tom knew that within minutes water would flood the engine compartment and kill the motor. They looked over at each other, but didn't say anything. Fifty feet ahead, Tom spotted a road climbing up from the creek. If they could just make it that far... "Mari, look to the front. See the canyon opening? There's a road climbing up from the creek on the left." She said nothing.

In the distance a rumbling sound like a locomotive coming full on vibrated through canyon. Almost immediately after they started their ascent, a wall of water eight feet high, hauling trees and debris, slammed through the narrow slot canyon where they had been seconds before. Silent and white-eyed, they continued moving up the hill as the water rose behind them. It was getting dark. He wasn't sure the road would climb fast enough to stay ahead of the rising water. Tom gunned the motor and went non-stop to what appeared to be the highest point on the hill, 30 feet higher than the canyon below. The water continued to rise. Quickly they perused the area. Mari spotted a small plot of ground higher up. Tom moved the Trooper, with the tires slipping, ten feet higher and prayed the water wouldn't continue to rise. By now it was dark, cold and windy. The lovers had become quiet. They both moved to the back of the Trooper and waited looking through the window. Folding down the rear seat, they made a place to lie down, occasionally poking their heads up to see.

Tom broke the silence, "Well if we die, at least we get to go together." Mari barked back, "You mean we came all this way to die, here in the middle of nowhere?"

"I hope we have more time."

"You're acting like nothing's going to happen, but I can feel your heart beating like it's going to jump out of your chest."

"I think we're going to be all right, but I'm not sure."

"I told you we should have waited."

"I'm sorry, you were right. I should have listened. You always have such good intuition for these kinds of things. I know. I always rush in hoping to discover something. You must admit it's humbling."

A slight smile came on her face, "Put your arms around me and hold me. It is what it is."

That night they slept little, if at all. They took turns looking with a flashlight at the water level and fell asleep just before sunrise. The next morning, they stepped from the Trooper to see that waterline had come within ten feet of sweeping them away. Tom heard dogs barking in the distance, "Mari, did you hear that?" "Yes, I can't imagine, maybe someone's out here." They climbed to the other side of the peak and looked across a tiny valley to a farmhouse nestled in the hills a quarter mile off. Smoke was rising from the chimney. Mari said, "My God, somebody lives out here."

On foot they made their way down a muddy dirt road toward the farmhouse. The morning sun had already baked the ground and steam was rising up from the mud. Everything smelled of wet earth. As they approached, two large dogs came from around the barn, barking and yelping. The sound echoed through the valley. Then a third dog appeared, a puppy dog, all ears, running forward, barking, and then dashing back to its mother's side. The lovers squatted on the ground greeting the largest of the three and were soon joined by the mother and pup. Mari was petting the pup when suddenly the dogs' ears rose up and they ran toward the front porch of the farmhouse. There, wrapped in blankets, were two children, a boy and a girl ten to eleven years old. They looked over at Tom and Mari and scurried back inside. Soon a large man wearing a cowboy hat and carrying a shotgun appeared. He calmly walked up within 20 feet of the lovers and asked what they were doing there. Waving a hand-drawn map, Tom told the man that they were trying to find some old friends that lived somewhere in the area. The man laid the shotgun across his left forearm and reached for the scrap of paper Tom stretched out in his right hand. He replied, "Who are you looking for?" Mari said, "Rusty and Betty."

"Well, you got the right place, but they don't live here anymore. They moved out about a month ago. They were staying here with us, but Rusty got drunk... anyways, there was trouble. I asked them to leave. How in the heck did you get out here, its impossi... how'd you get through the canyon?"

Tom replied, "We came in last night just as it started to rain. We just made it to the top of the hill when a wall of water came crashing through."

The man pointed the shotgun to the ground and relaxed. "My name's Earl. I live out here with my wife Lorna and the two kids. You guys are lucky to be alive."

Mari replied, "Yeah."

Earl went on, "It could take a couple of days before you can get out. Come on in and warm yourselves by the fire. You can meet Lorna."

When Tom and Mari walked in, Lorna was busy over the stove and the kids were eating at the breakfast table. Earl set his gun next to the fireplace as he introduced everyone.

That night the lovers slept in the Trooper. During the day they played with the kids and did chores around the farm in exchange for meals. On the third day Earl led the lovers out through the canyon with his son Jesse in a four-wheel-drive power wagon. The lovers followed them to a secret turn-around point. There they all waved goodbye as the Trooper waded its way through bumper-level water to safety. When they hit the pavement at Route 40 Mari said, "We sure get ourselves in some out-there predicaments." Tom replied, "Something to tell the grandkids."

From there they headed for Sedona and spent three days camping at Medicine Bowl with rattle snakes, then on to Jerome and finally Phoenix and home again. Two weeks later they bought a puppy dog and named him Didger, short for Didgeridoo. He was part McNab, part Australian Shepherd.

Mari dreamed of riding a horse. So Tom bought her a cowgirl hat, boots and a snaffle bit and they started riding once a week at a stable just off Old Redwood Highway. She kept the bit hanging from the banister in the hallway downstairs, just so she could see it when she walked by.

In September of '93, Mari was in the back yard watering her flower garden. Adam and Jacob kept running back and forth across the yard chasing Didger in circles, giggling, while she sprayed them with the hose. Tom had just returned from the hardware store and sat down on the back steps. He watched her swing the hose one direction, then the other. The dog chased the stream, biting at the water, while the boys danced and splashed barefoot through the wet grass. He watched them play, so full of joy, so full of life. Spinning in circles, spraying the water high into the air, she noticed Tom sitting on the steps. She smiled and winked. Flipping her sodden black hair to one side, she turned the hose toward him and smiled again, drenching him from head to toe. After loud cheers from the boys, she sat down next to Tom, momentarily placing her head on his shoulder. Lifting her white skirt above her knees, she said, "We should talk." The boys continued playing with Didger, tromping, zigzagging, and yelling, "Splendid, splendid." She turned toward Tom with puppy-dog eyes and said softly, "I think it's time to start our search."

Mari looked over at the two rusted iron balls sitting side-by-side on top of a cement plate, next to the oak barrel that housed the waterlilies she had planted months before. Tom had found the iron balls by an old quartz mine in Grass Valley. She raised her head toward the sky and said, "Remember the time at the Malakoff Diggings when you took me to the top of the summit and we made love in the sand and the eagle flew over. You were on top of me when it cried out—none of it made any sense. That's why I trust it, even if I die."

She laid her head on his shoulder and tears ran down her face. A few minutes later she got up, lifted her head high and slowly walked to the kitchen, removing a terracotta pitcher from the cupboard. The handle was stained and weathered with hand-oil from years of use. Dew formed on the outer surface as she mindfully filled the jug that had watered her plants 1,000 times before. As she moved from plant to plant, giving each a prescribed amount, she held the jug to her breast, blessing each one. Just as she finished, Tom walked in barefoot from playing with the boys. She marched over smiling and stood on the tops of his feet. They raised their arms, clasped hands and began gliding about the room. As she rode the tops of his feet, all their cares seemed to drift away. They took turns pushing the ends of their noses into each other's eye sockets, an endearment taught to them by the boys. Staring at each other—it was in that moment that they fully comprehended the change. A change so permanent it could not be gone back on; an amendment to regular life whose purpose was to find a cure for malignancy. It was no longer in the background; the "C" word would now permeate every household activity, every dream.

Several days later while folding clothes on the bed, she picked up a pair of Jake's underwear and turned to Tom, "You know, I think we should explain to the boys the real situation as best we can." Later that evening they all gathered in the front room.

Mari and Tom sat on the floor; the boys sat on the couch. Mari looked over at her twins. She watched them squirm about in unison as if some invisible string tied them together. As she started to speak, memories of giving birth flooded her mind; how their father Beto had taken so much care, how his fear in labor transformed into a proud father, how she almost bled to death during the delivery and how surprised she was when she found out there were two babies, calling them "A" and "B" for months. She seemed to drift off for a moment while the boys became even more anxious.

Jake said, "What did you want to tell us?" Tom could tell she wanted to cry, but she didn't. She gathered herself in elegant form and began to speak, "Boys, you know I have cancer." They stopped squirming and became serious. Adam took on the persona of a man-boy; Jake looked on in disbelief then quickly shifted his body to a compassionate posture. All joking had ceased. For a moment, in their own youthful ways, they fed back to her a spark of something that was beyond description, a transmission that defied any doubt of their love for her. It was profound and very beautiful. Tom sat silent, amazed at the depth of Adam's and Jacob's understanding.

Mari went on to describe her condition and prognosis. "I may only live a few more years. I've decided not to take conventional therapy because the doctors say the type of cancer I have doesn't respond well to the medicine, and the medicine would just make me sick. I want you boys to be close to each other and help Thomas as we go along." Jake interrupted, "Jeremy's mother has cancer and she's taking medicine?" Mari replied, "She has a different type of cancer. See, my cancer is very slow growing and the medicine works better if the cancer grows fast. The medicine makes you very sick and there's no sense for me to be sick if the medicine won't work." Jake seemed to understand. Adam looked over at Jake, a silent communication took place and they commenced funning again. Mari became relaxed in their humor and was happy for their strength, and happy that they were not devastated. They all hugged each other and went out onto the front lawn and began playing "grass ball," as if no one understood; yet they all did.

As the months went by, the boys continued with their humor, giving strength to all those around them, but Tom knew deep down inside their inner lives had been altered by the reality of it all. They seemed to be grownup beyond their years. They discovered cars and girls and began filling their lives with every exciting distraction possible. They seemed to understand the impermanence of life, how each moment gives birth to the next, and the importance of the moment. Being in the NOW became their way of being—living life to its fullest. They surrounded themselves with friends and did all the things teenagers do, yet there was something profound about who they had become. Everyone wanted to be in their presence. Outwardly they had become the "Blues Brothers"; inwardly they knew more than most. They had the *q'uecha*, the magnetism naturally gifted them by their mother and father and perhaps Thomas.

A year later, Didger was running through the tall grass barking at shadows cast by branches overhanging the creek in the field out back. Mari ran to the great oak tree in the middle of the field and Tom stayed near the edge. Didger was confused; he hardly ever saw the lovers apart. He kept running back and forth between them. Mari would say, "Go get Daddy" and Didger would run to Tom. Then Tom would say, "Go get Mommy" and Didger would run back to Mari. They had discovered a new game. When Tom first heard her say "Go get Daddy," it made him wish they had had a child together. He remembered wishing that once before, when Mari told him about the baby she lost in her early 20s. Even though she had two incredible boys whom she loved very much, he knew she yearned for a little girl; perhaps it was the little girl she had lost.

By now the frills of Jumby Bay and the things normal people put importance on had drifted away. There was nothing left to be frilly about. They were now on a mission for reprieve and regardless of the outcome, they would walk the path together.

Tom came home one day with a white-board and hung it in the kitchen. Mari wanted to know what it was for. He told her that it would help organize the different régimes she was undertaking. She liked the idea. With felt-tip marker he began listing them; what she had tried, what was current and ideas for the future.

Several months earlier she had sent away for information on the Gerson Diet, a vegetarian fresh juice/coffee enema protocol from Mexico that had kept her friend Solay, who had vaginal cancer, alive for six years. Mari stayed with the diet for a year, until discovering an auxiliary tumor under her right armpit. She opted for surgery, almost hemorrhaging to death in the procedure. She gave up the Gerson Diet for macrobiotics and radish soaks recommended by a tall thin Asian man who diagnosed her by reading her face at a clandestine meeting in Berkeley, California.

In the years to follow came the macrobiotic specialist from Hawaii, and the bloodroot "Purple" man who claimed all his patients got well. Then shark cartilage, Essiac tea, the Russian herbalist from Marin, the pendulum man who was dying of kidney failure but believed attitude was the answer, the English laying-on-of-hands healer that told her not to worry "She would be cutting the lawn next year," the husband/wife team from New Mexico that made their claim prescribing fine adjustments in herbal routines using a radionics machine. Then came the Sonoma County spiritualist couple that helped relieve her of an attached entity they maintained was at the root of the problem.

In their search for an alternative cancer cure, they spent much of the time on the road. It had become an excuse to be together in search of something. One summer they took two months exploring hot springs in four states. They attended scores of workshops on the latest cancer cures, death and dying seminars, and most every other event surrounding the spiritual that they had time for. It all seemed so serious in the midst of it all, but from a deeper perspective, it had become a journey for journey's sake. In between expeditions, she created a wonderful vegetable and cactus garden; she would say, "Dig here" and Tom would dig. She landscaped the back yard with beautiful flowers and trees. Now she had a place to sit and watch nature "be" and every year they'd go off to their cabin in Oregon and plant 2,000 ponderosa pine trees.

By now they had amassed enough research material to fill a large cardboard box and were ready to start another phase. Next came the homeopathic cure "Cancel" from South America, and the renegade biofeedback psychologist who alleged it was all in her head. After that came months on end in San Francisco's Chinatown where a Chi Gung master, who was sure it would be only a matter of days before the tumor began to shrink, prepared long lists of exotic herbs for purchase at the local apothecary. They spent countless days wandering San Francisco's North Beach where Tom loved the coffee. But most of all, he loved watching her stroll through Italian Town transforming into Euro-woman; taking on the part so well that she appeared foreign in America. It's been three years since her diagnosis, and two surgeries later, Tom was beginning to see the cancer taking its toll.

On Christmas he wrote the following letter to her:

"Something for Christmas—Coming out of the ground, little shoots that reach for the sun, next years' adults. They live among the drying brown leaves, food for next years' crop. You can be sure that beneath them lie the seeds for next years' children. We have traveled so far and what have we found—a gracious moss-covered rock to sit on. The oaks of my childhood are here, young energy looking for the mother, strength of my heart.

"The Sun is on my face and my mind soars up over the Valley—everything is empowering everything else without being threatened. It seems that this must be a part of Love and the spirit of Christmas. I watch the birds play; they don't seem to question, they're just being a part of the moment. This reminds me of a story. When I was a young boy hiking in the hills of Newbury Park, I was sitting up on a hill that overlooked a small valley called Hidden Valley, sitting very quietly just looking. A small deer that looked like she was hurt came out of the woods. She was trying to run—just then a pack of coyotes appeared. They took her down. I could feel as she cried out how much she wanted to live. Then as the coyotes tore into her flesh, she had a look of acceptance. The spirit of what was a young deer seemed to leave her, leaving her body to become food for the coyotes and their young.

"This confused me, I thought, "How could such things be?" Later I thought that from the deer's point of view she wanted to live, and the coyotes were only taking food for themselves, and from nature's point of view everything was as it should be. I thought in my young mind, how could I see from nature's point of view, what about compassion, where does it find its place on this earth, and where does love fit in?

"Years and many dissolutions later—is it only for our closest people, our sweethearts, our family, does it extend to the neighborhood and the community? Is it just for a country or does it extend out into the world and perhaps beyond? It seems to have something to do with being so well-connected with the source of life that we are unafraid of becoming, of living, or dying, that we can empower all that is around us without feeling threatened. Often we get this feeling in brief moments, when we are feeling secure without fear or care. I remember one evening just a few weeks ago when we were all four cuddled under a blanket on the front room floor. It was so comfortable that I felt there was abundance, something left over to give— sort of like a Christmas present. Perhaps it was my Christmas present from you.

"A wise person in the form of Rudy once told me that "going away" is the first lesson we are taught and the last lesson we learn. From a moss-covered rock overlooking the Valley, God Bless you Mari, Adam, and Jacob. Merry Christmas, Thomas."

A few months later the boys began asking about their biological father. They had come to the age when they felt they needed to know him. Tom and Mari made arrangements and the boys flew to Arizona.

Two weeks later, when the boys arrived back home, Tom asked Adam how it went. He said, "We went camping, it was all good. Jake and I instantly recognized him." Tom said, "What do you mean?" Adam replied, "He's just like us."

In 1994 the lovers left again for a Midwest search for remote hot springs and camped like gypsies through the summer. They danced in the moonlight and drummed alongside the road. In the fall they spent two weeks on the Hawaiian island of Kauai camping near the Kahili River. Mari watched Tom surf at Poipu and Kalapaki. They walked the sugarcane fields together, sailed with the dolphins, and toured the island by helicopter, while the boys took care of the house on Neo, throwing wild parties late into the night until the neighbors called the cops.

When they returned from Hawaii, Mari kept talking about a baby girl. Two weeks later she started sponsoring a five-year-old girl in Mexico named Marisol (Mari's sunshine.) Just about that time, she started doing Dream BodyWork with Arnold Mindell and working part-time as a salesperson at a contemporary art outlet in Calistoga, called the Artful Eye. She worked there with her girlfriends Gabriella and Paula until the pain wouldn't allow her to work any longer. Then she started sitting with the dying in nursing homes, while managing her own pain through music and meditation.

Several months later, one evening while sitting on the back porch Mari was going through her purse looking for a brush and set a small black book on the steps. Tom asked her, "I noticed you've been carrying that address book around with my picture on the back. You've written on the picture, 'Mari's Muse'?" Picking up the book, he said, "Why do you think I'm your MOOSE?" She replied, "You silly. That's 'muse', it means inspiration." They both laughed at his ignorance. Then Mari's face grew serious, "Tom, I've been talking with the boys' father, I think it's important that he spend time with them."

"Yes."

"He called yesterday."

"Is he in town?

"He's staying over at Jose's, the boys have been going over there."

"Why did you wait until now to tell me?"

"I don't know…."

Tom could tell things were hard enough for her; she didn't need any of his bullshit.

"I was thinking maybe we should invite him over."

"It's OK with me, I've always wanted to meet him."

"Will you call him and invite him? I think he's feeling uneasy about meeting you."

Tom called that evening, but Beto turned down the invitation. That night they discussed the situation. Tom was dozing when Mari came in and rang the meditation bell on the windowsill, and then sat on the bed.

"Tom, would you feel all right if I took Adam and Beto up to Frog Pond so Adam can spend a few days camping with his dad?"

"How about Jake?"

"He's got to work."

"I guess so."

"If you're feeling uncomfortable I could have…"

"No, you go ahead, it's OK."

"What is it?"

"Well…I keep thinking about all the things you said, how he was when you were married."

"That was a long time ago, we were both very young."

"If you're OK, it's OK with me."

"I'll pick him up around noon over at Jose's and take them up there."

"OK, are you feeling strong enough?"

"Yes…it's an important time. I need to talk to Beto, he needs to know, I need to know that all is forgiven. And if something should happen to me, I hope you'll support him with the boys. You've been a good father to them and they love you and I love you. You understand—I need to have closure."

"I understand,"

"I've raised the boys until now. If I die, he should have his turn even for a short time, do you understand that?"

"You're not going to die."

"Let's not go into that."

Tom took a deep breath, "OK."

"Do you understand?"

"Not completely, but if that's your wish, then…"

"Promise me you will use your heart when the time comes. We are all just playing roles here for each other."

"There's a part of me that finds…"

"We've traveled so much ground together, it's the last mile I'll need you the most."

"All right, don't give up on me sweetie, I'm with you."

The next morning Mari took Adam in the Trooper and picked up Beto. They drove to Guerneville. At the stoplight, from the back seat Adam was telling Beto how the town had become "gay." Adam and Beto went back and forth about "it's all good, as long as they don't try anything on us." Then Mari said, "I like those people, they're happy." Mari's hand was gripping the gearshift. Beto placed his hand on top of hers. They gently touched thumbs and held hands. It reminded Beto of the old days when they first courted. But it was more than that, it was a release, a closure, something that took place without words—a moment of forgiveness.

In the spring of 1995 the lovers took their last trip to the cabin together. They knew it would be their last trip and had planned for 12 days alone together in the wilderness. Three days into Shangri-La they were called away after being notified by cell phone of a death in the family. Mari's 19-year-old nephew Tony had passed away. After the funeral she built a shrine for him in the backyard and continued to place flowers there for months.

They continued their trips to Chinatown and sought out a new Chi Gung master to no avail. A friend told them about a Chinese acupuncturist in Oakland named "Doctor O," increasing their hopes for another reprieve. Time went on. Even though Mari wasn't getting any better, she loved the woman doctor from Beijing for her encouragement and spiritual strength.

One afternoon after leaving Doctor O's office, they strolled down Grand Avenue toward the manmade lake in the center of town. As they walked the circular promenade, Mari stopped beside two children and their mother feeding ducks near the water's edge. Mari stood there for a second then squatted down beside them. The mother looked over and smiled. No words were spoken. Mari basked in the moment then stood lifting her head into the air as though she had smelled something. An idea seemed to be pouring into her mind. She smiled back at the mother and the lovers continued on. Mari turned to Tom and said, "We need to go to the ocean." Tom, not knowing why, replied, "Yes."

Two days later they packed up the boys and a small bundle and headed for the Sonoma coast. After passing the Candy and Kites Bait House on Highway 1, they pulled over and stood huddled on a grassy highland plain. Looking out at the thin line separating ocean and sky, a deep rumble echoed off the rocks below. Shades of green and blue swelled across the water. White foam trimmed the sandy beach north of Portuguese Gulch. Seagulls crouched low from the north wind. Adam and Jacob stood with their hands in their pockets. Mari took a deep breath and nodded at Tom to bring the bundle from the car. The bundle contained clothes and items from different eras in her life; things from her childhood, her teen years, her hot tamale days, her marriages, and travels throughout the world. Tom handed her the bundle. She looked back with faraway eyes, then smiled, placing it to her forehead. Without notice, she turned and walked to the trail leading to the sea. Tom and the boys watched while she walked away in a ritual moment with herself. Didger scurried after her, casting shadows along the eroded cliffs. The boys followed Didger on the run, arriving at the beach before her. Tom hung back and watched.

Mari's lead was slow. It was difficult for her to walk without assistance and her breathing was labored. She took smaller steps now. Even in her condition, she remained the most beautiful thing he'd ever seen. Seagulls followed overhead with their antic cry as she turned the corner onto the beach. A gust of wind blew her hair to one side as she bent over to remove her shoes. She continued on barefoot, leaving footprints in the sand. Tom looked down to catch a scouting party of black ants crossing in a crack across the trailhead. Waves crashed on the shore echoing off the cliffs above. The air was moist and salty. The surf pulled in and out, underscoring life itself. Mari stood at the water's edge letting the foam skirt around her feet. Moments later Tom walked to her side ringing a Tibetan bell. She raised the bundle over her head and tossed it into the sea. He heard her whisper, "This is the mother." It was at this place that hope lessened. The raw truth had begun to reveal itself in the face of the woman standing by his side.

Others began to see what Tom had already seen. Her father started taking note of her wisdom. Her sister became more kind and open. Her mother's face told a story of what a mother must bare. Mari was having a magical effect on all those around her. She always did, but this was deeper. It was as if something spiritually beautiful was rising to the surface, touching anything near it.

Mari's father Didi owned racehorses and would race them at the Santa Rosa Fairgrounds. She loved horses but hadn't been involved with racing and thought parts of it cruel. One day Didi asked her if she would come see the horses, because a colt had been born and he wanted to give it to her. For the first time, she went to the ranch where Didi's horses were stabled and played with the colt. She could no longer ride, but loved watching them run the endless expanse of yellow mustard weed.

A few months later, on September 10th, 1995, Tom was commissioned to return to Antigua to help restore the island's infrastructure two days after Hurricane Luis, a Category 4 hurricane, devastated the island. He received a fax from John Mariani's headquarters in New York along with a UPI report stating, "...at least 13 people have been killed, 155 are missing and thousands are homeless..." With a request to depart immediately for the Leeward Islands, the lovers consulted with each other and Tom left the next morning. He arrived at the Antigua International Airport that evening and was put up at Jolly Beach, one of the few hotels still inhabitable.

A warm wind blew across his face as he climbed the stairs to the second floor of Jolly Beach Hotel. The elevators were out and most of the island was without power. He carried two small daypacks. One contained 30 cans of sardines, waterproof matches, five candles, a small flashlight, his log of previous island contacts, paper and pen, a few tools, a small first aid kit, and several bottles of electrolytes. In the other pack was a Polaroid camera and film, clothes, shaving gear and such, a voltmeter, hat, sunglasses, and a lock of Mari's hair. Laying the packs on the bed, he began scribbling notes for tomorrow's logistics.

The next morning, from the second-floor balcony he looked out across the mainland—not a single tree was left with leaves; giant palms lay sideways on the ground. To the east lay three large fishing boats blown inland a quarter mile, piled one upon the other. Packs of dogs sniffed violently through the debris of what used to be a hotel kitchen. He received a Red Cross report that winds in excess of 155 miles per hour had hit the island and stayed for 18 hours; in some areas entire villages had been demolished. He was anxious; anxious about the destruction and what he might see, and anxious about being away from Mari at such a critical time. He felt an internal hurricane tearing at him, devastating any semblance of peace that may have been left.

Visiting with other emergency workers, he grabbed a sandwich from the hotel lobby and managed to make a call to Mari by satellite phone before catching a ride to Shell Beach in a beat-up cab with no windshield. On the way in, he looked around with awe. He pondered, *If Jumby Bay looks anything like this, I'm going to be here for months.*

At the Shell Beach dock, boats lay splintered on the rocks like boxes of matches. A telephone pole near Jumby Bay's dispatch hut was embedded with fragments of glass, tin and strands of wind-driven straw; some had passed completely through the pole. A large tin structure lay collapsed near the dock. In the distance the gurgling resonance of a motorboat's approach interrupted the sound of water slapping against rocks. The smell of diesel and sewage filled the air. He continued to the end of the dock and boarded a speedboat for Davis deepwater harbor at Jumby Bay.

Bill Anderson, president of Jumby Bay, greeted him. They toured the island by electric cart while Mr. Anderson briefed him. There was no power on the north side; only one 100KW generator remained online. All microwave communications were out. The undersea freshwater pipeline had broken near the beach, the freshwater reverse osmosis plant was down and the sewage treatment plant north of Harbor Hill Villa was only partially operational. Near the northwest shore, at the high voltage transfer station, a transformer appeared to be breached with salt water. The underwater telecommunication cable lay torn and twisted on the beach west of the harbor. Roof and building damage was extensive throughout the island.

After looping the island, Mr. Anderson stopped near a string of villas and pointed across the sea, "Oh, and one more thing. East of the Parham dock, about a quarter mile inland, in the mangrove swamp, is the Petit Bleu." The Petit Bleu was a WWII landing craft used to carry supplies to the island. Tom smiled, "That should be a challenge. Where are the rest of the boats?" Mr. Anderson replied, "We've got one operating, the others— bits and pieces." Tom reacted, "And Parham?" Mr. Anderson turned his head to the left, "Bad."

The next day Tom set up headquarters at Harbor Hill Villa, organizing a twelve-man crew to document the conditions of the infrastructure and wide-ranging structural damage throughout the island.

Two days later he left in a speedboat, hoping to look at the Petit Bleu and check on the village of Parham. As the boat approached the dock Tom turned his head toward the village, glancing at a little girl dragging something from the water's edge. He smiled grimly to himself. He loved the children of Parham. He knew nature had been tough on them, guessing that 60% of the village had been destroyed. He instructed the driver to pull alongside what was left of the dock and proceeded toward the little girl. She was pulling a dead pelican from the water as he approached. He knelt down next to her and noticed her eyes. They seemed glazed. He wasn't sure if it was hunger or shock. Pulling a can of tuna from his pack he placed it in her hand, she smiled and ran off. At first glance he couldn't believe his eyes. Next to the sea, where an elderly man had lived for many years in a handmade house fashioned from wooden crates and tin, were piles of logs and debris washed up from the harbor. Large projecting objects, pieces of metal and wood and fragments of steel cable, surrounded the front of the old man's house only 50 feet from the sea. Yet the house was still standing. Debris was piled up three to four feet high on three sides of the house, stopping just a few feet short of either side. It was a miracle.

Tom stood in amazement for a few minutes then continued toward the village. Several Antiguan men approached stating many houses had been destroyed. Tom motioned for the men in the boat to come ashore. He asked passing villagers if the old man by the sea had been in the house during storm. One man replied, "Ya mon, he wodna leave, me assk, he no go." Later Tom found out that the old man's prayer had been to take the house, with him in it, or spare it from the sea. All the men assembled. Tom walked with them through what was left of the village. On one side of a cobblestone street were three houses looking like a bulldozer had ran over them, while a fourth stood standing with the roof still on. This random destruction repeated itself throughout the village. Tom and his men and other men from the village spent the afternoon putting houses back on their foundations.

Ten to 15 men would get on one side of a house and lift it, while others slid logs under the bottom frame. Then they'd do the same on the other side. Then they'd push one side of a house, rolling it on the logs, replacing logs as the house made its way to its original resting place. They continued moving houses, fixing roofs and distributing food until dark. Tom was amazed how the people helped each other without thought of reimbursement or any other reward. They didn't wait for assistance from the government or any other agency. They knew there would be none. Not even the Red Cross came. They sang with purpose as they worked, happy to be alive.

The next day Tom arranged with Bill Anderson to provide aid to the village.

Back at Jumby Bay, one of the main issues was the transformer at Pond Bay. The casing had been rusted over after years of exposure to the elements, and seawater driven by the hurricane might have entered the transformer. He knew if any moisture had breached the case, regardless of which way the bypass switch was thrown, water mixed with the nonconductive fluid around the leads feeding the windings could result in an explosion when powered up, damaging the high voltage cables and possibly killing the men who would be working on it.

Robin Leach of *Lifestyles of the Rich and Famous* and homeowner Peter Swann had been on the island since early September and had been without water or power since the storm. Tom had been approached several times by Robin, wanting to know when their services would be restored. In the meantime, they were using the facilities at Harbor Hill Villa to shower and bathe. One of the three main water pumps had been damaged by salt water and the pipeline had cracked near the road on the north beach. The sewage lift station at Pond Bay was without power, backing up sewage to all the homeowners on the north shore, forcing a shutoff of potable water to all the homes. Tom managed to airfreight a pump in from Florida and repaired the main line, but until the sewage lift station at Pond Bay had power, water would remain shut off. He flew in an electrical engineer from Orlando, Florida for a second opinion and he agreed with Tom's assessment.

Tom told Robin Leach that the transformer would have to be replaced and was on order, but would take several weeks to arrive. Robin become understandably upset and told Tom he should order it from Graingers. Tom contacted Caripak, Inc., Jumby's Florida buyer to follow up on Robin's suggestion. Graingers referred the buyer to Square D stating, "Grainger does not carry transformers that large." Tom had already put in an order with Square D a week before and was awaiting shipment. He then got a third opinion from Harvey Brooks, a high-voltage specialist in Antigua. Harvey stated, "Better be safe than sorry."

While Tom spent days sizing up the damage on the island, making repairs, and working with insurance companies, back in Santa Rosa Mari received the results from her latest X-rays and prepared to join him in Antigua.

She arrived in Antigua one week later. It was not an easy trip for her. She stood on the dock at Shell Beach waiting for her sweetie to arrive by boat, looking around, drawing parallels between the outside world and what was going on inside her. As the catamaran approached, Tom could see her standing, a silhouette, aloof like a Greek goddess. Then she saw him. She smiled slowly lifting her arm in a wave. Noticing the motion of her arm, he realized the journey had been long. His heart was so glad to see her. The boat reversed its engines and pulled slowly next to the mooring. Stepping from the boat he greeted her. They touched foreheads and kissed as if no one else was watching. He felt a soothing, friendly influence occupy his mind. Standing next to her was Robin Leach, Robin's girlfriend and Peter Swann. Once underway, Tom introduced Mari and then proceeded to stare into her eyes without blinking the entire ride back. She wore sandals and a long white dress that ruffled in the wind just above the ankles. Her eyes were deep yet they told a story of a more permanent thing. Tom was stirred with a sensation of a far-off world, where no one else could journey, save her.

She seemed older, as if she'd been away for years. He could tell that something profound was about to be told. When they arrived at Davis Harbor she took him by the hand and walked to the water's edge near the fueling station. She stood for a moment with her hand over her mouth taking in the panorama and then seated herself on a soiled wooden platform near the dock. She adjusted her elegant white dress and looked out across the sea. Ships' horns in the distance echoed across the sound when she began to speak, "Remember when we stood by Happy Isles at Yosemite watching the water gushing downstream over the rocks?"

Tom said, "Yes."

"Well, I seem to be moving downstream."

"What's that mean?"

"The cancer is in my lungs."

"O my God, sweetie."

She stared over at the boat captain slapping dominos on the deck with a tall muscular black man, and then gazed back out at the water, "I don't know—keep paddling." Tom pressed his nose into her hair, "We won't give up. We are both water, you can't leave without me."

Looking into his eyes she smiled, "And fire. Let's make the best of what time we have left."

"I don't like the sound of that."

"Cherish the memories of your love, like a garden of beautiful flowers."

"I love the way you say that, but can't we leave it for when the time comes?"

"We'll keep trying, but water flows downstream to the sea and every moment is precious—that's all."

"I understand…I don't understand."

"What's to understand? It eventually happens to every living thing."

"How can you be so calm?"

"I've had a lot of time to think."

"I feel so bad I wasn't there when you received the news."

"It's OK. Much of the journey is inside of me."

"I'm asking *why*. I know it's dangerous."

"Lookit, my sweet man, if we start…start grieving now, we'll lose what we have left."

And with that they rode off toward Harbor Hill Villa in Tom's electric cart. They set up housekeeping in a villa overlooking the sea. Mari rode with him everywhere, encouraging him in what seemed to be an impossible task. Three days later Didi showed up on the island and stayed in the upstairs bedroom. The next evening they all drove to the west shore by the Beach Pavilion and swam in the clear waters of the Caribbean. Didi remained on the shore while Tom took Mari in his arms and walked into the sea. It was a mysterious moment, Didi watching his daughter that he loved so much being held in the warm blue water by the man she called her husband. They kept calling for Didi to join them. He never did.

Mari and Judy, Bill Anderson's wife, started spending time together. There was something about Judy that seemed so much like Mari. When they sat together talking in the sun, their bodies spoke with the same language. They were twins in manner and understood the depth of life's meaning; it was as if they were sisters. There was a lot of politics going on amongst the movers and shakers and Judy and Mari created a calm in the midst of it all.

Water had damaged the path lighting throughout the island and many of the structures had electrical problems. Tom sent for his brother Ray in California and two other electricians, Franz Delhez and Lew Stark, to handle the situation. They showed up with their wives Jayne and Ramone and stayed in one of the villas at Harbor Hill for three weeks. They did an excellent job of documenting and repairing the damage. After hours, they spent time riding around the island on bicycles and hanging out with the Turtle Girls. The seawater had inundated the Estate House wine cellar, leaving much of the wine and champagne with cork damage. Ray and crew made friends with the cook, who kept bringing them bottles of $200 champagne.

One afternoon, Tom and two Antiguan electricians were working on transformer #3 near Harbor Hill. When they opened the door on the transformer housing an ozone smell filled the air, a sign that the terminals had been arcing inside. They began the process of cleaning the terminal blocks. Tom asked the men if they had experience with the procedure. They said they had worked together before as a team and were familiar with the process.

The first man removed the cable-boot from the transformer terminal on one of the 7,000-volt lines with a six-foot hot-stick and insulated gloves, while the second man grounded the boots and placed them on the stub-rack. They continued one after the other until all three lines were on the stub-rack. Mari watched from a distance. Tom stood next to the second man. They cleaned the terminals with a hot-stick adapter, then began cleaning the inside of the boots connected to the dead cables. After the cleaning procedure, the second man picked up the first cable in his bare hands and handed it to the first man. Placing it on the hot-stick, he put it back on the transformer. Without realizing the danger, the second man squatted and reached for the second cable, again with his bare hands. Tom screamed "NO" as the second man's hand came within inches of grabbing the cable. Simultaneously Tom kicked the man in the shoulder, knocking him back onto the ground just before the man's hand touched the cable.

What the man hadn't realized was that after placing the first cable back on the transformer, 7,000 volts would be coming back up the line through the down-line transformer, making all the cables hot. After finishing the procedure Tom scratched out on a piece of paper what had happened so the men would understand in the future. Dismissing the men, he told them to meet him back at the maintenance yard.

Tom walked over to Mari and continued to the side of a nearby building. She followed for a distance and said, "What Happened?" As they walked he said, "I feel sick." They walked around behind the building and he threw up. Mari put her arms around him, "What is it sweetie, you all right?" Tom replied, "Yes, I almost lost a man today."

The hurricane had stripped all the sand off the beach on the west side of the island. A week before, Tom had arranged with a Texas outfit in the Gulf of Mexico to bring in a sea-going tug and dredging barge to put back the sand. In the meantime he was trying to get the Petit Bleu out of the mangrove swamps. He and Mari met with the Port Authorities at St. John's Harbor to charter Antigua's largest tugboat, the *Sea Way*, to come set up a 2,000-foot hawser and try to pull her out. Tom borrowed 1,000 feet of three-inch eight-braid from Theo Francis at Crabs Marina, and he and Mari and a small crew of men rendezvoused at Parham dock the next day in a speedboat.

It was afternoon and the Port Authority's tugboat hadn't arrived yet. The men were hungry and there was no food; some hadn't eaten for two days. Tom pulled 16 cans of sardines from his backpack; it was oily and sloppy but everyone ate during the wait. Soon the tug showed up and anchored in the bay. The crew climbed into the speedboat and motored out behind the tug. A man on the stern of the tug tossed a three-inch nylon hawser line on a buoy, sending it splashing into the sea. The speedboat circled around, picked up the line and motored toward the mangrove swamp east of the bay. From the tugboat, men fed the line from the deck as the speedboat pulled it to the edge of the mangroves. Tom let the crew off and they continued on foot through knee-high stagnant water, dragging the borrowed line some 1,000 feet to the Petit Bleu.

There she sat, the lifeline of Jumby Bay. She was 56 feet long, weighing in at 64 tons, converted from a World War II diesel-powered landing craft made of plate steel with a front-loading gate. Part of her bow had sunk into the mud, the hull listed to port and her screws were out of the water. She was a rusty old bucket built for utility, not looks. Tom radioed to the mechanics to try to start her engines. After several tries, only the starboard engine fired. That would be good enough to get her home. He signaled to shut down the engine, tied the hawser to the bulkhead and returned to the speedboat. With all the crew aboard they sped off into the bay, hanging about a quarter mile from the tug line. Once in position, Tom radioed the tug captain to slowly move forward and tighten the line.

Antigua's *Sea Way* is the most powerful tugboat in the Caribbean. She's 81 feet long and has twin diesel locomotive engines. When the line was taut, he radioed again and signaled full throttle. Black smoke poured from her stacks, the roar was heard clear across the sound. Water boiled up behind her as her mighty screws churned the water. The hum of the towline twanged like a guitar string, echoing across the bay. The captain radioed Tom, "She's not moving, you want us to let some slack off and take a running start?" Tom thought for a moment then pressed the talk button, "Go ahead, we're clear." Tom turned to the crew, "Stand by, the line could snap. We'll have to retrieve it if it does." The tugboat slowly backed up, taking up about thirty feet of slack. The *Sea Way* paused for a moment. Then her engines went full throttle. When she came to the end of the line, sound snapped across the bay like a rifle shot. The line had broken midway. Tom and crew sped toward the towline and rolled in the torn hawser from the tug. He radioed the *Sea Way*, "Thanks, Mr. Green. This isn't working. I'll call you in the morning—we need to think on it." The men standing on the deck of the *Sea Way* waved as the tug churned through the channel and moved out of sight.

The next morning the sea-going tug that Tom had sent for from Texas pulled into to Davis Harbor. She was the *Devcon*, towing a 100-foot barge with dredge and derrick. Tom and Mari joined Captain Marshall for breakfast at the Beach Pavilion. They discussed moving the sand back onto the west beach, and then went to the harbor to look at the rig. Tom started talking about the Petit Bleu. Captain Marshall responded, "I've got 3,000 feet of one-inch steel cable; if it'll reach, we can pull her out with my rig." Tom replied, "How much?" Marshal replied, "Let's go take a look."

They jumped a speedboat to Parham for a look-see, and then returned to Jumby. During lunch Captain Marshal spoke, "I've talked it over with my partner. $5,000 if we can't get her out, $10,000 if we can. You provide the labor to get the line out." They shook hands. Marshal replied, "It will take a day to set up and a day to pull her out. Meet us at Parham Dock tomorrow— we'll start pulling the following day."

Two days later, in the morning, the lovers walked up the cement path from the Beach Pavilion towards the Estate House. Mari stopped several times to look at flowers that had miraculously bloomed after the hurricane. As they made their way past the turn at the estate house Tom stopped and bent over pointing at bricks lining the walkway, "See this Mar, 'Homer loves Joan.' Homer put it here in 1982." She replied, "Are they still in love?" He went on, "I don't know, I think they split up. I remember when we got the island up and running in '83, Joan and Homer came to the island. They were very in love at the time. I was rather ragged in those days with long hair, beard and bare feet, and Joan wanted to take me into Saint John's and get me a haircut, shave and dress me up. I kept hemming and hawing; suddenly Homer showed up and saved me. He and I walked around the perimeter of the island. He was happy that the resort was up and asked me how he could thank me. "I said, 'See that little island out there?' pointing to a small island just off the coast of Jumby Bay. He replied, 'I own that island—you want that island, then it's yours.' He paused for a moment then said, 'Where would Tom

Sawyer be without an island?' We both laughed—it was a happy time."

Mari replied, "It makes me sad when I think of how in love people can be with each other and then it's over." Tom replied, "I'm still in love with you." She put her arms around his neck and whispered, "I know, and I've been waiting all these years thinking it would go away, but it hasn't." They put their arms around each other and continued walking toward the dock at Davis Harbor.

There they boarded a speedboat, along with the crew, for the Bay of Parham. In the boat were seven other men: Tuki, Bushes, Lenroy, Billy, Franky, Solomon and Percy. When they arrived at the edge of the mangrove swamp east of the bay, they found the *Devcon* and winching-barge pushed partly up onto land. Large anchors were set with lines going into the water. Men were moving about the deck of the giant tug while others scurried back and forth setting lines and testing the barge's engines. The *Devcon* was stationed behind the barge in shallow water. Between the roar of the big diesel engines running on the barge and the engines of the *Devcon*, Tom could hardly talk and resorted to hand signals. As the speedboat approached the tug, the captain came from the pilothouse and motioned them to stay clear of the port side. The tug had both its port and starboard screws full on. If the speedboat got too close it could be sucked into a boiling whirlpool and pulled under into the massive propellers. They made their way around the watery vortex to the swamp's edge. The crew got out in knee-high water. It was warm and smelled stagnant. Mosquitoes were everywhere. Once the men were out of the speedboat, Tom and Mari took the boat to Parham Dock and picked up more men from the village.

After several trips, 30 men were assembled in the swamp. Everyone was careful to stay clear of the acid-producing mangrove trees that could sting the skin, burn holes in clothes and even blind a man.

Everyone seemed to be ready for what would happen next. The *Devcon* momentarily shut her engines down while Tom brought the speedboat alongside the tug. Mari boarded the tug to watch from the pilothouse while Tom went out with the men. He and Percy Fiedtkou led the pull. They began heaving the steel cable from the barge's winch and treaded, sloshing foot over foot, towards the Petit Bleu. Every six feet another man joined in until 30 men were pulling. Halfway to the Petit Bleu the weight of the cable swaying in their arms was too much.

Percy had spent years in the bauxite mines of Guyana and was no novice to danger. He was a master of men, in an era when men were men. He looked over at Tom with steely eyes, "TAKE CHARGE." In that moment Tom's soul stood still. He was no longer in the 20th century. Thirty capable men sat along a chain in high mud and hot sun—salty sweat poured from their brows as they waited for a sign. In a primordial transformation he yelled in a rasping guttural voice not common to him at all, "TURN AROUND, USE YOUR LEGS, PUT YOUR BACKS INTO IT. TOGETHER NOW...PULL." The "heave—ho" of 30 men pulling cut into the sound of the diesels running in the background. Repeatedly they pulled in unison, the flex of their biceps thrusting their bodies forward. The next half hour was without equal to any Tom had experienced in his lifetime. By the time they reached the Petit Bleu many of the men were bent over with bleeding hands, including Tom.

Tuki and Bushes connected the cable to the bow turnbuckle of the Petit Bleu with ringbolts. The men all boarded the Petit Bleu and made their way in behind the rusted pilothouse. Tom instructed the men to move to the stern for ballast and to lay low, out of the way of the cable. He explained if the cable should snap, it could cut a man in half. He signaled the *Devcon* to start the winch pulling. With eight anchors set and the *Devcon's* engines in full reverse the massive winch on the barge began to turn. Slowly the line tightened, sending a guitar-string like sound echoing through the swamp. The men on the barge and Petit Bleu began to flinch and duck. They kept looking over at Tom hoping he would call it off. The captain of the *Devcon* radioed Tom, "Is she moving?" Tom radioed back, "Negative." The captain returned, "The clutch is slipping on the winch." Tom replied, "Shut it down." The sound of whining engines rolled to a faint idle. The captain radioed again, "Standby." Tom hit the mike key twice signaling that he heard the message. For several minutes the faint sound of birds fluttering through the trees echoed through the swamp, a peaceful thick quiet in the wake of the deafening danger felt moments earlier. The radio sounded again, "Tattoo, I think we have a solution. We're going to set up the derrick and pulley system. It's going to take about an hour, over." Tom replied back, "Roger that."

With tension now off the cable, the men moved forward to the open hull of the Petit Bleu to escape the sun. Tom radioed the captain, "How's Mari?" The captain replied, "Standby." Mari voice came over the radio, "I'm having fun." Tom, still sporting his In Command voice replied, "Good on you. When we start pulling again don't stand in front of the window, over." Tom's radio sounded again. Mari replied, "Yes Dear!" The men began to laugh, "Ya mon, she iry." It was the perfect relaxant. Everyone on the Petit Bleu began talking amongst each other while the barge crew winched up the derrick in the distance. Tom radioed back, "All right, pretty lady." and clicked the mike–key twice.

Time went fast. Soon the captain radioed again, "Tattoo, if this works we're going to have to cut the cable with a blowtorch every 20 feet. You'll have to eat the cable. You all right with that, over?" Tom replied, "Go ahead, we'll pay for it, over." The captain ended the transmission, "Roger, standing by."

From the Petit Bleu, they could see the derrick rising high above the barge deck in the distance. Tom instructed the men to take cover on the stern and pushed the mike-key, then suddenly let it off again. Pausing for one last look, making sure everyone was safely positioned behing the wheel-house, he hit the mike-key, "Go ahead, we're clear." The sound of engines revving up in the distance once again filled the swamp with thunder. The slack came out of the cable and began to tighten. This time it sounded like an E-string pushed beyond the breaking point, twanging an eerie echo across the mangrove swamp. Black smoke rose from the diesel stacks in the distance. The whine of the cable and the rumble of the engines drew on the nerves of every man. Suddenly, just as Tom was about to hit the mike-key to call it off, the Petit Bleu slipped forward. Over the roar Tom radioed the captain, "*Devcon, Devcon,* she's moving, I repeat the Petit Bleu is moving." Everyone cheered over the roar of the engines.

Three hours later the Petit Bleu sat floating in the bay of Parham. Captain Billy prepared to get her underway. As they pulled away, they waved at the *Devcon's* crew and the captain blew its enormous horns. The Petit Bleu limped back to Davis Harbor on one engine with the speedboat following close behind. She looked seaworthy enough, but appeared to be listing to one side. She pulled into Davis Harbor 30 minutes later and docked at the refueling station. Tuki and Billy remained with the Petit Bleu while Tom and Mari made arrangements for the men to be fed and paid.

At lunch Tom received a call on the radio, "Tattoo, Tattoo, the Petit Bleu is sinking, come now." Knocking his plate from the table, he ran on foot to the harbor. She was listing to one side with her red waterline raised above water. She was a few feet from sinking. He instructed the men to turn on the bilge pumps; Billy replied, "They're not working." Tom snatched the cook's electric cart and headed for the maintenance compound, "Men, get as many portable bilge pumps from the warehouse as you can fit on this cart. The Petit Bleu is sinking in the harbor. Bring extension cords." The men scrambled, returning with bundles of power cords and pumps, piling them onto the back of the cart. Tom raced off for the harbor with several men running behind. A few minutes more and she'd be on the bottom of the marina. Men climbed aboard and set pumps while others laid electrical lines from the refueling station. A few minutes later the pumps were running. Within an hour she sat upright and the onboard bilge pumps were repaired. That evening, using flashlights for running lights, the speedboat and the Petit Bleu set out across the sea for Crabs Marina where she was dry-docked for repairs.

That night the lovers sat on the veranda overlooking Davis Harbor. Mari said, "How do you do it?" Tom replied, "I don't know. The men do it—I could do nothing without these men."

A few days later, in a discussion with Buck White, Buck told Tom that his brother Ben's wife knew about a lady who had survived breast cancer through the help of native Antiguan herbs used by healers; bush medicine dating back to the slave days. Mari was very interested and wanted to follow up on the story. They arranged to meet Ben's wife Mary and set out two days later by boat for Parham village.

They arrived around 6:00 in the evening to find Mary not there. Instead a young girl, about 12, was sitting on the front porch. From thirty feet away the girl yelled out, "You Tattoo?" Her face changed to a smile; assured by the colors needled permanently into Tom's arms. She went on, "Me moder be rit bock." Mari sat on the porch with the girl and made conversation while Tom paced back and forth on the grass in front of the house, staring up at what was left of the tin huts lining the foothills above Parham.

Soon Mary showed up apologizing for the delay and suggested they get a taxi. Tom radioed dispatch at Jumby and a taxi showed up. Mary and Mari sat in the back and Tom in the front. Mary instructed the driver to go to the village of All Saints. Once off the cobblestone streets of Parham, the road leading out of town turned to dirt and continued for several miles, passing herds of goats and withered cattle. Winding through the countryside with the dust blowing up behind them, Tom spotted Freeman's Village on the right and asked the driver to stop. He was thirsty and figured everyone else could use something to drink. As they entered the town, an outpost of about 160 inhabitants along the center part of the island, which used to be a mill yard during the sugar cane days, Tom spotted a "super market" on the left.

They all got out of the taxi laughing and talking. Mari and Mary had hit it off and stood by the door in conversation. Tom continued walking toward the super market, a building with one window and no glass. He greeted the proprietor and ordered four Tings, a West Indies bottled carbonated grapefruit drink. The shop owner apologized for the drinks not being cold and explained that the village was still without electricity. Tom tipped the man handsomely and distributed the drinks, passing one to the driver from the back seat as they pulled away.

Two miles south of Freeman's Village small houses began to appear, a sign that they were on the outskirts of All Saints, a community of 2,200 descendants of the slave trade. Mary instructed the driver to turn onto a narrow road behind a cricket field. They entered slowly on the soft gravel and turned left along a row of brightly colored houses. The sound of tires snapping on the rocks overrode the reggae music from the corner bar and brought people to their doors. Down the street, houses dwindled into a poorly lit neighborhood. They passed one or two more smartly-decorated dwellings and pulled over in front. Tom asked the driver to wait.

Dogs barking along the street brought more neighbors out onto their porches. A donkey's bray blending with the sound of reggae music rushed in as they opened the car door. They walked up six wooden steps and knocked. A barefoot girl ten years of age opened the door, followed behind by a tall thin sincere-looking woman in her 40s wearing a black skirt and red top. Mary introduced Tom and Mari and they were invited in.

Everything in the house seemed to have a purpose. Everyone was busy. There were no men. The lady brought them to an empty bright blue painted table in the center of the room, motioning them to sit. The patina showed through where arms and plates and spoons had rubbed for a thousand meals. As they sat, the lady and Mary talked in Bewee while the lovers glanced around the room. In the corner of the kitchen a small boy was reading a book by kerosene lamp, a teenage girl was stirring a cast-iron pot over the stove, an elderly lady on the exposed back porch was washing a small child in a galvanized washtub. In the front part of the three-room house, a girl in her 20s was making a dress with needle and thread. Herbs of all types hung from the ceiling and glass apothecary containers lined the walls leading to the shared bedroom.

Suddenly the lady turned to Mari and began speaking in the King's English. She spoke of her traditional roots and talked about her own personal experience with cancer. She said when she was Stage 1, she went vegetarian and started taking two herbs, Monkey Apple (noni fruit) and Guanabana (graviola). She had been cancer-free as far as she knew for three years. Mari explained that she was much further along, but wanted to try.

She gave Mari two paper bags containing the herbs and showed her how to prepare them. Even though the lady did not ask for compensation, Mari slipped her a $20 as they hugged goodbye. They just made it to Parham before the last boat to Jumby Bay pulled away. Mari knew she was Stage 4 and anything short of a miracle wasn't going to do much. She loved meeting the lady and took the herbs until they ran out, with no significant change.

The following week, for the first time Mari allowed Tom to change the bandages under her arm.

One afternoon Mari watched Tom turn down the cement path near the maintenance area and wrote the following in her diary, "He was soon among the men. He always seems like one of them, never afraid to dirty his hands. Many of them spoke to him, but their openness has failed to wipe away the unrest in his mind."

Robin Leach kept flagging Tom down, wanting to know when they would have service again. In the meantime, Tom had one of the old 75KVA transformers, stored at the Bone Yard, rebuilt using parts from other transformers. He installed the rebuilt transformer at Pond Bay, successfully restoring water and power to the north shore. Both Robin Leach and Peter Swann seemed happy.

Ironically the next day, on October 24th at 4:00 AM, lightning struck the newly installed transformer, resulting in a complete meltdown and 820 feet of high voltage cable lying fried underground. Robin and Peter were again without water or power. Tom felt badly for their loss after their being without services for almost a month.

This time it was a big deal; to repair the damage they would need to replace 2,460 feet of high voltage cable, removing portions of the street and breaking up the concrete sidewalks near the bridge at Pond Bay. That morning Tom received a call on the radio, "Tattoo, Robin Leach and Peter Swan are on their way to your house." Moments later an electric cart pulled up in front. Robin and Peter walked past Didi sitting on the porch and entered the house. Tom was sitting on the couch going over some files on the coffee table. He stood and greeted them. After reviewing what needed to be done to restore power to their side of the island, they left disappointed. Tom arranged with his old friend and master electrician, Harvey Brooks, to start the restoration, and told him he would have to finish the job. Tom would be leaving the island in two weeks.

In mid-October, Mari gave a Buddha casting she had made to Bill and Judy Anderson and said her goodbyes to Hans of Ballast Nedam; the look in Hans's eyes said everything. A few days later she flew back to Santa Rosa with her father. Tom returned to the States one week later.

In November Mari began trying a cancer treatment designed by an El Salvadorian biologist that used bacteria to create a fever that was supposed to kill the cancer—to no avail. This was followed by the crazy quack lady pharmacist gone mad in Tijuana who stood Mari in front of some machine and told her that she no longer had cancer, even though she had an auxiliary malignant tumor under her armpit the size of a baseball. On their return trip from Tijuana they parked the Trooper in a campground near Encinitas and visited a monastery overlooking the ocean where Paramahansa Yogananda had spent his later years writing his discourses.

Now settled in Santa Rosa, Mari began making statues of *Tara* (the Tibetan Goddess of Compassion and Mercy) and giving them to friends. She was now on small amounts of morphine every four hours and would often mumble things. On one of their evening walks, she was explaining what had happened the day before when suddenly she caught herself mumbling and retorted, "Forget that, it's my morphine mumble." Somehow the word of her cancer had spread to the neighbors and she became quite upset over it. She never wanted anyone to know her condition for fear they might pity her. When walking in public she would walk straight up as if nothing was wrong. For reasons only known to her, it was paramount that no one alter their plans for her.

One day as they turned the corner near the driveway from one of their walks, Mari stopped and looked into Tom's eyes— a timeless look, like the time when she told him about putting the kids and the dishes and the clothes in the shower, when he first fell in love with her. He knew she had something to say, "What is it sweetie?" She replied, "It's time to find you another woman. I don't think you're going to do very well, besides, I could help you pick her out." He said nothing—pieces of his reality began falling apart. *Is she telling me she's going to die? I can't believe she said that.* He softly replied, "I could never do that." It was never spoken of again.

She used to run her feet up and down his legs, hooking toes before falling asleep. She would push down on the tops of his feet with hers, using the ball of her foot as he lifted back against the force. They would laugh and giggle until one of them gave up, then take turns pushing their noses into each other's eye sockets. They would scratch backs searching for zits, kissing and spooning before falling asleep. In the morning they would do the same thing again and take turns cleaning the goop from each other's eyes. Then Tom would remove a brush from the nightstand, Mari would sit up in bed and he would brush her hair. Most of the time they would shower together in the morning. Sometimes he would kneel and shave her legs with a Princess shaver while the water ran off his back; this usually took place if she hadn't had her private candlelight bath the night before.

Often during her bath she would call for him to bring her a cup of hot tea. When invited, he would sit with her in the candlelight; sometimes they would talk, other times he would just sit quietly next to the tub and wash her back—she loved that. Most of the time she took a book in with her, but occasionally she would ask him to come in and read a story, or dry her off afterwards.

She liked to sew with needle and thread and on nights she couldn't sleep he would wake up in the middle of the night to find her repairing a garment. It was not unusual to find them sitting back to back meditating on the bed after the boys went to sleep. Before the lovers fell asleep they would have long conversations, whispering into each other's ears for no other reason than they enjoyed whispering. Sometimes he would clip her toenails and she would do the same for him. If they were barefoot, she would always come over and step on the tops of his feet.

Once a month he would trim her split ends and assist in dying her hair. Before they got a dryer they used to hang out the clothes on a clothesline together. They washed the dishes together when it wasn't the boys' turn. Mari mostly did the cooking except for an occasional stew that Tom would make. They always went grocery shopping together; Tom pushed the cart and brought the food in from the car and she would put it away. On the windowsill she had miniature baskets filled with wishbones and tiny crystals; the kitchen was a sacred place to her. Every night they would "bug" each other's toes and argue which ones smelt the worst.

But now much of that was gone—her body no longer had the strength. No more motorcycle rides, no more Albany Sauna, no more walks down Telegraph in Berkeley, no more dinners out, no more basketball at the school with the boys, no more swinging on the swings, no more long walks with Didger. They were now itinerant in a land less traveled.

Even though they were given much help from family and friends, and had saved enough from their work in the islands to travel the course of successive approximation, in reality it was a path of futility and hope. But more than that, it was a deepening of self, a desperate yet wondrous voyage through the unknown—a quickening. It didn't have much to do with a cure; it was about spiritual triumph and fortitude, a discovery of the deeper parts. Somewhere along the line all the "woo-woo" had disappeared.

16

*"I have come to measure spiritual advancement,
not alone by the light that surrounds one when they meditate
or by the visions they have of saints
or during heighten moments
or by church-going-ness,
but by what they are able to endure with love
in the hard cold light of day."*

Sri Gyanamata

Just Passing Through

Searching for a new Tintin adventure for Mari, Tom stood in the corner of a used-book store spinning a rack of comic books, when his cell phone rang. It was Mari, "Where you at?" Tom replied, "I'm at the Tree Horn. Are you OK?"

"Yes, but I just got a call from Didi. He doesn't sound good. Will you go over to the house and see if he's OK."

"What's wrong?"

"He says he's dizzy and has pain in his back. I think it's serious. Maybe you better call 911 and go over there right now."

Tom arrived before the ambulance and went into Didi's bedroom. Didi was sitting up on the edge of the bed half-dressed. He looked white. Tom helped him finish getting dressed and heard the ambulance pull up with the siren on. Tom went to the back door and let the EMTs in. By then, Didi had moved from the bedroom to the kitchen. Medical personnel started taking his blood pressure and asking questions about prescription drugs. Although he appeared conscious and alert, his eyes seemed glazed. Suddenly one of the EMTs said, "We need to transport, **now**." As they carried him out the side door, Didi looked at Tom and said in a strong voice, "You're the last one out. Secure the house and let Noni know they took me to the hospital."

That evening the doctors told the family that it didn't look good. The main artery feeding Didi's kidneys had ruptured; they performed surgery that night and put him on life support. Family and friends from all over came to pray. Mari left her bed to be with Didi. Over the sound of a respirator she bent over and whispered in his ear, "Didi, I love you." He passed away three days later on January 9th, 1996.

Five days later Tom and Mari left on their last journey of hope. They left Santa Rosa accompanied by their dear friend George Shepard for two weeks of hyperbaric oxygen treatments in San Bernardino. There, in the waiting room, they met the visions-of-grandeur Indian who was going to heal her by injecting her tumor with battery acid and spray-bottle chants, which Tom emphatically refused. After that they stopped in Venice to meet with the LA "coyote man," who after being left for dead in the desert was fed fresh meat by wandering coyotes, returning with a vision that raw uncooked meat was the answer.

Back from their trip and somewhat disillusioned, Mari remained in bed except for her jaunts with Tom to see Ellen Galford, her spiritual sister. Through the month of February he continued to consult for Jumby Bay by phone and fax.

Come Valentine's Day, which had always been a special day, probably more important than their birthdays, she gave him a card that no one knew how she got a hold of. It pictured a place where Tom would have loved to wander. The sky was blue with scattered clouds, purple mountains poked up at the skyline, and a great river snaked through a valley in the fall. The trees were golden. Inside she wrote, *"A three-eyed man is hard to find, I got lucky, both gentle and loving-kind, please be my special valentine. I love you, sweetest, kindest, bravest, bestest, husband, lover, friend and fellow traveler. Love, Mar."*

That same day he gave her a card of a Goddess standing in tall grass in the moonlight deep in an oak forest. A flute was tied with a scarf around her waist and she had flowers in her hair. Around her danced elves and wood nymphs in the middle of the night. Tom wrote, *"Dear Mari, How are you forest lady? Like a waterfall you drench me with wet colors. My heart is neither below nor above, but in your heart. A sweet Dharma, ever-changing, so refreshing. Not so nice that there is no truth. I thank you for all your truth. I am so fortunate to be with one like you. Like the road that turns, to turn back home, the fire of years of experience says, I love you. Will you be my Valentine? Love, Thomas."*

And so it went. The days passed on. Returning from one of his routine evening walks with Didger, he strolled to the end of the block near the school and stood on a manhole cover beneath the tree that had flowered last spring, where he and Mari had stood holding hands 1,000 times before. The cast iron letters read, "STORM." The tulip tree no longer had leaves. The edge of the field, where they once ran like children, was wet and brown, asleep for the winter. Staring off into the meadow with its single great oak, he contemplated the things he would need to do tomorrow and returned to the sidewalk.

As he walked toward home, Didger scurried out in front. Tom looked back over his shoulder, catching a glimpse of the rose-colored streaks in the sky. *How glorious,* he thought, as he passed over the concrete Bell System cover embedded in the sidewalk. He closed his eyes and continued his walking meditation. One, two, three, four, five, six, seven, eight, nine— suddenly he opened his eyes feeling a shadow pass by. He looked back. He'd missed running head-on into the School Zone sign by only inches.

Turning the corner at Neo, he noticed the patches in the cement sidewalk that did their best to hide the cracks from the fault lines running through the valley. He remembered tripping there last year and Mari laughing at his absent-mindedness, saving him from falling to the ground only because they had been walking arm and arm. As he approached the front of the house Didger ran back and forth hoping Tom would chase him. He opened the front door and Didger bolted up the stairs. He now knew Tom's every move. At the top of the stairs Tom quietly turned the corner into the bedroom and looked over at his sweetheart lying on the bed.

Her eyes were closed, slumbering with a peaceful look on her face. Behind her was a chest-of-drawers doubling as a headboard/shrine/medicine cabinet covered with a brilliant colored weaving from one of her El Salvadorian adventures. Atop the chest sat a statue of *Tara* that she had made weeks before, a Tibetan bell, a bird's nest found in the field behind the house last fall, a little glass lamp she could turn on without sitting up and a myriad of other small objects Tom had collected to show her from outdoors. On the wall to her right was a pencil drawing of *Tara* from a monastery in Bhutan, next to that was a framed photograph of Khyentse Rinpoche. The wall facing her was mostly window with a painting of an American Indian Christ and a Virgo Yantra (spiritual geometric shape) and below that hung a set of Catholic rosary beads. Suspended near her head by the chest-of-drawers were sandalwood meditation beads given to her by Ananda Moyi Ma in India, fourteen years ago. To the left of the window hung a picture of Paramahansa Yogananda. On the wall to her left was a bookcase that went to the ceiling, with various yantras mounted next to it. On the floor near the bookcase were boxes of medical supplies and a small oak filing cabinet. To her right on a little table sat a small TV, which could only play VHS tapes brought to her by friends.

Without a sound, Tom walked over and knelt next to her side of the bed, "Hello sweetie. It's time to change your bandages." She slowly opened her eyes, "What day is it?"

"It's Friday."

"No, I mean what's the date?"

"It's February 16th."

"Oh, where are the boys?"

"I think they're over at their girlfriends."

"Did you go to the pharmacy?"

"Yes."

"You doing OK?"

"I'm doing OK sweetie."

"How's your shoulder?"

"Oh…it hurts when I'm awake."

"Let's change your bandages first, then I'll rub your shoulder."

Looking around, it dawns on him like every other time; the room is part hospital, part spiritual sanctuary. Sliding open the chest of drawers that once held clothes, he glances inside. Arranged in neat little compartments are Epinephrine adrenalin chloride solution to stop bleeding, Lidocaine numbing solution, Lorazepam for muscle spasms, Bacitracin ointment and Neomycin polymyxin sulfate for infection, topical Clotrimazole and Metonidazole for surface fungus growing on the tumor, black elderberry extract for cough, and Lotrimin for the skin around the tumor. In another drawer are bottles of MS-contin (oral time-release morphine sulfate), Roxinal (liquid sublingual morphine), Dilaudid, Codeine, Hydrocodone, Buspirone hydrochloride and various other painkillers. Next to that are rolls of Micropore first aid tape, a bottle of sterile packing strips, a pair of hemostats, surgical scissors, boxes of throwaway scalpels for trimming off the dead skin and packages of 6" cotton-tipped applicators. To the right are small boxes of Chinese White Flower remedy that he sometimes uses to stop bleeding, Vaseline, packages of surgical 8x10 sterile dressings, and rolls of sterile gauze. Lined up in the back of the drawer are envelopes of absorbable gelatin sponges, and stacks of Tendersorb 5x9 ABD pads. On the floor next to the bed are boxes of Curad non-stick pads, Kendall ABD pads and calcium sodium wound dressings.

While he gathered up the necessary medical supplies, she opened her eyes wide to peer out the window and said, "No birds, a bunch of birds came in before you went on your walk." Tom replied, "I found a crow feather in the field, I'll just put it here." Her only view is the tops of the mulberry tree in the backyard. Occasionally a bird will land on a branch, exciting her for the day.

Placing a thermometer in her mouth he looked into her eyes, "Are you ready sweetie?" She smiled and muttered with closed lips, "Yes."

"OK, here we go." Gently rolling her partly to one side he placed a folded blanket under her waist. Carefully he removed the tape from across her chest and detached the bandage under her arm. Turning her head to one side, she said, "I can't get used to that smell." Tom replied, "Me either, but what the hell." They both smiled as if it had just been the odor of a common fart.

Next he cleaned the tumor under her arm and the parts that were now growing in and around her scapula in back. Then he applied the various topical medications and re-bandaged. The last step was to replace the plasma-soaked towel under her back with a fresh clean one without hurting her. Looking at the tumor had almost become second nature, but to hurt her during the process was unbearable. As time went on, he got really good at changing bandages. She would often comment, "You'll make someone a fine doctor someday." Seriousness moved from Tom's face to a slight unassuming smile, like a little boy's. Then he leaned over and kissed her forehead.

Next he jotted down notes in his medical log, administered the proper amounts of pain medication and glanced at the day before: "The yellow/red/gray tumor attached under her right armpit has grown to 6 cm, the size of a hardball. Arm lifts upward compensating for the malignant intruder, continuous pain shoots up her right shoulder into back ... 8:15 AM .5m Roxinal, 14 drops + AMOX (amoxicillin). 9:30AM .25m Roxinal, neb and sip, 10:37 .25m Roxinal. Fruit salad – breakfast. 1:30 .25m Roxinal, bleeding under arm, change bandage, 2:00 .25m Roxinal, chicken and corn lunch, 4:00 .25m Roxinal. 7:45 MSContin, change bandage, cooked carrots, beef, bread, pain in axillary, temp normal. 9:15 .25m Roxinal, 10:15 .2 Roxinal ... "

After her backrub and a short story, she drifted off to sleep. Getting up to wash clothes and clean the kitchen, he moved softly across the floor toward the door. Mari woke up announcing, "I want it removed." As he continued down the stairs he replied, "OK, I'll call Doctor Reed in the morning."

Three days later they had an appointment with the surgeon. Tom brushed her hair, bathed her, shaved her legs and dressed

her in Levis and a pretty flowered blouse; carrying her 5' 8",
115-pound frame down the stairs to the car, he gently placed
her in the back seat with a blanket. She liked to wear flowered
tops. It made her feel comfortable since no one would be able
to notice the bloodstains that would sometimes appear on an
outing. They drove to Dr. Reed's office. The medical staff
immediately recognized her and helped her to a private
examination room. Mari was quiet, then looked over at Tom
clowning in the doctor's adjustable examination chair, "I sure
hope they can take this thing off." He looked down, stuck his
hands in his pockets and glanced back, "Me too, sweetie." It
wasn't long before Doctor Reed appeared, "Hello Mari, how
you doing?" Mari replied, "Not too good. I was wondering if
you could remove this growth under my arm?"

Optimistically he replied, "W-e-l-l, let's take a look."

Tom helped her remove her blouse, lifting it just right to
avoid hurting her. She reclined onto the examination table with
a slight wrench. A large bandage covered the main tumor under
her arm; there were two smaller tumors protruding from her
right breast and one small one on her left breast. Dr. Reed was
silent; a momentary stun vacillated in his eyes, "Let's take this
bandage off." Nothing could have prepared him for what he
was about to see next, save having seen it before, "Oh...you
didn't have chemotherapy!" Mari replied, "No, that's the way
I wanted it." Looking away to put on rubber gloves, Dr. Reed
looked back and began examining the entity living under her
arm, "Does it bring you much pain?" Mari replied, "Sometimes."
That was an understatement. On occasion it would take her
breath away. He palpated around the yellow-gray mass where
protruding blue veins and arteries had made their way to the
surface. Moving his eyes away, he gazed out the window then
peeked back at her, "I'm sorry dear. We won't be able to operate.
There are too many arteries. I'm afraid I'd lose you on the
operating table." Mari just smiled as though she were a million
miles away, estranged from the infected body lying on the table.
Tom looked over with puppy-dog eyes. She rolled her eyes
upward with a slight smile and matter-of-factly changed the
subject, "Dr. Reed, did you put in a garden this year?" He

replied, "Yes, mostly string beans." They went on about gardening for 15 minutes. Tom drifted off into his favorite daydream—he and Mari walking hand and hand through a field of wildflowers, high up in a mountain meadow. He didn't even hear the doctor leave the room until Mari sat up from the table with a groan, "Will you help me with this blouse?" Slowly they walked through the clinical corridors and across the parking lot to the car without saying a word.

That evening they made a pact. She wanted no 911, no trips to the hospital, no doctors. If she was going to die, she wanted to die at home. Over the next week they took care of the paperwork making it all legal.

In March, Tom started making sourdough bread from a starter given him by the neighbors across the street. He was getting quite good at it. He had punched down the dough for the second rise and decided to do some work on the computer while the dough rose. After checking in on Mari, finding her asleep, he entered the "Computer Room" just around the corner from the bedroom. He was deep into some software engineering design when he heard her say something in a sleepy whisper and replied, "OK, I'll be right there, you OK?" There was a pause; he continued typing code. Again she said in a more audible matter-of-fact tone, "Something's not right." He stopped typing, "OK honey, be right there. What is it?"

"I feel wet."

Thinking she had spilt her water, he continued to type the next line, "OK, here I come." He got up from the computer and walked five steps into the bedroom. What he saw next stormed into his present reality like a torrent wall of water. His knees almost buckled. He gathered himself; he couldn't let her see how shaken he was. Then an outward calm appeared over him as she spoke in a calm soft voice. "I feel wet, it's making me cold." What he didn't want to tell her was, she was soaked from head to toe in blood. He slowly pulled back the blanket exposing a pool of blood puddled under her back and arms. He began to speak in a calm even voice, "Sweetie you're bleeding, I need to remove the bandage and take a look." In an endearing little girl's voice she replied, "Oh, is it bad?"

"Well, we need to take a look."

As he began removing the bandage, he noticed large amounts of blood running down her arm in surges. Moving back the bandage from the tumor, he located the problem. With every heartbeat came a stream of blood shooting from the tumor ten inches into the air. "Sweetie, you're hemorrhaging. I need to stop the bleeding. I need to get to the epinephrine. Can you hold your hand like this for just a second?" He placed the middle finger of her left hand over the hole in the tumor and quickly returned with gauze patches, a bottle of adrenaline and a container of shark cartilage. Whispering, "OK, remove your hand, honey." Turning the bottle of adrenaline upside down onto the gauze, then dipping it in shark cartilage, he counted, one, two heartbeats, pressing the adrenaline-soaked gauze into the hole in her tumor in between beats. Holding pressure against the tumor he assured her, "Honey, the bleeding's stopped, but I can't take my finger off for a while." In a simple sweet voice she replied, "OK."

"I'm going to hand you the adrenaline, can you hold it in your left hand?"

"Yes."

He reached for more gauze with his right hand, "Pour some on here." With his left hand on the tumor and his right hand across her body she poured adrenaline onto the gauze. He then placed it over the first gauze on the tumor and said, "We make a good team," She smiled. He continued to hold pressure for 45 minutes until he noticed her body starting to shake. He gazed at her pupils; she was going into shock. He needed help. "Mari, I need to get you some electrolytes and you need some warm dry blankets. Can you reach the phone with your left hand?"

In a wobbly, nevertheless articulated voice she asserted, "Who you calling? No doctors!"

"No sweetie, I'm going to call Pauline. I just can't reach things. I need to have someone reach things."

Mari reached for the phone and said in a calm undertone, "OK," and placed the black portable onto the red-stained blanket above her lap. He dialed with his right hand. Pauline answered, "Hello." Tom calmly replied, "Paul, I need your help."

"What's wrong?"

"Just Come."

There was a silence then Pauline replied, "I'm on my way."

Pauline arrived a few minutes later and walked into the room, "What should I do?"

Tom began giving instructions, "Squat in around behind me and put your left hand on top of mine. See, we have to keep pressure on this." His hand was covered in blood; he wanted to make sure Pauline wasn't going to pass out at the sight. "Hold your hand gently on top of mine. You OK with this?" Pauline seemed calm and willing. A few minutes later he lifted two fingers away, replacing them with Pauline's. "Hold it here. Not too much pressure. That's right. I'm going to get some blankets and electrolytes, I'll be right back." Pauline nodded.

Tom returned with a handful of medical supplies and blankets. He glanced over at Mari. She appeared pastel and weak. "Sweetie, I'm going to change your blankets now." Mari replied, "OK." Removing the wet blankets, he quickly soaked up as much blood as he could in a large sponge and placed the new blankets over her, tucking them in around the edges. He checked the color in Pauline's face. She seemed OK. Opening a bottle of electrolyte capsules, he said to Mari, "OK, take six of these, here's some warm water. Drink lots of water." Mari drank half the glass then put it down, "Sweetie, drink the rest." She peered back at him with a disgusted look and drank the balance. He reached over and pulled down one of her eyelids. Noting how white they were he said, "I'm going to give you a B12 injection."

"OK."

He lifted the blanket slightly exposing her right thigh and proceeded with the syringe. Mari didn't bat an eye.

"OK, here's some iron and folic acid," handing her another glass of water.

A half hour later he could see color coming back into her face. Tom and Pauline took turns holding pressure on the tumor for two hours. Then he took his hand off. The bleeding had stopped.

He looked into Mari's eyes and pondered; what was on the other side of them—a little girl riding a tricycle, a beautiful teenager turning heads, an intellectual college girl challenging minds, a mother raising twins, a spiritual older woman, an explorer of depths.... They all seemed to peer back at him.

As the weeks went on the lovers made sure they said goodnight with a kiss, knowing she could hemorrhage while they were sleeping and neither might not wake up.

Mari used to sneak out of bed when Tom was away shopping. She would crawl to some location in the upstairs part of the house, working her way up the wall to a standing position, and go exploring. In early April, she made her way to the computer room next to the bedroom and found Tom's paper he had tacked to the side of the bookcase. It read. "You can't leave without me. We are both water." Underneath that she wrote with an indelible Sharpie marking-pen that soaked through into the wood, "and fire." A few days later he wrote under that, "We will dance any way we can." Soon after that she wrote in pencil, "In your heart."

One gorgeous day in April Tom had returned from his bi-monthly run for medical supplies and entered the house with an armload of medicines and cartons of bandages. Running up the stairs, he entered the bedroom. It was dark and silent. He looked toward the bed; Mari was gone! He panicked, *Had she hemorrhaged? Had an ambulance taken her away?* Then he thought, *Maybe she's made her way to the bathroom.* He checked, no Mari. After checking the entire upstairs he started to call Noni, then hung up the phone. The thought pressed through his mind, *Could she possibly be downstairs?* Diligently he explored every room in the house, calling, "Mari!" No answer. He started toward the downstairs phone. Suddenly as he turned the corner, there she was, curled up under the kitchen counter looking up at him, smiling. Dropping to his knees to match her height he said in a crimped, worried voice, "What are you doing here?" She replied, "I came to take a look at what's down here, it's been so long. Don't you think I look wiser now? I looked in the mirror. I look wiser now."

Staring curiously he noted the thinness of her face, the pronounced wrinkles across her forehead, "Yes, you do look wiser. How did you get downstairs?"

"On my bottom. I scooted on my bottom."

"Why didn't you say anything when I was calling you?"

"I thought I would have to go upstairs again."

Sighing with unbearable compassion he said, "Oh, sweetie, I'm so sorry."

He helped her to the couch where she spent the rest of the day gazing out the sliding glass door into the backyard.

The next day he carried her to the car for what she called her Last Ride, making a nest in the back seat with blankets. As per her instructions, they followed the blacktop behind the airport, crossing a bridge over the river at Stanley to Whitewater Springs Road, a small isolated picturesque road that winds through the mountains to Armstrong Woods, passing out-of-the-way vineyards, gnarly oaks, giant redwood trees and rolling green hills.

Meandering for miles, she instructed the driver to pull over near a grassy meadow of wildflowers by a hillside creek. Observant to the signal to be lifted from the vehicle, he carried her into the pasture and sat her in the flowing grass. Spring was in full bloom. It was as if, for a moment, she had been pardoned from her prison. Glee filled her face with radiance, sunshine emitted from her once dark, partially grayed hair. She had been transported to paradise, some ecstasy known only to those who have lived without. A flock of blackbirds flew overhead, landing in the trees behind her. Blissfully she began to speak, "Look at all this, do you know what this is? I know what this is," Adjusting her long flowered dress, she turned toward Tom and said, "It's me, you silly, in a million other forms, coming and going, frolicking in the sunlight, dying in the night." She rubbed her face and tilted her head back, letting the light reflect off her forehead. She looked translucent in the grass. Then abruptly she said, "OK, take me back to my little nest."

Once on the road again, she had him roll the windows down and kept saying, "I can smell everything! Tom, I can smell e-v-e-r-y-t-h-i-n-g!" As they passed the campground where they had spent their first night almost ten years ago, he slowed and looked back at her. Her eyes were glassy; she pressed her lips together and turned away. They continued slowly, passing the place where the Goddess once whispered the constellations tenderly in his arms. They continued winding down the twisting mountain road to a gas station in Guerneville. Tom stepped from the car and began pumping gas; he noticed the attendant's face as he peered in the window at Mari in the back seat— there was a time when she thrilled and amazed people, now they were deepened in her presence.

Last month Hospice dropped by to introduce themselves, going over the usual stuff about options, what it's going to be like, medicines, phone numbers and such. Now the nurse comes by every couple of weeks. Today's visit seems normal. They're still waiting for her to stop eating, but she hasn't yet. What's curious is the rapport between this new nurse and Mari. The nurse is dressed in bright-colored street clothes wearing a stethoscope around her neck. There is something about her eyes, large and bright, consistently un-forbidding. Enthusiastically she moves to the bedside, reaching out with fearless compassion she holds Mari's hand. She looks earnestly at Mari, wanting her to share her feelings. Appearing almost angelic she says, "Do you believe in angels?"

Mari replies, "Yes."

"Well, I'm your angel for today." They both chuckle.

She went on taking temperature, blood pressure, asking questions about food and water intake, urine output; all the things that the other nurses did. But what made the difference was the way she contacted Mari's soul. She somehow understood that her body was only her vehicle and her spirit would be moving on soon. It really wasn't anything she said, it was more how she was. Just before the nurse left, Mari told Tom to show her the angel book. The book of watercolor angels captivated the nurse. When the nurse left the room, Mari whispered to Tom, "When I die give her my angel book."

Mari had numerous visitors—some came anxiously, others came with compassion, while others were quite open and cheerful in her company; she preferred the latter. Ellen came often, sitting at the foot of the bed massaging Mari's feet. They would have long conversations about *P'howa* and other Tibetan spiritual practices. Noni and Pauline would come to bring food and encouragement and prayers from their path. Her lifelong friend Janet from the hot-tamale days would come every week to bring videotapes and music. Carl and Sharon came respectfully to give her love. Gabriella, who she had worked with at the Artful Eye, came every day, bringing her fresh flowers and funny jokes, driving 30 miles each way. Ritma and Shanti, Mari's old Rajneesh friends, came by every so often to give Tom a massage, relieving Mari from his constant doting. Anila, who had known Mari for lifetimes, and her partner Anunado came as often as they could, to massage her shoulders and tell stories and share silent loving space. Lots of folks dropped off food and were then on their way. Several of Mari's old lovers came to visit. Even Moses, one of her old flings that Tom disliked fervently, stopped by and in the midst of the visit, all Tom's rancorous jealousy disappeared in her presence. Curt Paulson, a remarkably wicked saxophone player and childhood friend of Tom's, came and performed at her bedside. There were times when she would say, "That's enough," but for the most part, no matter how exhausted, she was grateful for every contact.

Days flew by, the calendar turned in the wind. She now required more pain medication and constant monitoring. Tom asked Hospice about a morphine pump. They replied, "When the time comes we'll see that you get one."

Previously, in early May, he had begun to sense the glass cracking. It would come and go, but now he could feel the hammer pounding on the vessel that contained who he was.

On Saturday morning in the first part of May, he came from the shower and picked up his jeans off the bed. As he began to put them on Mari interjected, "Tom, I've been meaning to ask you, why do men lift their heel like that when they're putting on their pants? I've seen lots of guys do that." Tom replied, "I bet you have!" She smiled. He went on, "It's no big secret; when you're tucking in your shirt, by lifting up one heel it keeps your pants from falling down." She replied, "Oh, I never knew that! All these years I wanted to asked someone, but didn't want to seem dumb."

That evening he cuddled up next to her and was reading the traditional bedtime story when the phone rang. It was Russ, their oncologist. He was hoping to drop by Monday morning to see how Mari was doing. Mari replied, "I'd love to see him, I have a couple questions." Russ showed up about 10:00 and performed the examination. The tumor around her scapula had started to die and they were speculating whether she was going into a remission. Russ took Tom into the hallway. Tom whispered, "Do you think she's in remission?" Russ slowly turned his head from side to side and answered, "I believe an artery has died inside the tumor, killing off just that portion. You have to understand that the cancer is systemic. It's in her lungs and looks like it's in her right ribcage. She appears anemic and it may be in her liver. Do you understand?"

Tom looked down and replied, "Yes."

Russ gazed at Tom and went on, "You don't look so good yourself. Are you getting any time away?" Tom looked puzzled and replied mournfully, "How can I do that?"

"Can you arrange for someone to relieve you once or twice a week?" Tom thought for a moment, "Maybe Pauline." He wouldn't trust anyone else to be alone with her, but after the hemorrhage episode he knew he could count on Pauline. Tom thought again, "Maybe Hospice could come in more often."

Russ continued, "Can you call Pauline right now? I want to take you somewhere."

"I suppose so."

Tom made the call and Pauline showed up a few minutes later. Meanwhile, downstairs, Russ began explaining how fun mountain biking could be, convincing Tom he'd be a better caretaker if he took time for play. It was difficult for him to comprehend this. He went upstairs and asked Mari. She replied, "Yes, please, take some time."

"Are you sure?"

"YES, I need some time away from you too."

"That makes me feel bad."

"Look, you silly, it's OK. I would enjoy having different company. It's OK."

"OK."

Pauline sat by Mari while Tom and Russ went shopping for mountain bikes. That afternoon, and once a week for the next couple of weeks, Tom went mountain biking with Russ at Annadel Park. It was short-lived, but the timing was perfect.

A few days later, he had just slid a *Sherlock Holmes* videotape into Mari's TV, and was preparing to shave her legs. He kissed her feet and asked if she had done all she wanted to do. She replied, "Remember the sketches I showed you a few months ago?"

"Yes."

"They were going to be in my children's book. I've been writing a children's story about a little boy put down by his father for everything he tried. Then one day a neighbor realizes the boy's gift and the spell of discontent is broken. Most of it was going to be told through the drawings, but I never got to finish it—maybe next lifetime." She paused for a moment then went on, " I wish I could have done more for children in Mexico."

That night when Tom was coming back from his walk with Didger, suddenly a mother deer and two fawns bolted from the bushes and Didger couldn't help but chase them. The mother and one fawn ran for the field. The other fawn froze for a moment then ran toward the street. Didger was in full pursuit. The little one made the corner at Neo in a full run, looked back and ran right smack into the side of a parked car. It got up and ran across the street and collapsed between the curb and a truck. Tom went over to the baby; it appeared dazed with its eyes open. He brought the fawn into the house and placed it in the downstairs hallway. Running upstairs he spoke out, "Ma, guess what, I found a deer who's hurt, she's downstairs."

Mari replied, "What happened?"

"Didger chased it and it ran into a car."

"Is it all right?"

"I don't think so. I think it has a broken neck."

"O God. Can you do anything for it?"

"I'm just going to sit with her, it's a little girl. Let me know if you need anything? You OK?"

"Yes, I'm going to listen to the radio."

"I'll be right downstairs."

He sat with the baby deer. It died around 3:00 in the morning with its eyes open.

That night Tom dreamt he was on a beach. A large wave was rolling in. It became larger and larger, reaching high into the sky. It crushed over the top of him, pulling him out to sea. As he was about to drown it picked him up and threw him back onto shore. He woke up in a sweat amazed that he had survived the ordeal.

The next morning he took the fawn to the field and dug a shallow grave. Placing the sweet limp body of what was once life, expressing itself in the form of a deer, into an earthen hole in the ground. He covered the grave with dirt and piled up brush. He positioned a piece of petrified wood near the site and said a prayer for its spirit. He was solemn, yet thankful for the moment. He thought, *Was this an omen of what was about to happen?*

Making his way back upstairs he stopped in the hallway and looked intently at Mari from a distance. She had drifted off, holding the *Course in Miracles* in her left hand. He knelt down and kissed her forehead. She opened her eyes. He noticed they were sunken but still bright and full of life.

"Honey, I'm going to make you a fruit plate with tuna for lunch. Do you feel like eating?"

"Just a little. Maybe I'd better take one of those THC tablets." He helped her take the appetite stimulant and went downstairs to the kitchen. There he prepared a dish of sliced bananas alternated with slices of Kiwi fruit, encircling the edge around a small mound of freshly cooked albacore, on a small white china plate and brought it upstairs.

"Are you going to be OK for a little bit? I need to run to Food for Thought and pick up some groceries."

Normally she would take the plate with a little smile. She seemed distant. As he set the plate in her lap she became short and visibly angry.

"Something wrong? Just eat what you can. You don't have to eat it all."

She glanced out the window for several seconds and then began picking at the banana slices. Without looking up she said, "I don't like you taking care of me."

In that instant he felt as though his heart had been stabbed and ripped open. His hands began to shake. They looked at each other. Their eyes locked and grew dark. All that was good and loving, normally making its way to the surface, retreated to the core and stayed fixed in the center of their beings, while they collapsed downhill handcuffed together.

All the brutality and sporadic abandonments of Tom's childhood, the rejections through his teen life, his attempts as a outlaw to find acceptance, his betrayal of his first wife, the infidelities delivered to him by others, his lies for love, all the poorly lit packages neatly wrapped in camouflage wrappings; all he knew to be darkness, surfaced.

All Mari's childhood disappointments, her father's habitual crushing of every creative idea afforded her, every point of self-expression traded in for something that should have been better. The duplicity and blatant infidelity of her first real love, her failed experiments in lesbianism, the devastating disloyalty by the oriental man she considered her mate and spiritual teacher, the games of the Bhagwan, the erotic get-backs laid upon men through out her life; all surfaced to form a dark cloud.

Their shadow selves had become completely exposed in one dark truthful moment. Placing a napkin over her lap, he looked into her brown eyes and saw anger. Time stood still, blank without substance, there was nothing to say, broken only by his calmly spoken words "Would you like someone else to take care of you?" She stared back devoid of sound and continued to fiddle with the banana slices. He left the room without a word and walked to the field and sat by the grave of the fawn. As he walked he felt the drag of a large black cord attached from his stomach to hers. He thought to himself, *For all that we have been through, how could this be?* He sat crouched with his head between his legs and began chopping at the cord with an ethereal axe. Inside the cord were layers of life's darkest experiences, distributing themselves in neatly contained boxes, tiered like an onion. He reviewed the darkness. His intention was to sever the cord completely. He continued to hack away until coming to a place that could not be penetrated by anger. It was glowing.

In an epiphany he realized, in spite of all life's ugliness, he had found the place where their love had retreated. It was resting in the core of their beings, in the spirit, the part that existed in more dimensions than darkness could dream of; it was the love they had for one another from the first moment they met.

With that he looked up at the sky and thanked the Goddess and returned to Mari's side. He laid his head in her lap and whispered, "Why do you not want me to take care of you?"

Mari replied, "I feel guilty; this ever-unforgiving guilt that has terrorized me all my life. I wronged you."

"How have you wronged me?"

Mari went on, "I had a fling, I never told you. Remember we promised to be honest, even if it hurt? Is this what I'll see when I die?"

Tom whispered, "I want to take care of you. I love you more than anything."

In a strong voice, Mari continued, "A few minutes ago I was nauseated by the very contrast of my pain and your gestures of kindness. It makes me angry."

Tom spoke out, "I brought all my baggage to you when we came together. At least you warned me of yours." Mari interrupted, "I didn't show you everything. Neither did I tell you the truth. I kept from you the darkest parts of myself." She took her hand away and pushed his head from her lap. Without looking up he slipped his head back onto her lap and began talking, "You think I didn't know, I knew all along. As much as you tried to hide, I pretended." Mari cried, "Is that supposed to help?"

A sad look came to his face and he went on, "Those parts in me that I'm ashamed of, I knew you knew. All those trips to the garage to take care of my distorted dirty hurt self, I knew you knew. I'm as guilty as you are. Don't you think, all we have gone through, that we've traveled beyond this petty stuff?" He kissed her hand and continued, "I think we should judge our life by its entirety, not any one event. I love you for all that you are, the goods and the bads."

As she replied her voice seemed to be coming from the very space around her, "I've turned off on so many roads I never intended to travel, and now that I look back, I hope I haven't caused too much pain, in searching for myself. I hope that all I have wronged will be right, and grace and love will be with them. I have been given so much in this life."

With that she placed her swollen right arm across his back and they wept. During that cry and in the moments to follow something seemed to be happening that rivaled description. At first it came slowly, and ended in a white flash surrounding them. As they gazed into each other's eyes they could see all that was good between them; their unshakeable love, their desire to be together whether in body or spirit, every kindness and tender moment revealed itself in a clear luminous tunnel extending outward from who they really were.

She told him she wasn't angry about dying, and that she only felt bad she had to leave the boys and him behind. Past all the shadows cast by the light shining through the ego's arrogant reservoir they had discovered the truth resting in the depth of their love, a friendship only spoken of by the masters of the world. It wasn't "forgiveness," the ego wasn't even involved. It transcended all pardoning. In that moment they had discovered a Divine symbiosis, a perfect understanding of purpose.

That night Mari started talking about how she wanted some way of having her loved ones involved in the preparation of her body, the making of the casket, the cremation—and most of all, she didn't want her body to be touched or transported by anyone who was not near to her.

A few days later Ellen showed up with a lady named Jerry Lyons, founder of the Natural Death Care Project. She showed the lovers how to navigate a maze of paperwork and red tape to make Mari's wish come true. Later that week, state law made Tom, Mari's legal funeral director.

Not long after that, two Tibetan spiritualists, Rigdzin Tromge and Jigme Tulka Rinpoche, started coming by to sit with Mari. They had heard of Mari through Ellen.

On May 6th Tom was lying on the bed beside Mari when he heard a knock at the door. He went downstairs. There, he stood face to face with a man seemingly not from this world, almost ancient at first glance. Against the backdrop of the neighborhood, Tom watched the man for several seconds. There was something fierce yet compassionate about him. Tom shifted his head and peered into the slits of the man's eyes. The man wore a broad Indian red rag belt around his waist with a tassel at his right hip. The wide belt made him appear strong and fearless. The man stood not more than 5'8" tall. His untamed hair was silver-white bordering the sides of his balding head. His boots were colorful and made of brown leather, disappearing under a reddish-brown skirt. A golden silk chemise covered his upper body. Hanging loosely around his neck was a gold medallion on a red string. Over that he wore a crimson-embroidered robe trimmed in black with long sleeves, opened in front. Everything appeared handmade. His features were weathered and distinguished. He looked to be in his late 70s. His Mongolian eyebrows slanted upward. His white Fu Manchu mustache and long beard made him appear primeval. He stood in a relaxed pose with fearless black eyes and said nothing. The two men stood eye to eye for a moment. Tom's brain did not know how to compute the meeting.

Suddenly the man stepped around Tom without a word and began climbing the stairs. All Tom's senses told him that whatever it was, it was good. Just as Tom was closing the front door, Rigdzin Tromge appeared. Tom asked her who the man was. Rigdzin replied, "That's His Holiness Chagdud Tulku Rinpoche from Tibet. He has come to bless Mari."

As they walked up the stairs Rigdzin went on, "This is very uncommon he should come." As they entered the room Chagdud Tulku was already standing near the bed gazing at Mari. He turned to Rigdzin and said something in a foreign language. Tom asked what he said. Rigdzin translated, "She is a spiritual warrior, emanations of the Goddess *Tara* are close within her."

Tom knew a little about *Tara* through conversations he had had with Mari and other encounters from his past; however, there was much he didn't know, and would find out later.

Up till now Mari had not been aware of the man standing before her. She had been sleeping and was awakened by his words. She caught a glimpse of him and turned her head fully to meet his eyes, then broke into tears, exclaiming, "There's a saint in my room, Tom, there's a saint in my room." She continued to weep, placing her hands, as best she could, in *pranamah* across her heart, making eye contact with the holy man. He began uttering in low melodious tones. He was praying.

After a short time he stood silent and remained that way for 45 minutes. Afterwards he turned to Rigdzin and spoke again, glancing over at Tom. Once more Tom asked Rigdzin to translate. She replied, "His Holiness wishes for you to make 21 *Tatsa* (small statues made from human ashes) from Mari's cremation ashes in the form of Green *Tara*. When you have completed this he will take them and place them in temples in India, Tibet and Bhutan. Also, at the instant of her death, there should be *P'howa* (the transference of consciousness at the moment of death to states of higher awareness) practiced." Tom remembered the term from a meeting with Ellen, but never believed it would come to pass. Rigdzin went on, "While making the *Tatsa* you are to recite the *Tara* mantra." As suddenly as the holy man came, he left. Tom ran down the stairs to keep up with him. He climbed into an old rickety car filled with monks and Tibetan children and momentarily looked back. Tom reached his hand through the front window of the car toward the master. Their hands locked together and they smiled. Tom said, "Thank you, it meant so much to her." The holy man nodded and looked away, signaling the driver to move on.

A few nights later, Tom noticed Mari walking to the bathroom. She insisted on making these pilgrimages on her own. She was thin, thin like a concentration camp survivor. Not long ago she walked with pageantry like a racehorse in her long hourglass figure—sophisticated and beautiful. Now her gait was slow and labored as she made her way hand-over-hand along the wall. He knew soon it would be her last walk.

On June 8th she went on oxygen. She wasn't ready to die yet and the oxygen provided comfort to her struggled breathing. The boys set up the oxygen pump in their room to keep the noise down. A long clear hose reached from their room to hers. They took turns changing the filters and keeping condensation from building up in the line. In case of a power failure, they assembled an oxygen bottle backup system and kept the pump in good working order. They had become young engineers in charge of the lifeline.

Tom noticed that her bedsores were getting worse. No matter how often he hand-bathed and turned her, the pressure sores wouldn't heal. He started using hydro-active dressings; they helped some, but it wasn't until he got an alternating-pressure air mattress that the wounds got better.

It was the 12th of June and Mari was growing weaker. Her pain seemed to be increasing, and her breathing labored. He'd called Hospice for a morphine pump but none had arrived yet; they're waiting for a return. As he sat by the bed changing her bandages, Mari looked over with sad eyes and began to speak, "Time is getting near, don't you think?" Reluctantly he replied, "I don't know." Sternly she responded, "I think so." They were silent for a while, then Tom said, "Do you have any words of wisdom to pass on?" Immediately she said, almost matter-of-factly, "Don't worry, be happy." He asked, "Do you have any regrets?" She thought for a moment, then responded with remorse in her voice, "The way I've treated men." They were silent, then she went on, "Tom, I want to tell you…" He interrupted, putting his fingers to his lips; a moment he would regret for the rest of his life. He knew she wanted to make a deeper confession and he stopped her.

He was weak, weak from watching her waste away, inch by inch, day by day. He felt he would break into a thousand pieces, one more tap on the glass and he would break. She just looked at him with sad eyes and pressed her lips together as if to say, *All right, I understand.* They held hands and looked at each other until she drifted off into a slumber.

That night, just before falling asleep, he rolled over and kissed her and said, "Goodnight sweetie," like he always did. Just then he felt her break. She broke into tears and wept openly. He kept repeating, "I'm sorry." He knew; she knew; anytime now he could wake up in the morning and find her gone.

The following day, Father Dennis of St. Rose Church came and gave her the last rites in the presence of Noni and Pauline. Even though she was no longer a practicing Catholic, she accepted the rites respectfully with an open heart and love. In the afternoon the boys came. She had Tom leave the room while she spoke her last words to her sons.

Afterwards the boys went downstairs and she called Tom into the room. "I would like for you to make a list of things that I want you to do when I'm gone." He swallowed as he reached for paper and pen. He sat on the bed near her and said, "What would you have me do?" She went on, "First of all, do you still want to live?" He replied, "I think so, yes I still want to live— I've taken it day by day. I have no idea what's going to happen to me without you." "Good," she replied. She went on giving dictation as if she were merely leaving on a trip.

- "Be watchful and love the boys, help them to find their way, but don't crowd them. Even though they appear not to know, inside they know.

• Bobby (the boys' biological father) will probably come. If he comes, help him, do not interfere with his efforts to be reunited as the father of his sons. Step back and allow him his turn. Love him if you can.

• Stay close to my mother.

• Make my memorial as I have lived. See if Nana will come.

• Sing a song for me at the memorial.

• At the end of the ceremony I want Dan Taft's brass band to play. See if you can get Kurt Paulson to come play the sax.

• When the boys turn 25, flip a coin; one boy will get the drawing I did when I was five years old and the other will get Baba's (Mari's grandmother) purple ring.

• Give the little green chair to my mother.

• Janet gave me a small bamboo chair, see that she gets it.

• Keep my house plants alive for as long as you can.

• Make sure that I am cremated, don't let anyone talk you out of it.

• Do what you can for Marisol.

• Take my ashes and put some on the Hill, give some to my mother and the rest you can make *Taras* and give to people.

• Take care of yourself and don't forget to eat.

• Make sure Ellen gets paid.

Will you do these things for me?"

"Yes, sweetie."

Mari went on, "Also I have marked my black address book with a star beside each name for people that should be notified."

Tom replied, "OK."

He felt a fog roll in around him. It didn't seem real that they should be talking this way. He noted everything she said, not fully realizing the impact it was having on him.

The next morning she asked for a cup of coffee. Tom brought it to her in her little blue baby cup. She was so weak she could barely bring it to her lips, "I can't even hold my little blue cup anymore." She made her last entry in the checkbook on June 9th.

June 16th, she was hardly eating. That morning while he brushed her hair, she asked if he would call a physical therapist to the house, in hopes it would help her walk to the bathroom. Compassionately he massaged her legs and feet, and reluctantly told her that the cancer had wasted away her legs, keeping her from walking. She seemed to understand and canceled the idea. In the afternoon he found her sleeping peacefully and looked at her face for a long time. In a whisper he uttered, "I love you" as if she were leaving on a train never to return—unable to wave goodbye. Beside the bed he found two poems she had written during the day.

WHAT IT'S DONE

Look what it's done to live-
drowned by a sea of
blackberries & rhododendrons
(unusual neighbors)
backed by a house
that cut off all light.
Look how it's stretched &
distorted wandering
reaching for two years
to be touched by the light.
Its long spindly
calla lily stalks
unrecognizable & yellow.
It lives
bloom aching
the ancestral dawn to be
felt again.

WHEN I DIE

When I die there'll be
no mockingbirds outside
the window
shades drawn and
no glimpse of morning light
flooding pink azaleas.
There'll be no strawberries
& cream borne by strong
weathered hands that whisper
I want you here.
The playground will be silent
the dog away somewhere.
When I die there'll be
no sweet voices downstairs
being twenty with their ladies
no lawnmower smell
or carved rocks
no silent moments
no peace.

MQ

The following day, he noticed her ability to speak was failing. She could say "Yes" and "No" but didn't have the energy to go much beyond that. She motioned Tom to bring his ear near her mouth. He whispered, "I love you." Faintly she whispered back, "I love you too. Water every ten minutes." The next morning he read to her a note he had written the night before. It would be their last verbal communication.

MARI MY LOVE

You're over there and I'm over here, it's how we started out. I did not come to you a whole person. I came to you broken. God guided me to you. I knew you before I saw you. We have always strived to be together and for the most part we got to have that dream. I didn't get my dream of you and I holding hands and walking the flowered wilderness forever, what I did get was to be made whole again. You have taught me about unconditional love, you taught me not to be possessive (jealous). We look for God together it seems in everything we do. Even though your body looks like it's failing, you still have that presence about you that I fell in love with. If you go, prepare a place for me in the light. I have no idea what it's going to be like without you – I've taken it day to day. I'm always with you, that part of me that knows. Peace, Love, Strength and Wisdom to you. Thomas.

After he read, she smiled, motioning his ear nearer her lips and whispered, "You should write more often." Those were her last words.

The next day per instructions from Ellen, Tom performed a preliminary *P'howa* ceremony and blessed Mari in preparation for the Journey. The following day Mari took on a paralysis; only facial expression and arm movement remained. She stopped taking food or water. In the afternoon, Pauline and Noni came to visit. Tom had just finished changing the bandages, and was having a conversation with Pauline and Noni while sitting on the foot of the bed. Suddenly Mari started waving her arms, moving her head from side to side and rolling her eyes back in her head. Pauline tried to comfort Mari by placing a pillow under her head. Tom shouted at Pauline, "Don't you see? She's turning blue." Pauline moved away as Tom moved over Mari's face. Removing a pocketknife from his pocket, he placed the handle between Mari's teeth, pulling her tongue forward, clearing the airway. Turning to the window he shouted, "My God, she's swallowed her tongue," as if God should have had mercy on his helpless sweetheart. He recalls, "It wasn't pretty. I didn't want her to die like that, turning all blue suffocating to death." Mari resumed normal breathing, but her fingernails remained blue. From then on he placed her head turned to one side to keep her from swallowing her tongue again.

Later on, downstairs on the patio Tom apologized to Pauline and asked her forgiveness for such an outburst. Pauline hugged him; he could tell it had hurt her; amazingly, he could feel love coming from inside her.

Mari could no longer speak, but could tap her fingers for "yes" and "no" to his words. When she lost her ability to tap a finger, she moved to blinking her eyes. One blink for "yes," two blinks for "no." They continued communicating like this till she could no longer open her eyes.

Mari has now been in a coma for two days and Ellen has come to sit with her. Tom asked Ellen if she would watch Mari for a little longer, he was going to take a shower. Ellen lovingly agreed and Tom went into the bathroom. When he stepped in under the water, it came to him in a charged explosion—a grief deep inside was coming up. It ran up his spine like a freight train exploding in his head. He cried out openly. Something within him gave permission to cry, now that no one could hear his screams over the sound of the rushing water. Suddenly Mari's face appeared in front of his face. She was angelic, younger and more beautiful than he had ever seen her. Her presence stayed for only a minute, but in that minute his cathartic grief vanished. Mari's spirit remained with him during the breakdown and was gone again in a bat of an eye. After drying off, he came back in the room and Ellen said, "While you were in the shower Mari opened her eyes and was looking all around the room." Tom replied, "How could that be, she hasn't opened her eyes for two days?" He noted the event, but didn't tell Ellen what had happened in the shower until later.

The boys came that evening and joined them. Adam and Jacob took turns wetting her lips with swabs to keep them from cracking. Later in the evening Mari's lungs began to fill with fluid. Her breathing was labored and gurgling. Removing the stethoscope from his neck, Tom looked at her and got a mental message, *Not yet.* Then he went to the garage and brought up a foam rubber tilt-ramp that she had purchased the year before for exercise. He placed the tilt-ramp on the bed and covered it with blankets. The boys helped him gently move her body to the ramp, but in the process she cried out and opened her eyes. He felt so bad he almost couldn't bear it. In that moment he thought, *Have I gone too far?* With her head downhill on the ramp, all the fluid in her lungs ran into her throat. He removed the fluid every half hour with a turkey baster.

She was now breathing easy again. He spoke to her, "Honey, if you can hear me then hold your breath." Tom turned to Ellen,

"Did you see that?" Ellen replied, "Yes." Tom exclaimed, "She held a breath!" Ellen was surprised and replied, "I saw it." Tom went on, "Mari, if you can hear me, hold a breath for "yes" and breathe normal for "no." Then he continued, "Mari, I love you, do you still love me?" which was a dumb question, but that's what he said. She held a breath.

They continued to communicate this way for several more days. Pauline and Molly Brennan, (a RN in training and Mari's cousin) arrived at the house on the 25th to help with the morphine "pushes." Without a morphine pump, they now had to manually inject 5cc of morphine epidermally every half-hour. Tom kept a running record of morphine intake and watched her breathing, keeping a balance between normal relaxed breathing and the pain expressed by the tension in her brow. He didn't want to lose the curve; if he gave her too much it would suppress her breathing, if he didn't give her enough she would go into pain and he'd lose the curve.

He needed some relief. He'd been up 36 hours with hardly any sleep and was asking Molly and Ellen, an experienced LVN, to take over, when the phone rang. It was Hospice. They were returning his call to tell him, "No morphine pump." Numb with fatigue, he didn't argue. He told them he only had enough morphine for "pushes" till morning. They reluctantly told him; they were out of morphine but would call around to hospitals and see if they could get more. Hospice ended the conversation by saying, "You keep saving her life. You need to let her go." Tom became short, "Maybe I should have let her bleed to death, maybe I should have let her suffocate and turn blue. Maybe I should have let her drown in her own saliva, but it didn't seem right. I'm hoping her body will just shut down in peace. I'm concerned about the quality of her death. I asked for a morphine pump a month ago and you said we would have one. I'm now having to move the injection site every three hours because her skin circulation is giving out..." Overall, Hospice had been supportive and kind during the entire process, but they didn't know how to respond to Tom's outburst and reiterated they would continue their efforts to find more morphine.

After hanging up the phone, he checked with Molly and lay down on the couch downstairs around 3:30 AM. Pulling a blanket over his head, he closed his eyes and drifted off. Waking up, he looked at his watch; it was 4:05 AM. He lay there staring up at the ceiling, praying that she would just go peacefully. *My God, hasn't she suffered enough*, he thought. He lay there another half hour until he thought he heard her calling his name. She was gurgling so loud he could hear her from downstairs. It sounded like, "T-O-M." When he arrived at the bedside he knelt down next to her and said, "I'm here sweetie, honey I'm here." She appeared to calm down at the sound of his voice. Molly said it sounded like she was yelling something but couldn't make it out. Somehow they had lost the curve. With a stethoscope he listened to her lungs. He looked over at Pauline and then at Ellen, then slowly looked away. Mari was getting ready to go. He gave her a 10 cc muscular injection and watched her brow relax. Her breathing normalized and she continued to breath normally for another 30 minutes. After that, her breaths became farther and farther apart.

She took her last breath at 5:11 AM. Her heart continued to beat a few more minutes and then stopped. To him, a golden explosion occurred in the room at the time of her passing. There was a peace, the kind that's present after a storm. She died with her eyes open on June 26, 1996 at 5:15 AM on the same day her passport expired.

Tom kissed her on the forehead and Ellen closed her eyes. As he held her hand, he thought, *Of all the atoms in the universe, these atoms, these molecules, these cells are holding this hand and these atoms, these molecules, these cells are holding this hand. She's going home.* He began his prayers for her journey and Ellen immediately induced the *P'howa* with a loud scream. Ellen and Pauline went downstairs and Tom held Mari until dawn's first light. He kissed Mari on the forehead and went downstairs and hugged Pauline, Molly and Ellen. Soon Pauline and Molly went home and Ellen came upstairs and sat with Mari while Tom went for a walk in the field.

Mari always remained a mystery; it was one of the things that made her so beautiful. It wasn't until this walk in the field, under the oak tree, that he understood for the first time the meaning of the screen-divider they had made nine years earlier: Her older self, watching her younger self, dancing on the bow of a boat from the shore. The thousand steps to heaven, her wave goodbye at the top of the stairs and him sitting under a great oak in the grass, alone in the moonlight with an eagle flying overhead—painted on three silk panels by her in the form of a screen-divider.

After he returned from the field he and Ellen began washing Mari's body. Suddenly Tom picked Mari up and started walking toward the shower and was stopped by Ellen. Ellen thought perhaps they should simply give Mari a sponge bath on the bed. Tom agreed. When he rolled her body over to clean her back he noticed it was all black and blue. He was upset by the sight and asked Ellen what she thought it was. He got mad at the tumor and before Ellen could explain, he opened his pocketknife and was preparing to cut off the tumor under Mari's arm when Ellen stopped him again. She told him it was normal for the blood to pool up in her back like that after her heart stopped beating and if he were to cut off the tumor her body would bleed out and make a mess. Again he agreed and drifted off into a memory.

We loved being on the road together and just sitting on the back porch was enough. There was something that made me whole, something that overlapped us whenever we were together.

After bathing her body they brushed her hair and Tom dressed her in the silk dress he had given her when they were first going together. He placed the matching butterfly belt around her waist and fastened her beaded Huichol ankle-bracelet onto her left ankle—the one she was wearing when she walked in the door at Linda Wren's house nine years before.

While he was dressing her, a thought came in. He remembered, *In February, just four months earlier, while rubbing her feet she had said, "In the summer I will give my dog a bath." She never did. She never showed any fear, even unto the end; so amazing she was.*

Gabriella and Shanti Devi showed up later and put lipstick and mascara on Mari's face and painted her fingernails. Gabriella kept adjusting Mari's fingers so they looked like she was "flipping the bird." Tom didn't like it, but thought later that Mari would have chuckled. Afterwards Tom placed Mari's hands across her heart and put a flower there. He kept her body on the bed upstairs for three days. During those hot summer days people came and sat with her in prayer. At no time did rigor mortis set in or any odor ever emit from her body.

On the second day, people were coming and going, bringing things, food, and items to make the casket. The house began to look like a beehive with every worker knowing exactly what to do with no one in charge—at least no one visible. That afternoon Noni and Tom stood on the front porch. Noni said, "When should we have the memorial?" Tom thought for a second, the words *Tuesday Lobsang Rampa* flashed through his head and he replied, "Tuesday, we'll have it on Tuesday." Noni nodded and went off to start the arrangements. People would come up to Tom and say things like, "How many people, I'm lining up the food." Tom would reply, "Oh, maybe 300" and not even know why he said it.

On the third day, Paula Camacho who Mari had worked for in Calistoga and Noni, Pauline, Adam, Jacob, Ellen, Theresa, Dan Taft, Henry Métier, Molly, Jane, *Teta* Nevinka, Patti, Gerry, Shanti Devi and Gabriella came to be with Mari during the making of the casket in the backyard. Paula just happened to drop by with 50 gallons of rose petals. The casket was made from strong cardboard and painted with designs sacred to Mari. Her closest friends and relatives worked all day designing her carriage back to the elements.

Afterwards the boys carried the casket upstairs. Together they gently lifted their mother's body into the cardboard casket, laying her to rest on a bed of rose petals, and carried the casket downstairs into the front yard. Adam and Tom crossed her arms over her heart. Everyone covered her with roses so only her head and hair were exposed. Pauline, Jacob, Shanti Devi, Adam,

Tom and Henry Métier carried the casket in a procession to the Trooper while her relatives, friends and neighbors looked on. Didger jumped in and lay down beside her. Unfortunately the casket stuck out six inches too far. *Teta* Nevinka shouted, "Use my station wagon." The boys made wisecracks about Tom's measurements, getting him to crack a smile as they moved the casket to the station wagon. Everyone waved goodbye as Tom and Gerry Lyons slowly pulled away.

Passing Laguna de Santa Rosa through the little town of Sebastopol they turned left, passing Luther Burbank's farm, into an old graveyard. Continuing down a narrow road with tombstones lining either side they arrived at the crematorium and pulled around in back. They were greeted by the proprietor and introduced to the man who ran the furnace. Tom, as the funeral director, prepared the necessary paperwork and said his last goodbyes. The cardboard casket was placed in the furnace and the door closed behind her. Through a small window in the door Tom watched as the body of his sweet lady ignited into flame, viewing something he could never have imagined—body returning to dust.

Below is an excerpt from the obituary placed in the Press Democrat:

Mari Quihuis-Sawyer 1950-1996 also known as Shetima, Ma Nirdosh Santosh, Mari or Ma, spent most of her life searching for God in all forms. One month before her passing His Eminence Chagdud Tulka Rinpoche, Jigme Tulka Rinpoche and Rigdzin Tromge visited her. His Eminence said that she was an emanation of Green Tara. The former Chief of Protocol for the Dalai Lama spoke at her ceremony. Portions of her ashes were formed into twenty-one Tsatsa Green Taras and placed in temples in Bhutan, India and Tibet by His Eminence Chagdud Tulka Rinpoche. She gave instructions that a portion of her ashes should be fastened into Tsatsa art in the image of Green Tara and distributed to those who seek Love, Peace, Wisdom, and Joy.

Her memorial began at 3:00 on a warm Tuesday afternoon at Saint Rose Hall. Nearly 350 people attended. Speakers from all paths came across the country to honor her, including Lama Gytsu, Chief of Protocol for the Dalai Lama, and Jaichima and

Rutury, Huichol shamans from the Sierra Madres of Mexico. Many friends and family spoke. Tom sang his promised song and told stories and Kurt played the sax and in the end, people ate listening to Dan Taft's 27-piece brass band.

However imperfect she may have been, for the most part her path was traveled by sacrificing outward situations for the sake of the truth. When she was done she was no longer religious, she had become spiritual. Institutions of men did not move her, only the little truths spoken by the masters of life— very simple to understand, very hard to do.

She was born into Catholicism wanting to be a priest at the age of six. She studied the "self road," Kali, the body beautiful, mindfulness, Tantra, motherhood, Cabalism, Shamanism, Buddhism, Rajneeshism, the Sufi path, Hinduism, Vipassana, Bhakti Yoga and relationship; her journey ended with *Tara*, the Tibetan Goddess of compassion and mercy.

She said, "When you think that all has forsaken you, *Tara* will come. The Divine Mother is *Tara* and Mary and Radha— all love that emanates as the love of the mother (in Nature) is Divine. Find something, anything and be kind to it. Love is the highest thing we can experience on this planet."

17

Musical Medicine

It's been a couple of weeks since Mari's passing and Tom's beginning to feel the walls closing in. His sense of home is scrambled. He's been wandering the last two days, walking the streets at night—lost.

Cars whiz by as he sits on the curb at Mendocino and Fourth downtown, looking at the American flag flying atop the SSI tenant building across the street. With his life's training, he figures he'll be all spiritual and everything, emulating the quintessential Buddha, and accept Mari's passing without attachment, viewing it as just another event in the Universe. He's sure he'll be back to normal soon. He can still feel her presence, but that too is beginning to fade. Turning his head to catch a glimpse of an elderly woman in rags and tennis shoes, pushing a squeaky shopping cart with all her possessions down the white line in the crosswalk, he ponders, *Even though I have a home to go to, I feel homeless, akin to this gray-haired lady in conversation with herself.*

Though he saw Mari's body burn in the crematorium, he passes in front of the kitchen window on his way home from walking Didger, believing he will see her standing over the sink. He's having trouble believing she is actually gone. He's got the idea that maybe if he goes back downtown he might find her walking amongst the crowd.

He parked the Trooper at the bank and was walking toward Mendocino Avenue when he saw a woman who resembled Mari dart into a clothing store, *Oh my God. There she is. Could it be her?* He quickly caught up and slowly entered the store, walking up behind her. The hair seemed the same. Suddenly the lady turned around; it wasn't her. He apologized and walked despairingly out to the street in an attempt to hide his broken heart from the world. Continuing down Fourth Street, he came to the park at Courthouse Square and stood in front of a sign. He was beginning to see things he'd never seen before, even though he'd driven by there a hundred times. Things intended for the troubled and homeless, things that normal people pass by and never register as something for them. The sign read, "The following is prohibited: Riding of Skateboards, Roller-skates, Roller-blades, Bicycles or Motorcycles, Unauthorized Vehicles, Frisbee or Ball Playing, Dogs, Glass Containers or Alcoholic Beverages."

He sits on the cement embankment encircling the park, next to a man in a red baseball cap, and looks around. An older woman carrying a baby doll is lying on the grass, not far away. She keeps talking about how the wolves protect her from harm. A teenage couple with a baby approaches asking if Tom could "Spare 50 cents for a phone call?" He's always striven to be compassionate, but something has changed; he feels everyone's pain. He can hardly bear it. An invisible megaphone goes off inside his head, *Doesn't anyone care about these people?* He reaches into his pocket, depositing a dollar in change into the young girl's hand. Bouncing her baby, she smiles and says "Thank you," and walks away.

Little sounds seem loud. All of a sudden, clanking bottles being drawn from a trashcan next to him by a plainly dressed middle-aged man startle him. Down the way a boy in his 20s is making paper flowers stuck into used Coke bottles, panhandling them to passersby. Tom stares up at the signal pole on the corner and notices paint peeling from the "NO LEFT TURN" sign. A motorcycle cop conveniently concealed behind a parked car waits for another fish. To the side of him, is a proud Indian Vietnam Vet twiddling his thumbs, looking intently into space.

Speakers in the park's trees blast out chamber music to keep the teenagers away. A fat man with a large white beard is talking to a gentleman pushing a furniture dolly with all his belongings attached. Two large plastic bags with used clothes sit near the intersection. The sound of a crying woman turns Tom's head to see a woman with a scarred face fishing frantically through her purse for antidepressants, openly shaking the empty bottle. Tom had enough and returned home to hide.

He spent the next week crawling around on the floor in his own snot, continually crying and eating very little. He was afraid to come out of the house, even to buy food, in fear that the neighbors might see his condition. He would sit up all night rocking back and forth in different corners of the house until the sun came up, and then fall asleep out of exhaustion. Each time he fed the dog, he would say to Didger, "Where is she? It's time for her to come home now."

Most everyone he knows, even the boys, seem to be back to normal. He is determined to go it alone, and is now writing letters to her every day, which has helped considerably. In desperation he has found a woman on the Internet in Yugoslavia named Mari and has written several emails with no response. He's making it from one minute to the next, astonished when an hour has passed. He's losing weight and the ability to do the simplest of tasks. He's been taking Didger for walks at night when no one can see, but is yearning to venture out earlier to catch the sunset.

He realizes one evening, that what made things appear beautiful, was her. It's as if he's looking through different glasses, ones he's never worn before. Occasionally he passes by the rosemary bush in front of the house, picking and squeezing the needles between his fingers. Bringing them to his nose, he says out loud, "O Honey—Albany Sauna." He misses Noni's Spaghetti Night, but most of all he misses seeing Noni and Pauline. He thinks he has to have a reason to go over there.

A month has passed and lately he's been praying for a drive-by. Whenever a car drives by on his walks he imagines the bullet entering his back; falling to the ground in relief. He's no longer afraid to die; he has become afraid to live.

One evening he went to the closet and methodically loaded the 30-30. He stuck the barrel in his mouth and pulled back the hammer. As his thumb moved slowly toward the trigger, thoughts flooded his mind, *What kind of mess am I about to leave for my children to clean up? What kind of departing legacy is this? Hasn't this family suffered enough? What disrespect am I giving Mari's memory, her spiritual courageousness and fearless death?*

Over the next week, both his sons Larry and Adam kept calling and checking in. Possibly Tom's condition was being monitored over an ethereal network, open only to those who could tune in. His daughter Tiffany kept calling for no apparent reason, other than to say hello. People were dialing in, but he'd always say he was OK, repeating, "Oh, I miss her, but I'm doing fine."

Lately he's been going through the cupboards checking the food supply. Most everything's gone. Although he hates going to the store, he's going to have to do something.

That afternoon he got up enough courage to enter the corner grocery store and came back with a box of Quaker Oatmeal.

After noticing Tom putting something in a pan, Didger circled the stove, wondering what his master was up to. Could it possibly be something for dogs, or was it just for dads? Tom cooked for ten minutes, stirring with a wooden spoon, then grabbed the pan and walked toward the sliding glass door leading to the backyard steps. There he sat with pan in hand, eating cereal with a ceramic Chinese spoon like his sweetheart used to do. Tiffany kept coming into his mind. For a moment he lost track of where he was and endearing memories flooded in.

"I made a tree swing in front of the cabin from an old truck tire. Tiffany used to walk down those precipitous chainsawed steps with her little legs, dressed in a tattered bathrobe, shouting, 'Daddy, swing me.' She was three years old.

"Larry and I made a pipe bell and strung it up on an oak branch out in front of the cabin. When I was in the garden working, I would hear the slow repeated gong of the dinner bell sounding through the trees. As I came up over the rise, there she would be standing barefoot next to the great oak, pounding on the pipe bell with a large pot-iron spoon. I would pick her up in my arms and carry her into the cabin, saying, 'You and Mommy got something good to eat?'

"When we were living on the Hill, we started having an annual horserace and picnic. Hill folks would come from miles around to participate in the spring celebration. All the women cooked a big spread and the men would busy themselves marking the route for the race. During the figuring of the route, I put Tiffany on the saddle in front of me and rode out across the ridge. She said to me, 'Daddy, let's go here.'

"One summer we were all out front cutting firewood. The yellowjackets were bad that year. Someone had set a Coke can on the porch and Tiffany picked it up and started drinking. She was too little to realize that the can was filled with sugar-seeking meat-bees. They stung her inside her mouth. I picked her up in my arms and carried her to the pond and washed her mouth out. She kept crying out, 'Bad bees, Daddy, bad bees.'

"Before we had an outhouse, we used a 'slit trench' with a coffee can stuck over a toilet paper roll on a stick. Sometimes the dogs would be there, waiting, gobbling it up as soon as we walked away. One day Bango had his fill and came into the cabin to lie down. Suddenly his eyes turned green and he up-chucked his steamy banquet onto the floor. Tiffany ran over to help clean it up and got it on her feet. She kept saying, 'Bad dog, bad dog,' while my wife cleaned the spoilage from between her toes.

"Tiffany and Larry would always be down in the garden helping us weed and such. Larry would pull weeds and Tiffany would carry them to a pile. When we took our lunch breaks, the kids would usually eat peanut butter and jelly on homemade bread. For some reason the yellowjackets would land and gather on her sandwich. She'd always end up eating a few.

"We cooked on an old wood-burning kitchen stove. My wife would bake bread in the oven. I would cut the right size kindling for what she was baking and Tiffany would carry it to the stove and place it in the burner.

"In the winter we used a large galvanized bucket to bathe the kids in. Eventually we graduated to a small plastic swimming pool. I remember one day, reading Tiffany a story while my wife bathed her. The peace and protection in her eyes melted my heart. It snowed six feet that year.

"Larry and I would cut ice blocks from the pond in the winter to keep our spring hunt fresh a few extra days. We often made jerky and Tiffany would help with the preparation. But most of all, at the end of the day, when the work was done, I cherished hearing her say, 'Daddy, read me a story.'"

All these flashes of his little girl came rushing in. He thought, *Why am I having these thoughts? Am I going to die soon? Is my life going to flash in front of me?*

Several days later he started cleaning out the medicine drawer and found a bottle of liquid pharmaceutical cocaine he'd used to stop Mari's hemorrhages with. Holding it to the sunlight he pondered, *Maybe this could help?* He'd been there before. He went to the bathroom and pulled out a Q-tip, dipping it into the blue liquid. As his hand carried it toward his nose, he stopped. His mind caught up to the somatic reaction and said, *What a disgrace to Mari's memory. If she could see you now, she'd have you for breakfast.* Standing over the toilet he poured the entire bottle down the flusher and muttered to himself, "That was close."

In late July, Tom received a call from Jacob saying that Bobby (Robert, or Beto as Mari called him, Adam and Jake's real father) had arrived from Arizona. He was at a gas station in Santa Rosa and needed help to find his way to the house on Neo. He wanted to come see Adam. Adam was staying with Tom at the time.

Bobby had traveled a long circular journey to come back to his boys. Before meeting Mari in 1975, he worked at the Kaiser open-pit mines as a young man, then moved to Mission Beach, California at the age of 22 where he worked as a gas station attendant. Mari had just returned from a six-month stint in Mexico and was living in a converted chicken coop in Ocean Beach, when she drove her '68 Karmann Ghia into the gas station looking for directions to a Yugoslavian folk-dance class. Beto, a youthful strong innocent Huichol Indian boy, set out to clean her windshield, when the magic began. She left the station and returned, leaving her phone number on a book of matches. Two weeks later he moved in with her, took a job as a tow truck driver and Mari became pregnant. Several months later they moved to Arizona where he worked as a carpenter and truck driver and she waitressed. They were married January 12, 1976 and on February 9th she gave birth to twin boys, calling them A & B, later renaming them "Adam" and "Jacob." Bobby and Mari loved each other but had dissimilar ideas about how to travel life's journey. They considered each other soul mates and were able to dive deep, but had different destinations. They divorced in 1981, traveling separate roads.

Mari set out on her voyage to find herself in India while raising the twins, and Bobby, missing his family, broken-hearted, never forgetting the love, set out on a path of "when men were men." He was looking for success, independence and adventure to test him to the extreme. From Arizona he moved to a boomtown in Texas and worked as a carpenter/ironworker/roughneck in the oil fields, later moving to an offshore oil rig in the Gulf of Mexico. From there he moved to Okalahoma City until the oil crash of 1981, when the oil-shale boom suddenly went bust. He left Okalahoma bound for a boomtown in Louisiana, then back to Arizona where he picked up the building trade once again and worked for 14 years as a journeyman carpenter.

He never lost hope that sometime in his life he would rejoin his boys. Mari and he stayed in touch over the years sharing snapshots of what it was, but for Bobby, all those years were empty years and now they were about to be filled.

Tom put Didger in the Trooper and headed for Steele Lane and Mendocino. There in the back of the gas station was an old Chevy pickup with Arizona license plates, loaded with tools and possessions for survival. Behind the wheel sat a muscular man with a mustache and red bandanna. He turned as Tom pulled in alongside. He looked cautious and dazed from being on the road. Thoughts of old stories told to Tom by Mari flashed through Tom's mind. One story in particular kept hammering in his brain. They were not good, but he continued, out of respect for Mari's memory to connect with the man behind the wheel. Bobby followed and they drove to the house on Neo. When they entered Adam was sitting on the couch. Adam stood, greeting his father in an embrace, then sat back down. Tom stood in the hallway giving them space to reunite. The story wouldn't go away. Suddenly, Tom interrupted their conversation, "Beto, let's take a walk." Bobby replied, "OK." His voice was kind and soft from seeing his son. Tom's voice became stern, "I want to talk with you, let's go to the field." Tom opened the door and they cut across the grass to the sidewalk. Adam stood at the hearth with a concerned look as his two fathers walked away side by side.

The air thickened. Halfway to the corner Tom started talking, "Why are you here?" Bobby replied, "I'm here to be with my boys." Tom went silent until almost reaching the corner and then burst out aggressively, "You're the guy who blew up her van with dynamite." *(Years later Tom found out that Bobby never did blow up the van; according to Bobby it was washed away in a flood in Texas, but for now Mari's story was Tom's reality.)*

Bobby slowed his walk and positioned himself two steps behind and replied, "I don't like your tone." Tom replied, "Whatever," and continued walking with Bobby at his back. Tom went on, "Well, did you?" Bobby said, "I don't remember." Tom burst back, "How could you not remember something like that, and what about the way you treated her when you found out about Cecil." Bobby didn't respond. Tom was praying for a fight, win or lose—anything to move him out of his torment.

Tom expected the first blow to come from behind but it didn't come. They continued to turn the corner to the field. Tom walked into the field; Bobby stayed on the sidewalk by the bridge. Tom called, "Come out here." Bobby responded back in a rough voice, "This is far enough." Tom said, "Fine," and walked back to the bridge. The two men stood facing each other.

Tom had converted his grief into anger; now he had a purpose. Just as his emotional adaptation began to switch itself to something ugly he heard Mari's voice whisper, "Love him if you can." He had almost forgotten the promise. By the time he stopped the adaptation, he had reverted to a biker persona and responded, "You're a brother; I know who you are." Bobby came back, "What's that mean?" Tom replied, "You've been there and so have I." Bobby just looked back with steely eyes. Tom, still not quite finding his heart, went on, "I'm not going to help you; you're on your own."

As they walked back to the house Bobby answered back, "I never asked for help. I'm here for one reason only, to be with my boys." When they entered the still-open front door Adam was sitting on the couch crying. Tom had never seen him cry before, even after Mari died. Tom knelt down and put his arms around him. Tom's heart softened. Bobby remained standing as though he hadn't earned the right. Seeing Bobby and Adam apart, Tom's heart broke even more as he hugged the 20-year-old son of both of them. He so wished he hadn't talked that way to Bobby and that Bobby would join them in the moment, but he didn't. Standing, Tom looked at Bobby with soft eyes and walked up stairs to silently cry. Adam called out up the stairs, "Love you Thomas," as he and Bobby made their way to Bobby's truck.

Bobby temporarily set up housekeeping at Jose's (a friend of the boys and surrogate son to Tom) until Bobby and the boys found a place on Lincoln Street. As time went on, Tom and Bobby became friends. Actually they became more than friends; they were now like brothers, helping each other with their common loss. They started hanging out together, telling Mari stories late into the night. Tom and Bobby (who by now preferred being called Pops or Robert) gave each other something that no one else could give. They both knew the Goddess intimately and would often cry in each other's arms. And Tom needed to cry. His chest was getting so tight, it was getting difficult to breathe.

Tom would soon find out how incredibly wise and big-hearted Pops was; the journey Pops had traveled had taught him more about life and spirit than any scholastic endeavor or spiritual workshop.

In the future the boys would venture off and make their own way. Pops would search the newspapers and find a little place on Slater Street near the college. He wouldn't realize until later, when Jake told him, that he had unknowingly moved into the same apartment complex where Mari had lived 15 years earlier, when the boys were babies.

A few days later, under the oak tree, Tom concluded, *Everyone out there is searching for love; their compensations are what everyone sees. Whether they're in the boardroom or on the street, their impressive actions are the result of their inability to find love.* The whole idea of having to impress someone to be loved seemed to sour inside him.

He began making more trips downtown. One day he spotted an old man bending over a grate reaching for a cigarette butt. The man looked up, catching Tom's glance. The man smiled at first out of embarrassment, and then looked Tom in the eye. Tom thought, *Have I been a fool all my life? I can't seem to find anything more important than people's hearts.* They continued to smile at each other, almost turning to laughter, when suddenly a car turning the corner honked at an old lady moving slowly in the crosswalk. Tom looked away to see a rather chubby Jewish-looking man run from behind a hot dog stand on the corner and help the lady cross. The man returned to his stand matter-of-factly and continued to talk to people gathered around him. He was joking and bobbing his head back and forth—everyone on the street appeared to know him.

Now Tom started making more trips to the hot dog-stand, watching the man from a distance performing his kindnesses to those wandering in his territory. Tom was amazed. The man was stern and tough to the bullies and kind and loving to the disheartened. Tom figured he'd found a genuine soul, a *bodhisattva* (a compassionate soul in disguise). He didn't approach the man, but watched him almost daily. He was becoming impressed by what he saw.

One day Tom decided to start cleaning the house, the best he knew how. He had made up his mind to give most of Mari's clothes to girlfriends she had known, and what they didn't want would go to the Goodwill. In the process of going through her drawers he found his father's clarinet. He remembered playing it when he was just a boy in college. Back then he had fallen in love with a girl named Janice, his first real love—so he thought at the time. He was so moved by the newfound feeling that he would go to the handball courts by the college at night, for the acoustics, and play Pete Fountain's, "Stranger on the Shore."

Removing the clarinet case from the bottom drawer, he put all the pieces together, fixed the reed and headed for the shower. He began playing "Stranger on the Shore." It came right out, as if it had only been yesterday. This was good, really good. It gave him the best form of peace he'd felt in a long time. When he felt he could no longer go on, not even for another minute, he would go to the shower and play the clarinet. He thought, *If this works, how about my old accordion?* He scrambled to the garage, shifting boxes around in the loft; there it was, still in its broken-down case covered in dust. He carried it to the house and started playing. For the first time in months he had a moment of fun. He remembered making a deal with his mother when he was seven. If she would stop making him take tap dancing lessons, he would practice the accordion. He became silently overjoyed that she had insisted that he practice—music had become his medicine.

Not long after that, Pauline called. She had an old piano that she wanted to store at the house. Tom was elated, a clarinet, an accordion, and now a piano! He wrote a blues song and played it repetitively. He wrote a round for Mari hoping she might hear it, playing it late into the night again and again. Later he wrote a song called "Kickstand Man" and a piece for his daughter Tiffany, "The Outhouse Song."

KICKSTAND MAN
(Ageless Lady)

She picked me out of trash and made me a jewel,
I was a jokester, just a fool,

I can almost do everything that I can,
just like a biker, an old kick-stand.

How many times have you been through here before,
O ageless Lady, you finally found the Door.

She was pulled from my arms and taken away,
they left me to die, day by day,
O magical Indians and bicycle seats,
walks on the ocean, down on the creek.

How many times have you been through here before,
O ageless Lady, you finally found the Door.

It was down by the jail yard when She walked by,
She looked back at me and said, "Why?"
I looked into Her brown eyes and said goodbye,
She was the Love of my life.

THE OUTHOUSE SONG
(When I was Ten Years Old)

Chainsaw steps, a meadow look, flowers long the row.
A stack of newspapers by the door,
that been read many times before,
a bucket of ash, an old wooden cup
Mama taught us how to flush.

Uncle Willie told me about the widow
that lived just under the seat;
I'd stare at the pictures and the dust on my feet.

Candle-lanterns in the middle of the night,
an old torn bathrobe,
Daddy built an outhouse
when I was ten years old.

The music helped, but the train kept coming into the night. Now that he had passed through what he considered the "worst rapids" there was something even deeper than music. It was the gaping hole in his heart—the void left by her departure. Spreading a portion of his sweetheart's ashes at the base of the oak tree in the field behind the house, he commenced with daily meditation. He prepared to contact his guidance through lessons taught him long ago and almost forgotten. In meditation under the tree he came to a plateau where he could sit in peace. He recalled one of his teachers saying, "Dive deeper, come up faster, it's dangerous down there." He needed to go to the bottom of his pond where years of mud and sediment had settled—all his demons lived there.

One afternoon while under the tree, something Mari had said came back into his awareness, *What she had been trying to teach me all along was, soul enjoys and the ego owns.* He remembers her saying, "Enjoy me, don't own me —you can't own me any more than I can own this body; some day it will break down into a million other things. My soul will go on forever, enjoying it all.'"

Through his pain he's beginning to get bits and pieces of the truth. Immediately he went home and converted the boys' old bedroom into a meditation room, a place where he could go deep, without concern of interruption—a spiritual launching pad.

On one of his many trips to the oak tree he pondered about anger and wrote the following note to a friend in trouble.

"I've been on many journeys; Anger is just another form of Fear, I know it well. Anger is what we get when we don't get what we want. Spirit doesn't burn; ego burns. What we want most of all in this life is Love, and if we can't find it, we will settle for Purpose and if we can't find Purpose we will settle for Power and Respect and if we can't find Respect we will settle for Sensation. I myself struggle through the passages and turns in the road and that's probably why I have so much tolerance for the rest of the vandals of the world.

"If we are lucky enough to find Love even for a moment, it gives us a Place, a vantage point, in which to view life that is different than those who have forgotten. Love allows us to transform Anger.

"One of the illusions of Anger is, it provides us with a sense of real Purpose, allowing us to direct it without conscience at whomever we deem wrong. If we don't transform it, it internally crystallizes as Purpose for our Actions, leading us on its long hideous journey through self-destruction. What is going on in the world right now is but a small example – 'an eye for an eye, making the whole world blind.' Anger begins in the ego very near the soul, and manifests itself outward into the physical like a virus. Ultimately it is the teacher, calling us to action in one of the more painful houses of learning.

"The highest thing we can experience on the planet is Love, it is without Want – it transcends Purpose, Respect and Sensation. Love, Tom"

In August, Henry Métier, a precious-stone sculptor for the Dalai Lama, gave Tom six small *Tara* molds, showing him how to make the prescribed *Tara Tatsas* from Mari's ashes for Chagdud Tulku Rinpoche. Tom spent the rest of the week making twenty-six *Tara* statues and gave them to Jigme for Chagdud Tulku to take to India. In addition, Henry gave Tom two large molds, ten inches high and eight inches wide. Steve and Linda, the neighbors next door, put in a new fence along the property line and Tom used the old wood to make a bench from where he began making *Taras* from the larger molds. The process, prayers, and ceremony he kept secret. He would go on to make over three hundred *Taras* containing portions of Mari's ashes and her blessings, just as he had promised.

The pain comes in waves. One day he feels normal, the next devastated in grief. He's been keeping a diary addressed to Mari. Every day he writes to her, which helps considerably. The episodes are getting further apart but still present. Each anguished moment seems to include all the uncompleted griefs experienced throughout his life. He walks a course not knowing when something, a memory, a smell, will trigger a hollow piercing pain in his chest affecting the way he breathes. It's getting more difficult to cry, which he discovers, is the key to breathing easy. If he goes more than a day without crying, the intercostal muscles around his ribs tighten so tight it makes it difficult to pull in a complete breath, followed by a dull pain in his heart. Something is dying inside of him. He's now beginning to think he will not live out the year and deeds all his assets to his children.

He becomes housebound and doesn't know it. When he ventures out, he can't wait to get back to the house. From his diary of August 10th he writes,

"Today was an interesting day of drop by's. You must have sent your sisters to heal me. Linda Fiori and Penny Chamberlain came over and told me about their trip to England. They showered me with female energy. Ritma and Bronwen also came over and did the same. Then my mother called. Then Ellen came over and invited me to the Furlongs Institute. Today has been such a healing for me to have the blessings of your sisters. I wish so much that you could have been here in body. These are your people of the earth. God bless you and send you Love, Peace, Wisdom and Joy. Goodnight my love, Thomas."

Four days later, Ellen called in the morning. She would be camping at Salt Point on the coast and invited Tom to join her. He found it ironic in that this was the first place that he and Mari had camped, where they sat back to back waiting for the phone booth, where he had felt the indelible feeling of home that changed his life forever.

He decided to take the long way and went up over Tin Barn Road passing the Buddhist temple at Odiyan, on to Stewarts Point, a road traveled many times by the lovers. Eight miles south along Highway 1 he reached Salt Point, pulling into Ellen's camp. After visiting with Ellen, he decided to check out their Original Camp Site, #11, and reenact past moments with Mari. Returning to Ellen's camp, he told her that he had brought *Taras* and Tibetan bells and some of Mari's clothes for a ceremony near the sea. Ellen was excited and off they went in the Trooper till the road ended by the beach.

They packed the ritual items in daypacks and walked along the sand, listening to the seagulls cry above the crashing breakers. Turning east they crossed a meadow of wildflowers near a large complex of boulders jutting upward from the grass. There they climbed to the base of a massive rock and went in around behind smaller rocks that formed a small cave. Tom started clearing rocks from the grotto, making it deeper. Ellen watched in standing meditation while Tom removed a long flowered dress from his backpack. He placed it in the newly made indentation, sprinkling ashes from a small glass container onto its lap. There he placed a solid gold *Tara* given him by Henry, folding the dress neatly into a crevice. In front of the crevice he placed a large *Tara* made from Mari's ashes and covered the indentation with stones he had removed moments before.

Ellen and he stood in front of the site in silence, then began chanting the *Tara* Mantra, "Om Tare, Tu Tare, Tu Ra, So Ha," 26 times. Immediately after the chant, Tom rang Mari's *Dorjee* bell 49 times, one bell for each day she had been gone. A great energy moved through them. Tom began singing "Radha-Govinda" as he placed more rocks in the opening, sealing off the grotto. Energy swirled around, first at the base of their feet, moving up to their heads, and then through them. They turned, climbing down the rocks to a clearing and sat meditating, facing the grotto. Tom could feel it, but Ellen could see it. She described great masses of purple colors surrounding white and pink, then gold, silver and turquoise blue. Ellen saw deities moving up from the rocks. Tom kept hearing, *Worship Divine Mother first, then me.* All loneliness and grief passed from him in that moment.

One afternoon he bumped into another of Mari's girlfriends in the grocery store and figured it was some kind of sign. That night, August 16th, just before dusk he made his way to the field and sat under the oak tree with Didger. Didger explored the grass while Tom prepared a spot at the base of the tree for meditation. He sprinkled more of Mari's ashes in the fork of the trunk and kissed the tree. Sitting in the lotus position he contacted his master Sri Yukteswar in prayer and drifted into the surrounding space. It had been 51 days since Mari passed on.

Tom's awareness moved above the field into the clouds. He could see the neighborhood from above. He looked to the heavens and discovered he was sitting in an ethereal field of flowers. In front of him was an image of the Goddess *Tara*. He began chanting and noticed Mari sitting directly in front of him—behind her was another form of Mari slightly different, then another and another till in the distance sat *Tara* holding her left hand to her bare breast and her right at one knee. Around her were glowing flowers, seemingly suspended about her head. He bowed and kissed the feet of the Goddess, exploding him-self into tiny pieces; reassembling forms of his known body sitting under the oak tree. Deeply moved, he gathered up Didger and walked away from the tree. They danced back toward the sidewalk, crossing the field toward home. Didger stopped at several celebrated pissing spots and pranced down the sidewalk to Neo wondering what his master would be up to next.

It was still light out and Tom went upstairs and stretched out on the bed like he always did when returning from the field. He kissed his hand and rolled over touching Mari's side of the bed. When he rolled back, there stood Mari. She was standing there in the skirt he had cremated her in, adorned with a white scarf around her neck. She did not waver or flicker. She was as real as flesh, and in such detail, he could see the threads in her clothes and the pores of her skin. It lasted for only a few seconds then she was gone. He was filled with joy.

Three days later, Tom decided to wander the streets again. He always parked the Trooper at the bank then walked downtown. He was still having trouble breathing easy and thought people might notice. He pulled his shoulders back and walked briskly, compensating for what was really going on inside. Passing by Wolfe's Coffee House, he headed for Fourth Street and Mendocino hoping to get another look at the hot dog vendor who had so encouraged him back in July. He crossed the street, stood in front of the bank against the wall and observed the scene. From the bank he could see across Fourth Street to

Courthouse Square in plain view of the hot dog stand on the corner.

The hot dog stand was uncomplicated and made of stainless steel. A hand-painted sign of a hot dog dressed in a tuxedo and stovepipe hat was bolted to the frame. Above that, in black letters, it said, "Ralph's Courthouse Classics." On the left, underneath two large red-and-green Hebrew National umbrellas, was a small chalkboard displaying the prices for various types of dogs. Behind the portable metal booth stood a rather large Jewish man with mustache and beard, bobbing about, bending over, standing up, twisting to grab napkins while carrying on a conversation with a man with a cigar in his mouth. To the right was a young lovely dark-haired woman in a short skirt and red low-cut tank top, sitting on a fold-up wooden chair getting a shoulder massage from a white Rastafarian. To the right of her sat a black woman dressed in Gypsy clothes, next to a fold-up table ornamented with colorful coffee cups and a napkin holder. Further to the right was a punk rocker in her 20s with long brown hair, dressed in see-through black lace, sporting tattoos on her legs. To the left of the stand, tucked in the background, were two policemen on bicycles.

After watching the jovial *Hotei* Buddha sell hot dogs for a half hour, Tom crossed the street and approached the stand. He was greeted with a Bronx accent, "Hello brother, dining out today? What can I getcha?" Glancing at the chalkboard Tom replied, "Give me a Giant Classic with sauerkraut." The man replied, "You got it!" A few seconds later the man handed Tom a steaming dog wrapped in wax paper. The man went on, "Have I seen you before? Just passing through?" Tom responded, "No, I live here. Are you Ralph?" The man smiled and replied, "Who's asking?" Tom took a breath and said, "Tom Sawyer." The man replied, "T-o-m S-a-w-y-e-r, bet you've heard that a hundred times before?" Tom repeated, "You're Ralph?" The man laughed, turning to the people around him and said, "That's me."

They instantly liked each other. Tom ate his hotdog and watched Ralph work the street. Everyone seemed to like him—

more than like him, they loved him. He was a grounding presence for everyone around him. Tom asked him if he knew of a shoe repair shop in town. Ralph told him the best shoe repair shop in Santa Rosa was Tate's Shoe Service, just one block away. Tom thanked him and proceeded to Fifth Street. Continuing a little ways down Mendocino, he walked front of a narrow building. As he entered the doorway, on the left was a black man shining shoes. To the right was a long glass counter with stacks of shoes. The proprietor glanced away from the machines running near the back room and moved towards counter. He looked like one of Santa's Helpers, a gray-haired man with rough hands and kind eyes. Tom asked if he could wait while the man put new heels on his boots. The man, who had never seen Tom before, looked up through his spectacles and said, "For you, I could do that. Take 'm off. Be 'bout 20 minutes. Sit down, you can visit with Homer," referring to the shoeshine man by the front door.

Homer and Tom hit it off right away. Tom started reminiscing about when he used to shine shoes in Inglewood and Pershing Square as a kid. Homer listened intently. Tom told him about how he was inspired by the older boys shining shoes and selling papers, eventually getting a job himself pulling a newspaper wagon on an early morning route that paid ten cents. He told Homer how he visited places like the Statler Hilton and the Biltmore Hotel just to spend time in the basement lobbies talking with the shoeshine men hoping to pick up a few pointers, and how when he was a kid he wanted to become a shoeshine boy.

Homer told Tom his story. How he put his children through school shining shoes, finally putting himself through school with a degree in sociology, and worked as a jailhouse chaplain until he retired. Now that he was 80 years old he had come back to what he loved, shining shoes. He had known Martin Luther King and grew up during the Depression shining shoes in Ailey, Georgia where he and Walker Smith (Sugar Ray Robinson) played as kids.

Homer moved Tom. Secretly Tom wished he could go back to the corner where he too once shined shoes. He thanked

Homer and Mr. Tate and headed for home in his brand-new fixed-up boots.

The next morning Tom went to the garage for a private conversation with Ol' Gal. He'd been working on the front brakes and there was deep frustration as to whether he was going to be able to put it back together—he's thinking he's lost his touch. As he tightened the axial bolts with a torque wrench he remembered how Mari used to sit on the bike and hold the handlebars steady, smiling and asking questions. After wrenching up the last bolt he took Ol' Gal for a test run. Pulling out of town, he thought he could hear Mari's voice whispering in the wind, instructing him toward another journey.

Through an unusual set of coincidences, a beautiful lady named Kathleen ended up on the back of Tom's motorcycle. They found their way to a diner on the east side of the city and sat at a table near the window. Over lunch he found out she had been present at Mari's memorial and had come to the house with a friend to sit with Mari while she lay in state. He couldn't remember; there had been too many people. But before the meal was over he had respectfully fallen in love with Kathleen. Her beauty and no-nonsense persona reminded him of someone dear to him. Kathleen suggested Tom meet her husband, who was also named Tom, for a cup of coffee.

Two weeks later the two Toms met for coffee at a clandestine gas station next to the Coke machine in an industrial part of town. Both Toms seemed to have pasts that sprang up between the cracks in the concrete and before long they were buddies.

In September, Theresa, Ellen, and Tom and Kathleen (known as T&K) surprised Tom Sawyer on his birthday with a candlelight dinner at Neo. Good things were beginning to happen if he would just sit up and take note of what the Universe was trying to provide—good friends and people to love. Shortly after that T&K started inviting Tom over for "Movie Night." Soon the two Toms started hanging out and eventually built a tree house in the woods.

On the 20th, Tom and Ellen went to Dog Mountain for Mari's Birthday. Somewhere off Coastal Highway 1 they turned off on a gravel road winding through Pomo Indian land to the base of a mountain. They both carried packs filled with food, water and ceremonial objects. Ellen hadn't been there before and was charmed by the beauty. As they climbed the narrow path winding through cathedrals of redwoods and cedar trees, Tom pointed to the Russian River cutting across the valley below. He commented how he and Mari used to come there every year with Didger and climb to the plateau.

Reaching the top at the last bend, a great oak stood twisted by the ocean wind. Tom pointed to a small cave not far from its base. There he and Ellen placed *Taras* and clothes and personal objects from Mari's life, covering them with stones and brush. They went to a ledge overlooking the sea and sang "Somebody Prayed for Me" and "Happy Birthday." Then they sat quietly in meditation listening to the coastal wind howling through the branches. An eagle cried out, echoing across the rock outcroppings. Tom turned to Ellen, "Mari told me she had lived here in this valley 200 years ago." Ellen didn't respond. Tom moved to the grassy plateau just below where they were sitting and began dancing with Huichol ceremonial rattles given to Mari by a tribe in Mexico, then disappeared, climbing a rock to sit alone. Ellen joined him for the trip back and they put their arms around each other; she too had become Tom's spiritual sister.

In October, Tom and Pops and the boys went to Dog Mountain and celebrated Mari's journey with an ash ceremony, binding the two boys and the two fathers together in an invisible force of growth and caring.

Tom couldn't keep away from the hot dog stand. His Grandma Sawyer had a hot dog stand on Crenshaw Boulevard in Los Angeles when he was a boy, and hanging out at Ralph's Courthouse Classics brought back many memories.

Tom was sitting on one of the fold-up chairs next to Ralph's one afternoon, when a bright-eyed lady who came to get a hug from Ralph smiled at Tom as if she had known him before. Ralph introduced her as Potenza the artist. Come to find out, she worked with the United Nations. Using acrylics, she morphed hearts into the flags of countries on large canvases and presented them to leaders of different nations each year, calling it "Hearts of the World." She encouraged Tom to come to a Christmas celebration at her home with a group of supporters. For some reason not known to him, he brought what he considered his security blanket, his father's clarinet. He really couldn't play it that well, but, like a bull in a china closet, without measuring the consequences of an uninvited public performance, he pulled it from its case and began playing Christmas carols. Two songs and several missed notes later, red-faced, hoping no one had noticed, he packed up the instrument and began to mingle. Before the evening ended he financed Potenza's "Hearts of the World" presentation for Greece.

Tom spent most of the winter holed up at Neo. He kept Mari's plants alive, as promised, and walked the dog and fed the cat, but something's stuck and he still can't breath right. He feels he has to yawn all the time and his chest is tight. It's getting harder and harder to cry and that was his only real medicine besides music. Now even that doesn't seem to work. His only relief is to sit in meditation escaping the world he's in, but each time, soon after leaving the ecstatic state, his body responds to signals left in his heart, where she used to sit. He's trying to get the idea "she is with me in spirit" but it is not enough to satisfy his body's response to the loss.

Thank God for Movie Night.

In March he hung dried pieces of seaweed Mari found two years earlier, attaching them on strings high up in the mulberry tree in the backyard, along with purple ribbons from her clothes drawer. He put her bird feeder and cast-iron chime on a lower branch and then fastened her childhood swing to a large limb running toward the fence. A few days later he took a steel hoop from one of the oak barrels she once planted flowers in and stuck it up in the tree. Occasionally, when he walks out the back door, his peripheral vision will catch a glimpse of the purple ribbons flagging in the wind and for a moment, he believes it's her—for a split second his mind is put at rest.

A few weeks later he needed to go to Berkeley on business and he was dreading the trip. He left Santa Rosa in the Trooper traveling south on Highway 101 toward San Francisco. By the time he reached Mill Valley his chest had become so tight he figured he was having a heart attack. He turned around and headed home. As soon as he returned north he noticed the symptoms lessening. By the time he pulled in the driveway at Neo he felt almost normal. Once in the house, he hugged Didger and lay on the couch pondering, *What was that all about?* His doctor voice answered, "You're having a classical anxiety attack." His patient voice said, "You mean I'm not having a heart attack?" His doctor responded, "No and furthermore, if you don't start to get out more often you're going to develop a phobia and become housebound." His warrior self heard the conversation and piped up, "Pack your stuff, you're going to the Hill for a month by yourself. Get your shit together." His patient became frightened, "Are you crazy? Something might happen. What if there's a medical condition, problems on the road?" His warrior responded, "What if, what if. I don't give a shit; you're going to the Hill. Look wimp, start packing, because if you lock yourself in here, you are going to die."

Tom arranged with Dorothy across the street to feed the cat, checked in with Theresa, T&K and Noni and Pauline and headed north the next day for Oregon. By the time he reached Redding his thoughts were scrambled and his breathing rapid. A big part of him wanted to turn back. At 65 miles an hour he looked over at the off-ramp and pondered. The warrior was right on it, "Lookit, a year ago you wanted to die. Now you're sniffling about being on the road. Die, live, I don't give a damn. If you want any resemblance of a spirit carrying on in life, stay the course." He passed the off-ramp and continued north. At Weed, California he'd become surprisingly relaxed, but it didn't last. As he passed Mount Shasta on Highway 97 it started up again.

Several hundred miles later he rolled into Bend, Oregon, numb and bewildered. The only thing pushing him on was pretending she was sitting next to him with her bare feet up on the dash while he played with her hair. He cut a small locket of hair from his own ponytail and began rolling it back and forth between his thumb and index finger, making believe all the way across the desert to The Dalles, Oregon. There he stopped for supplies and continued climbing out of the valley toward the Hill. When he heard the tires shudder as they passed over the first cattle guard on Ketchum Road, he relaxed and turned to Didger, "You hear that buddy, we're almost home." Didger wagged his tail while keeping his eyes fixed on the road. Winding around in the dark for another 20 miles on dirt roads, through prairies and mountains, they finally arrived at the cabin.

The next morning Tom made breakfast and headed to the outhouse, with Didger following close behind. As he passed in front of the Trooper's bumper near the woodpile on the north side of the cabin, suddenly, from five feet away, he heard the hiss and rattle of a North American Diamondback. He jumped back, waving Didger away from the snake. She was a big one, four feet long. He counted ten rattles, one for each year. Tom ran to the cabin for his snake stick. He usually catches them, letting them go in the canyon about a mile away. Thinking Didger was right behind him, he grabbed the stick from the corner of the cabin and before he could take two steps he heard Didger yelp. With stick in hand, he ran for the snake. Didger was facing it, sitting up on both hind legs with his front paws in the air. Tom knew right then he'd been bit. Dragging Didger away from the snake and checking his right front paw, Tom found the entry wound. Removing his T-shirt, he made a tourniquet just above Didger's elbow. He put Didger in the back seat of the Trooper and sped down the hill towards The Dalles as fast as he could go.

When he reached Lookout Point he was in cell-phone range and placed a call through Information to the nearest vet. He knew it would be another 45 minutes before reaching the little cattle town and asked the vet if he had anti-venom. The vet said he didn't have any, but would go to the emergency room at the local hospital, get the anti-venom and meet Tom back at his clinic.

By the time Tom hit the blacktop at the edge of town, Didger was foaming at the mouth, breathing rapidly, and limp. His eyes rolled back in his head, his right leg was swollen up the size of a quart Mason jar and his chest extended out past his lower jaw. A few more minutes and Didger would go into convulsions and die. Tom pulled in front of the vet's and was taken right in. He placed the limp body of his buddy on a stainless-steel table and stood back. The vet immediately administered an injection of antihistamine and adrenaline and started an IV drip of electrolytes. The vet then placed a few drops of anti-venom into Didger's left eye, testing for an allergic reaction to the serum. Didger's eye remained un-irritated and the vet proceeded. Slowly he injected a few drops of the serum into the IV line every five minutes. Within 30 minutes, except for the swelling, Didger was up on all fours as if nothing had happened. He spent the night at the vet's and Tom went back to the Hill.

When he arrived the snake was still there. Tom walked to the cabin, loaded his 30-30 Marlin and walked back to the snake. He explained to the snake he was sorry, "My grandchildren are coming in the morning." He didn't want to take the chance of the snake disappearing into the grass if he tried to catch her. Taking careful aim he blew off the head of the reptile. It was a big gun for such a small animal. He searched for the head, knowing it could be poisonous if stepped on barefoot; he only found bits and pieces.

The next morning Tom's son Larry arrived with his children, Damon and Natalie. They all pitched in and built a stone-pile grave marker for Mari on the northwest pasture overlooking Mount Adams, just as she had wished. Tom placed some of her ashes there while the kids gathered prairie flowers from the meadow. He and Larry said prayers and Natalie placed wild irises on her grave. That afternoon they all went to town and got Didger. Larry stayed on for one more day. That night they made a campfire in front of the cabin and Tom told stories to his grandchildren of what it was like for their father growing up in a log cabin. How they had all slept in a tent for seven months when Larry was a boy, cooking over a campfire while building the place. They talked about horses and harness and hard work. Larry told them the same ghost story that Tom had told him when he was a boy; about the Daffodil Lady up on Shelton Ridge who could be heard screaming across the canyon on moonlit nights.

Tom and Didger stayed for three more weeks on the Hill. Everything that he and his sweetheart had done there, poured back into his heart. He went to a remote canyon on the south side of the property and sang endlessly to her. Afterwards he wrote this poem:

Angel on the Ground

Passers-by wonder if you're coming by tonight.

They sat up all day on a dusty dirt road on Sunday watching a child play with a box and wondered.

Your tricycle still sits in the street near Coddingtown, played with by time.

The lady in a far-off town next door wonders if her husband will live through the night, up at all hours, holding her elderly body waiting for first light.

I look at the heavens and wonder what is moving, earth or sky, there are no answers to why.

Pieces of flight not moving through time hold me in you.

I think I'm the wave and you're the sea,

someday I'll get it,

you are me.

What he went through in those three weeks is beyond description, only that in the end the tough-love warrior was right.

Back in Santa Rosa he dried the snakeskin with alum (made from oak balls he found in the field behind the house), sea salt and flour paste, and fashioned the rattle to the back of a hat that he wears to this day.

His house needs cleaning and he could use a good sit-down dinner. Most of the time he dines standing up over the sink or squatted on the back porch eating out of the same pan he cooked in. Wieners and beans are his mainstay.

A few days later at the hot dog stand he met a lady. Her name was Leslie. She's kind of a tomboy. Part of her reminds him of someone. She's on-call and may go out to sea at a moment's notice. She studies the Kabala at night and sells hot dogs for Ralph on odd days. She's a professional cook and has traveled the world. On her last voyage she was the cook for 12 men on a seagoing tug out of the bay of Alaska. Tom hired her for six weeks to cook for him and provide perspective on how to clean the house. She hadn't worn a dress since she was a little girl, so he gave her several of Mari's best dresses. She was a very deep lady and deeply misunderstood by the mainstream. She was what he needed, to find some sense, some momentum for the domestic role of householder. Before she came, he lived in his two-story home as if it were only a shelter. He lived mostly out of baskets and cardboard boxes in a four-bedroom house filled with dust-covered memories.

Now he shares his time between working on medical software and being a clinician at a naturopathic clinic, hoping activity will dull the pain.

Thank God for Movie Night.

Tom loves it, because when the movie's over Kathleen always opens the floor with questions that inevitably take the conversation deep into the heart. She's not afraid to travel any terrain no matter how light or dark. And seeing his buddy Tom sitting next to her, loving her so deeply, reminds Tom of when he and Mari sat like that. What he sees in Tom and Kathleen encourages him to go on.

In June of '97 he tried his hand at dating. He went out with an astrologer, a flute player, a massage therapist, a florist and an artist. Through no fault of theirs, several months later he was confused and disheartened. Mari was the baseline and no one could fit the mold. He could find parts and pieces in this woman and that, but never the total.

He gave up on the idea of dating and spent months wandering the house not knowing what to do with himself, moving in and out of present time. Sometimes he can be so in the moment he can sense the molecules of a dragonfly's wing in full flight, fast frozen in time, and then the next, the slightest tap will carry him off to some far off memory.

One afternoon he walked to the driveway and picked up the newspaper. As he carried it to the backyard he kept snapping the rubber band. He sat on the back steps and removed the rubber band, snapping it one last time. Suddenly he was carried off to 12 years old. He was on his Schwinn bicycle riding down the sidewalk at 15 miles per hour. He reached into the basket on the front and tossed a paper toward a house. It spun through the air in slow motion landing on the porch some 30 feet away. It was a good feeling—he could live here for a while.

In October, Potenza invited Tom to a friendly poker game at her new home in the valley. There he met a stunning Jewish Gypsy lady from Forestville. Infatuated with her long dark wild hair and boundless energy, he made several attempts to woo her to no avail. In early December, Potenza sent him an invitation to her annual Christmas breakfast, noting that the Gypsy Woman would be there. After several casual meetings fraught with romantic background chatter, her fear of "he's just a redneck biker" wore off. She asked him up to her posh estate nestled in the woods outside Forestville. She lived there by herself on enchanted holdings deep in the forest where she kept a secret garden. She practiced white witchcraft at night and taught school during the day. They became "boyfriend girlfriend lovers" for about nine months, reverting to "brother sister friends." Now he understands how Mari maintained old lovers as friends. He had somewhat accepted the idea, but never really understood it until now.

In April Tom's buddy, and his son, Casey, along with Tom and Gabriella went to the Hill in Oregon. Planting trees had been a tradition started by Tom and Mari years ago, and now it seemed like the same people came each year to celebrate the earth by putting their hands back into the ground. Larry and

Kim, Tiffany and Curt, David and Shawn, Kim's mom, George, all of Tom's grandkids, and now, three new souls, three old souls. That year, they planted 2,000 ponderosa pine trees.

After returning from the Hill the medical software company was starting to roll. They had naturopathic evaluation systems operating in 11 clinics in five states. Tom acquired investment capital from a friend and the company grew at a smooth pace. Ellen arranged to put on seminars for local doctors and interest was increasing, when Tom's partner decided he didn't want to do the seminars and furthermore "was no longer interested in selling the system." He told Tom a few days later that what he really wanted was to have a system for his clinic, but didn't care to sell the system to other doctors and moved to dissolve the company. The investors suffered a substantial hit and Tom lost six years of work.

A week later, T&K and Tom along with Don Hyde met up with Lionel and Victoria for the Bob Dylan concert in San Jose. In the afternoon they gathered around an isolated group of tables off the main ballroom in a fancy hotel. It just happened that Tom Sawyer and Victoria sat next to each other, meeting for the first time. They seemed to hit it off right away. Victoria was beautiful in body, mind and spirit, and had tremendous intuition. She told Tom about his journey and that Mari was still providing guidance from afar. They talked for about an hour before leaving for the performance. Once there, they entered the musician's entrance at the side door of the venue. Noticing Tom's reluctance with the glitter of the scene, Victoria grabbed his hand, pulling him out front through a flood of guards and music personnel.

After the performance they all went backstage. Victoria and Tom huddled in a corner discussing the spirit world, while groupies scurried about ogling the celebrities. She told him things about Mari that no one could have known, except for Tom. She said that Mari's father had passed before her and was still hanging out. While people were milling in the midst of superstar greatness, Victoria took Tom under her wing, tuned into his heart and offered the kindness of a spirit's connection.

Tom's meeting with Victoria inspired him to find a psychic and two weeks later he met a lady named Nancy Tonilli.

Nancy told him, "Mari is thankful you gave the ring to her cousin" Angela, and a whole list of mind-blowing details that no one knew. Nancy went on, "I keep seeing gourds and bright colors. Did Mari plant gourds? She keeps saying thank you about the gourds. Does that mean anything?" Tom replied, "Yes, the year before she died, she planted African gourds in the garden. I put them in the garage to let them dry out. Last Christmas I sanded and painted the gourds and gave them to her relatives." Nancy continued, "OK, that makes sense, she's saying thank you for that. I'm seeing shoes, maybe sandals. Mari is holding a heart symbol. Do you do something with her sandals—touching your head?" Every day, Tom placed his forehead on Mari's sandals and prayed; no one knew this, no one.

Prior to Mari's passing, it seemed like every psychic the lovers ever went to, gave them general information, and if details were provided, they usually turned out to be wrong. But now through the help of Victoria and Nancy, Tom was open again. Nancy told him about a box located in the house on Neo that would contain a taped message about Mari that he hadn't heard. He found the tape where she said it would be and began to listen.

The tape was a channeling for Mari, six months prior to her passing. Keep in mind that the channeler had never met or spoken to Mari before the taping. Below is the exact transcription (imagine an East Indian accent):

"Namaste."

Mari replies, "Namaste,"

followed by silence...

"If we could basically live in a world that was not full of frills and distractions we could begin to find some of the depth and meaning and purpose we've been seeking for thousands of years. But the natural circumstance of life often lends itself towards surface elements; things that hold our attention, that grasp us, that keep us from going deeper. So we spend a great deal of our time focused only on the outer distractions. Every moment of life affords us depth. Sometimes we resent it. Sometimes the experience of having to live so much in the moment, so much with the purpose of the moment, it can be trying on us. But the truth is that for many generations people have been trying to experience truth. To be in the moment, to live these more depth-full times and when we have an opportunity that gives us the grace of that experience, where we are not so concerned about the up and down of the wave on the ocean, we are more likely to seek what is the ocean all together, then this is a tremendous opportunity.

"So I think that you are in a very life altering experience, something that yogis pray for, something that if people knew they would want it. It's the knowledge that we cannot live forever. We have a place where the mortality addresses the issue of the moment and that experience becomes precious, that we cannot be holding to frivolous experience, that we cannot for long get caught in minor distraction, because there is all too much to learn about from the depth of the moment. So this period of time is transition, this moving into a depth of the self, a knowledge of the self at a very deep level of taking life not lightly, but taking each step as important, each breath as precious, is a tremendous opportunity and believe it or not, even though we wonder why these things happen to us or why we are having this experience it is such a tremendous opportunity that we if we could see the whole picture, would have gratitude. We would have gratitude for what we are given in the experience of each moment. So I feel for you, you are as I said in an opportunity.

"There is time for you to figure out what you haven't figured out; there is time for you to play because that is certainly part of the depth and the picture of life, and there's enough time to say goodbye to the things that you need to say goodbye to, and there's enough time to realize the things you want to realize. But the most important thing is to take each day as if it is a blessing and when we can do this even when each day is not necessarily the way we want to feel or what we want it to look like, then we are really emerging into that path of transcendence. We are allowing life to become a teacher, very quality teacher and it keeps us very focused on the moment. So there are many blessings upon you, you have a never ending band of angels that flies around you that blesses yourself and your family, and so there is a great deal to be grateful for and yet in the experience there is the whole spectrum of what a human can experience, yes?"

Mari replied, "Yes."

"So welcome, tell me what questions you have?"

Mari asked, "I wondered if you can, if you had any guidance or help for my children during this time, knowing, watching their mom being so ill and realizing they may lose me soon, if there was anything that you could suggest that I could help them?"

"I think I would recommend that they write things down. I recommend that you write things down. I would recommend that everyone documents every experience whether they want to or not. You know, some things we don't want to document."

Mari interjects, "It's so hard to get things down on paper—there's so much going on."

"Yes but I…"

Mari continues, "changes and…"

"Yes, but I do think it becomes, as I said you are in a extremely important phase and as I said many yogis pray for this opportunity."

Mari responds, "Oh yes."

"…and it's just an incredible place."

Mari says, "I can see why."

"So to be able to document it, it will remain with them for the rest of their lives. It will be a way for them to look at the transition that they will inevitably go through, various kinds. And really an opportunity for you as well, to leave behind something that you feel is very important, which is the best part of yourself.

Mari said, "So you recommend writing and documenting?"

"I recommend writing. You know, now and then, it is important for families to talk, but I don't think is as important, if it happens it happens. If you want to you can do it. But it's not as important for your family, I think what's important is just to have the experience and what oftentimes happens, for instance, in the birth of a child we think 'This is so incredible— for all of my life I will remember these moments.' And then two weeks later we start to forget, three weeks later we start to lose that incredible place. So when we document it we can go back to it, we have a trigger that helps us. So I feel more than anything just to have some documentations, maybe pictures, maybe tape recordings if you resist the writing, maybe videos, but basically just, you know, it's similar to having a spiritual teacher. When someone has a spiritual teacher they want to experience the spiritual teacher as much as possible and this is, oftentimes, a problem; the devotees want to be every moment with the teacher. This is because they are representing something that is so important to us. We want to hold to it, we want to learn as much as we can from it. So the spiritual teacher often leaves writings or lectures or messages here and there, because the spiritual teacher cannot be with us every moment. So we must take the experience and utilize it in our lives. So the energy that you're with right now is very much like a spiritual teacher. It's a blessing to all those who are around you."

Mari replied, "Yes."

"Because it tremendously breaks down the immediate boundaries which we use to separate our selves from life and makes us completely open and vulnerable. And that's the way. The only way to realize God; is to be completely like a child, open and vulnerable and there is no nonsense, there is just truth. So it's very very important energy."

Mari said, "Yes. I've had some difficulty writing. It seems like I'll feel all these things or I'll awaken to these things, and by the time that I would write them, it all seems just so natural, so obvious."

"Yes, to you."

Mari said, "Yes."

"But not to everyone who reads it."

Mari replied, "Maybe not. I'll try, it's a good suggestion. Any guidance for at the time of death or preparing for death?"

"Well, it's a very good question, I wish more people would ask this question. They're so busy in life we do not consider the energy and the movement. I think for you Mari, the most important to embrace it with joy, to embrace the living with joy, to embrace the transition with joy, because as I said, a band of angels watches over you. And life is incredible, you have lived an incredible life, you have brought to this body many experiences, some neutral, some positive, but very much brought life to this body, it's only a body. It's like, some trees grow and they seem to go on forever and ever and some trees grow and they're not around for a very long time, but the essence of the tree and the beauty that it brought, everything that it brought to the planet will live on and on and on. So for you, the living is about truth. Your whole life, this whole journey has been about truth and has taken you in various studies and I think here you are encountering the most amazing way to realize truth there is, which is the experience of the moment. So life gives you support, death is not something we do alone. It is such a frightening thing to many people 'cause they think there is nothing anybody can do to help us through it, but just as we are supported with every single breath in our body, we are also supported as the breath leaves the body. So just embrace it with joy. You will be greeted, you will be honored, you will experience the likeness of your body, you'll be freer, you'll find friends, you'll find joy, you'll find the experience is very easy and you want to seek the light, you want to seek the primal sound, you want to seek the highest energy that you can experience and then that carries you over the threshold into basically merging with light."

Mari said, "Is there anything I can do for this tree, this body, is there any way that I can help it—be stronger or with less pain or fear. Is there anything I can do on the physical plane that would help?"

"Well observe it, because it is a vehicle, it has served you as a vehicle. It's a very good time to listen to anything you might not have listened to, so it's a good practice especially when you're just laying down, just observe it—from a gratitude perspective 'thank you, anything you want to tell me' and listen to it pretty regularly. Listening will help because we open to inside what the body might need or what the body might be telling us. As far as a physical regime for yourself, it's really a day-to-day process at this point. So listen, one day you feel it's very important to have light, you know, where you're attracted to light, to sound, another day you may find the need to enter deeply, some days it may feel good to stretch, some days it may feel good to lie, every day's different."

Mari responded, "That's true. In the moment."

"So you have to listen and pay attention to the moment. I think in general I would stick with foods that are fairly warm. You want to enjoy life, so that doesn't mean to avoid all foods that you enjoy that are not warm, but I think that you'll probably feel stronger if your basis is soups and grains and very warm foods."

Mari said, "OK. I have a lot of fire inside I feel, you think I should make attempts to cool that down like with aloe vera or something like that. 'Cause I notice there's a lot of fire—I just can feel a lot of heat inside?"

"I think it's an indication of movement, there's a lot of energy moving. It's a very alive energy in your body, it's almost like all the molecules are very very busy, so they're all moving around quickly. So it's a quickening experience that translates into heat—so what can you do about that. I think the coolness I recommend is the stillness, the meditation, the tuning into the body, the visualization, the bringing of blessings—I think that tends to slow the energy down more and therefore does not create as much heat."

Mari responded, "OK. All right, I think that's all the questions I have. It's all written down."

"Well, basically I would say that you are an incredible woman. Just as there are those who have loved you and have embraced you in your life here, there are those who love you and will embrace you as you continue to live without the tree.

In the meantime enjoy every moment as much as possible, learn from it, grow from it, because you leave behind an incredible experience for those that you love in doing in this way and the opportunity to share with someone that we love very deeply, a passing, a transition, or a death is an incredible blessing. Most people are in such fear that they will lose the person that they love and yet oftentimes the choice becomes then, someone will leave in order to give the blessing of what that transition is. So this is one of those things, you are blessing many and you're an incredible person to make that choice because it takes a tremendous amount of strength to be willing to do that and to serve others as part of the karma of our life. So take one day at a time, smile as much as you can and just seek to embrace enjoyment because bottom line that's all there is."

Mari said, "Yeah—that's true."

"I think that you'll hear bells at the time of your passing and you spent a lot of time in your past life—Buddhist temples. So there is a conscious connection of spirit to bells, so look for them."

"OK.'

"I think they will help to guide you, all right?"

"All right."

"Do you have any more questions?"

"No, I don't."

"Well then, God bless you, may you live in peace, may life continue to express the peace of your tremendous spirit. Don't give up hope, all of life is meant to be a teaching and you're in the midst of one of the tremendous teachings that we can ever have—so gratitude, 'cause the creator watches over us always, all right."

Mari agreed, "All right. Thank you and thank you for this work."

"Namaste."

"Namaste."

After hearing the tape, pieces of what he had learned through life began surfacing in his mind. He could feel something good growing inside again. The friendships he established were giving him profound souls to reflect off of, and providing love to fill those vacant spaces in his heart where Mari used to dwell.

In September his buddy Tom asked if he would record a song with him that he'd written when they were up planting trees on the Hill. Tom wanted him to play the accordion in a song about a woman from the Old West. He spent two weeks practicing the part. Then one sunshiny day in October, he pulled through the security gate at Prairie Sun Studios. Passing the chicken coops to the right, he stopped to let a mother hen usher her baby chicks across the road, then drove around in back. He wandered through the converted poultry barn/recording studio, looking for the control room. He could hear in the distance, what seemed like a blacksmith banging on a piece of steel with a sledgehammer...? Someone found him wandering the halls and took him by the hand to Studio A. Placing a headset over his ears, they said, "Stand by, get ready to play." The first take was bad—he couldn't hear himself play. They weren't feeding the sound back to his headset. They tried again. This time it was better. He looked up through the control room window to see his friends Tom and Kathleen clapping. That was all he needed. Something in that moment gave him a confidence he hadn't felt since Mari.

In November T&K and Ellen and Tom went to listen to Tibetan bells in San Francisco's Castro district. Music now fills those parts he longed for from his past. Nancy told him music would be coming back into his life over the next two years.

In December Tom and Louise, an accordion-playing friend of T&K's, went out to buy new accordions together. They stopped off in Cotati where Tom used to live in a water tower when he was first going with Mari. They went to the Mexican restaurant where he used to walk for his daily burrito. Over lunch, Louise, an eccentric intelligent woman with a dry sense of humor, cracked a smile. Then smashed a paper-straw jacket from her soft drink on to the table and balanced the saltshaker on its edge using her secret sugar-granule method. Followed by her live worm trick: She dipped the straw into her Coke with her right thumb cupping one end, releasing the liquid onto the accordioned paper-straw jacket, causing it to come alive, expanding outward like an earthworm crawling across the table. She turned to the waiter as natural as lifting a spoon and asked for another straw, repeating the process. After lunch they went to the house of an old accordion man associated with the Cotati Accordion Festival. There they bought twin accordions.

Tom started playing the accordion in the square by the hot dog stand once or twice a week, attracting passers-by to Ralph's Courthouse Classics.

Thank God for Movie Night.

That Christmas he played the accordion at Noni and Pauline's Christmas dinner. Afterwards everyone retired to the couch in front of the fireplace. They watched TV, which fascinated Tom because he had his cable disconnected a year ago. After the football game the boys and Pops left and Tom set back to watch the fire. Although he loves being there, sitting in the house where Mari grew up is sometimes haunting for him. He feels Mari's in another part of the house and will be coming out of the bathroom soon. He heard water running in the kitchen and turned. Mari always helped with the after-dinner dishes. As his head rotated toward the sound, there she was standing in front of the sink. His heart expanded into his throat and uncontrollable tears ran down his face. He watched her for several minutes. Abruptly she turned to grab another plate from the counter, and then he saw—it was Michelle, Mari's niece. From the back she looked exactly like Mari; even her body language was the same. Turning, Michelle caught Tom's eye. She shut off the water and walked toward him, smiling, and sat down on the couch next to him. She put her arms around him and said, "I know."

With family and friends he had found a safe harbor. The wind moved in and out of his sails, breathing spirit back into his life. He remembered saying the line to Mari, "Why are you being so nice to me?" She answered, "Because you're letting me."

In April 1999, he started thinking about what Mari had said about Marisol. Mari had started sponsoring the little girl when Marisol was five years old and now she was 11. She lived in a village 400 miles south of the boarder and Tom kept getting feelings he should pay her a visit. Many letters had gone back and forth since Mari's passing and he continued to sponsor Marisol. He asked his buddy Tom, who spoke Spanish, if he would help him take a set of picture book encyclopedias on animals, written in Spanish, to Marisol and accompany him to meet her family.

The next thing they knew they were on an airplane headed for Ciudad Obregon, Mexico. FAI (Foundacion de Apoya Infantil, "Save the Children" in Mexico) met the two Toms at the airport and took them directly to a day camp outside of Ciudad Obregon where 600 children were dancing and making paper baskets. Luis Leyva from FAI introduced Marisol to Tom Sawyer. Marisol showed the two Toms how to make baskets from rolled-up newspaper. They ended up buying a truckload of watermelon and everyone ate *sandia.* The children crowded around them and asked their names. They said, "Thomas and Thomas." The kids giggled and yelled, "Oh, Tomás y Tomás." Through the gracious help of Luis and Anna Leyva, the next day they drove 90 miles across the desert to the village of Alamos. On the way they passed a large rock formation where a 100-year-old shrine had been built to the Mother of Guadalupe.

They met Marisol's six brothers and sisters and their parents, who live in a little government brick house about the size of a bedroom and do all their cooking outside on iron plates heated by wood. When the Toms gave the encyclopedias to Marisol, she immediately shared them with her brothers and sisters. Tom said, "It was easy to see how much the books meant to them from the joy on their faces." Marisol's mother, Tomasa, told them that her husband, Jaime, played the accordion for a living and asked if they would go and see him play at the local cantina. Of course as musicians, that was heaven for them. It turned out, Jaime had been playing the accordion since he was 12 years old. He and his group of musicians put on a performance that touched the deepest part of the two Toms' hearts.

In the tiny town of 6,000 people, who mostly farmed, providing there was enough rain, the children were not only hungry physically, but mentally as well. As the two Toms walked through the village, they started talking about things that they could do that might benefit the children. They ended with an idea of starting a library for kids.

They went to Lazaro Cardenas del Rio, the school in the village, and met with the principal, Juan Zoilo Lopez Delapaz and Maye Corral, head of children's services for FAI in Alamos. They found out that neither the school nor the village had a library. They spoke with the principal about starting one. He said that the school would be happy to provide a building to house it. At that point they decided they would start a nonprofit organization to build libraries for children in Mexico and the village of Alamos would be the first project.

In August 1999, they received an official letter from the school board of Alamos, Sonora, Mexico stating that the board was providing a schoolroom to house the library. After forming a non-profit, calling it "Tomas y Tomas" which literally means, "Drink and Drink," they began raising funds by putting on plays. With help from Rosemary Ward and Wild Child Productions they produced two plays written by Susan Hunt, *All I Want is Serenity and Some Really Good Mascara* and *He's Got My Car and I Have No Lipstick.* Through the success of these shows, and private and public donations, they got enough money to purchase 1,100 books written in Spanish and headed for Mexico. *The rest of the story can be found at www.tomastomas.org.*

In June, Tom's buddy asked him if he would transport a piano to Los Angeles for some kind of gig. Tom Sawyer's son Jacob, along with a bunch of guys from Jake's rugby team, loaded the piano into a U-Haul truck and Don Hyde and Tom Sawyer hit the road south. On the way they ended up telling long stories and arguing about whose dress style was the most attractive to women. That night they bunked at a non-English-speaking dive in North Hollywood and Don showed Tom the town.

The next morning Don hung out and Tom took the piano to the prescribed address; someplace called Center Staging in Burbank. He entered the parking lot of what looked like a football-field-size production studio, a far cry from the converted poultry barn he had recorded in a few months earlier. As instructed, he parked the truck in back near two large doors and walked around to the office. As he passed through the set, he couldn't believe his eyes. Crews of 30 or more were constructing tracks that circled the central stage, carrying large cameras that moved about on wheels. Larger cameras mounted on massive hydraulic booms sat on opposite sides of the tracks. Bays of sound equipment under test sat to the left in the enormous hall. Hundreds of lights lay on the floor for mounting in the overhead. Cords and cables were strung everywhere. Stopping to ask for directions, he continued toward the office.

As he approached, a woman behind the desk wearing a headset and mouthpiece glanced up, "Can I help you?" Tom stood there in T-shirt and dirty Levis with tattoos exposed, looking homeless as he replied, "I'm with Tom's crew." "Oh," she replied, stopping what she was doing, "We better get you a laminate." Tom didn't know what that was, but waited to see what she came up with. Stirring through a drawer she said, "Oh, here it is, we only have one. What's your name?" "Tom Sawyer." Looking him up and down she said, "OK, let's see some ID." When he showed her his driver's license something shifted. She hung the laminate around his neck as if he had been knighted and got on the phone, "Tom Sawyer is here!" Within seconds two men showed up escorting him to a loading dock. Inside they opened the huge bay doors suggesting he pull the truck in. A few minutes later four more men showed up and began carefully unloading the piano. They treated it like a priceless ceramic from the Ming Dynasty. Once unloaded, Tom stood at the keyboard and went through the octaves. To his surprise it appeared to be in tune.

It was beginning to dawn on him; he was about to see a side of his buddy he'd never seen before. A large man who appeared to be important came over to the piano and announced himself, "Are you Tom Sawyer?" Tom looked up from the keyboard and replied, "Yes," and continued testing the keys. The man said, "Are you a friend of Bill's?" "Bill who?" The man looked puzzled and said, "I'm sorry, I was thinking of someone else." Satisfied that the piano was in tune, Tom shook the man's hand, climbed in the truck and drove back to North Hollywood.

Back at their motel he and Don decided to visit a few places on Hollywood and Vine that Don knew about. They were sitting in a corner restaurant discussing the move when Tom said, "So we pick up the piano tomorrow and head home."

Don said, "Aren't we going to the show tonight?"

"What show?"

Don snapped back, "Tom's show."

"You mean we're invited? You mean that whole thing is for Tom?"

"Yes."

Tom went silent for a moment and replied, "Well, yes, but they only had one laminate."

Don said quietly, "That's OK, you go, I'll hang out here."

Tom replied, "No, we'll both go and if anyone asks, I'll say you're with me."

Don agreed. One hour before showtime they entered the office at Center Stage and made their way through a wave of busy people running around in all directions looking like something big was about to happen. Tom and Don stood against the wall in the back lot behind the stage and watched the scene. Security personnel were everywhere, testing their walkie-talkies and going over logistics, while movie stars and entertainment executives lined up in the cold outside the gate waiting to be part of the audience. Don was standing, shifting from side to side, puffing on a cigarette like a European and Tom Sawyer squatted against the wall jailhouse style.

Fifteen minutes before show time a security guard approached in a cocky manner, "Who are you guys, what are you doing here?" Tom moved from his hunkered position unzipping his jacket as he stood. When the zipper exposed the laminate, VH1—Storytellers—Tom's Crew, the guard almost fell to his knees. He backed away, walking backwards, muttering apologies as he disappeared into the crowd that had built up around the gate. Tom noticed the guard saying something to a plain-clothed lady with a walkie-talkie.

The word spread. As people walked by, they smiled and nodded as if the two scruffy characters leaning against the wall had become instantly important. The whole thing humbled Tom; he hadn't felt those feelings since Jumby Bay—to be deemed instantly important by association. Tom and Don entered the set, a theatre in the round, and sat three rows back from the front. A few minutes later their buddy entered the stage amid hundreds of cheering fans. Soon other backup musicians entered.

The maestro of musical contraption gave a paramount performance as the cameras rolled, filming for VH1, and bright lights appeared out of the dark from every angle. For a moment Tom Sawyer felt foreign. He couldn't relate to the man on the stage; he only knew the man as a friend, someone he could tell his heart to. The feelings moved in and out, touching him deeply, expanding his knowledge of who the man was.

After the show Tom and Don went backstage. As they approached, record company executives and security staff surrounded Tom and Kathleen. Tom Sawyer wasn't sure how to approach the musician. He glanced over and connected. Tom waited for Tom to finish a conversation with Epitaph Records then extended his hand in congratulations. His buddy ignored the handshake and opened his arms.

18

*"Get down on your knees
and brush your blues away."*

Gerry Rafferty

Shine Mister?

People, mostly women, were calling Tom asking for *Tara* statues. Several art shops and Goddess outlets wanted them. He continued to make *Tara* statues on the bench out back. It became a spiritual practice.

One day, on one of his trips to the garage for more cement, he stopped to talk with his motorcycle when he spotted a wooden crate stuffed in the corner behind a tennis racket covered with spider webs. Mari had used it years ago for flower arrangements. It still had the label on one end, "Tasty Treat Washington Asparagus." It was the right shape, but needed a little reinforcing. He looked over at Ol' Gal and said, "Well, what do you think?" Answering, he replied, "Yes, I think so too. It's the perfect box." He rummaged through the shelves in back trying to remember where he saw that piece of wooden dowel a week ago. Muttering, "Ah, there you are," he gathered his carpenter's tools from the back of the Trooper and began to go to work.

An hour later, he walked from the garage carrying the box by its new handle and set it on the back porch. Standing back to take a better look, he exclaimed, "Yes. You're the perfect shoeshine box." He liked the feel of it and walked around it several times, "You will do."

Earlier, while searching for the dowel that became the handle, he remembered spotting a special aluminum container with a black screw-off cap. He remembered how Mari liked to carry the little bottle in her backpack. It would now become the urn for his special clear polish he called "secret sauce." He already had some brushes stored somewhere in the house. Rummaging through the upstairs bedroom closet he found them in a box. Noticing Mari's shoe rack still hanging on the closet wall, he began to cry. "O sweetie, we need to give these away."

He grabbed the box and ran downstairs to the back porch, smiling at all the little finds. Digging through them, he discovered two jewels right off—a genuine Cadillac Star horsehair brush and a larger 100% horsehair brush made in China. Under some rags, at the bottom of the box, he uncovered a Star 100% horsehair applicator made in Brazil, then two more of the same, followed by a real (made in the USA) Esquire Shoe Dauber. Then came the thing that made him the happiest, a Panetela Largas cigar box from Honduras. He opened it and found a toothbrush, a few dimes, quarters and a couple of nickels. He figured it was a good sign and continued outfitting his newly-crafted shoeshine box. He made a list of things he would need to get started: shoe polish, lots of shoe polish; some black leather dye for side-soles; and buffing rags. Then he thought for a moment. He remembered Mari getting upset when he used one of her massage table face-guards as a buffing rag. Those, he recalled, made the perfect buffing rags.

Back into the garage he went, flipping open a brown wicker basket filled with sheets and various massage paraphernalia. Halfway down, there they were, two massage face-guards. He asked Mari for forgiveness and ran back to the shoeshine box, folding them carefully into one corner. Didger kept coming over and sniffing everything, wondering what his master's newfound energy was all about.

He needed one more thing, a shoe stanchion for people to place their feet on while he shined their shoes. It came to him, Didi used to have one. He called Noni and asked if he could use it. She told him, yes.

He jumped in the Trooper encouraged and excited; it was all coming together. He picked up the stanchion from Noni, gave her a big hug and set out for the shoe repair shop, where he knew he could find genuine Lincoln shoe polish. There he purchased an assortment of colors and a bottle of black leather dye with applicator. He now had everything he needed to start the little business and rushed home to put on the finishing touches.

In the back yard he set the shoeshine box and stanchion next to each other by a bench under the mulberry tree and stared at them. He noticed that the stanchion had brass hinges on it. It dawned on him, *It opens up.* He jockeyed open the latch and found various shoeshine paraphernalia along with a small can of Bright & Shine brown shoe polish, made in Jamaica. He seemed curious; *Wonder where Didi got this?* It made him reminisce about his days with Mari in Antigua.

He needed a sign, something he could attach to one end of the box that would tell passers-by how much it cost. He pondered, *I don't want to charge a lot.* Then he remembered he used to do a shine for two bits, 25 cents. "That's it," he said, "25 cents." Didger looked up, like he understood.

The next day Tom went downtown and found one of the locals who frequented the hot dog stand, named Tugboat Billy. Billy made a fashionable 8" x 11" plastic-coated sign that said, "Shoe Shine 25 Cents," and Tom tacked it to the shoeshine box on one end. He was ready.

He started shining shoes on a Wednesday at the hot dog stand and is now going once a week when the weather's good. It keeps him in touch with the street and he feels he's providing a service. Because the price is only 25 cents, homeless people can afford a shine. He works on everyone, bag ladies to bankers. It's become a *sadhana* for him and it feels right, shining the shoes of the homeless, seeing them walk away a little taller.

A month later, for bread and butter, he's started a small web design business out of the house, working for artists and non-profit companies.

On September 22nd while shining shoes, he and Tugboat Billy (William Cosgrove) got to know each other a little better. Billy, a colorful discard on SSI, who made his way to Santa Rosa via Oregon from the Bronx, told Tom his story.

Billy was a tugboat captain at the Long Island docks back in the '60s. He had traveled all over the world on a seagoing tug, making stops throughout the Caribbean, and at one time was stationed in Kingston, Jamaica. He was injured in a maritime accident and had to retire early. He sold all he owned and set up a cabinet shop in Beaverton, Oregon. Several years later he came down with emphysema. He lost the business and moved to Sonoma County to escape the cold. He ran out of money in Santa Rosa and was forced to go on SSI to survive. Now he has a small graphic business he runs out of the tenant building across the street from the hot dog stand, but has to keep it secret or he might lose his SSI—he's locked in. Billy makes stationery and cards on an antiquated computer and sells them to passersby. He made a portfolio, showing his work to people that came for hot dogs, and lately had picked up some nice printing jobs, but all underground. Because of Tom's love for the Caribbean, they were able to reminisce about the good old days and dream of other faraway places. Occasionally Billy worked the hot dog stand for Ralph while peddling his wares, but he had to be careful. He had trouble breathing and had to walk slow or his heart would pound.

One afternoon while Tom was shining Billy's shoes, Billy started talking about an idea he had. He told Tom that many of the people in the tenant building across the street hardly ever came outside; they were "shut-ins." He wanted to do something that might get them out of their rooms and brighten up their lives. The idea fit right in with Billy's fantasy of being a stand-up comic. He asked Tom if he would come and play the accordion at a talent show he was organizing with the owners of the building. Tom thought it was a great idea and was happy to come.

The next week, Tom got a call from Billy to come to the rec room at the tenant building on Thursday, around four in the afternoon. That Thursday, along with Ralph, Tom entered the building carrying an accordion over his shoulder. The place was full of people. Billy had opened a door for these people, "Share on stage your talents," talents they would have never dreamed of exposing. Guitar players, singers, harmonica players, storytellers, poets, dancers, a stand-up comic and an accordion player performed that afternoon to a crowd of 25.

The raw unadulterated talent that came from these people that society considered outcasts was unique and extraordinary. Later, after the show, Tom saw a man he had seen walking by the hot dog stand many times before, but had never heard him speak. He was a young man. His face was badly damaged and normal people were afraid to look at him. Tom approached the man because he was so surprised to see him in conversation with one of the other performers. Tom introduced himself. The young man could barely talk but what he did say was very intelligent. He told Tom he'd been an engineering graduate before being in an automobile accident, and knew people didn't like to look at him and that he found it difficult to talk in public. Billy's idea, this seemingly small act, touched and brightened the hearts of people who would have otherwise never ventured out to express their hidden talents and share the music inside.

One afternoon Ralph approached Tom with an idea. Ralph's plugged into the Luther Burbank Center for the Performing Arts, 'cause he sometimes sells hot dogs in the lobby. Taking Tom aside he said, "How about you and I playing the Smothers Brothers Children's Show at LBC." Tom said, "For real?" Ralph answered, "Yes, I'm not kidding. I'll sing, "When I Was a Rich Man" from "Fiddler on the Roof" and you accompany me on the accordion, what do you think?" Without thinking of what that really meant, Tom replied, "Sure, let's do it." Tom got the sheet music and began practicing. Ralph figured they could be ready in a week; Tom told him, "More like a month." He told Ralph, "It's one thing to play to the wall and a whole different thing to play to 1,500 people!"

After a few dry runs in front of friends, Ralph realized what the difference was. Neither of them had played to a large crowd and it scared them both. The largest group Tom had ever played to was 60 people in a biker bar called The Doll Cage in Norwalk, California when he was 21 years old and he was playing bass in the group, not accordion. Ralph would be the only vocalist and he'd never done it before, and for Tom to hit a wrong note in front of 1,500 people, in a song that everyone knows, would be a disaster.

One day after practice Tom asked Ralph again, "Are you sure this gig is on?" Ralph replied, "Yeah, I checked yesterday and we've been given our sound test schedule." Tom replied, "Now look what a fine mess you've got us into," quoting Laurel and Hardy. They both laughed.

Once they memorized the music Tom suggested they play to people on the streets and find the most embarrassing places to play. They played in the lobby of a bank, to a group of punk rockers gathered outside a coffee shop, to sophisticated women walking briskly down Fourth Street, at 31 Flavors, and on selected days to just about anyone who came to the hot dog stand. Tom said they needed a larger crowd to test their courage; Ralph suggested the stage in the park at Courthouse Square. That went great, but only 30 people showed up. They thought about doing it in the Santa Rosa Shopping Mall, but figured they'd probably get arrested. It's only one week away and they're practicing every night. It's a long song, they won't have sheet music to read, and they'll have to stay on beat.

It's one day before show time. Tom enters a grocery store in Cotati and just starts playing. He's scared to death. Soon a group of shoppers gather around. He expects the management to come at any moment with a long cane and pull him off the stage, but being that Cotati was the home of an annual accordion festival, people seem to like it, even the management. That little experience helped.

They're as ready as they're going to be and today is the day. Show time! Their sound check has been bumped and they're not going to get one. Backstage, other entertainers are busying themselves for the "Really Big Shoe." Everyone is receiving their numbers for what order they will go on, and the energy is beginning to wind up. The sounds of people gathering in the auditorium, and the smell of popcorn, triggered Tom to remove his accordion from its case, when Tommy Smothers walked over and said, "You know how to play that thing?" Tom responded, "I hope so." Mr. Smothers chuckled and stepped back, adjusting his bowtie. Tommy's a pro and knew right away who the virgins were.

Tom hears the emcee announce the first act. He and Ralph are number four and his heart is starting to beat fast. His hands become sticky wet. The first act is over and he hears the applause. Sweat begins to bead up across his forehead. He looks over at Ralph; he's quieter than Tom's used to seeing him. Tom wipes his forehead with the back of his hand and says, "Ralph. You doing OK?" Ralph, brass-ing it up, replies, "I'm good, you all right?" Tom says, "I don't know, it keeps getting bigger." Ralph smiles, but his cheeks are quivering.

Act two is over and act three just went on. Tom and Ralph are in the chute entering stage left standing in the dark and Tom is rocking back and forth. Ralph is behind Tom and can't see the audience, but Tom can. His heart is pounding so hard he can feel it in his throat. He keeps saying to himself; "It's going to be OK." He turns around to look at Ralph, who is frozen; he's not breathing and turning blue. Tom responds in a loud whisper, "Ralph, you need to breathe. Take a breath." Ralph started breathing rapidly. Tom replied, "It's going to be OK, don't hyperventilate. Who gives a fuck anyway?" That seemed to help them both.

They hear the applause for the last act and they're about to go on. The announcer broadcasts the act as "Ralph and Tom…" That's their cue. As Tom walks from the chute to center stage, spotlights hit his eyes and follow his every move. He can hear the audience clapping but can't see them. He keeps looking around for Ralph but the lights are blasting in his eyes. Tom makes his way to the microphone. The left mike is set up wrong. He begins to adjust it to pick up bass notes from the accordion and knows he needs to say something. The delay has been too long and he can't find Ralph in his peripheral vision. While making the adjustments, the following words come out of his mouth through the right mike, "Things seem to be more like they are now than they've ever been." The audience laughs, as Tom notices Ralph entering in front of the main mike. They turn to each other and Tom counts, "One, Two, Three," and away they go.

They didn't miss a note; Ralph remembered all the words and the audience clapped. They bowed, waved themselves off the stage and giggled like little boys through the side door into the night air. Tom turned to Ralph and said, "Holy shit, that was like jumping out of an airplane." Ralph hugged him; they put their arms around each other and sat down on the concrete curb near the door, wiping the sweat from their eyes.

It's February 2000 and things are getting better for Tom. The waves of grief have lessened considerably, but every time he dials Noni's phone number, he has the urge to say, "Is Mari there?" But he doesn't.

Archery and Bikram Yoga have become Tom's passions. An old friend put a straw bale in the backyard and now he shoots arrows from the kitchen sink, out through the sliding glass door, over the tops of the roses, to a tennis-ball target against the back fence 70 feet away. Instead of waiting until his bladder is screaming for mercy, he's created a ritualistic break from the computer. He walks away from the keyboard, goes downstairs, grabs the bow, and shoots two dozen arrows.

One afternoon he hit the tennis ball and instead of pulling the arrow out, he fastened another arrow to the bow and drew back. He figured he'd be lucky to hit the ball again. But as luck would have it, it not only hit the ball, it entered the shaft of the previous arrow, piercing it, coming out the other side. Both arrows were damaged. So he hung them, ball and all, from the branch of a large potted plant he doesn't know the name of in the family room. It reminds him that extraordinary things can happen with a little intention and a whole lot of luck.

Lately he's been working on getting the library started in Mexico. Through the Hispanic Chamber of Commerce he met Dr. Brian Shears at Sonoma State University. Dr. Shears provided connections to various book publishers in Mexico and things were about ready to commence.

A month later, over 900 books have arrived in the village of Alamos and are now stored at FAI awaiting his arrival.

Everything's ready to go. Tom's buddy, Tom has been busy in the recording studio, and Tom needs to find a Spanish-speaking volunteer to go to Mexico and help set up the library. He's been putting the word out, but hasn't found anyone with that much adventure in their blood.

He had just curled up next to Didger on the bed, when the phone rang. It was Shea, his massage therapist; "I think I have someone who might go to Mexico with you." Tom replied, "Great, who is it?" Shea gave him the name and number of a woman who lived in the Mohave Desert, who had lived for two years in a remote village in Chiapas, Mexico. Tom jotted notes as they talked and later called the woman. Her name was Robin Flinchum. In discussions, he found out she had actually lived for a while next to Adam and Jacob and Pops when they lived on Lincoln Street several years ago. Tom and Robin made the deal over the phone and met for the first time at the LA airport on their way to Mexico.

They flew to Obregon, Mexico on March 1, 2000, and were greeted by Luis Leyva of FAI, then drove 90 miles to the village of Alamos to begin setting up the new library, calling it Biblioteca de los Ninos de Alamos.

The library was a success and FAI and local people from the village helped make it so. They refurbished an old school building, did minor repairs to walls, painted, put in glass windows, electrical, lighting, and installed eight tables and 42 chairs. George Shepard, Tom's buddy from Oregon, who is a muralist, came to Alamos on his own ticket, riding the buses all the way. He painted animals and children on the inside walls. They installed 16 bookcase modules and through the tireless efforts of Robin Flinchum, cataloged 937 books including encyclopedias, atlases, and dictionaries.

Children, organized by FAI in Alamos, did much of the work. The local children actually got to help in the building of their own library. The library opened on March 13th with over 200 children attending the opening. The superintendent and directors of schools in Alamos, in conjunction with FAI, put on an educational fiesta with music, puppet shows, children's dancing and poetry.

Tom wasn't sure how it was in other schools in Mexico, but the elementary schools in Alamos had no books for students. Only the teachers had books and taught from the blackboard. Tom met with some of the teachers and suggested that they include assignments that would require the students to use the library. The children who attended the opening didn't want to leave the library—that was a good sign.

For details see Robin's Log at www.tomastomas.org "The saga of building a library in Mexico."

In April of that same year Tom made his annual pilgrimage to Oregon to plant trees and was going more often on day trips to the coast with Didger. Time passed and he continued to make *Taras* from Mari's ashes.

One morning in May he was awakened by a bird. Seeing its own reflection in the upstairs window, it kept slamming itself against the glass. It happened again the next morning. It made him think, *Is there something I don't like about myself?* or *Should I try to wake up earlier?* He figured it was a sign of some kind, but wasn't sure. But whatever it was, it made him remember all the times he got in trouble—and that usually had something to do with females. He rolled back over sinking into the pillow and drifted off into daydreams of his early childhood.

He remembered being in Grandma's post office. She was the postmaster for Newbury Park at the time. He was six years old and his mother and dad had come for a visit. He remembered the smell of the unlit kerosene heater in the lobby. While his parents were with his grandmother behind the counter, he snuck off and wandered into the barn next door. As he walked through the massive double doors he saw a haystack to the right. The smell of alfalfa permeated the air. It was warm that day. The bales scraped his elbows and knees as he climbed the stack. Curiously, he could feel heat on his feet coming from inside the freshly cut bales. He climbed to the top and looked around. Looking back, he saw a little girl about the same age standing in the doorway. She was barefoot too, wearing a yellow dress.

She looked up and caught his eyes. They looked at each other for a few minutes. Then she said in snotty tone, "This is my daddy's barn." Young Tom said, "Come on up, it's nice up here." She climbed to the top like she had done it before and sat a few feet away. Tom told her that his grandma ran the post office next door.

They started running around the top of the stack playing-catch-me-if-you-can. The little girl tripped and was covered with alfalfa straw. She started brushing the straw off her legs and then removed her dress to get at the rest. Tom thought that was a good idea and removed his clothes too. They continued to run around the stack naked. Suddenly her father appeared at the door below and started yelling, "Put your clothes back on." He yelled so loud that Tom's dad, who was already looking for him, heard the racket and came into the barn, to find the little girl and young Tom standing naked at the top of the stack. The little girl climbed down and was quickly ushered off by her father. Tom's dad shouted for Tom to come down, but he wouldn't. His dad had to climb the stack to get him, dragging him to the ground below. Once on the floor, his father removed his belt and proceeded to beat him with the belt on Tom's bare skin; it was a beating he would never forget. It was his first lesson in "the shadows of your own reflection."

Other memories seemed to flood in. His dad was a plumber but didn't make all that much money. He went to a school where most of the kids were poor. When Tom was in the second grade his mother decided to dress him up. She would, in her own loving way, take him on the Red Car streetcar to the department store to have him outfitted. He loved riding the streetcar with her, holding hands, but as soon as they entered the store, he'd have a fit. He hated dressing up because he always got in trouble for getting his clothes dirty. He'd just as soon wear dirty clothes. That way, if he got dirty, well, they were already dirty and no bad things would happen. She loved dressing him up, sending him off to school in the very best; it made her feel good that her son was well taken care of. The problem was, no other kids dressed up so nice and they would pick on him and a name like Tom Sawyer didn't help.

One day a kid on the school grounds started teasing and tearing his new shirt, saying he was a mommy's boy. That didn't set well with young Tom and he slugged the kid in the face. The kid went and got a baseball bat and whacked him in the leg. Tom jumped on the kid, but was pulled off by the playground teacher. The principal called his mother at home to come pick him up, stating, "He's out of control." His mom came and got him. On the way home she kept saying, "Tom, Tom, the piper's son, stole a pig and away he run, the pig got loose and caught a goose and Tom got put in the calaboose." He didn't understand the poem until later in life. When he got home of course she would "have to tell your father." When his father got home, he got a worse beating than he already had. It was his first memory of really being mad at someone. As far as he was concerned the kid on the playground caused all his misfortune.

The next day the kid drove by on a bicycle in front of Tom's house, yelling from a safe distance. Tom went to the back porch and got a broom and proceeded to the front yard. The kid went to the end of the block shouting obscenities and turned around for one more drive-by. When he did, Tom was ready. As the kid peddled by at full speed yelling, "Tommy is a mama's boy," Tom ran to the street shoving the broom handle into the spokes of the kid's front wheel. The spoke caught the handle of the broom, allowing the front wheel to make one more revolution before being abruptly halted by the bicycle forks. The bike flipped over, throwing the kid through the air. He hit the pavement with his face and slid to a stop. He was crying and bleeding from his nose. Inside Tom felt bad for the boy, but kept bellowing, "That's what you get." All the neighbors came out including Tom's mom. She grabbed him by the arm, dragging him away making sure all the neighbors could hear her saying, "Just wait till your father gets home." Lesson number two in "the shadows of your own reflection."

It seemed like he was always getting in trouble. Apparently he didn't learn much from the "naked girl in the barn" episode. A few months later the girl from across the street came over and they went behind the incinerator in the backyard and played I'll-show-you-mine-if-you-show-me-yours.

On the bed, he continued drifting through a whole succession of strung- together memories. For some reason, unknown to him, he was riding a convoluted stream of consciousness into childhood. He was in the back yard in Inglewood, 20 feet from the clothesline his mother used to tether him to. By age seven he realized that the clothesline was really meant for drying clothes and that its previous purpose was only used to keep him from wandering into the street. To the right of the incinerator, where he was busted for sexual curiosity, sat a large pile of wood, mostly rough boards with nails sticking out, remnants of an old chicken barn long forgotten. Santa Claus had brought him a tool box and he was in the process of building a doghouse for his newly gifted puppy he had named Chico, as suggested by his uncle Joe who was half Italian and half Mexican. His four-year-old sister, Theresa, whom he figured would "tell" the prime authorities if he did anything outside of the box, was playing in the distance. He was torn between his love for her and her wanting to hang out around him and his suspicion she may "tell," resulting in dire consequences to his body.

As he hammered and sawed she watched from a distance. She knew he was in the middle of creating something, but had no idea what it was. Her curiosity pulled her closer for a better look. He hadn't asked permission to build—there was no building permit. If she "told," he figured the project would be set back or even halted. As she approached within ten feet of the construction site he sent out a warning. He told her to "stay back," that there were nails sticking up out of the boards and she was barefoot. She stayed clear of the invisible ten-foot boundary but pranced back and forth chanting, "Tommy, what you doing," over and over. He stood for a moment with hammer in hand signaling a warning to stay back.

She continued to taunt, "Does Mommy know?" He was silent and continued his work. She approached closer, "I want to help." Again he told her to move away. She could tell, whatever he was doing, it seemed to have some importance about it, which gave her the power. She repeated, "I want to help." He replied, "I said get out of here," and slammed the hammer on a board next to him creating a loud bang. She bolted back beyond the ten-foot limit and turned around. Placing her hands on her hips she announced, "I am going to tell." He replied, "You better not." She began dancing in the distance, "I'm going to tell, I'm going to tell." He didn't say anything. He continued working, hoping something else might grab her attention.

She watched for a while then started up again, "I want to help or I'm going to tell." He continued working as she approached. She passed into the ten-foot demarcation line prompting him to stand. "I said to get out of here, if you come any closer I'm going to throw this hammer at you," smashing the hammer again onto a board. She ran and as she ran, she yelled, "I'm telling, you're going to get in trouble." He only wanted to scare her off, but as she ran reciting, "I'm telling," he threw the hammer, expecting it to come close but not to hit her. She ran as fast as her four year-old legs would carry her. The hammer sailed through the air in slow motion. Something told him it was not going to be a near miss. The hammer continued to sail, tumbling repeatedly. She was in the middle of the words, "I'm telling" when it struck the back of her head. Her body fell to the ground limp. Tom ran toward his sister and picked her up. By now she was coming to and his mother was on the scene wanting to know what he had done. His mother was so astounded by the act that she ignored his explanations and carried her four-year-old daughter into the house, instructing Tom to remain in the back yard.

It turned out that Theresa was only knocked out and no permanent damage had occurred. It was during those two hours in the back yard with himself, awaiting news as to the condition of his sister, that he realized his own concept of karma. And it wasn't more than two weeks later that he was beaten up by two neighbor kids, receiving a blow to the back of the head with a red brick. At a young time in his development, his concept included the Universe, and at the age of seven, he was able to recognize the lesson. Something happened during that period that helped him to love both himself and his sister with deeper insight. He realized that his love of anything was because he wished it so, not because he was supposed to, and began to search for the source of that wish.

When he was eight years old, he fell in love with a gypsy girl and was chased away by her father; he never went back there again. When he was nine he almost died from a cyst that had been forming since birth, that no one knew about. It had formed on his right kidney and had wrapped itself around the nerves in his right leg and had tentacles reaching up into his lungs. He was saved by surgery and spent two months in the hospital. He didn't realize it at the time, but without the surgery the doctors had given him six months to live. During surgery he remembered traveling down a spiraling tunnel; they almost lost him on the operating table due to loss of blood. He was on the table for almost four hours. He remembers waking up the next day on the ward in a baby bed with sides. As he came into consciousness, it bothered him more and more that he was in a "baby bed!"

On his right side were 63 stitches and two large clamps. A drain tube came out from inside his right side, connected to a pump. Various IVs and other tubes were connected to his body. A catheter tube ran up inside his penis and down the side of the bed to a pan on the floor. The more he thought about it, the more he didn't like being in a baby bed. He wasn't a baby and how could they put him there? They must have made a mistake. He proceeded to pull out all the tubes from his body. He managed to edge up over the bed and was crawling down the hall when a nurse spotted him. She went to the wall and set off an alarm that brought people dressed in white. They took him to an operating room to reinsert the tubes in his side. Before they put him out the second time, he uttered, "I don't want to be in a baby bed." A few hours later he came to in a standard hospital bed with a young nurse at his side. So it went, another reflection in "the shadows of your own reflection."

Back on the bed, in real-time, Didger started licking his face, signaling it was time to get up. He needed to get ready. He jumped in the shower, shaved and put on bib overalls. He's excited; he and his buddy Tom are going to stack firewood today and he loves to split and stack firewood. After driving up a long private road to the twisted oaks atop a mountain, he turned, and parked behind a '57 Cadillac. His buddy was there to greet him with a cup of tea and they went right to work. He and Tom were swapping childhood stories, when Tom said to Tom in a gruffly voice; "I've got a friend who lives in Jamaica, his name is Chris Blackwell. He's got a water problem. I don't know that much about it, but several companies have tried to solve the problem. You interested?" Tom replied, "Very." The other Tom went on, "Send Kathleen a resume, we'll see what happens."

Tom sent the resume and two weeks later received a phone call from Chris's executive administrator, Cathy Snipper. She wanted to know if he had experience with water wheels and aqueducts. He told her he did and they scheduled a phone meeting with Roger Brown, who ran Chris's Jamaican operations.

This year seemed to be arranged by the Universe. He was not in control. It's not so much what Tom tried to do, it's what the Universe put on his plate. He'd had periods in his life before like that, where he never knew from month to month what he'd be doing. It all seemed to be coming out of grace.

In June he received a call from a man named Ken Rose who was a private jet pilot for Jim Warren, who had helped in the past with the library work in Mexico. Jim had offered to fly books into Mexico and Ken was looking for logistical details to schedule the adventure. Over the last year Tom had been collecting books through donations from various sources in the U.S. including the Sonoma County library. A friend of Rosemary Ward's, Jennifer Mann, had been helping him translate and catalog 400 titles in Spanish for inventory and Ken had offered to fly them in.

Two days later, Tom received a verification fax from his connection in Mexico that everything had been cleared, and to proceed with the shipment.

Ken flew in from Scottsdale, Arizona in a Trinidad GT and landed at the Sonoma County Airport. Tom was late by ten minutes and Ken had already gassed up the plane. He'd been waiting upstairs in the pilots' lounge for 20 minutes and wasn't real happy.

Tom, Kathleen, Sullivan, Rosemary and Don came to see Tom off. Everyone's cars were full of books. Each box was numbered and they were about to load them on the plane. Ken made it clear he was on a schedule. Everyone went to work packing the boxes in cargo compartments aboard the Trinidad. Sullivan, a nine-year-old boy, climbed up on the right wing to look at the controls. When Ken spotted him, he became visibly upset with Tom, asking him to get the boy off the wing. Tom understood the seriousness, but was now wondering what it was going to be like spending six hours in the air with Ken, whom he had only met on the phone. Everything was packed and Ken, aside from being a little curt, was very methodical about performing all the ground checks before taxiing to the runway. Ken and Tom boarded the plane, and Ken shouted, "Clear," as he started up the engine. Ken instructed Tom to put on a headset and fasten his safety belt. He set the radio for the various frequencies required for the flight and contacted ground control for weather and taxi instructions. As Tom and Ken taxied towards runway 19, everyone waved them off.

When they reached the runway, Ken went through the run-up list and Tom checked them off. Ken seemed curious that Tom was familiar with the procedure. Ken called the tower and announced, "Sonoma County Tower, Trinidad 4368 number 1 for takeoff on 19," The tower came back, "Trinidad 4368 cleared for takeoff." The Trinidad's turbo-charged 250 HP engine revved up and off they went down the runway, destination Mexicali-Calexico border, near El Centro, California. Once in the air, Tom figured there would be hours of silence, in that the two men didn't appear to have much in common. A half hour into the flight, Ken spoke his first words, "You've flown in a private plane before?" Tom replied, "Yes sir, I have a pilot's license." Ken looked over from the controls with a slight grin, then looked back at the maps in his lap and continued setting navigation frequencies into the autopilot. At that point Tom figured they did have something in common and began to speak, "I don't have a lot of hours and anything you might want to point out, I'd love to learn." That did it. Tom became the student and Ken became the instructor. It was great; they instantly moved into their roles and became friends. Ken loved teaching and was good at it. Ken also flew Lear Jets and had considerable experience with flight instruments. Tom was honored to spend the hours next to such a master.

When they arrived at Calexico International, an unmanned airstrip next to the Mexican border, the sky had become dark and warm. From the city lights below, it was obvious what side of the border they were on. After a smooth landing, they tied down the airplane and checked into a dingy motel ten blocks from the airport. It was still early. They decided to wander into Mexicali, on the Mexican side, for something to eat at an all-night cantina.

Ken wanted to get an early start; he'd called for a weather briefing before Tom woke up. Raising Tom from his slumber, Ken said, "Let's go, I want to try to beat the weather building up over Sonora." Tom opened a can of sardines from his pack as they sped toward the airstrip in a decked-out Mexican taxicab. They gassed up the Trinidad and were in the air in less than 20minutes. The sun was just coming up over the horizon as they flew down the western coastline of mainland Mexico. The desert seemed to go on forever. Changing course about 50 miles down they headed southeast, destination Hermosillo International, Sonora, Mexico.

Four hours later they touched down behind a jet "on final," catching some of its wake turbulence, and taxied to customs. Tom couldn't speak Spanish, but had a letter from an official contact in Mexico he hoped would grant swift passage. He handed the letter to one of two armed men dressed in plain clothes approaching the plane. The man looked curiously at the letter and began to speak in Spanish. Tom asked Ken what he said. Ken replied, "They want us to go through the check-in procedure." As Tom and Ken chalked the wheels, one of the men wanted to see what was inside the plane. Ken opened the storage compartment and the man looked in, saying something.

Tom picked up on the word, "Libros" which he understood to mean "Books." The men motioned for Tom and Ken to follow.

Tom had been in the airport many times before, but never to the area the men were taking them. They entered a small side door. Rows of non-air-conditioned booths lined the outside windows. Each cubicle contained a man behind a desk with an antiquated manual typewriter and stacks of papers. Each man required a fee. Each man would make change from his pocket and then stamp their papers requesting them to move to the next cubicle. Tom and Ken went from booth to booth, filling out papers and paying fees. It took an hour and a half and $175 US to pass through the gauntlet. They had finally arrived at the last booth, when a well-dressed man who spoke English entered the room and said, "Gentlemen, please come with me."

They followed the man to a plain-clothed car and were instructed to get in the back. They were then driven to another part of the airport and entered a two-story building made up of mostly offices and air traffic control equipment. They followed the man upstairs and entered a fancy office waiting room. The man requested that they wait and to have a seat. A few minutes later a very beautiful woman appeared, announcing she was Head of Customs. Cordially she explained to the two wary pilots that they could not take the books on to Alamos and that there was a law prohibiting the import of books into the country without first having them inspected. She said the inspection would take several weeks and the books would have to be impounded. Tom asked Ken to tell her that he was president of a US non-profit organization that built libraries for children in Mexico, and that the books were for children in the village of Alamos, and that they did not intend to sell them. She thought for a moment and said that she was very sorry, but that was the law. Tom then asked if they flew directly back to the US, could they take the books with them. Sympathetically she nodded her head, yes. The man drove them back to the Trinidad; they gassed up the plane and resubmitted a flight plan for Scottsdale, Arizona.

They landed for US customs on a isolated airstrip in Nogales and tried to explain to the lone agent that they were not bringing in the books from Mexico, the books had originated in the US The customs guy was the perfect bureaucrat and wasn't sure how to handle something so complex. Finally Ken was able to facilitate him on how to fill out the paperwork and they were in the air again.

After landing at Scottsdale they went to Ken's house and Tom started making phone calls. He thought perhaps the clock could be reset by flying back the next day, if he could just figure out what had gone wrong with his connection. He asked Ken about flying back the next day, if Tom could get things ironed out. Ken agreed. Tom talked with his connections and explained what had happened. His connection told him that there had been a mix-up and if they flew back into Hermosillo in the morning, there would be "no problema."

Ken received an emergency call from Jim Warren and had to cancel the flight back to Mexico. He and Tom stored the books in an airplane hanger in Arizona and several months later made another attempt.

This time Tom assured Ken that he had double-checked his political connections and "all systems are go." With a planeload of books they headed south again. Upon approach, Ken radioed the Hermosillo Tower and requested landing instructions. This time as they taxied off the runway toward the customs area, the Director of Hermosillo International Airport greeted them. He apologized for the previous mix-up and instructed two well-dressed customs men to check the Trinidad for its contents. They opened the cargo door and closed it. Tom and Ken were then escorted and hand-walked through each check-in process, gassed up and were back in the air in less than 15 minutes.

Northeast of Obregon they started to run into weather. Cumulonimbus clouds were building over the barren foothills and they had to climb to 11,500 feet and pass between thunderheads. The plane hit downdrafts dropping 100 feet in a second and then bouncing back up. It was a wild ride until just outside Navajoa. Descending to 2,000 feet, a few minutes later they passed over the basin leading to a dry valley surrounding the village of Alamos and circled twice. Locating the small airstrip to the north of the settlement, they followed the runway downwind for a "right base" and made final approach at 500 feet. Ken made a perfect landing and they taxied to the other end where Maye from FAI, Tom's son Adam, and his sweetie Molly were waiting to greet them.

Adam and Molly had taken the bus down into Mexico on an adventure and were planning to go further south the next day, but had organized their trip so they could meet up with Tom in Alamos. Not many planes land in Alamos and the whole town had seen the Trinidad circling—including the Federales. An army jeep loaded with men carrying automatic weapons approached the runway and scrambled down the parallel dirt road. As the jeep got closer to the plane, a man dressed in a green khaki uniform in the front seat glanced over, holding his finger on the trigger of an Uzi 9mm machine gun. He noticed the FAI symbol on the side of Maye's truck and motioned the patrol to turn around, disappearing down the runway toward town as fast as they came. Tom hugged everyone and he and Ken started unloading boxes from the plane to the truck. Adam and Maye joined in and within a few minutes they were heading into town. They zigzagged up into the foothills on dirt roads, passing over several dry creeks before reaching a small outpost where FAI had set up headquarters.

At FAI headquarters, they visited with some of the children and checked in before heading to the school where the library was housed. At the school, the principal, Juan Zoilo, greeted them and they started moving the precious cargo across the schoolyard to the library building. Everyone went instantly to work.

Ken had to get back. He wanted to fly out before dark. Molly and Adam started putting books on the shelves while Maye updated the inventory log. Juan, Ken and Tom visited and caught up with the news. Tom asked Juan for a wish list and discussed possible improvements for next year. Three hours later, all the books had been cataloged and put away.

It was a quick trip. As Ken revved up the Trinidad, Maye moved close to Tom's ear and said in Spanish over the roar of the prop, "Goodbye my friend, until we meet again."

19

"See mi fa'ce in de wa'ter."

Lyon, holy man of the Martha Brea

Jamaica

Back from his Mexican adventures, Tom settled into silence. He roamed the backyard on Neo wondering where Mari might be. He often checked the old garden site and the bench out back where she used to do her Chi Gung exercises. He equated the breeze ringing the wind chimes in the mulberry tree with a hello from Mari, and then went about his chores of keeping her plants alive.

One day while sitting on the bench, he gazed over at the *Taras* stacked on pieces of wood behind the Buddha statue and contemplated whether any more chapters were left in his life. Would there be more adventures? Or was he to simply slip into old age and die? Things his psychic Nancy was telling him were encouraging, but doubt had crept in. He pondered, *I've raised my children, experienced the love of my life, and now I'll attend to my own demise. Where can I go from here? It certainly can't be some mainstream, stick-your-head-in-the-TV, idea. It's got to be something outside the box.*

He thought how he loved the old ways and how his idea of adventure seemed to come from another time. What he loved was mystery, things that involved commitment, loyalty, excitement, risk and vision, stepping outside his normal self to become a person that perhaps lived 100 years ago.

He had almost forgotten about his conversation with Cathy Snipper a month ago when the phone rang, interrupting his "poor me" contemplation on the bench. He ran inside and picked up the phone. When he answered, he noted "Out of the Area" on the call-number display and almost hung up, thinking it was just another telemarketer. When the voice said Chris Blackwell's name, Tom replied, "Oh, yes, Chris Blackwell, yes, this is Tom Sawyer." It appeared he might get the job; they wanted him to come and look.

A few weeks later, a small jet that had been flying over the blue waters of the Caribbean Sea for several hours has just made a turn, dropping close over the water for a landing. Tom has come to take a look-see at a water system problem on a remote estate located somewhere in the interior of Jamaica. All he knows is Roger Brown, Chris Blackwell's man, said that someone would pick him up at the airport and take him to a place called Golden Eye.

After clearing customs carrying only a small backpack, he stood in the lobby among scores of Jamaican taxicab drivers descending on tourists, and looked for someone holding a sign. After an hour he asked a passing flight attendant where he might find a phone. A friendly lady behind a desk in one of the adjoining offices allowed him to use the phone after he mentioned Golden Eye. It seemed to be a magic word. From a small notebook he carried in his back pocket, he called the number Cathy Snipper had given him prior to leaving Santa Rosa. A lady's voice on the other end answered, "Golden Eye, may I help you?" He replied, "Hello, my name is Tom Sawyer." A sweet Jamaican accent replied, "Oh, yes. Where are you?" "Montego Bay." She explained, there'd been a "confusion" in the timing and he should hail a cab for Golden Eye.

Out front he asked an all-too-willing cabbie how far Golden Eye was. The driver's eyes sparkled and opened wide as if he had struck gold, replying, "Sixty, seventy miles." Tom inquired. The fee was reasonable. He jumped in the cabby's private car; he presumed it might be able to make such a journey, and set out down the coastal highway, east along the northern Caribbean Sea.

The driver pointed out famous spots, engaging in historical conversation most of the way. They passed Little River,

Falmouth, Runaway Bay, Saint Ann's, and Ocho Rios. The cabbie seemed intelligent and knowledgeable about the area. After 60 miles, Tom asked, "What is Golden Eye?" The driver gave him a curious look, as if to say, *You mean you're going to Golden Eye and you don't know what it is?* The driver was quiet for a few minutes then started in, "The writer Ian Fleming purchased the property from Mr. Blackwell's mother, who owned substantial holdings in England's food distribution empire in the late '40s, when Mr. Blackwell was a boy."

"Ian Fleming, like in 007?"

"Ya mon. Fleming wrote all his books there."

"Does Chris Blackwell live there?"

"I don't know. Mr. Fleming became like a father to Mr. Blackwell and I believe he owns Golden Eye."

"What is Golden Eye now?"

"It's a private meeting place for famous people from all over the world. You've heard of Bob Marley?"

"Seems like I've heard the name. Who's Bob Marley?"

The driver removed his sunglasses and looked back curiously in the rearview mirror, taking a second look at the tattooed man carrying only a backpack for luggage. Wondering if his passenger would be able to afford the fare, he said, "You have business at Golden Eye?"

Tom replied, "I'm not sure yet." The cabbie said nothing and continued to drive.

They had been traveling for several hours now and just passed through the town of Oracabessa (Golden Head) in the province of St. Mary, when the driver broke the last 20-minute silence, "Not far now." For the last eighth of a mile Tom had been noticing an eight-foot-high stonewall fence surrounding a compound to the left. The car slowed and turned into a driveway, stopping in front of a large iron gate. A rather large well-dressed Jamaican man departed the gatehouse and walked toward the locked entrance. The driver announced, "Tom Sawyer has arrived." Leaning to one side looking through an opening in the bars, the gatekeeper peered into the back seat of the cab as he swung open the gate and waved the car through. Suddenly he motioned the car to stop. Tom rolled the window down. The guard said, "Mr. Sawyer, please continue to the office area straight ahead, they are expecting you." Tom thanked the man. The cabbie looked relieved and pulled forward slowly.

Manicured lawns on either side of the road extend outward and seem to go on forever. The road is paved with white granite stones and lined with intricate rock edgings and coconut trees. Brightly colored tropical plants dot the area with purple and red flowers. Warm salt-sea smells of the West Indies flood in the opened car window, lighting up recollections of remote island places. The cab continued on for what seemed like a long time and pulled in front of an office lined with banana trees.

As the cabbie opened Tom's door, a beautiful Jamaican woman came down the stairs apologizing for the mix-up at the airport. Tom looked over at her. He felt a sense of familiarity and took the liberty of hugging the woman. Gracefully she embraced him announcing, "I'm Hope, the property manager here at Golden Eye." Tom replied, "Good to meet you." He tipped the driver handsomely and thanked him for the historical journey. Hope immediately grabbed Tom's arm and took him on a tour of the grounds, pointing out that Chris Blackwell was not there, but Roger Brown would be joining him soon. She showed him to the villa where he would be staying and excused herself.

Tom wandered the grounds. He found rock steps descending to the sea next to a cave and walked the beach for an hour. He was there, but he wasn't there. He marveled how he had arrived at such a place—so magnificent, so classic, a place where time seemed to have no relevance. He went back to the cave, followed a rock trail leading inside and gazed back at the blue calm waters of the north Caribbean. He's still working on it, the tendency to attach all beauty to his sweetheart. He continues to say things in his mind like, *O sweetie, look at that.* While imagining a tall slender lady in lavender walking the beach, with her hand pressed against her cheek, looking back, a thought boiled up from inside, *Stop it, you're breaking my heart.* At once the mirage went away.

Returning to his villa, he lay on the bed listening to Jamaican tree frogs barking in the distance and drifted off.

Two hours later Roger Brown showed up. He was a tall handsome man, half Irish, half Jamaican with strong features and a steel-trap mind. He carried an air about him, both mysterious and in charge. Through the open window Tom saw him enter the porch and knock. Rising from the bed, Tom said, "Come in. You must be Roger?"

Roger replied, "Did you have a good trip?"

Tom motioned him to sit at the table by the window facing the ocean and went on, "Yes, it's great to be here."

Roger opened a small briefcase and laid out several papers on the table. Tom asked, "What you got there?"

"This is a map of Pantrepant…"

Tom interrupted, "Where?"

"Pantrepant, it's where Chris Blackwell lives. It's a 2,000-acre cattle ranch in the province of Trelawny about 50 miles from here. It's where we're having the water problem."

"What kind of problem is it?"

"The pumps keep burning up. There's an aqueduct," pointing to the map, "here, that runs from the Martha Brea river to the main house. It was built 300 years ago and still operates. At the base of the aqueduct in the jungle is a pumping station that pumps water out of the aqueduct to a holding tank 600 feet up the mountain."

"Where does it go from there?"

"It comes down and fans out through the property, servicing different facilities on the estate."

Tom began asking technical questions about pipe size, elevations, etc, when Roger stopped him, "I don't think it's going to require rocket science."

"Do you have a survey of the property?"

Roger glanced away from the map and went on, "And by the way, you don't seem to look the part. You and your resume don't go together."

"Yes, I sometimes wonder about that myself."

Several seconds of silence ensued. Then Tom said, "Well, we'll need to take a look." Roger walked to the opened bay window and stared out at the sea grapes winding their way up a post by the veranda. From across the room he announced, "I'm leaving for Ocho Rios; if you need anything, contact Cathy Snipper. She's staying here at Golden Eye."

No words were spoken as they passed over the teakwood porch to the steps, exiting the villa. Roger continued, then stopped on the steps with one foot higher than the other. Rotating his head to one side, he said, "Chris will be arriving in a couple of days from New York—in the meantime, enjoy the place." Tom nodded. Roger took ten paces down the walkway, turned around, smiled and disappeared into a grove of coconut trees.

Tom decided to walk the perimeter of the 30-acre beach estate. While he meandered, a waiter named David stopped by Tom's villa and left a note inviting him to attend a poolside dinner with other guests who were awaiting Chris's arrival.

Tom was traveling down a path towards the beach next to a group of banana trees. Between the passing trees he spotted a woman in the distance crossing the lawn near the seawall. She was moving toward him but didn't know it. He froze. She was elegant and stunning; the way she moved almost took his breath away. His heart skipped a beat, and then began pounding. Watching her turn at the pool and pause in a classic serene pose made him pleased that he could still feel. She stood there several seconds by a large Grecian pot ten feet away from the pool, looking into the water, and then quickly vanished behind the media building.

That evening as he walked toward the pool, he hoped she would be attending the dinner. The thought frightened him. Nancy, Tom's psychic, had told him he would meet a beautiful Jamaican lady; she would have a daughter, but would not be married. As he sat down introducing himself to the table, he noticed the woman coming toward the pool and became tongue-tied in the middle of his preamble. The guests noticed his withdrawal and looked to see what had startled him. He blushed quietly as the woman joined the table.

Everyone at the table seemed to know who the lady was, except Tom. The guests were curious; he didn't look like someone who belonged. He remained quiet until another woman asked who he was. He told the table he was an engineer and was going to look at a water problem at Pantrepant. When he mentioned Pantrepant the Jamaican beauty said, "You're going to Pantrepant! I've never been. Hardly anyone gets to go. What's it like?" Tom replied, "I've never been there, I'm supposed to go in a few days." There he was, he had found another magic word, and the Jamaican beauty wanted to know everything about him. She introduced herself as Terry O and began telling him that she had a ten-year-old daughter and how difficult it was being a single mom. Suddenly Nancy's words surfaced and he uttered to himself, *O my God, what's going on here?*

The next day the energy began to pick up. People were running here and there preparing for Chris's arrival. The cooks were making up something special and more people were arriving. Some seemed like music entertainment people, dressed down. Other stylish executives appeared to be in the film industry.

From his villa he could see general help scurrying about the beach below, setting up tables, beach lamps and barbeque equipment. Maître d's, waiters, and cooks moved trays of exotic foods across the sand to a hut ten feet above the water line. At the other end of the beach was a curved stone wall extending out into the water. Atop the wall, back in the trees, was an open grass *tuki* shack where cooks turned lamb on a barbeque. Smoke rose into the air as helpers placed items from the fire onto large tables covered with white cloth.

An hour later he saw guests making their way down the stone steps to the beach and gathering around a portable cocktail lounge. Tom continued to look from his window, hoping to see Terry O. Noticing the crowd build, he pondered, *Maybe I can get a sandwich brought to my room; it looks kind of scary down there.* Putting the thought aside, he unzipped his backpack, lifted out a *Tara* statue wrapped in an old T-shirt and set out for the beach.

Walking across the sand in his brown polished combat boots he passed a table where no one was sitting and continued through a group of four larger tables. Sitting at the last table, he placed the T-shirt-wrapped *Tara* in his lap and looked around. He didn't know anyone and pretended to be interested in the ongoing conversation. He gazed around, noticed Terry O sitting at the table to the right and wished he had sat there.

Several minutes later an entourage of executive types entered the beach and moved across the sand. The man out front, wearing shorts, T-shirt and sandals approached an empty table somewhat set back from the group and was greeted by an attendant. The others remained standing until he was seated. Tom knew it was Chris Blackwell from Kathleen's description.

He said something to one of the maître d's, sending him scurrying across the sand. Before long, men dressed in white wearing white gloves brought cocktails to the table. The atmosphere changed to clinking glasses and conversation.

After an exquisite dinner of local crab, lamb, and beef from Chris's ranch, people began engaging in jovial chat. Tom stared over at Terry O, making extended eye contact, then looked over at Chris's table. Chris wasn't there. Continuing to rotate his head, Tom noticed Chris pouring a drink at the portable bar near the seawall. Tom stood up from the table with the *Tara* statue in hand and walked over to introduce himself, "Hello Chris, my name's Tom Sawyer." Chris replied, "Yes, I know. You're friends with Tom and Kathleen. How are they?" Tom stumbled for words, "Oh, they're doing good. They said to send you their love. I brought you something." Unwrapping the T-shirt, he passed the statue to Chris's hands, "I make these *Taras* and thought your wife Mary might enjoy it." Chris smiled and held it up, "Thank you. She's not here right now, but I'm going to Pantrepant tomorrow. I'll leave it for her." Tom smiled and walked back to his table. He noticed everyone staring. All eyes focused on him. They were wondering who was this tattooed man speaking directly to Chris in such a familiar way. As soon as he sat down some of the men began queries. Tom politely evaded the questions, preferring to glance over at Terry O, while skim-listening to the conversation.

A few minutes later Chris stood up from his table and invited everyone for a nightcap at his "hideout." Tom didn't know where that was. He tagged along behind the stragglers, up stone steps from the beach following a path around the pool to a gravel road, and continued 200 yards to a wooden fenced area. They entered, winding back and forth on narrow cement paths to a terrace overlooking the water.

The hideout had very few exterior walls and kissed the bay. A warm balmy breeze slapped water from the inlet against an intricate stone seawall. Carved wooden Balinese sculptures sat on a floor of brown marbleized Italian tile. For a minute Tom stood by himself looking out at the bay. The sun had just dipped into the sea creating a pink/blue flare at the horizon. Servers moved in and took orders while everyone mingled. Tom felt comfortable with Hope, the Jamaican property manager, and sat next to her on the terraced rail overlooking the bay. He and Hope were in an interesting conversation regarding Nelson Mandela, when he noticed Terry O standing three feet away with no escort. He pretended not to notice but checked in every so often, occasionally making eye contact.

An hour later people were beginning to leave. He turned from the conversation and saw Terry O standing by herself on the steps. Tom excused himself and walked over and stood beside Terry, but was afraid to speak. They both just stood there, frozen, looking out at the water. Suddenly she lifted her arm, placing it on his shoulder. In turn, he put his arm around her waist and pulled her close. He couldn't believe it. There he was, standing with his arm around an unbelievably beautiful creature, gazing out over the blue waters of the Caribbean in a billionaire's enchanted hideaway, trusting the moment would never end.

They stood like that for what seemed an eternity—five minutes with no words, just feelings. Then they looked at each other like they had been together for years and turned and walked away in concert. She knew her way in the dark, giving instructions now and then, "Not that way, this way" until they reached her room. Standing at the door, looking at him with inviting eyes, she asked, "Where's your room?" They peered into each other's eyes for a moment, and then hugged. Tom kissed her on the cheek and whispered goodnight. Back in his room he pondered whether he'd done the right thing. The feeling was so strong he couldn't sleep. He went in the dark and sat in the cave he had found the day before on the beach. Like a schoolboy he drew in the sand, "Tom + Terry" encircling it with a heart.

The next morning before breakfast he heard a helicopter land momentarily and take off again. He walked to the pool, where he was greeted by one of the estate aides carrying a note, "We will be leaving for Pantrepant after breakfast," signed Roger Brown. He acknowledged the note and proceeded through a maze of vine-covered trellises near the shoreline to Terry O's back door. He knocked. She appeared in the doorway barefoot wearing a white summer dress with full-length sleeves and a thin silver arm bracelet. *How auspicious*, he thought. Her hair was pulled up with sunglasses, her ears adorned with pearls. She smiled studiously. They small-talked for a bit, and then Tom asked, "Can I take your picture?" She posed with her hands clasped, looking away with a smile. When he pushed to know more about who she was, she looked away with sad eyes and said clearly, "You better do your project and I'll keep my job." These were not the words he had hoped for. They hugged and said goodbye.

Roger joined Tom for breakfast in the Tiki Room without a lot to say. Thirty minutes later they were in an ATV headed west, down the coast highway for Trelawny. Even though Tom had spent years in the Caribbean, he had never gotten used to driving on the left side of the road. They were both quiet. Just after St. Ann's Bay, Roger sped up, passing a long line of cars. Tom looked over. Roger was intense; his eyes glared as he continued on the wrong side through a blind corner, daring all head–on traffic. Up ahead, Tom saw the daylight shine of flashing headlights from an oncoming car. Roger held his ground, determined to pass the next car—he was playing "Chicken" with a stranger, no matter what. For Tom it was OK; today was as good a day to die as any. At the very last second, at 70 MPH, Roger passed the last car and jammed back into the lane, just missing the approaching vehicle by inches.

Tom looked over and said in calm voice, "That was pretty good." Roger's scorn turned into a smile. Tom figured it had been some kind of rite of passage. What Roger didn't know was that Tom had lost the love of his life, and had just been misled by a stunningly beautiful impossible situation, and deep down he really didn't give a shit.

It broke the ice and these two unlikely men began to share their life stories with each other. About 40 miles out, they turned off at Falmouth, passing small settlements dotting the road. Tom didn't know it, but they were headed for "The Cockpit Country," the jungle of Jamaica. Most people think of Jamaica as a beach on the Caribbean; sipping rum to steel-drum music. Actually, Jamaica is 140 miles long and 50 miles wide and at her center lies an uninhabited jungle 40 miles long and 20 miles wide.

They continued till the blacktop turned to dirt, and for miles they traveled through green rolling hills and panoramic views of simple countryside. Tom loved it; the people he saw walking alongside the road seemed to have no concept of time. Life appeared uncomplicated and sweet.

A few miles after leaving the last settlement, he noted an 18th-century Georgian style great house on the right with estate gardens and a roadside split-rail fence that seemed to go on forever. Several miles past that, they came to a bridge, where a beautiful river flowed. Tom asked Roger, "What is this river?" Roger replied, "It's the Martha Brea." Being an engineer, Tom was fascinated by the bridge made of steel and stones. Except for the I-beams supporting its under-member, it could have been built 200 years ago. Further on, he noticed a large ruin with trees growing through it. Stones hand-lifted by men 300 years ago were partly falling over, yet standing in testimony of a time when men were men. It appeared to be an old rum factory. The grounds around the ruins were well kept. Coconut trees speckled the landscape. As the road bent to the right he saw a long line of coconut trees and what looked like great oaks reaching into the Jamaican sky. The place seemed enchanted.

As they went on, the road merged into an expansive well-kept lawn bordering either side of the road, carpeting up a hillside. A two-story structure painted powder blue with a tin roof poking into the heavens stood atop the hill. Below the building was a Jamaican woman in blue, hanging garments on a clothesline that stretched the length of the building. A hundred yards to the left, across a vast lawn, sat a quaint two-story house painted maroon with green trim. An expansive covered veranda surrounded all sides. Between the two structures was a great tree, a tree so large he couldn't believe his eyes. Its branches cut into the sky, extending from one structure to the other.

Roger made a sharp turn to the left and parked. Several Jamaican men came to the car window and started talking patois, a Caribbean language consisting of African, English, French and other local dialects mixed in a clipped African rhythm. Tom was somewhat familiar with it, if spoken slowly. To his surprise, Roger spoke back like a Rasta then turned to Tom and said in English, "This is Pantrepant." Opening the car door, they walked in front of the large two-story blue structure that Roger called, "the office/guest annex," and continued across the lawn to a set of stairs.

When Tom first saw her, he knew he had seen an angel. There at the top of the stairs stood an English woman in her 60s holding a cane in each hand. As she moved down the stairs, one step at a time, he could see her ankles were swollen and she traveled slowly. He literally saw light coming from her heart. Halfway down she suddenly lifted one cane. Using it as a pointing stick she yelled in a Jamaican accent with the voice of an army sergeant, "Andrew, go fetch Mr. Anderson," and continued down the stairs. Tom and Roger moved towards her. Her presence was so strong, Tom almost instinctively bowed in reverence. Roger introduced her as Mary McFarlane, the property manager for Pantrepant. She looked at Tom intensely; he felt an unexplainable familiarity as she said, "You can call me Miss Mac."

Roger and Tom were chit-chatting on how long the pumps had been burning up when Miss Mac abruptly turned on one cane and faced Andrew, Chris's right-hand man. An older man approached. Speaking to the older man she said, "Mr. Anderson, this is Tom Sawyer. I want you to take him to the pump station."

Lifting one eyebrow she glanced back at Tom and said, "Mr. Anderson is the ranch foreman, he can show you." Mr. Anderson replied, "Yes, Miss Mac." All four men walked toward the jeep.

They drove to the road near the river and continued up the hill, then carried on down into the jungle, crossing several more bridges over the snaking Martha Brea. Beside the lane for most of the way ran an old open aqueduct made from hand-fitted stones during the slave days. Tom could see water rushing towards the ruins and figured it must feed the waterwheel that Cathy Snipper had talked about on the phone.

They continued another 100 yards into the jungle and stopped near the river. Leaving the jeep, they went on foot across a narrow bridge to the aqueduct wall, walking 50 yards atop its edge, foot-over-foot, to a ramshackle pumping station. Two elderly Jamaican men were sipping tea over a campfire nearby and mosquitoes buzzed everywhere. Tom looked at these men; their faces showed toil and hardship beyond what most could understand, yet a great humanity came from their presence. One of these men, Apollo Joseph, would later bestow many kindnesses on Tom. Tom looked down at the water traveling the aqueduct, finding it hard to believe it had been running there for over 300 years. The sound of cuckoo birds and Jamaican orioles merged with different frog sounds. Other noises deeper in the jungle struck him with a sense of wonder. It was hot and humid under the jungle's canopy. Beads of sweat formed on his forehead. The smell was like a hundred shades of green.

Tom walked up a small embankment near the edge of the aqueduct and followed a pipe for 50 feet, watching it go straight up the side of a hill and disappear into the jungle. He asked Mr. Anderson where the pipe went. Mr. Anderson replied, "To de tank." Tom took a few pictures, made some measurements and asked several questions. Jotting notes, he motioned to Roger; he wanted to look at the water storage tank on the hill. They made their way back down the aqueduct, crossed the footbridge and climbed into the jeep.

Moving out of the jungle, they pulled the hill by the main house and took the road branching to the left by the ruins, passing the office on the left. They continued 50 yards to a large wooden gate and stopped. To the right were stables and a cafeteria used by the 70-some men and women working the ranch. Roger told Tom that most of these people came from the village of Unity a mile away on the other side of the river. Mr. Anderson got out and swung open the gate, motioning Roger to pull forward. The smell of horses and hay drifted into the opened door. Cowboys near the stables were moving about, each with a job to do. Mr. Anderson closed the gate and got in. Roger moved the jeep forward slowly, so as not to spook the horses crossing the road in front, and then gunned it down the dirt road, pulling a grade into the foothills. They crossed pastureland and rolling hills till the jeep could no longer move up slope. From there they went on foot for a quarter mile on an overgrown road, zigzagging at a steep rate to the top of the hill.

There on the hill, in a mountainous jungle, was a natural plateau extending 50 yards in either direction. Set back on the flat was a large brown steel water tank. Tom took measurements and calculated the tank to be 55,000 gallons, noting it in his logbook. They followed the pipe coming from the tank to the perimeter of the forest. Tom stood on a boulder gazing along a steep descent to the jungle below. The pipeline to the pumping station appeared poorly anchored to the face of the cliff. He wondered what it would be like to work with men on such an incline.

Tom made a few more notes and they headed back. At the corral, Roger dropped off Andrew and Mr. Anderson and continued past the ruins to the main house atop a knoll, and stopped. Tom could see a table being prepared out on the main lawn by a Jamaican lady, under the great guango tree. As they departed from the jeep, Roger looked over, as if to say, *Follow me.* There was a man already at the table. Approaching closer, Tom could see it was Chris Blackwell.

When they arrived they stood silently by the table waiting for Chris to finish writing something in a book. Roger commenced with the introduction when Chris stopped him,

"Yes, we met last night." Chris motioned them to sit. They began talking about Tom's background, the history of Pantrepant, and Jamaica in general, while a sweet older Jamaican lady named Mamaji served a delightful lunch. As they dined Tom could tell that Chris cared about his people by the respect and appreciation he gave Mamaji; a sign Tom always looks for. Everything about Chris seemed genuine.

After eating they were sipping on Jamaican Blue Mountain coffee, when Chris turned to Tom and said, "Can you fix it?" Tom said he understood why the pumps were burning up and proceeded to explain. The mile of underground wire from the Switch Room going to the pumping station was too small and the pumps were insufficient to push the water to the tank at any significant rate, even if they had all the power they needed. It was a compound problem. Not only would the pumps need to be larger, but the wires supplying them would have to be a great deal larger. Chris responded, "What's something like that going to cost?" Tom replied, "I won't know until I get back to the States and model the system on a computer." Chris insisted, "That's OK, just give me a ball-park figure." Tom replied, "I really don't want to guess at this point." Chris changed the subject and took another sip of Blue Mountain coffee.

Chris suggested they go look at the waterwheel. As they walked across the lawn toward the ruins Tom noticed a huge wicker basket in the shape of a fish, hanging from a rope high up in the great tree. He noted the ruins on the left, but didn't see any waterwheel. Then it came to him, as they got closer. Where the aqueduct spilled over, running down past the gardens among the ruins, he saw the base of what used to be an undershot wheel. Chris stopped at the site and said, "This is where the waterwheel used to be." Tom walked closer, amazed at how ancient it all seemed. He had had experience with other waterwheels, but this was an old undershot wheel; he had never seen one before, but knew of them.

Chris turned to Tom and said, "How much water do you think is coming down the aqueduct?" Tom picked up a twig and asked Roger to pace off ten feet upstream. Tom instructed him to throw it in, while he counted the seconds it took the water to carry it downstream to the base of the wheel. He told Roger to throw in another and watched it again. Tom measured the width of the aqueduct and the depth of the water and looked up at the sky mentally calculating a guess. He turned to Chris and said, "Around 1,300 gallons a minute, maybe a little more." Chris wanted to know how much it would cost to restore the wheel so that it produced electricity. Tom gave a knee-jerk number and then explained, "The wheel at most could generate 1 to 2 horsepower, not enough to offset the cost of restoration, unless it is just for esthetics." Chris smiled.

They had all started walking back towards the main house when Tom noticed the tree swing again. He turned to Chris and said, "Is that your tree swing?" Chris answered, "Yes, you want to swing?" Tom replied, "Yes," and walked over and climbed in. Chris grabbed the wicker fish-basket with Tom inside. Pulling it back, he ran forward until the arc of the fish swung behind him, letting go, swinging Tom high into the air. Tom closed his eyes for an instant then looked out through one of the eyes of the fish, watching the ground spin underneath him. He felt like a child swinging in an ancient womb.

When he climbed from the swing, he and Chris shook hands. They all walked to the main house and sat in chairs underneath the veranda overlooking the Martha Brea. Mamaji brought them drinks and they sat quiet for a time. Tom asked Chris if his wife liked the *Tara*. Chris said that she hadn't arrived yet. He got up and walked inside. Returning with the *Tara*, he said, "Tell me, who is *Tara*?" Tom replied, "This is Green *Tara*, the Tibetan Goddess of compassion and mercy," pointing to the statue, "*Tara* has 21 aspects, but this is Green *Tara*. See, she has her right leg down and only two arms, with her left arm over her heart." Chris lifted the statue up exposing the back and said, "What's this on the back?" Tom replied, "It's the *Tara* Mantra, *Tara's* prayer written in Sanskrit, blessing the mother force in nature. See, you can hang it if you want," pointing to a small metal loop on the back. Chris got up and went inside again taking the *Tara* with him. A few minutes later he returned with a hammer in one hand and the statue in the other. Walking to the east wall under the veranda, he placed a nail near the back door and attached the *Tara* statue to the side of the house.

They completed their business and said goodbye to Pantrepant. Roger and Tom made a few stops at nearby villages to drop off messages and made it back to Golden Eye in record time.

The next morning, Tom received a note requesting him to meet with Sue Morris, head of maintenance for the estate. Sue was passing the message on, "Chris asked if you would do an engineering evaluation of the stadium at Oracabessa." Sue took Tom to the site and they spent the morning going over the infrastructure. In the afternoon, Cathy Snipper took Tom around Golden Eye to meet the community working there: Alton, Cladets, Clayton, Myleen, David and Rowshine and a host of others.

Cathy suggested that he try the jet-skis and that Alton would set him up. Tom informed her that he had no swimming trunks, but thanked her just the same. She looked puzzled and said, "Wait right there." A few minutes later she showed up with a pair of brightly colored swimming trunks that fit perfectly. Tom asked, "Where did you get these?" She replied, "They're Chris's, I don't think he'll mind."

Tom had just returned from a jet-ski trip around the bay at Golden Head when he saw Cathy sitting at the patio table overlooking the bay talking with another girl. Drying himself off as he climbed the steps, he turned onto the patio and sat down. "I want to thank you for that Cathy, that was really fun." Cathy replied, "Oh yeah, thank Chris." They started talking and Cathy asked, "I saw on your resume that you worked at Jumby Bay. When was the last time you were down there?"

"The last time was in 1995 for hurricane restoration; Bill Anderson was running the place."

"That's right. He came here and ran Golden Eye shortly after that. You've been going to Antigua for quite some time?"

"Yes, I started in the early '80s and been going on and off for almost 20 years. I ran the utility operations for the island in

'90, but…until my wife discovered she had breast cancer and we came back to the States in '91."

"Is she OK now?"

"No… well yes, I think she's OK now. She passed away on June 26, 1996."

"Oh, I'm sorry…that must have been hard."

"Yes, it was. She was such a great lady," pulling a picture from his wallet, "I really loved her a lot. We were best friends, lovers, everything wrapped into one."

"That's what I hope for someday. Did you meet her in Antigua?"

Realizing that Cathy was sincere and genuinely interested, he began to tell her the story of how he met Mari. An hour later, when he was through, Cathy turned to him with an extended heart and said, "I've never had a man talk to me like that." Tom turned his head to one side and looked away, wondering if he'd spoken too candidly. Cathy went on, "No. Have you ever thought about writing it down?" The words lifted his heart; she was the second person to mention that. Tom's niece Angela had made the suggestion four years earlier. He reached across the table and grabbed Cathy's hand, tenderly squeezing it with both hands. That evening while walking on the beach it came to him—there would be a book someday.

The next morning he received instructions to depart for one of Chris's resorts in the Blue Mountains, called Strawberry Hill. Strawberry was built there years ago by Chris and was famous for its restaurants and spas. Tom was to meet a man named Johnathan and spend two days there, then fly out of Kingston for the United States. Those were his only instructions. Cathy arranged a cab to pick him up at the main gate at Golden Eye. He walked one last time to the entrance road and stood on the grassy lawn looking back at the sea.

The cab gathered Tom up and turned left down the coastal highway. Tom had no idea where they were going and took comfort in the young cabbie's smile. As the converted van sped outside Port Maria the sea disappeared behind them. All he knew was that Strawberry was somewhere on the other side of the island, high up in the mountains with a view of Kingston. At White Hat they turned left heading east, passing through Water Valley back towards the coast and entered the highway at Annotto Bay, passing Windsor Castle to Bluff Bay. From there they began a winding run into the mountains.

They'd been traveling an hour on twisted blacktop, passing through little settlements with names like Rose Hill, Tranquility, Bangor Ridge, Soso, Bimam and Wakefield, deep in the interior of rural Jamaica. Tom was riding in the front seat. Somewhere between Wakefield and Green Hill the cabbie decided to pick up the pace, rounding blind corners on the wrong side of the road, passing every car in sight. The prospect of getting the project has given Tom a reason; he feels purpose coming back into his life and the thought of dying doesn't seem as palatable as it did a few days before.

On one of the corners they missed a head-on collision only by sheer luck. He wasn't sure what the cabbie was using to tell if another car was coming—it appeared to be intuition or maybe faith. He was trying to enjoy the view when again the fear arose; he almost said something. The fear moved back and forth between his heart and his gut. They had just gone over a bridge, when he looked down and saw a group of women washing clothes on the rocks by a river. It was an ancient sight. Right then, he felt a change; he wasn't afraid to die and he wasn't afraid to live. Suddenly everything turned to Technicolor. His sense of smell increased, his eyes could see details he never thought possible, his body became relaxed, and his mind had no thoughts. He had slipped into a state of peace on the wrong side of the road at 40 miles per hour. He had given up all need for control and was in a state of surrender, yet fully alive.

With his head now hanging out the open car window, he paid no attention to oncoming traffic or any other concern for safety. Only joy and beauty filled his heart: the countryside, colorfully dressed people, brightly painted handmade houses flashing by, the rust on tin roofs, old men sitting on porches, the rural Jamaican air blowing in his face, women with their children in front yards, the crevices in the bark of trees, the flicker of strong men stacking wood as they passed.

He remained in an altered state all the way to New Castle. Something had changed. He felt lighter, energized and full of life. From New Castle they traveled through Red Light to Irish Town and began an even steeper climb. Tom looked off ten miles to a large city below; it was Jamaica's capital, Kingston, a city of 1.2 million people where 900,000 lived in poverty. They continued to wind into the Blue Mountains. Rounding a bend, they saw it near the peak; Strawberry Hill, built into the side of the mountain with stone stairways seemingly touching the sky.

Exiting the taxi he wiped the toes of his boots down the backsides of his soiled Levi's, tucked in his T-shirt and tipped the cabbie goodbye. Climbing the concrete drive from the blacktop he continued uphill to a building marked '"Office.'" He asked the lady at the counter, who looked at him curiously, "Is Johnathan here?"

"Is he expecting you?"

"I believe so."

She looked perplexed and asked him to wait as she scurried to another room. A few minutes later a cheerfully dressed, concerned woman appeared with a large muscular Jamaican man. "I'm Jenny Wood, the manager for Strawberry Hill. Can I help you?" Tom replied, "Yes, my name is Tom Sawyer, I'm supposed to meet Johnathan here." Her posture changed. Enthusiastically she reached out, greeting him with a handshake, "Oh, Tom! We've been expecting you. Johnathan is not here right now, but let me take you up to the restaurant, I'm sure you must be hungry."

They climbed a series of interchanging crafted-stone walkways bordered by colorful flowers and tropical trees. He began to get a sense of how luxurious and romantic the place was. Elegant 19th-century cottages tucked into the surrounding hills, with their verandas peering out over the Blue Mountains, connected magically with a system of walks and trellis-covered corridors. He would soon find out why Strawberry is famous for its restaurants and spas.

Jenny took Tom to the main lounge and introduced him to the bartender, "Take care of him." Tom ordered a Bailey's on the rocks and wandered out onto the veranda to gaze at Kingston 12 miles below. An hour later a bearded man carrying a cigarette and a beer approached from around the side of the restaurant. His hair moved from side to side, spilling over his shoulders as he walked. He pulled out a chair at the table, reached across and shook Tom's hand, introducing himself as "Johnathan, Chief Engineer." Tom liked him right off. They were both mavericks on the outside, but underneath was a pocket protector and a bunch of pencils.

Johnathan gave Tom a tour of the resort from an engineer's perspective. They started at the "back of the house" finishing with the generator room. Not only were both of these guys characters, but they liked to look at the same kind of stuff. Most resort operators liked to think that the "front of the house" is everything, but if the guest can't go to the bathroom, take a shower, or turn on the lights, the reputation meter starts running backwards. In Antigua Tom had always told his men, "This is not the 'back of the house'; it's the 'foundation of the house.' "

Johnathan and Tom covered everything from grease traps and underground drip systems to path lighting. Over dinner Johnathan brought up websites. He described a web system he was developing for Island Outpost that covered all seven of Chris's resorts, bouncing questions off Tom here and there. Tom loved it. Later, in the cool of the evening, they walked the gardens and stairways, visiting every *jolie chose* on the grounds.

The next morning Johnathan left on business. Tom spent the early part of the day taking in the surroundings. He walked out on a ledge overlooking the east side of the island and peered down into the valley where Bob Marley once lived. Just before lunch he sat by the pool watching it spill over the edge facing the skyline, giving him an impression that the water was disappearing into the sky.

Tom sat by himself on the restaurant veranda eating the soup of the day when he noticed a beautiful redheaded woman walk in from the lounge and sit alone, one table away. He thought he had seen her at Golden Eye but wasn't sure. She was striking and full of spunk. He watched her order, then said, "Were you just at Golden Eye?" She replied, "Why yes, I thought I saw you there too. My name is Suzanne." They talked from one table to the other for a few minutes, then Suzanne said, "Would you like to join me?" Tom was delighted and started gathering up his plates and utensils like a schoolboy when suddenly a server appeared offering to reset a placement at Suzanne's table. She told him she was a scriptwriter for a film being produced by Chris Blackwell and was living at Strawberry while working on the manuscript. They told stories for two hours over a dramatic panorama 3,000 feet above Kingston.

That evening Cathy Snipper showed up with Roger and a whole group of people. Everyone ate dinner outside on the patio next to several distinguished-looking guests sitting two tables away. Next to them was another table of diplomatic types all maintaining proper conversational protocol. At Tom's table, things started to get a little boisterous. There was a man who lived on the south shore, a somewhat isolated and notorious place, who kept telling loud dirty jokes. It wasn't that his jokes were so funny; it was Cathy, trying to get him into proper etiquette. The more she would try to shush him, the louder he would be. It was like a Laurel and Hardy act, compounded by Tom's effort not to laugh, which made him laugh even more. The more Tom laughed, the louder the man got and the more Cathy tried to correct him. It went on and on like that until Tom almost split a gut.

The next morning Tom grabbed his backpack, said goodbye to everyone and caught a cab for the Kingston airport. After an hour of trying to explain to security that he had brought the tools in his backpack into Jamaica at Montego Bay as carry-on, and had no luggage to check, he finally opted to place them in a cardboard box and check them at the last minute, running out onto the tarmac seconds before the plane closed its door.

He arrived back in Santa Rosa on July 15th and began engineering the project for Pantrepant in late July. Design drawings, surveys, cost analyses, budgetary assignments, specifications, equipment, material lists, manpower requirements; all sorts of information started pouring back and forth. In late August he started the procurement. Equipment and materials began streaming to the freight forwarder in Miami for a container ship bound for the Caribbean.

Sitting on the cement steps in the backyard on Neo he looked over at the triangular planter box Mari had cultivated years ago and pondered, *O purple, white, yellow iris, planted so long ago by loving hands, you have so many children, where do you send me now?*

20

"A kind of golden hour one remembers for a life time...
Everything was touched with magic."

Margaret Bourke White

Pantrepant

Two weeks ago a cargo ship set out from Florida across the Caribbean Sea and docked at Montego Bay on the island of Jamaica, carrying a 40-foot container destined for Pantrepant in the central jungle of Trelawny. Jamaican Customs are still processing the equipment and materials sent to a freight forwarder in Miami almost a month ago.

Tom had just received a fax stating the subcontractor has completed the first half-mile of underground pipeline and is awaiting his arrival. Running for last-minute stuff on his 44-item carry-on list, he's determined not to have to check anything. He's managed to put everything into three bags: one large duffle bag that looks like it might fit in the overhead, but will really have to go in one of those special closets; a camera bag filled with almost everything but a camera; and two large daypacks strapped together to look like one, with a makeshift shoulder strap attached. In them is everything he'll need for his three-month construction adventure.

At 3:00 AM he caught a bus from Santa Rosa to San Francisco and boarded a plane for Jamaica. His plane is just now landing at Montego Bay. A summer thunderstorm has forced his plane to circle twice over the runway. It's been 14 hours and the sun is still shining.

He made it through customs in 25 minutes and walked to the frontage road facing the airport. A handful of tourists scampered about trying to figure out the system, while taxi drivers descended from every direction hoping for the catch of the day. Brightly dressed women with children swarmed along the road greeting their incoming relatives. Andrew and Justine, whom Tom had many phone conversations with, were waiting just outside the door. Although they had never met, Justine hugged Tom, provided a last-minute briefing, and waved goodbye. Tom is to ride to Pantrepant with Andrew.

They drove the coastline for a half hour to Falmouth, a former sugar port of 10,000 with its Victorian markets and parish churches nestled amongst buildings built during the turn of the 17th century. It was Saturday night. The streets were teeming with brightly garbed inhabitants milling about with rum bottles waving in the air. Women danced outside in front of a makeshift tavern while men gathered on corners looking on. It was hot and muggy. Crowds roamed the alleyways, sprawling out into the streets, forcing all vehicle traffic to move at a snail's pace. The air was still and smelled of sea and rum. Andrew slowly moved the truck through the swarm and continued on. At the edge of town the street turned from blacktop to gravel as they bounced over ruts in the road. After 16 miles, they sloshed along a mud-covered road blending with dark water channels pouring in from the sides of flooded pastureland, a course thinned by a world of jumbled erosion.

On a slightly downhill left curve, they passed Good Hope, exploding into a view of foothills. Not far ahead lay the fertile mountains of the Cockpit country. Traveling the last two miles in first gear, they crossed over the Martha Brea, passing a windswept flat of thick jungle forest; an endless canopy of a thousand tints of green, flowing into the rolling hills of Pantrepant.

At Pantrepant Tom was welcomed back with a handmade card from Miss Mac. Andrew showed him to accommodations upstairs in the guest annex overlooking the valley. The building was a clapboard structure with heart-pine floors, mahogany doors and ceiling fans. The balcony looked over antique brick pathways leading to a lanai and on to a botanical nursery to the right of a sprawling lawn.

Andrew reintroduced Tom to the beautiful Jamaican lady, Mamaji, who would be Tom's housekeeper and cook for the next few days.

Tom stood in front of the window at dusk. A slight mist filled the air, making the valley appear diffused like a watercolor. From the north he could see the Martha Brea rushing below the main grounds. Through the open door leading to the veranda, rolling hills disappeared into the jungle. The room was faux-painted with pastel blue and peach. A 17th-century farm scene on canvas hung on the wall at the front of the bed. To the right was a vintage roll-top desk next to a hand-carved nightstand with a phone on top. A mahogany reading table sat near the window. Beyond, an entryway opened up into a kitchen and dining area. Off the east wall was a hallway leading to a bathroom and shower.

A sense of home surrounded him. He threw his bags down on the bed and went with Andrew through the dark to meet Keith, a strong kind-hearted Jamaican man and head of security. He asked Keith where he might locate a man named Sleepy, who he hopes will know where the 40-foot container is. Keith replied, "Axe Mr. Anderson."

Walking across the road toward the stables, Tom found Mr. Anderson, and asked where he might find Sleepy. Mr. Anderson pointed toward several new construction sites and Tom walked on. As he passed near the nursery he saw seven 1,300-pound spools of 350MCM copper wire sitting on the lawn and figured the container must be on the property somewhere.

Climbing the steps to the new office, he found Sleepy, a reliable hardworking carpenter's foreman, placing sheetrock against the west wall, lit by makeshift floodlights. Sleepy took him to the container site and unlocked two large steel doors. He shined a flashlight inside, exposing all the materials needed to start the project.

Tom felt he could sleep easy now and returned to his room. On the bed was a note: "Chris Blackwell has already gone to bed. He would like to walk the property with you in the morning. Also, Barry Cowan of Cowan Electric will be arriving early."

Tom set the alarm for 5:30 AM and turned in. A thousand things spun through his head before drifting to sleep.

The next morning, up before the alarm, he stepped from the shower just as Mamaji came to make breakfast. Putting on his socks, he looked out the window. The sun was poking up over the tree line. Across the way, cowboys had already saddled up their horses and were trotting into the valley.

After breakfast, near the nursery, he inspected the wire spools brought in from Montego Bay the week before. He noticed consistent cuts in the insulation on one of the spools, then another and another. All the spools had been damaged by what looked like the teeth of a front-loading tractor. Anxiously he double-checked to see if the correct wire had been shipped. Sure enough, 37 strand, .68 copper, 13/16 thick with 600-volt fuel-proof insulation. It's "all good," except for the damage. He figured they'd have to pull 100 feet of wire off each spool and repair the nicks with high-voltage tape and epoxy.

At 9:00 AM it was 75 degrees. Barry Cowan, one of the Jamaican subcontractors, showed up with his crew. They went over the specifications and scheduling for next week. Tom spent the rest of the morning sizing up what was damaged or missing. After lunch, he and Chris walked the pipeline that would carry the massive wires out into the jungle to the new pumping station a mile away.

Toward evening Tom walked to the great tree behind Chris's house and as he did, he noticed a beautiful Jamaican woman working the flowerbeds around its base. Something seemed special about her. He moved in closer for a better look. Her skin was almost glowing. Her eyes were bright and full of life. He remembered seeing her somewhere, but wasn't sure. Then it dawned on him. As he approached he said, "Are you Mary, Chris's wife?" She looked curiously shocked. Placing her garden trowel next to her bare feet, she turned and looked up, as if to say, *How could you tell me from any other Jamaican?* Then she replied, "Yes, how did you know?" Tom went on, "I saw you before." She replied, "On this property, or one of the others?" He answered, "In a fashion magazine Kathleen told me about."

Mary smiled and said, "You must be Tom Sawyer." She continued to plant flowers as they carried on a warm conversation about Pantrepant and what he was doing there. She seemed more curious about who the tattooed man with long hair was, than the details of what he was going to be doing for the next three months.

Excusing himself, he wandered on. A misty rain had begun as he continued his walk around the grounds. At the edge of a large organic garden, behind the nursery, stood a gorgeous Rastafarian woman talking to a nurseryman and another gentleman gathered near the stone wall. Her hair hung down to her ankles in large twisted locks. Her eyes were deep. He couldn't help but approach. Introducing himself he embarked upon a trade. If she would let him touch her hair, he would let her feel his tattooed skin. Her name was Dianne, a Rastafarian priestess and entertainment attorney. Her large bearded Jamaican friend was To-To. Tom and To-To temporarily exchanged knives as a sign of friendship. To-To smiled and looked away. Glancing into Dianne's eyes, Tom ran his fingers down one lock of her hair, while at the same time, with the tips of her fingers, she touched his forearm noting the Goddess tattooed there.

Around six, Chris came over to the guest annex and invited Tom to the main house for drinks. They sat out on the veranda with Lion, a holy man who lives in the jungle and wears nothing but a loincloth. Chris gave Lion a cigar and a small glass of brandy. They had just taken a sip when Mary came out onto the porch. Everyone stood as she entered. She wanted to know more about the *Tara* that Tom had given Chris at Golden Eye on the trip before. She became concerned when Tom told her it contained Mari's ashes. He reached into his pocket and handed Mary a sheet of paper explaining who Mari was and her words to the world. Mary was apprehensive at first, but as she read, her face changed. She seemed pleased and honored to have the *Tara* in her home. Mary excused herself and went upstairs and Lion disappeared back into the jungle. Chris made grilled-cheese-and-tomato sandwiches and the two of them sat in the front room watching Palm Pictures productions into the night.

The next day Tom had steel stanchions fabricated by a local blacksmith to hold the heavy wire spools. They needed to repair the damaged insulation on each spool by pulling 100 feet off each one. Each spool weighed 1,300 pounds and he figured it would take 12 men to lift one spool onto a stanchion. He had two men place a stanchion in front of the spool, slid a 20-foot length of 2-inch steel pipe through the hub and instructed six men to take position on the left and six men on the right. He counted, "1, 2, 3, heave." In unison both teams lifted, raising the steel pipe into the air. There was only one problem. The spool was still on the ground and the pipe had been bent in the shape of a U. Everyone started laughing. Tom laughed too—it was a great icebreaker. Trying another approach, they cut the bent pipe from the spool and inserted another pipe. This time, they tilted the stanchion back to meet the horizontal pipe and moved the men right next to the spool. Using this method was more dangerous. If the stanchion should collapse, the men closest to the spool would be crushed. Tom took one of the inside positions and synchronized the men; "1, 2, 3, heave." Up it went. The stanchion held. The rest of the day was spent testing and repairing the spools.

The next few days brought everyone together. The crews had been lined out and knew what to do. The job was moving forward nicely. Between Natalie, the office secretary, Andrew, and Miss Mac, Tom was able to get local resources organized and was becoming familiar with what it IS.

Yesterday a German Shepherd-Doberman started following him around, disappearing now and then, and reappearing again. It's as if the dog knew Tom missed Didger and purposely followed him everywhere he went. One afternoon, Tom sat on the edge of a water trough near the guest annex splashing water on his face when Mamaji walked by and said, "Dimswitch him like you." Tom replied, "Dimswitch? What Dimswitch?" Mamaji replied, "De dog." Excitedly he said, "Oh yeah, he follows me everywhere. I call him Dog." Mamaji smiled, "Him name Dimswitch."

Over the next three weeks men pulled the massive wires, two at a time, through the conduit across the valley toward the jungle. At times 20 men pulled barefoot in the mud, moving the 2,600-pound load only a foot at a time. Barry told Tom that in Jamaica men didn't say, "pull" they said, "TU." Tom asked, "What means TU?" Barry replied, "It means to pull with all your heart."

One especially warm afternoon, just after a rain, men were assembled along the conduit. Ten men on a chain, two gangs either side. Tom joined the chain and pulled with the men. He yelled, "TU"; 20 men pulled, their bare feet digging into the mud. It was an ancient, much-respected sensation. It seemed to transport him to another time, perhaps a time when men died of their toil. Tears flowed down his face as 20 men leaned into it with all their hearts. He would never forget how honored he felt to work beside these men.

A few days later, he had just come from the jungle onto a grassy knoll overlooking an expansive pasture. It seemed to go on forever, a sea of swaying green, blown by a warm breeze. He'd been under the jungle canopy for ten hours. He was soaked in sweat and his arms were swollen from mosquito bites. He paused to watch the last few men disappear across the valley to their homes in Unity Village. As he walked toward what he now called home, he couldn't remember how he got there. He thought to himself, *How did I get here, have I always been here, did I live somewhere else before...* All his past seemed to disappear from memory; he wasn't sure what century it was. He looked over at Dimswitch scampering in the tall grass and said, "Hello my friend, are you ready to go get something to eat?" Dimswitch wagged his tail and they meandered on. As they approached the guest annex he saw Cynthia, his new cook, waving from the balcony. She always hopes he'll be on time, but never complains. He was two hours late for dinner. She still had to feed him and then walk three miles to her village and make dinner for her family.

As he climbed the stairs, Dimswitch ran right past him to the top of the landing. Wagging his tail, with his tongue hanging out, his big eyes said, *What's taking you so long, I smell food?* Tom could hear singing coming from inside; he knew Cynthia was already working over the stove. She always sang gospel songs while she cooked. He removed his muddy boots and collapsed onto the bed. From the kitchen Cynthia paused from her music, "Mr. Sawyer, hope you like oxtail, me make yam and yoyo fruit too." She continued singing, stopping now and then to tell stories about growing up in her village. Tom rolled over and picked up his harmonica from the nightstand and began to play along. It was something they did just about every night.

Lately Mamaji and Cynthia have been taking turns cooking. They are competing to see who can feed him the most. One day he had just gone out the door, to find Mamaji and Cynthia talking on the veranda. They both turned to him and laughed, patting their bellies. Cynthia said, "You get fat," and they both laughed again. Tom rubbed his belly and said, "I don't want to go home with a big belly." They laughed even more.

One day he noticed Cynthia hanging clothes on the clothesline. She seemed tired. She and Mamaji did all the laundry and ironing for the ranch as well as taking care of Tom. He came over and gave her a hug and said, "Don't worry yourself about making me lunch any more. I love your cooking, but I'm going to start eating with the men, I can get more work done that way." She smiled and continued hanging clothes.

Each morning Tom assembled the crews on the lawn reviewing the day's work. For the last three days a man had been coming every morning looking for work. Tom asked another man who he was. No one seemed to know. Tom would just say, "Not today." That night Tom asked Cynthia if she knew the man. She told him his name was Paston and that he walked seven miles each way from another village hoping to find work.

The next morning the man came again. The crew was gathered on the lawn when the man approached. Tom stopped talking and turned toward the man, "What's your name?" The man replied matter-of-factly, "Paston." Tom asked, "Have you come far?" The man spoke back in barely understandable patois. Tom replied, "We could use another good man today, it pays $J600 per day," US$13. The man nodded. Tom excused the crew except for Paston, and motioned him to remain. He looked at the man. His locks were pulled up in a bundle and tied with a black-and-white scarf with stripes of red. He wore a tattered clean white shirt that hung over in back, covering a 14-inch knife tucked down in his pants. The knife shimmered through the thinning cloth in the sunlight, perhaps a reminder of how hard life could be. His pants were clean but holey and his feet were bare. He had a full beard and appeared to be in his 30s. He looked thin but strong. Tom said, "It's hard work, have you eaten?" Paston looked down. Tom told him to stay there; he would be right back. He went to the refrigerator and broke off a large piece of cheese and two pieces of bread. Returning, he told Paston to eat as they hurried to catch up with the rest of the crew. Neither one said anything as they walked. It turned out that Paston was a devoted Rastafarian; he supported a family of four and was a loner at heart. He spoke very little and worked hard, gaining the respect of the other men in two days.

That night Tom was so exhausted he came back to his room, removed his clothes and collapsed onto the bed naked, with the door open. Nicola, a lady carpenter who was staying in the next apartment, saw him and woke him up. She said, "Are you going to sleep all night with your door open?" In a daze he thanked her, thinking *How sweet, she doesn't want me to get eaten alive by mosquitoes,* and rolled over, drifting off again.

Normally he's been rising before breakfast to take Dimswitch for his morning walk, but for the last couple of days Dimswitch has been disappointed; they haven't gone for their usual jaunt. This morning Dimswitch walked through the open door and started licking Tom's face at 5:45 AM; his tail wagged profusely as he moistened his master into consciousness. Tom skipped his shower and they set out north for the Wilson River Bridge. Cutting across a field of wild sugarcane, they came to the riverbank not far from where two rivers came together. Making his way along the edge, Dimswitch darted back and forth following an invisible trail of something that was no longer there. The sun rose over the tree line, reflecting off the water. Morning doves cooed to the sound of a tractor starting in the distance.

When they reached the east side of the bridge, Tom sat squatted, staring out at the rushing water, splashing a stick up and down, imagining the river was standing still and he was moving. He turned and looked under the bridge, noticing a yellow bucket, a blue plastic tarp, several white jugs and a blanket-roll. Suddenly an older Jamaican man appeared, introducing himself as Mr. Nelson. He said he had lived on the property since he was a boy and took care of the cattle. They both sat under the bridge and talked for a while. Off in the distance they could hear the whine of helicopter blades winding up. They walked out from under the bridge just in time to see Chris fly over, destination unknown.

It's been several weeks now and three crews are working. One is enlarging the pump house at the base of the embankment with instructions to stay clear of the cliff, one is making the uphill pull along the power line across the valley, and 14 men are working the face of the embankment rising 650 feet up from the pumping station to the tank.

A 10-man crew had been carrying pipe, by hand, up a zigzag path to the tank when Tom looked across the basin and saw they were no longer working. He went to investigate, figuring they should have moved it all by now. At the base of the hill he picked up a 20-foot length of galvanized 2-inch steel pipe. He lifted it onto his shoulder and began to climb the hill. Each pipe weighed 82 pounds. Halfway up the quarter-mile climb, he had to set it down. Resting for a few minutes, he went again, setting it down at the three-quarter mark, resting even longer. His heart was pounding. Then he went again, finally reaching the top where a man descending the hill saw him. The man turned and ran back toward the tank, notifying the foreman that the boss-man was coming, carrying a piece of pipe. The foreman scurried toward Tom saying, "Please sir, let me take that." Tom replied, "I needed to feel how hard it was. Please put two men on a pipe next time."

He noticed the men had gathered in the shade around the tank and were cooking something, "What you cooking?" The foreman, Millerman, replied, "Jombi Rundown." Tom asked what it was. Bushes, a Rastafarian plumber and Millerman's right-hand man piped up. Taking a long toke from a spliff in his right hand, he started speaking patois. He said Rundown was made from fresh coconut milk boiled down to a thick sauce with banana, country pepper, johnnycakes and tubers from the jungle. Tom asked if he could try a little. Bushes smiled and picked up a tin cup near the campfire, washing it out under the faucet near the tank. He stirred the blackened pot twice and spooned in the brew. They all sat leaned-up against the tank eating Rundown, in a moment of talk and laughter.

After lunch the men were installing steel water pipe on the face of the embankment, at times hanging on with ropes to keep from falling 600 feet down. They were anchoring the new lines with chains and spikes every 20 feet.

Tom had left the piping crew to go back and do calculations, when Millerman, the crew foreman, appeared shaken at the door, stating, "Mi tink we haff a problem mon." Tom calmly looked up from his papers, "What kind of problem?" Millerman twirled his locks and said, "A problem mon." Tom was curious to see what this man thought a problem was. They jumped in the jeep and headed for the tank. Millerman was quiet the whole way and didn't want to explain what the problem might be.

When they arrived Millerman took Tom to the edge of the embankment. Looking down 650 feet into the jungle below, he saw the problem. One of the couplings on the old line had rusted through and a man working the face had bumped it with a wrench. All 650 feet of old pipeline had collapsed, falling down the hillside, and was wrapped up like spaghetti at the base of the pumping station. Tom immediately checked to see if any men were injured down below. Thank God, no one had been under the pipeline when it went. Trees as thick as a man's arm had been cut completely in half by the crushing pipe as it made its descent. To make matters worse, the line that had collapsed was the main line and by morning the entire estate would be without water. They spent the rest of the day and into the night with flashlights, bringing up pipe and reconnecting it.

Tom had lowered himself on a rope to assist a threader working 300 feet above the valley floor. He stood in the moonlight for several minutes on a rock outcropping listening to jungle sounds coming up from below. Millerman came up alongside of him and said, "Yu like it hir in de nite." Tom replied, "Yes, I love it here." and went back to work.

From then on, when Millerman used the word "problem," Tom listened intently.

One evening he heard music coming from far off in the distance across the river and was curious. A few days later Millerman offered to take him to Unity Village. Tom had heard about the bamboo bridge called One Tick and until now could only imagine what it would be like to cross it.

Bushes, Millerman and Tom had traversed the west pasture and were approaching the river when the smell of cool moss mixed with cow dung permeated the air. Mosquitoes thickened as they moved closer. The buzz of horse flies blended with the sound of the river below. Following 30 yards behind Bushes and Millerman, Tom spotted the bridge up ahead. It nestled itself in the trees growing along the bank and was made of three 9"-wide bamboo timbers tied together with ropes, spanning 50 feet across the Unity River. Two smaller bamboo bars about head height acted as overhead railings. The trick was to slide each hand along the guide rails while walking on the timbers. Care had to be taken to avoid falling. The rounded timbers were moist and slippery in the constant mist boiling up from the rushing water 15 feet below. Millerman and Bushes scurried ahead, leaving the initiate to cross as they waved him on.

Tom went hand-over-hand. After reaching the other side they patted him on the back and cut through a cane field to a small path leading to the village. There they met up with Yotan, a massive gentle giant of a man who worked on the pipe crew, coming down the trail. It seemed strange to see these men outside of work, living in their own environment. While Tom, Yotan and Millerman stood by an old ruin, talking, Bushes climbed a nearby coconut tree with a machete in his mouth. Everyone turned to watch as he pushed himself upward barefoot, with a T-shirt tied between his ankles. Reaching the top, he cut several coconuts and watched them fall to the ground with a thud. Yotan gathered the nuts. Drawing a machete from his side, he began cutting the green husk away. Tom walked closer to watch. By now Bushes had climbed back down and they all stood in a circle watching Yotan. Yotan held up a coconut in his left hand and swung a three-foot-long machete with his right, cutting off a small portion with surgical precision, exposing the milk inside. As is the custom, he who climbs gets first drink. Yotan handed it to Bushes for a cool sweet drink that spilled over his lips and ran down the front of his chest. Tom was guest; he was next. They stood passing the drink from one to another until it was gone, then Yotan cut another until all the coconuts were empty.

With full bellies they walked on toward the village. Passing a neighborhood of small brightly painted tin houses, they turned left onto a dirt path and continued along a stick fence for a hundred yards to a white house set back from the road. By now people had gathered around, curious about what a white man was doing in the village. Millerman seemed to have pull. People only approached to a subconsciously-agreed-upon distance.

Drawing near the white house, Tom could see two elders, a man and a woman sitting under a covered porch, singing. The woman was playing a small piano, the man sat close to her in a wooden chair; both were harmonizing gospel music. The woman appeared to be blind. When the old man saw Tom, he stood, quickly putting his right hand on the woman's shoulder, partly out of respect, partly out of a response stemming from the old days when a white man meant trouble. Millerman introduced them, "Dis is mi mudder and fadder." Tom told them he loved their music and asked if they would sing another song. As they sang, a small girl got up from the yard and entered the house, reappearing with chairs.

For a half hour the couple sang songs of faith to their implausible guest. Millerman, who is a Rasta musician when he's not working, asked Tom if he knew how to play the piano. Millerman had heard Tom play harmonica from the balcony at Pantrepant the week before. Tom said he knew very little, except for a little blues tune, the one he played repeatedly after Mari passed on. Millerman whispered not to play anything Reggae; his mother didn't like Reggae. Tom played a Ray Charles kind of "Doll Cage" blues, rocking back and forth. The old woman made her way to the little piano bench. Putting her hand on Tom's back she said, "I have a good son." Feeling her way back to her bench on the porch, she smiled at her husband and sat back down. Everyone touched hands as a sign of farewell. Millerman took Tom back to One Tick and waved goodbye.

Late in the afternoon the next day, Tom was making line inspections along the edge of the jungle when he heard something moving through the bushes at a rapid velocity. He jumped back. A group of men working the pipeline saw him jump and giggled among themselves. He couldn't imagine something moving that fast through the bushes. He turned to one of the men and said, "What was that?" The whole crew responded, "Mongoose."

On the way back from line inspections, he noticed two men in the valley working hard in the hot sun. They were lifting concrete blocks for the new manholes along the line. Tom watched from a distance. Even though they were drenched in sweat and breathing hard, they continued to work at a strong pace. As he approached he could see the glaze in their eyes. He stopped, "Do you men have water?" They replied, "No sir." Tom walked back to the annex, brought the men cheese and water, and then found the foreman and chewed his ass.

A few days later when men were laying pipe down the steep incline from the tank, they found loose stones precariously balanced on ledges the last 200 feet. As they worked, boulders started falling along the embankment to the base of the pump station.

Tom asked Millerman to clear the rocks off the cliff before installing more pipe. Millerman wanted to bring in another man who knew more about "falling rock." He told Tom the man's name was Daimmy and that he was a holy man who had lived for years with the Nani, an isolated tribe of mountain people living in the western region of the jungle. The Nani stay purposely isolated to preserve their traditions in folk medicine and spiritual practice. Tom found out later that Daimmy had survived alone in the jungle for years serving an apprenticeship given him by his teachers, and had lived in the region for over 70 years.

The next day, Tom walked the valley to the jungle and traversed the aqueduct west of the caves. Walking along its face to the pumping station, he noted the clear water of the Martha Brea rushing over rocks to Chris's natural swimming hole, some 40 yards across. He stood for a moment on the aqueduct wall and looked across the water. Next to the swimming hole was Chris's meditation gazebo with a six-sided gabled roof, topped with an ancient crown from some long-lost civilization. He stared into space; *Millerman is bringing Daimmy today, a holy man. What will that be like?* When Tom arrived at the pumping station he saw Twini, a mason, smiling with no teeth, mixing cement for stonework along the aqueduct. Behind him was a man wearing an East Indian turban tending a campfire of large boiling pots. Roots and tubers gathered from the jungle were spread out on cloth beside the river. Clouds of smoke filled the air from men carrying smoke pots. Tom asked Apollo Joseph, an old man in his 70s who frequently brought Tom tea, what all the smoke was about? Apollo answered, "Mosquitoes bad today." Men squatted on the ground fashioning rope into nets. Several men were carrying large sledgehammers and picks across their shoulders.

A few minutes later Millerman showed up with Daimmy. They shook hands and discussed how the boulders would be removed. Daimmy was quiet, speaking only when there was something to say. He looked wise and agile for his age. Tom asked if he could take his photograph. Daimmy said he didn't mind, but said it probably wouldn't come out. Joseph the Carpenter (who was really a plumber) sitting with his legs crossed on the aqueduct, straightened his pink and green hat to one side and said, "Daimmy is *juke-ti-fied*," (respected for his magical powers). Kingman and Millerman, along with a crew of Rastas, began removing boulders from the face of the embankment, coordinated by Daimmy. The men wrapped the largest boulders, some the size of Volkswagens, in handmade nets, permanently attaching them to trees above.

Then they began swinging hammers and picks to Daimmy's rhythm. A big man standing on the hill yelled down to the cook, "Mi wants long pot." The cook yelled back, "Mi cook short pot." The cook yelled again, "Nigger, nigger swing," as the large man with massive muscles swung the hammer, crushing a large rock with a single blow. Everyone started laughing.

Tom spent the afternoon watching boulders being lowered to the base of the embankment. There was something magical, almost spiritual, about the event that kept him captivated. When the crew had finished, he felt he had just come from church. In the days to come, on occasional Sundays, he and Daimmy would sit in the caves above the Martha Brea for hours, enjoying the peace. Three weeks later, when Tom had the photographs developed, the East Indian cook and the campfire showed up, but no Daimmy.

One especially warm misty night Tom sat outside on the veranda sipping tea. He heard a deep sonorous bass sound coming across the valley from the jungle, and then it stopped. Then it sounded again. He walked inside, calling for Cynthia. She poked her head around the corner from the kitchen with a curious look. Tom asked, "What's that sound coming from the jungle?" Cynthia smiled and said, "Fog." Tom reiterated, "Yes, I see the fog. No, I mean the deep bass sound, what is that?" Cynthia replied again, "Fog." He finally got it, she was saying "frog." They both laughed. He picked up his little Bhagavad Gita and lay down on the bed to read.

After a few minutes he looked over at the nightstand. Sitting near the phone was a metal-flake candy-apple green praying mantis five inches long. It was motionless. Its legs spread apart like a piece of heavy construction equipment. In front of its body were its praying hands, clasped together in position to strike. Slightly back, along a pole-like structure extending several inches above its body, was its head with beady all-directional eyes. Tom watched it for a minute, waving his hand. He watched its eyes follow the motion like a crane operator. It looked like a little guy sitting in a tower attached to heavy machinery. What freaked him out was that it appeared to be so conscious. Suddenly it began to rock back and forth in a hypnotic motion. That was it. Tom uttered out loud, "You're going outside." He removed the pillowcase from the bed, making a makeshift butterfly net trap. Catching the creature with one swing, he walked out onto the veranda. As he shook the pillowcase over the edge, he said, "Sorry fella, you're just too weird," and watched the mantis fall in slow motion through the air. One foot above the ground its armored body opened and wings came out, gliding it safely into the grass.

A week later as they started to pull wire through the jungle along the Martha Brea, Sam, Barry's right-hand man, came to Tom and said, "Will you miss me when you're gone?" Tom replied, "No, but I will miss your spirit." Sam had been in a car accident years ago, and both his legs had been crushed and broken in several places. The pins holding the bones together literally showed through the skin along his shins. He could outwork any two men and never complained.

Later on that afternoon, Tom was working with the men along the river. The mosquitoes had been exceptionally bad that day. Having to go to the bathroom, he grabbed the smoke pot that Apollo Joseph had made for him out of a coffee can and baling wire, and set out for a private spot away from the river. When he dropped his pants, thousand of mosquitoes swarmed his private parts. By the time he was done, his legs, butt and scrotum were bitten beyond respectability. He had been told before to put the smoke pot "very near." That night, in the quiet of his room, everything began to swell. Waking up continuously to scratch, he'd say to himself, "When they say, 'very near,' that means 'very near.'" He couldn't sleep and went outside to talk to Keith, the night watchman, who grinned while advising him to place the pot up wind. The word had spread all around that day; everyone seemed to know, even the secretaries. That night he was definitely in his body and vowed never to make the same mistake again.

Now that he was eating lunch every day with the men, he would often eat at the farm cantina, an orange-peel-colored building with powder blue doors, green trim and tin roof. The kitchen opened to a large covered patio lined with rows of pastel green tables. He would sometimes play dominos with Barry G and watch the men slap them hard onto pieces of cardboard to keep from chipping the paint off the counters. Barry Cowan, "Sam the man," and Tom would usually sip ginger beer or Busta and talk shop till it was time to go to work. Most of the men who worked the farm wore blue khaki uniforms, shirts and pants with black rubber boots. Dimswitch always hung out under the tables just in case someone would drop a morsel.

One of the men started bringing his five-year-old daughter to the farm around lunchtime. She was full of life, with big black eyes that seemingly shone in the dark. Her smile was that of a beauty queen. She wore a Levi-blue dress with bright-colored flowers embroidered above the pockets, letting her shoulder strap drift down one arm. Her hair was tied in braids on either side with red and green ties. Often her father would chase her across the grass saying, "Hurry mi catch yu." She would run laughing until her papa caught up, lifting her high in the air in a spin. She was very photogenic and constantly urged Tom to take her picture. He called her the "Spirit of Jamaica."

One day, one of the cooks, who all dressed in white dresses with long light-blue aprons, opened the door leading to the patio and said, "Mr. Sawyer. Yu like ugly?" Tom replied, "Mi ugly?" She said, "No. Yu like ugly. Juse, mon!" Tom, pointing curiously at himself, said again, "Mi ugly?" She told him to wait there and returned a minute later with a large black gnarly-skinned fruit about the size of a grapefruit. She explained that "ugly" was fruit and she wanted to make juice for him. He finally got it.

When Cynthia found out he was drinking ugly at the cantina prepared by another woman, she and her daughter Jackie started making sweet *sarwee* juice made from the sarwir flower that grew around the farm. Each flower had to be picked and processed by pouring water over it, a procedure that took all day. She would often have a glass sitting on the table when he came home.

A month went by. The power line, running three quarters of a mile across rolling pastures and entering the jungle for the last quarter mile, was now complete. The new water pipeline extended from the pumping station to the tank on the hill and the pump house had been expanded and retrofitted. All they needed now were the pumps to finish the plumbing. Tom was making his daily pilgrimage to the pump station to supervise the building of a small bridge across the aqueduct, and making drawings for the plumbing system. On his way he stopped by the main house and dropped off Fire Balls for Mary. She loved them and couldn't seem to get enough. They're a spicy cinnamon/hot pepper/sugarcoated candy jawbreaker. He'd purchased 200 of them at the Yulupa Ace Hardware store in Santa Rosa before he left. He was just about out and was having to ration the delicacies. Mary smiled and watched him go down the dirt road. His backpack, filled with tools and fittings, swayed with each step.

Today he decided to walk through the west pasture; following the aqueduct to the plank bridge, he crossed the river at the swimming hole. He will sit on the bridge for a few minutes watching the water rush, and swing his legs back and forth. He will say a few prayers to the nature Goddess and continue on to the second bridge. He will do the same thing again at the river crossing, then move on to the aqueduct and walk several hundred feet along its edge to the pumping station. He has just traversed the aqueduct wall and is standing at the pump house on the opposite side. Apollo Joseph sees him and disappears into the jungle. Almost every time Tom comes, Apollo brings him tea made from roots and herbs. Apollo is a pump man; born in 1927 in Cuba and knows every medicinal herb in the jungle. Last week he brought Tom a tea called Bloodwitch that was supposed to clean his liver. Tom gave some to Barry and they both got so high they couldn't talk. Now when Apollo brings Bloodwitch, Tom says, "Oh, thank you sir, but I think I'm going to pass today."

Tom turned to see a line of men carrying 100-pound stacks of cement blocks on top of their heads, moving along the aqueduct to the pump house. Andrew's crew was building a bridge across the aqueduct using ironwood, a black native hardwood found on the property. Tom removed an assortment of tools and supplies from his pack and gave them to Andrew.

As Tom walked into the pump house, out of the corner of his eye he caught Apollo dropping something in the boiling pot next to the campfire. Apollo is such a sweet gentle soul that Tom never liked to turn down his hospitality, but always hoped, whatever it was, it wouldn't get him too stoned. Tom bent down to take measurements and was jotting notes in his log when Apollo appeared with cup in hand. Tom said, "Thank you sir," double-checking to make sure it wasn't Bloodwitch. He said, "What does it do?" Apollo said, "En-a-gee giv." Tom took a couple of sips, set the cup by the Red Head pump-mounts and went back to taking measurements. Apollo smiled, exposing his missing teeth, and started checking valves on the old system. Tom finished up the measurements and excused himself. Conveniently leaving the cup, he headed back down the aqueduct. He couldn't afford to get stoned today.

In a small meadow on the other side of the river, he pulled a calculator from his pack and began doing last-minute computations. A few minutes later, it began to rain. Two hundred yards away, the cave that he and Daimmy sat in on Sundays seemed to be a good escape. Hiking to the knoll on the east, he could see the entrance. He remembered that Daimmy had said Arawak Indians inhabited the island 2,000 years ago and lived in the valley, probably dwelling in caves along the Martha Brea. The entryway overlooking the river rose 20 feet at the opening. A small meadow descended below all the way to the river. Standing just inside, he watched the rain pour down over the entrance like the backside of a waterfall. Then he remembered seeing a cavity further back that opened up into another chamber. Moving deeper in, he pulled himself up onto a ledge and continued. Light from outside still lit the walls as he climbed. Once on top he could see the opening to the chamber. Hunching down, he crawled inside and sat down. For a half hour he listened to the rain pour over the entrance while sitting in a lotus posture. Glancing around, he noticed something carved on the wall. He removed a small flashlight from his pack and scanned the enclosure. There in front of him engraved in the rock was a figure. It had wings with a halo atop its head. Chills ran up and down Tom's spine. No wonder he had been internally urged to sit with respect in this earth-moss covered room.

Suddenly the rain stopped. He climbed back down and stood at the entrance looking out at the Martha Brea, feeling blessed in the moment. He thought whoever lived here must have lived in paradise: the river, the meadow, the cave, fish, jungle herbs and shelter. He set out across the valley. Coming up over the hill, he noticed Chris sitting under the great tree by the main house going over papers. He stopped for a minute to say hello. Chris asked how it was going. He told him, "Things are going good." Then he asked Chris if he'd ever seen the carvings in the cave by the Martha Brea. Chris said he had heard about them but never actually saw them. Chris stopped what he was doing and they walked back to the cave. When they arrived, Tom led the way into the upper chamber. Chris, who was in his 60s and in very good shape, made the climb without effort. They sat for a while in silence and then returned to the main opening. As they approached the exit, both stopped and looked down at the river. Chris began describing how the river surged up from underground caves deep in the jungle. Tom looked over at Chris and said, "This is a spiritual place." Chris, with a faraway look, replied, "Yes, it's a spiritual place."

Barry and Sam of Cowan Electric had been grooming one of the young men from the village to work on technical items. Tom had been watching the man being put through the wringer for several weeks, a very strict and demanding apprenticeship—old school. Barry would say things like, "Dammit man I said, number 12 wire, this is number 14, tear it out and start over again." Then he'd turn to Tom and wink. Tom had been inspecting one of the lines when he came upon the man working in a group of laborers. Barry was there and looked over at Tom, as if to say, *What do you think?* Tom walked over to the man and asked his name. He replied, "Tallus."

"Where you from?"

"Unity Village."

"What's 12 times 12."

The man thought for a moment, and replied, "144."

Tom looked over at Barry and said, "You'll do just fine," just as one of Tom's mentors had said to him 20 years before. Tallus was eventually hired on as the water systems manager for the estate.

One afternoon Tom was walking up the several miles of dirt road from the pumping station towards the main house. He had just crossed the plank bridge where the Martha Brea bends and meandered through a group of banana trees near the western plantation. Sitting at the base of one of the trees he began to think of Mari. He pondered, *Of all the people in the world, it would have been you that would have enjoyed the enchantment and beauty of this place.* He looked up through the ruffling broad leaves, watching white clouds peeking in from side to side as they floated across the sky. It seemed to take him out of time. Soon the clouds disappeared and the sun glared into his eyes. He rubbed his hands across his face and looked slant-eyed across the plantation to the 300-year-old aqueduct running alongside the road. As he gazed at the moss-covered stones making up its walls, he pondered what labor must have been involved in casting such a wonder. Again he moved deeper out of time into an almost dream-like state.

In a mist of consciousness Mari materialized in front of him, standing barefoot in a long white dress. The surrounding countryside disappeared taking on another form. She appeared to be walking a trail high up on a grassy knoll. They walked together for some time. She left the trail and walked across the tall grass toward a large Buddha statue embedded in the side of a hill. As she approached it, she turned and looked back, waving, and crawled into the mouth of the gigantic idol. Looking back at Tom she whispered, "Meet me in the mouth of the Buddha," and disappeared.

The following words came into his mind: *Soul mates separated by death are in constant communication at a subtle symbolic level, continually influencing the life of the other. Even when the pain of physical separation becomes unbearable they will not let go for years later, and even then maintain some sort of mysterious emergence. Often the survivor will take on the physical and spiritual attributes of the other in subtle ways, and in order to find a new mate, they must find a soul who would love them both.*

He stood up and leaned against a banana tree as the surroundings transformed back to their former shapes. Somehow he felt she was with him, guiding him along the way. Quickly he jotted the words down in his logbook and looked up. He heard conversation coming from the road—Mary was pushing a Honda motorcycle and Chris was walking beside her. Tom walked back to the road and moved towards them. They all met halfway, near a bubbling spring that had eroded its way into the plantation.

Chris inquired how it was going. Tom said, "Fine." Chris asked Tom, figuring he'd been a biker at one time or another, if he would ride Mary's motorcycle back up the hill. It had rained that day and the road was slippery with deep mud. Tom handed Chris his logbook and turned the bike around. He got on and gave it a kick. Slowly he fishtailed up the hill, stopping on the flats about 200 yards from the main house and waited. Soon Chris and Mary strolled up holding hands. Chris said they were getting ready to leave for New York and just wanted to say goodbye. Mary asked about Fire Balls. Tom said he was out, but perhaps Tom and Kathleen might send a new supply.

Sunday was a lazy day. He'd been waiting for parts to arrive. He decided to go for a walk by the river. As he strolled along the bank an idea came into his mind, *Go fishing!* Running back to the farm with boyish excitement, he asked all around; no one had a fishing line. In Jamaica it's called a "fish line"; a plastic bottle, some line, a couple of hooks and a nail or bolt as a weight. Then another idea came, *Go to Unity Village, you're bound to find a fish line there.*

He set out from the farm and headed across the north pasture for the Unity River, a tributary of the Martha Brea. After giving a bull on the path respectable bay, he crossed One Tick Bridge. On the other side, he walked about a mile and noticed a small boy, maybe ten years old, walking toward him. As the boy drew near, he saw that Tom was something he wasn't used to seeing. The boy froze like a deer. As Tom approached on the path, the boy just stood there, amazed and dazed. Tom waved as he walked by. The boy slowly waved—a delayed wave. Tom thought, *If this is the effect I'm having—then what awaits me?*

Dimswitch had followed. Suddenly an older boy came from the cane field on the right and yelled "Dimswitch!" He recognized the dog, but was shocked to see Tom and ran back into the cane, disappearing into the green.

Tom tried to remember when he was here with the Rastas. He finally got his bearings and found the little footpath leading across a wooded area towards the Community Center. As he walked, there were little handmade tin houses all along the way. People were out in their yards; some were smiling in fright, others went back inside their houses. He paid no mind, only to say inside, *I love you, even if you find me strange.*

He was almost to the Community Center, when someone started yelling, "Joe, Joe, hey mon." Tom turned and looked in the direction of the voice. Fifty yards off the path, a man standing next to a wooden handmade house was waving for Tom to come over. As he approached he saw he was no ordinary man. The man was battle-scarred. Knife wounds appeared about his body on his face and arms, stab wounds in his chest, stomach and back. A large keloid scar ran down his right bicep from his shoulder. Old bullet wounds in his right collarbone and left leg displayed permanent medals of valor and desperation. The man was holding a plucked yard chicken in his right hand as Tom approached. Tom continued towards the man's back porch and stopped ten feet away. The man wanted to know what Tom was doing in the village. Tom said, "I'm looking for a fish line."

Standing before Tom was perhaps the reincarnation of Taharqa, a fierce Egyptian warrior in black skin. A few glances into each other's eyes and they knew one another. The man said he had no fish line, but to "Cum." He took Tom to a mound of dirt and stacked stones 20 feet from where they were standing. He knelt on one knee beside the mound and told Tom his mother had died two weeks ago. Tom crouched to the ground next to the burial site. He picked up a small stone and placed it on the grave in silent prayer. The man began to speak. In a few words he told his life story. Then, noticing the tattoos on Tom's arms, he proceeded to read Tom's life with amazing accuracy. Tom thought to himself, *This highly sensitive man walks the path of the warrior. What blessing is this?* They dawdled back to the man's back porch and squatted near a chopping block.

The man began talking about what was going on in the United States. Tom replied, "You stay pretty tuned in, how did you know that?" Suddenly the man's expression changed and he raised his voice, "Why are you shocked that I know? Is it because you think I'm a little man?" Tom calmly replied, "You must have a radio. I have no radio." Looking into Tom deeply, the man paused for a minute then muttered, "Yes, my batteries went dead a few days ago." The tension seemed to dissipate.

The man then walked around behind Tom. Tom remained squatting on the ground, making designs in the dirt with a twig, as the man continued to talk. While behind Tom, the man called for his Rastafarian apprentice standing in the doorway to bring him a machete. Tom wasn't sure which one had the machete, but he picked up three small stones, one for past, present, and future. Several minutes passed with no one talking. The air grew thick. In a show of respect, Tom gave the man a warrior's honor; he didn't look back.

Several more minutes passed in silence as Tom tumbled the three small stones between his fingers. Everything began to intensify. He could hear small children playing in the distance and laughter coming from teenagers kicking a ball in a field nearby. He could feel grief coming from the grave 20 feet away. As joy and grief centered themselves in a point inside his heart something happened. For just a moment he experienced acceptance, a place of no fear. Whatever would happen next would be OK.

Suddenly, the man moved around in front to the chopping block with a smile on his face and began hacking up the chicken, swabbing it with a fresh lime. Tom asked his name. The man replied in the King's English, "Dimswitch. The same as that dog you're with." He warned Tom that he would hear many bad things if he mentioned the name Dimswitch. Tom asked, "What do you like to be called?" He replied, "Freddy."

They talked a while longer, then Tom stood. "I'm headed out now in search of a fish line." With blood and lime juice dripping from his hands, Freddy reached out in friendship. They shook hands in an eye-to-eye goodbye. As Tom started to leave the property, Freddy started yelling out again, "Hey mon, cum bak." Tom turned around to see Freddy walking toward him with a machete in his right hand. They both continued to walk toward each other. Two feet away Freddy raised his machete, making a fist, extending it out towards Tom. Tom put his fist out, touching fist to fist. Freddy smiled and shouted, "RESPECT" and waved Tom goodbye, instructing him to take the lower path to Millerman's.

Tom followed the path with Dimswitch trotting close behind. They made their way to the center of the village and Tom sat on a tree stump to rest. He could hear a woman yelling at a man in the front of a dwelling across the way. She kept yelling, "What's a white man doing in the village?" Tom refocused his attention to the children selling T-shirts out of the back of a broken-down pickup with no wheels. As he walked toward the truck, one of the kids came over and asked if there was something wrong with his arms. They wanted to know if they could touch his skin. He stretched out his arms for sampling as they leaped from the truck-bed, swarming him like a rock star.

Just then an old man on a bicycle drove by, wanting to know if he was looking for someone. He told the man he was looking for Millerman, pointing to the road where he thought Millerman's parents lived. As the old man pointed, Tom turned and looked at the house next to the truck. There was a familiar face. It was Joseph the Carpenter working on a neighbor's picket fence. Joseph took a double-take and smiled apprehensively. He was shocked to see Tom in the village by himself. Joseph came over, "Wha yu do here." Tom said, "I'm looking for a fish line." Joseph laughed, "You crazy mon?"

Joseph took him across the road to his house, and began apologizing for his house being so small. It's a simple sweet handmade house with a tin roof, comfortable quarters, quaint front yard with bench, and tire-swing. Tom told him he loved the house. Joseph reached into a milk crate covered by cloth on the back porch. Pulling out a complete fish line wound on a plastic Coke bottle, he said, "Dis won, mi go la'ter. " He told Tom to get some *swims* (crayfish) from Eddy at the farm. Tom thanked him and said he would return the fish line on Tuesday.

They waved goodbye and Tom and Dimswitch headed back through the village to One Tick, where Dimswitch got into a fight with three other dogs. Eventually Tom was able to stop the fight with a stick, and the two vagabonds crossed the bamboo bridge back to Pantrepant. He found Eddy and asked about *swims*. Eddy went to the freezer and gave Tom *swims*. Dimswitch and he went fishing that afternoon at Chris's swimming hole on the Martha Brea. They didn't catch anything, but had "long" fun.

Christmas brings up memories of his beloved. It's been a lonely Christmas Eve and he's missing his sweetheart. Tom and Kathleen sent a Christmas package filled with an assortment of wonderful things, including Fire Balls, which filled his heart with love. That's been the trick—to fill the void with love. He went over to Chris's tree swing and swung himself for about an hour. He could hear singing coming from the village and was almost drawn to go. Joseph the Carpenter came by and they went fishing at the plank bridge. Joseph caught seven and Tom caught one. Afterwards he wished Joseph a Merry Christmas and went to his room to call Noni and Pauline. He loves them; his heart feels good talking with them. Cynthia dropped by to wish him a Merry Christmas and said she would be back to fix him a special dinner. Brenten, who owns the Bamboo Bar in Unity Village, walked all the way from the village to bring him a leg of ham for Christmas. Feeling lonely, yet loved by all his new friends, he went back into the jungle that night and started working on the pump station plumbing.

He wrote in his log, "Joseph the Carpenter brought me more fishhooks today. Maybe I'll get a chance to go fishing again in a few days. Mosquitoes are bad tonight, hundreds of bites, picking ticks from my ankles and neck with knife Tom & Kathleen sent me for Christmas. Ticks under my arm."

Finally, the pumps arrived by special airfreight from Chicago and were expedited through customs. Each pump weighed 500 pounds. They were carried by tractor as far as it could take them. Then men carried them across the river and down the aqueduct a quarter mile to the pumping station without dropping them in the water. It was a time to celebrate. That evening, he went to the Bamboo Bar and drank Red Stripes with the men. Afterwards he wandered half drunk through the night for several hours before finding One Tick, crossing the river back to Pantrepant by moonlight.

After the pumps had been installed, Tom began making pilgrimages to the pumping station at night. Deep in the jungle with no one around, it had become a pagoda, a place not only for work, but also for worship. One late evening after working on the system plumbing, he shut off the lights and stared out at the water running through the aqueduct in the moonlight. He watched a leaf pass under the bridge and move downstream. In that moment he thought of his father, a 3rd-degree Master Mason who had worked hard all his life with the tools of the trade. Memories began to appear on the surface of his mind. All the teachings, the gratitude, the hard work, the craftsmanship afforded him from a master of the trade began to bubble up. He remembered his father giving him a list each night of all the pipe sizes his father would need for the following day's work. He would go to the garage after dinner and cut and thread pipe, placing them in wooden milk crates by size, for his father to put in his truck early the next morning. The transmission from father to son never left him. Even unto this day construction sites remain a holy place in his mind.

There he realized that Pantrepant had been a place that had brought him up, up from the bottom of himself to see beauty once more. The experiences given him in this time gave him hope that he was not forever lost, that there were still a few more chapters left in his life.

Two weeks later, the new pumps were now working, pumping 90 gallons a minute up the hill to the tank. He and Barry ran multiple tests on the system and found it performing beyond expectations. Tom wrote maintenance procedures for the water system and was preparing to give classes to several of the men the following week.

Mary and Chris arrived from New York to ready the estate for visitors. Helicopters have been landing and taking off all day.

It's New Year's Eve. There were still adjustments to be made to the plumbing at the pump station and hopefully in the next week or two all the paperwork, audits, and training would be finished. He was lying on the bed going over some documents when the phone rang. It was Ralph the "hot dog man" and Little John from Santa Rosa. They had called to wish him Happy New Year. Not long after that the phone rang again. It was Chris with an invitation to come over to the house for New Year's Eve dinner. A few minutes later he appeared un-showered at the door of the estate house, carrying a handful of Fire Balls. Chris, Mary, Patrick (the guy who does the un-Cola commercials "f_a_b_u_l_o_u_s"), his lady Nandhi, an East Indian goddess, and Tom enjoyed a magnificent dinner prepared by Chris and Mamaji. That night they all danced on the veranda to Bob Marley's music. Tom watched from a chair, rocking back and forth. Chris came over and said, "It's OK. You can dance with Mary." Out on the lawn Chris swayed back and forth with his hands in the air as Tom and Mary danced in between Patrick and Nandhi. It was a most memorable New Year's, one he'll never forget.

The next day Mary flew back to New York and Chris stayed on to take care of business. Tom was walking back from the pump station on the flats when Chris appeared with a group of people. Tom walked along carrying his backpack over one shoulder, passing through the crowd. He waved at Chris as they passed. Tom looked back and saw Chris had let the group go on and was walking back toward him saying, "Take a break. We're all going swimming." Tom told Chris he had a couple of things to do yet, but would show up soon. Back in his room he started looking for the swimming trunks Cathy Snipper had given him at Golden Eye, on his first trip over. He couldn't find them anywhere. Opening just about everything in the room, he found them at the bottom of a paper sack underneath a bunch of socks.

He set out for the swimming hole. Taking a short cut through the jungle, coming up on the other side of the river across from where everyone had gathered, he placed himself on the aqueduct wall with his feet in the water and stared across at the group. He removed his shirt and leaned back against the rocks. He'd been on the farm so long he felt like one of the men and was not accustomed to social get-togethers. He knew he could still communicate, but found the thought of mingling with the crowd of dignitaries across the water intimidating.

Minutes later a beautiful East Indian lady swam over towards him wearing only a T-shirt for a top. He was awestruck and couldn't talk until two little girls, he guessed about nine years old, who had followed the lady, came and sat on the aqueduct next to him. Curious as to how far his tattoos went, the girls walked around in back on the grass to get a better look. They started asking questions that broke the ice. The Hindu goddess swam closer and smiled, making eye contact. Tom stood and dove into the water and they both swam to the other side, where a picnic was going on. He mingled for a while, then decided to head back. As he was leaving, Chris came up and looked curiously at his swimming trunks. Tom offered up the explanation, "These are yours, Cathy loaned them to me. I'll get them washed and give them back to you tomorrow." Chris smiled and said, "You keep them."

A few days later a helicopter landed on the lawn and two guys stepped out. Tom had been out in front of the guest annex, casually feeding the chickens running wild on the property. At the main house Chris motioned Tom to come over. The two men huddled around Chris for a few minutes talking, then looked over at Tom. He continued up to where they were standing. Chris introduced them as Alex and Felix, and said they were all going to Golden Eye for R&R and wanted to know if Tom wanted to go along. They were music executives from one of Chris's productions and had brought tapes for review by Chris's Island Group that would be meeting at Golden Eye the next day.

Tom wasn't sure if he had any clean clothes. Chris smiled and said, "You've been on the farm for awhile now, just grab your swimming trunks, we're leaving in five minutes."

Once on the road, their first stop was Ocho Rios. On the way they told stories. Somewhere between Good Hope and Wales Potosi, Chris pointed at the road explaining that in the 1800s slaves from both properties had cut a road through the hills between two lands, allowing cane carts to pass without having to climb a grade. Each gang worked from its own side and met in the middle. The gangs consisted of 500 men each. Story has it that they completed the cut in 24 hours. There's a stone marker commemorating the event, called "One Day Cut."

At Ocho Rios, Chris met up with Roger at the office and told Alex, Felix and Tom to go up to the restaurant on the hill and wait. Chris repeated, "I won't be long." They made their way past ruins and brush as they climbed along a fence line that finally opened through a rusted gate at the back door of the place. An older blond lady with smeared lipstick, wearing a muumuu, stepped out the back and wanted to know what they were doing there. Alex said, "Chris sent us." That changed everything. She motioned them in the back door and sat the three men at the bar. She said, "Drinks are on the house. Chris owns the place." They picked up their cocktails from the bar and went out to a veranda overlooking the sea.

A half hour later Chris called by phone saying he was ready to go. They all scurried down the hill and were off again. Chris wanted to stop at Keith Richards', but he wasn't home. They continued on, to some guy's place who had built an exotic garden hideaway with waterfalls and crafted streams, high up on the mountain above Ocho Rios. The man was in the process of adding a recording studio to the property and Chris wanted to check it out. When they drove in, the owner and Chris strolled off down one of the paths in conversation, when suddenly a lady appeared beside Tom. She looked familiar. Suddenly he realized—she was the East Indian goddess he'd seen at the swimming hole at Pantrepant. She came right up to him and they walked off together with their arms around each other, like they had known each other for years. She started talking about a book she was writing on Ayurvedic medicine. Come to find out, she was a medical doctor doing research on medicinal plants. She wanted to know Tom's phone number. He told her he was staying at Pantrepant and could be contacted there and handed her a card. They walked and talked like old friends. They never connected again, but he often thought of her.

Chris and the man came back and Tom and the lady stood there with their arms still around each other. Chris smiled at the sight. Alex and Felix wandered into the huddle from another pathway and they all stood there talking. A few minutes later Chris walked to the car and they were on the road again.

When they arrived at Golden Eye, flocks of people started surrounding Chris, and Alex and Felix went off somewhere. Tom figured he was with Chris and just hung out. The whole group began going towards Chris's hideaway with Tom following in behind. One of the men in the group dropped back. Walking alongside, the man was curious who the tattooed man was. Tom still didn't get it. They continued to walk as Tom explained he had just come with Chris from Pantrepant. The man seemed interested and perplexed. Tom continued to walk innocently along. Once at the hideaway, they entered a room overlooking the bay and all sat at a large boardroom-style mahogany table. Tom sat down like he was supposed to be there, but was now wondering himself. Everyone seemed to know each other except for him. People started looking over at Chris, then back at Tom, signaling for an introduction. Chris looked up and said diplomatically, "Oh, Tom, have you tried the jet-skis yet, you might want to see Cathy and get a room." Tom felt the blood rush into his head; he finally got it. He had been on the farm too long.

The two music executives, Alex and Felix, and Tom hung out on the beach for the next couple of days basking in the sun and sipping rum. The next day, in the afternoon, Chris, Cathy,

Roger, Tom, Alex and Felix, Suzanne the writer, Dianne the beautiful Rastafarian priestess from the farm, and, Joe and Justine all hung out at the hideaway and jet-skied for most of the day. Roger and Tom raced across the bay, ending in a tie.

The next day Tom and Chris left for Pantrepant in Chris's car. They were quiet nearly all of the way. Chris pointed to a box of CDs on the floor. Tom reached in and grabbed one. Chris put it in the player, listened for a few minutes, popped it out and tossed it. If he didn't like it, he'd sail it out the window like a Frisbee for some lucky Rastafarian to find, and Tom would hand him another. They did this most of the way. Somewhere between Falmouth and Pantrepant, in the silence, Tom noticed how precious life had become. As they entered the dirt road to the farm he turned to Chris and said, "Thank you, Chris. Being here has been a healing for me." Chris turned his head curiously, "That makes me happy. I'm glad to have reliable water again."

The next day Tom went to the stables. He was to ride horseback around the ranch and inspect all the watering troughs. Mr. Anderson saddled up a tall mare and the two spent the day combing the countryside. In the afternoon, Roger stopped by for final inspection of the new water system and Tom said his farewells to all those who had cast so much love upon him. As he was getting ready to go, he saw Miss Mac sitting on the steps near the annex. He sat down beside her. Putting his arm on her shoulder, he looked into her eyes and said, "Until we meet again." He handed her a small white box containing a golden *Tara* and kissed her on the cheek. Tears came into her eyes. Standing, he squeezed her hand and waved goodbye.

On January 21, 2001 from Pantrepant in Trelawny near the edge of the jungle, he boarded a helicopter for Strawberry Hill. Landing on the resort lawn he entered the restaurant. There, by chance, he met his old friend Buck White from the fishing village of Parham. They drank and told stories till the sun came up.

The swishing blades of the ceiling fan blew cool tropical morning air over the top of the bar and Tom poured Buck another drink and continued. Buck interrupted, "How will I ever know the details?" Tom laughed and said, "I'll send you tapes!" Buck went on, "But what I want to know is, did you ever find another woman?" Tom mumbled, "No, I'm searching." Buck said, "What?" Tom replied, "I'm still searching." Buck placed his hand on Tom's shoulder and said, "You mean after all your travels you haven't found her?"

"Not yet."

"Describe her, who are you looking for?"

Staring up at a passing bird, Tom reached for his back pocket. He pulled a tattered napkin from his wallet began to read:

"She walks naked in the forest on a full moon night. She's a white witch with dark hair..."

Journey On

A great storm carried him down stream
to the next fertile valley, into another time.

Despite outward changes
the inward journey remains.

I witnessed Tom endure pain and joy.
I am his soul.

Love to you and to all those who love you,

Tom Sawyer
Santa Rosa - 2005

About the Author

photo by Julianne Deery 2005

Tom Sawyer is a pilot, author, and consulting engineer with 27 years in the industry and is a member of the Institue of Electrical and Electronics Engineers (IEEE). He spent 10 years with the Bell System and was a consultant to Intel Corporation for 11 years. He co-founded an organization that builds libraries for children in Mexico and currently designs water distribution systems in the US and the Caribbean.

In 1987, he started having visions of a woman he'd never met. Through a set of extraordinary circumstances he found the woman and her twin boys at a Huichol Indian ceremony. They were married in 1988. In 1991, he accepted a position as chief engineer and vice president for a world-class island resort in the Caribbean. He moved his family to Antigua, West Indies and hob-knobbed with the rich and famous until discovering his wife, Mari had cancer. It was after that, that he became inspired to write their story, "White Summer Dress."